Black Resistance to the Ku Klux Klan in the Wake of the Civil War

KWANDO M. KINSHASA

McFarland & Company, Inc., Publishers
Jefferson, North Carolina, and London

Library of Congress Cataloguing-in-Publication Data

Kinshasa, Kwando Mbiassi.
Black resistance to the Ku Klux Klan in the
wake of the Civil War / Kwando M. Kinshasa.
v.   cm.
Includes bibliographical references and index.

Contents: Things fall apart — The interminable conflict — Dialogues on human rights abuses —
Themes on racial conflict — Organized resistance — Literary provocateur : a case study of
John A. Leland — A planter's letter to the New York Times — Excerpt from The Prostrate State by James Pike —
Testimony of Elias Thomson regarding Klan activity — Remarks of Judge Hugh Bond regarding
Klan activity — Excerpt from the oral history of Mary Anderson — "The Lowrie bandits" —
Letter from General John C. Gorman regarding the Lowrie bandits.

ISBN 0-7864-2467-2 (illustrated case binding : 50# alkaline paper)

1. Ku-Klux Klan (1866–1869)   2. Reconstruction (U.S. history, 1865–1877)
3. African Americans — Crimes against — Southern States — History — 19th century.
4. Freedmen — Crimes against — Southern States — History — 19th century.
5. African Americans — History — 1863–1877.   6. Southern States — Race relations — History —
19th century.   7. Ethnic conflict — Southern States — History — 19th century.   8. Reconstruction
(U.S. history, 1865–1877) — South Carolina.   9. South Carolina — Race relations — History — 19th century.
10. Reconstruction (U.S. history, 1865–1877) — Sources.   I. Title.
E668.K58 2006   975.7'041 — dc22   2006010922

British Library cataloguing data are available

On the cover: A man representing the Freedmen's Bureau stands
between armed groups of Euro-Americans and African Americans.
By A. R. Waud, *Harper's Weekly,* July 25, 1868 *(Library of Congress
Prints and Photographs Division, Washington DC)*

Manufactured in the United States of America

*McFarland & Company, Inc., Publishers
Box 611, Jefferson, North Carolina 28640
www.mcfarlandpub.com*

To those who resisted terror silently,
and those who resisted with the fury of battle.

Acknowledgments

I wish to acknowledge the assistance and in many instances guidance given to me over the years to finish what originally was a master's degree thesis. My advisor at that time, Ruth Ramsey, professor of communications at Hunter College, City University of New York, was both wise and prophetic in suggesting that I pay close attention to micro-elements in my writing and noting that *both* the devil and angels reside in detail.

Often a brief but insightful discussion with a colleague is significant enough to focus one's attention on a process that would have otherwise been overlooked. In this regard I thank attorney and social scientist Gerald Horne for his questioning of specific material related to the Ku Klux Klan and my original research paradigm. I also want to thank my colleagues in the African American Studies Department at John Jay College of Criminal Justice, CUNY, who over the years have offered (knowingly or not) critical advice on various segments of this work.

A vast amount of my basic research material was acquired through the resources of a number of research institutions, especially the Schomburg Center for Research on Black Culture in New York City and its excellent supporting staff, who were brilliant in the face of my often endless queries about bits of data. I also want to thank the staff at Howard University's Moorland-Spingarn Research Center for their archives pertaining to Reconstruction. Similarly, during the latter stages of this project I was able to utilize the research facilities of the Laurens County Library in Laurens, South Carolina. The expert, patient and informed guidance of archivist Elaine Martin was invaluable. Similarly, I have to thank both Betsy Carter and Jane Yates of the Citadel Military Academy in Charleston, South Carolina, for identifying and making available crucial documents pertaining to one of its past faculty members and a central character in this manuscript, John A. Leland.

As a doctoral student at New York University I had the opportunity to study under the guidance of social psychologist Richard Sennett. This experience helped me understand the importance of micro-social analysis and how to utilize it as a means to better understand social history and the connections that give meaning to the human experience. Rigorous scholarly preparation of this sort helped me later to fully appreciate the writings of a late friend and colleague, Amos Wilson, who wrote extensively on the psychology of race and place in society. It is to his intellectual well that I often return.

Finally I would be remiss if the contributions to this work by my wife, Imani Kinshasa, were not acknowledged. Her research skills and overall understanding of this book aided me in identifying critical data that would have otherwise remained hidden in the nineteenth-century census records of South Carolina. Her contribution was matched only by the sacrifices of my children, grandchildren, and great-grands who understood that my closed door in the evening and on weekends meant simply, "Papa is working."

Contents

Preface

A man without force is without the essential dignity of humanity. Human nature is so constituted that it cannot *honor* a helpless man, although it can *pity* him; and even this it cannot do long, if the signs of power do not rise.

— Frederick Douglass, 1855

Throughout the latter part of the nineteenth century, the Ku Klux Klan's propaganda and its night-riding purveyors of terror existed as an American thesis of hatred which confronted its antithesis in African American economic political development. Acting as a political synthesis for a southern social order in total disarray and economic exhaustion, Ku Klux Klansmen and sympathetic elements propelled both black and white Americans toward extreme solutions as a way to resolve a number of post–Civil War exigencies. In this regard, for those Freedmen who were now on the path toward American citizenship and the franchise, civil and human rights were crucial enough to consider the use of armed defense and retaliation as a way to avoid becoming secondary citizens within white America's racial system of political hegemony.

While Northern political clichés attempted to obscure what was otherwise crass exploitation of the ex-slave at the end of the Civil War, racial interactions by the fall of 1865 were more accurately portrayed by the south's most virulent representatives, the Ku Klux Klan. From this perspective, Klan propaganda became the proselytism and expression of a vast array of fears and insecurities maintained by southern conservative whites: fear of foreigners and their strange customs, fear of Catholics and their supposed allegiance to the pope, fear of money-lending Jews, and most of all fear of Africans who were the embodiment of all that was evil. These anxieties, institutionalized by over two hundred years of racially centered nation-building and domination over an enslaved population, spawned a nationalistic mentality that despised any suggestion that the enslaved African or any non–European group had any rights that white Americans were *obligated* to respect. Emanating from this perspective arose an infamous racist Ku Klux mantra that effectively

1

sponsored, promoted and propagandized race-specific violence aimed at disregarding the human rights of blacks and others who disagreed or challenged what essentially was a national agenda against the ex-slave.

However, assessing the effectiveness of the Ku Klux Klan's propaganda and those acts that emanated from these racial zealots reveals an exposed and vulnerable underbelly of racist intrigue, subterfuge and fear. Ironically, Klan propaganda, intended as a threat, became an inspiration for its victims to organize against psychic and physical humiliation. Making the decision to organize armed self defense units and in specific instances seek retaliatory action represented a new social paradigm for the Freedmen and in a sense established a series of social and political nuances that forever changed the relationship of whites and blacks throughout the south.

Throughout the American Reconstruction era of 1867 to 1877, the Ku Klux Klan was intended to be both a violent sword of retribution for failed southern nationalism and a motivating tool for defeated Confederated ideologues who demanded political retribution and economic redemption. For these disciples of organized terror, to use the terms *civil rights* and *Freedmen* in the same sentence was an affront to the Constitution itself. Conversely, the existence of armed Freedmen in opposition to Ku Klux Klan–type organizations underscored the desire and ability of some blacks and their Republican allies to both psychically and physically combat various kinds of tormentors and thus to establish a semblance of personal justice and honor in the face of southern America's deadly racial fantasy.

The primary focus of this manuscript is to call attention to those levels of armed and unarmed resistance by Freedmen who in the years immediately following the Civil War found themselves within a boiling racial cauldron that was nineteenth-century America. Utilizing the syntax of the time, both victims and victimizers in a number of social contexts expressed concern about the exigencies they were facing, and as a result armed themselves against perceived threats and actual attacks. In an era where individual and community opinions were increasingly influenced by aggressive newspaper reporting that at times itself became labeled as either a coercive tool for terrorist plots or a social platform for human rights advocates, neither contradictory nor frivolous recollections were discarded or minimized as unimportant words. Even newspaper commentators of the day knew that gestures were but prologue to armed attacks and vicious reprisals. Consequently, spoken appeals increasingly reinforced by mass distribution of the written word vigorously seized, influenced and inflamed many southern conservative whites with an ever deepening level of secessionist sentiments about an evolving violent reality. As one letter to the Greensboro, North Carolina *Republican Press* put it, "assassination must be met by lynching, and midnight murder by midnight execution."[1] This sort of published appeal to armed retaliation certainly suggested, at least in Guilford County, North Carolina, in 1869 that retaliation might discourage Ku Klux raids, particularly in a county with a significant black population.

Though this certainly was the case in more than one post–Civil War county by 1870, it was the willingness by an increasing number of southern blacks to confront their history in a manner that now proclaimed "no voice should be louder than the sound of battle" that in turn aggravated southern white Democrats' fears about their increasingly precarious political situation.

Armed as best they could be, a nineteenth-century version of black minutemen struggled to survive amid determined southern white and some instances black conservative elements bent on their extermination. At the core of this vicious blood-letting was the reality that the Civil War did not end on April 9, 1865, but by June of the same year had evolved into an intense form of guerrilla warfare that would decide whether or not the African, now the Freedman, would remain society's servile, political, economic and social pariah. In many aspects this emerging armed conflict was as much about shaping the soul of a people and a nation as it was about retribution, political equity and social-cultural validation. In this respect, a close examination of written historical recollections from the Reconstruction era reveals that both blacks and whites attempted to transform a venomous southern reality into one that reflected their own sense of justice and social morality.

Introduction

Never threaten a man individually. If he deserves to be threatened,
the necessities of the time require that he should die. A dead radical
(Republican or Black) is very harmless — A threatened radical or one
driven off by threats from the scene of his operations is very troublesome, sometimes dangerous, always vindictive.

— Gov. Wade Hampton,
South Carolina, 1876

An examination of the Ku Klux Klan during Reconstruction requires the skills of a historian, sociologist and literary critic. These three perspectives, though seemingly different in their methodological constructs, attempt to study society utilizing their respective skills and in doing so complement each other.

For example, historians have traditionally concerned themselves with the task of dissecting past events, hoping to provide future generations with a deeper perspective of the past and present. Critical to this approach in conducting historical research has been an increasing recognition not only do events occur within specific, overlapping, and changing social frameworks but that language use in these time frames, particularly from the subjective perspective of the narrator, can either obscure or enhance our understanding of historical events. In this regard, nineteenth-century Ku Klux Klan propaganda continually attempted to draw on perceived notions of the south as a reawakening of "Old Greece" within the environs of North America. In researching this topic the inquiring historian must come to terms with those whose recollections and sentiments of a failed Confederacy are replete with explicit racial overtones that castigate the uplifting of the African slave as a destruction of civilization when they mourn, "'tis Greece; but living Greece no more."[1]

On the other hand, a sociologist probing into numerous aspects of human social behavior during the postbellum period would be ultimately concerned with understanding how recently freed slaves living within ex–Confederate states functioned in an institutional social structure that was very much committed to white political, social and economic dominance. Though social scientists doing this kind of research have continually found themselves hampered by a number of social variables and conditions that juxtapose contemporary linguistic standards, concepts, and mores with that of a past era, the challenge in this case is all the more difficult because the primary historical data itself is saturated with and premised by bias and conjecture. Efforts to develop dependable research data are made immeasurably more difficult if one forgets the political intent of the data itself. For example, one must realize that nineteenth-century Americans relied solely on the spoken word or printed reflections of orations transcribed into newspaper formats, letters, diaries and an assortment of official documents, all of which were written or compiled from the social perspective of the writer's or correspondent's views on race, class and social political positioning. Objectivity in nineteenth-century newspapers, journals, letters and diaries was not a necessary or expected characteristic, yet these items for contemporary sociologists are a primary source of data. Similarly, "reliable" material weaned from archival sources—for example, diaries and newspapers— is generally more representative of viewpoints from a self-interested literate class of white or black southerners rather than silent masses of blacks or whites.

Influenced by contemporary societal exigencies, sociologists studying nineteenth-century white racial terrorism or armed resistance by Freedmen must quickly recognize that archival data pertaining to social conflict between the races was often cloaked in secrecy, veiled in innuendo or otherwise disguised without explanation and compiled into numerous categories and characterized as minor criminal acts, outrages and social disturbances or labeled as acts of murder, robbery, assault, theft or mischief. Moreover, rarely will an inquiring researcher find nineteenth-century newspaper articles or legal correspondence that details political insurrection or acts of retaliatory terror by Freedmen after the Civil War. However, when incidents of this political nature did occur, they were reported on when it was assured that these incidents would be suppressed by a massive demonstration by the government and private actions of white citizens, for example, the Camilla (Georgia) massacre of 1868, the St. Landry (Louisiana) riot in 1868 or the Memphis riots of 1865 and 1866.[2] Not surprisingly, finding relatively few published articles underscoring successful Freedmen resistance during Reconstruction, many social scientists have concluded that none existed and that little if any political challenge to the dominant race and class by society's pariah class or race existed.

Southern white conservatives dominated the media in the Reconstruction era. Political analysis, social opinions and official proclamations in the newspapers of the time sanctioned what was acceptable and condemned, supported or questioned the mores of contemporary society. In doing so, the daily surveying of society by white-owned journals and newspapers established not only a cadre of informed correspondents but an official public venue for the discussion of important issues, thereby validating southern whites' right to rule by a process of continual public self-affirmation. In this case, newspapers played a critical role in establishing a context for social legitimacy as well as that which was antisocial and troublesome. Conversely, similar attempts of political analysis by Freedmen newspapers were either condemned by whites as foolhardy or at worst viewed as instigating racial hostility that would eventually lead to open attacks and riots.

At best, diatribe after diatribe in local conservative white newspapers such as the *Lynchburg Virginian* attempted to construct a negative image of blacks in general. For example, in a state where Ku Klux chapters were not known to be well established, sentiments against blacks were very evident. Consequently in response to a growing number of Freedmen delegates in the Virginian state legislature, a conservative newspaper editorial complained,

> white Virginians should [use] concerted measures without delay to fill the State with white laborers from the North and from Europe. They must crowd the Negro out. They must rid the State of an element that will hinder its prosperity, an element that under the influence of base white demagogues—themselves without property—would tax property of others to relieve themselves of obligation to educate their children an care for their paupers.[3]

Supporting the exclusive rights of white laborers, another Virginia paper, the *Petersburg Index*, asserted, "The Negroes are the last men who should complain if their white employers were to discharge them and supply their places with white men."[4] Understandably, at the core of the emerging violent contest between southern blacks and whites was the question of economic parity and participation in the affairs of state.

Heretofore, sociological analysis attempting to ascertain levels of resistance to racism during the postbellum and Reconstruction eras tended to ignore or marginalize the perspective of those at the lower spectrum of society. This being the case, stories about armed resistance by Freedmen to Ku Klux raiders or their willingness to confront white mobs through armed defense were rarely published in black-owned newspapers, and when mentioned in conservative white Democratic papers were characterized as criminal acts. Even when armed confrontations were cited in either in black- or Republican-owned papers they were written with a level of circumspection so that the reader would derive neither solace nor encouragement from the article. Conversely, articles depicting blacks being brutalized, killed, tortured, maimed or otherwise "helpless" against "night raiders" were published more frequently and in detail. In this regard, *sociological* analysis of blacks' armed resistance to racist persecution endeavors to circumvent the anxieties of earlier chroniclers and narrators of Ku Klux terrorism and instead examine how resistance was formulated and pursued. With this said, it is also acknowledged that although social traditions, values and desires of post–Civil War America are not directly transferable to today's time, clearly the antecedents of nineteenth-century racial conflict and resistance are very much a part of today's reality. By utilizing the *Literary Critic*'s analysis of the extraordinary material in chapter 6, I endeavor to extricate the reader from a quagmire of historical myth to proceed along a path toward deliberate assessment of the Freedmen's resistance to Ku Klux Klan terrorism.

When the last Civil War cannon was fired on a southern field, deeply felt impulses to publicly display one's indignation about the loss of life and material destruction were felt throughout the country. This emotion will be tested on both a philosophical and pragmatic level. In this regard, this book is premised on a delicately balanced social axis. On one side a plethora of southern white Democratic post–Civil War newspapers, pamphlets, diaries and books addressed the issue of social political realignment in terms of a "new southern society" and perennial white enfranchisement. However, from an opposing end of the spectrum, salient issues defining the concerns of Freedmen's civil rights, economic parity, the political franchise and one's right to armed resistance and retaliation in the protecting of their constitutional rights were of the utmost importance.

It was not enough, argued many Republicans, that the 1868 Fourteenth Amendment to the Constitution gave blacks some semblance of "due process of law," "property rights" and citizenship. Yet two years later these advocates for the Freedmen would also maintain that enactment of the Fifteenth Amendment to the Constitution guaranteeing "the right of citizens of the United States to vote shall not be denied or abridged by the United States or by any State on account of race, color, or previous condition of servitude" was insufficient if southern state governments chose to ignore or enforce these federal constitutional amendments.[5] Central to this issue was discerning if the federal government would demonstrate the *will* to enforce constitutional amendments, thereby ensuring that an independent political and economic growth for America's traditional pariah class would be set in motion, or if they would back off and let individual state governments settle the matter through violent internal political struggle.

Many southern and northern conservative whites argued that such a commitment was too extensive and expensive, principally within agriculturally based states, such as South Carolina, where by 1870 blacks constituted some 58.9 percent of the population; blacks also dominated Mississippi and Louisiana, respectively, by 53.6 and 50.1 percent.[6] It was further surmised that racial disparity in some states threatened whites' tenuous dominance throughout the southern agricultural regions of the country, while raising the politically sensitive and critical question of who would ultimately profit from mounting demands of a mercantile society if the newly empowered African Americans by 1870 dictated the development of the southern economy.[7]

For northeastern manufacturers, the stakes were even higher. There existed a possibility that politically ascendant blacks would seek an alliance with white laborers, thereby establishing a nonracial unification of southern farm laborers that would ultimately affect worker demands within northern urban centers. This possibility struck too closely at the question of socialism for many Republicans and Democrats.[8] More important was the perplexing social and political problem of the presence of a large number of southern men who, well schooled in the art of killing, had now grown sullen from tasting the bitterness of defeat.[9] This very serious reality was underscored by the fact that crimes of assault during the post–Civil War against the Freedmen, Republicans, conservative Democrats or anyone else not armed to protect themselves were rampant and showed little likelihood of abating anytime soon.[10] For example, in 1867 Republican officials in Kansas noted that "83 percent of the State prisoners had served full terms in the army before taking to crime."[11] In this regard, historian T.J. Stiles observed that after the Civil War, particularly in the guerrilla-style warfare in Missouri, "the incredible bloodshed of the war had put many soldiers through a social process ... [that may be called] 'violentization.'"[12] Stiles borrows the term from sociologist Lonnie Athens. Its application is insightful in defining a number of stages by which "dangerous violent criminals come into being."[13] Much of the south experienced some of all of these stages.

In the midst of this racial and economic strife, newspapers and books were condensing and summarizing events in treatises warning whites about the dangers in tolerating violated southern mores and "insolent" blacks. In essence, the intellectual cliques of a fallen southern aristocracy were being challenged to obtain in defeat what they failed to accomplish in the Civil War. Even the emerging technological innovations of war, particularly the rapid-firing revolvers produced by gunsmiths such as Samuel Colt, essentially placed into the hands of millions of Americans an enhanced ability to kill and maim. And thousands of Confederate soldiers were returning home with these weapons after their surrender at

"This Is a White Man's Government!" *Harper's Weekly*, September 5, 1868. LIBRARY OF CONGRESS PRINTS AND PHOTOGRAPHS DIVISION, WASHINGTON, D.C.

Group of "contrabands" at Foller's House near Cumberland Landing, Virginia, before the end of the Civil War. LIBRARY OF CONGRESS PRINTS AND PHOTOGRAPHS DIVISION, WASHINGTON DC.

Appomattox. A northerner in Mississippi noted, "a great majority of the country white people wore [pistols] strapped out side their pants, and many outside their coats."[14] Another correspondent observed that in Richmond, Kentucky, "all wear Navy revolvers strapped around their waist." More striking, he wrote, was that "this habit of wearing firearms is not confined alone to men, but boys scarcely fifteen years of age."[15] To claim that southern states post–1865 were armed camps would not be an understatement. To then suggest that both southern whites and blacks were mutually evolving through a period of economic, political and social post traumatic stress, albeit from differing vantage points, would also be fairly accurate. Their bitterness would frame the context for armed conflict and the reality of what some would call the second civil war.

When evaluating the defeat of a political elite, it is essential to comprehend what they see as the reasons behind their loss. In attempting to do so, difficulty arises in distinguishing fact from fiction, truth from exaggeration; truth becomes obscured and clouded by myth. In this respect, southern essayists describing their fallen society and the anguish of defeat could avoid excessive rhetoric and hyperbole when endeavoring to explain the loss of their Confederacy.

In the face of this development, numerous questions involving the sanctity of racial prerogatives come to the fore, particularly as they related to nineteenth-century white male hegemony in America and the fear of economic and political competition from a formerly enslaved black population. For instance, numerous white Americans, whether conservative northern Republican supporters of the federal government or southern Democratic secessionists, assumed notions of racial equality were naturally premised on *their* ability to dictate the terms of equality in the marketplace and in the political arena. They expected that whiteness automatically and naturally facilitated for them a favorable and appropriately skewed social policy, above all in the arena of military science. Within this framework Africans in transition to becoming African Americans realized that an inability to shape a favorable policy for themselves within the legal constructs of southern society was itself an injustice and a form of social inequality and stigma. This devaluation of Africans, this refusal to accept them as humans and fellow citizens was buttressed by an active racist propaganda and terrorist campaign that consciously endeavored to eliminate blacks as an economic and political threat to white Americans. Consequently, postbellum expressions such as "keep down the style of the niggers" represented more than philosophical orientation; they bespoke a conscious effort to confront an already threatening presence of armed black Union soldiers who represented a contradiction to traditional American mores, not only on who shall be armed, but on who will dictate authority.[16]

John Leland's 1879 book, *A Voice from South Carolina: Journal of a Reputed Ku-Klux,* provides a literary illustration of how racial tensions rapidly developed into a struggle between armed suppression and armed resistance. Setting his tale in the mythological trance of a vanquished Confederate States of America, Leland, an ex–Citadel Military Academy Professor of Mathematics and a Confederate major, envisioned a South Carolina no longer mired in military defeat but one anointed in its antebellum experiences. He anticipated that his revisionist view of history would energize social change in a manner more acceptable to the peculiarities of a disposed Confederate elite. Foremost, he presumed that most southern whites *knew* that increased African empowerment was the result of an uncontrollable sinister immorality conceived in a northern hell. In his political meandering, armed resistance by Freedmen to the dictates of whites' race and class presumptions was not an option to be considered. Somewhere, he pondered, there must exist a recourse for the social political redemption of southern whites.

However, as with many similar claims for redemption, there existed the pernicious collusion of envisioned virtue with actualized hypocrisy. For Leland and similar extremists, redemption meant the propagation of ideals, emotions and a philosophy of racial dominance, regardless of its cost in lives. This he argued was above all "divinely sanctioned."[17] In line with this philosophy, a Ku Klux thesis premised on fanatical notions on race was created to forge a desire among southern whites to not confront the contemporary political exigencies of the south, but instead circumvent the present by celebrating a supposed and imagined glorious past. Nostalgia, myths and behavioral codes were fabricated to engender fear, delusion and aberrant terrorist behavior among the Klan's own devotees as well as its intended primary enemy, the African American. Its envisioned success, however, was continually modified, dulled and in many instances negated by determined resistance from nonconservative southern blacks, allied white radicals and indigenous people. Examining this often ignored but critically important aspect of southern postbellum and reconstruction history helps us better understand the breadth and depth of freedom fighting within the American historical experience.

Things Fall Apart

Be frustrated all ye stratagems of hell / and devilish machinations
come to nought.
— Milton

A Deadly Ku Klux Fantasy

The social and political beliefs of the first Ku Klux chapter were very much reflective of the general mindset of southern whites and to some degree northerners after the Civil War.[1] This observation is supported by evaluating the consistency of opinions expressed in both southern and northern newspapers and the influence they exercised on their respective constituency on the question of black enfranchisement. It is also apparent that southern newspapers in general were not averse to reprinting Ku Klux propaganda that was aligned to support southern white grievances on Reconstruction, the Freedmen's threat and the Anglo-Saxon's natural right and responsibility to rule![2] From this genesis, Ku Klux propaganda tapped the daily economic and social frustrations of the average white southerner, and in doing so rationalized who the enemy was and how they were to be defined, fought, and eliminated as a threat. In this regard, the thoughts of historian J.T. Stiles reminds us that we should not forget that "Mythology Requires Effort. Achilles and King Arthur may have begun as men of flesh and blood, but Homer and sir Thomas Malory labored had to make them figures we remember."[3]

In its earlier years, Ku Klux philosophy as a form of armed propaganda embedded itself in the quixotic machinations and desirers of a militarily defeated southern white populace while abetting the development of a racism ideology that left little room for negotiation. Contrived notions of social behavior and development, many of which were premised on fundamentalist religious beliefs, coalesced into a form of social behavior that defined only Anglo American civil rights as synonymous with western civilization. Extrapolated from this thinking, a policy emerged aimed at eroding African American human rights with an unbridled violent display of Euro-ethnocentric antisocial behavior. Steeped in a belief that political violence was a necessary cost to pay for white racial hegemony, it was hoped that the mantle of guilt for the surrender at Appomattox would be psychologically transferred from southern whites to blacks.[4] It was also surmised that a process conducive to reforming the will of a dispirited white populace into accepting their *historical* if not *spiritual* duty could be encouraged to combat what many saw as the coming "dark despotism of African rule."[5]

In 1871, congressional investigations in several southern states including South Carolina were under way to examine the veracity of armed attacks by white gangs on essentially unarmed southern blacks. Termed "Ku Klux outrages" in national newspapers, these brutal attacks occurred during a period when after four years of civil war the nation appeared to be weary of "the Negro problem."[6] In addition, publicized testimonies into what many assumed were provoked acts of violence unwittingly contributed to an evolving mythology about terrorist gangs such as the Ku Klux, and as such provided legitimacy for their existence. For instance, Richard B. Carpenter, an ex–Republican who in 1870 changed his political affiliations to the Reform Party ticket that was composed of southern whites and dissatisfied Republicans but still lost to Republican incumbent Governor Robert Scott, testified before a congressional committee supporting the frustrations felt by many white South Carolinians. In a voice that rejected the demise of the Confederacy, Carpenter defined for all who entertained any doubts as to who the *present* enemy was: the "colored population." In doing so he positioned a humble southern white populace above that of the Freedmen when he asserted

> the colored population upon the seacoast and upon the rivers, in point of intelligence is just as slightly removed from the animal creation as it is conceivable for man to be. I venture to say that no gentleman here would be able to understand one of them upon the witness stand, or would be able to know what he meant. I have had to exercise more patience and more ingenuity in that particular, to have more explanations and interpretations, to find out what a witness meant to say, who had witnessed a murder, for instance, than to understand anything else in my life. They talk a very outlandish idiom, utterly unknown to me. They are very ignorant, and still have very strong passions, and these bad men lead them [Republicans] just as a man would drive or lead a flock of sheep.[7]

In the same spirit, John C. Lester, an original member of the Ku Klux in Pulaski, Tennessee, described his disdain for the newly emancipated African by proclaiming,

> The disturbing element was the Negroes. Their transition from slavery to citizenship was sudden. They were not fitted to the cares of self-control, and maintenance so suddenly thrust upon them, but many of them entered their new roles in life under the delusion that freedom meant license. They regarded themselves as Freedmen, not only from bondage to former master, but from the common and ordinary obligations of citizenship. Many of them looked upon obedience to the laws of the state — which had been framed by their former owners— as in some measure a compromise of the rights with which they have been invested.[8]

In a hierarchically structured multiracial society that was nineteenth-century America, racially charged statements as such were the oil that lubricated an intense violent competitiveness that vibrated throughout the country. Explicit attempts to define blacks as protagonist simply converted their past social condition, physical characteristics and heretofore suspected economic competitiveness into examples of evil. Once identified as such, negative attributes about the Freedmen's pariah status were codified into stereotypical characteristics that enabled many conservative southern whites to review their own role and place in society juxtaposed to others. Similarly 300 years of African enslavement in the western hemisphere and the almost 250-year history in North America alone had fashioned and concretely structured racially charged distinctions between Africans and Europeans into notions of common knowledge if not truth. As one historian put it, a major ambiguity existed in that freed blacks became slaves of *society* during Reconstruction, thus they were called and viewed as Freedmen — not free men![9] Commenting on this process, social psychologist Ernest Borman observed,

> Values and attitudes of many kinds are tested and legitimatised as common to the group by the process of fantasy chains. Religious and political dramas are tested. For example, if someone dramatizes a situation in which a leading political figure is a laughing stock and it falls flat, particular political attitude and value has been exhibited and not legitimatised. However, should the group chain-out on that drama [by] improvising on other laughable situations in which the politician has participated, the group will have created a common character which they can allude to in subsequent meetings and elicit a smiling or laughing emotional response. They have created an attitude towards a given political position.[10]

Borman's observation about those psychological factors that assisted white Americans in forging their own alleged common racial personality while in the midst of a social, cultural and politically displaced ex-slave population underscores Lester's recollections of early Klansmen:

> The members of [the] Ku Klux Klan are nowadays inclined to consider that their order comprehended all that took shape in resistance to the Africanization of society and government during the reconstruction period. As one ex-member said: "nearly all prominent men — ex Confederate — in all the southern states were connected in some way with the Klan." This is true only indirectly, nearly all white men, it may be said, took part in the movement now called the "Ku Klux movement." But more of them belonged to other organizations than were members of the Klan. The Klan had the most striking name and it was later applied to the white movement. The more prominent politicians, it is said, had no direct connection with any such orders. Such connection would have embarrassed and hampered them in their work, but more of them were in full sympathy with the objects of the Ku Klux movement, and profited by its successes. Many of the genuine Unionist later joined in the movement, and there were some few Negro members, I have been told.[11]

Within this social context, it was southern whites' fearful premonition of the Freedmen or more exactly *Africanization* that quickly became a major theme in southern white propaganda. This was apparent in South Carolina, where secessionist-oriented writers increasingly envisioned themselves as being violently overwhelmed by an irrepressible, unfit, ill-mannered, politically inept populace of ex-slaves. Some even claimed, "judging by the record they made, written indelibly in the official archives, continuance of their [blacks] rule would have meant inevitable and irretrievable annihilation of the fruits of two centuries of labor, thought, courage and aspiration."[12] With this as their social construction of reality, apologists, sympathizers and propagandists for the Klan constructed their version of what South Carolinian reconstruction should look like.

Throughout the postbellum years of 1865 to 1879, a variety of literary works emerged espousing Ku Klux Klan sentiments and the need for an armed response to the Freedmen's challenge. However as a result of questionable standards of literacy particularly throughout America's rural southern and southwestern territories, it is difficult to accurately determine functional literacy. Though the 1870 census indicates that 20 percent of the entire U.S. adult population was illiterate, of which 11.5 percent were white Americans and 79.9 percent African Americans, standards differed per state. However, irrespective of these variations by 1880, white illiteracy dropped two points to 9.4 percent, and the African American illiteracy rates dropped dramatically nearly ten points to 70 percent.[13] Whatever these figures might suggest for interracial relationships, literature or newspapers as a tool for mass mobilization were relatively restrained when compared with primary communication methods such as word of mouth and town hall meetings. If literacy in nineteenth-century America is understood to have enhanced a citizenry's ability to articulate and bear witness to perceived social needs, then identifying those segments of the populace that have readily obtained these skills is important when critiquing the development of privilege, power and political structure within a society. Commenting on this, linguist Harvey Graff posited that "the implications for the usefulness of popular literacy are clear: they were limited. More children were exposed to more regular and formal instruction, but learning could also be obtained informally, through daily life, interactions, work, recreation, and institutions, for which literacy was not always central."[14] It also has to be noted that post–Civil War America was not a static environment, as reading skills for both blacks and whites increased rapidly as the demand for highly opinionated information in an expanding commercial market became the benchmark for social recognition by the end of the century.

However, barring those financial problems generally associated with running a newspaper in postwar Georgia, where most newspapers were produced in small towns instead of cities such as Savannah or Atlanta, they had a direct impact on their readers, as one historian noted that "while newspapers may have not have been entirely comfortable reporting on the activities of the Ku Klux Klan or other vigilante groups that appeared in the postwar period, neither were they quick to condemn lynching of black Georgians."[15]

With a concomitant rise of southern anti–Republicanism, Ku Klux propaganda found a convenient platform in newspapers that were eager to publish what their customers considered were valid responses to primary social grievances. As many Southern and some northern newspapers became mouthpieces for a disgruntled and defeated populace, it was apparent to publishers that remembrances by Civil War soldiers, politicians, educators and plantation owners was a profitable and effective tool in articulating the frustrations of a southern white past. By becoming an instrument that allowed columnists to scrutinize and express sentiments that would otherwise not be heard or known of except by a few, postbellum southern newspapers were gradually able to exercise an enormous influence on an expanding readership. However, this ability to transmit opinions and interpret reality did not necessarily advance or heal the existing quandary of competitive racial relationships.[16]

For the volatile mass of despairing veteran Confederate soldiers, published disclosures of changing social norms, the eradication of human property laws, and the possibility that a narrowing and in some instances an evolving superior economic status of Freedmen provided a fertile milieu for resistance campaigns by those whites who saw social reconstruction as *their* displacement in the social order. In this respect, the printed word, utilized as a spiritual sword and verbal scimitar for a displaced southern Confederacy, now propagated a call for racial and economic retribution. Inherent to this clarion call was the compulsion to control a formerly enslaved race whose own perceptions of the new social order was just a rifle shot away.

In this manner many European immigrants whose concept of whiteness was traditionally subordinated to their ethnicity, the concept to "self-govern" meant to become functionally literate, "in the American sense meant to become American, which in turn meant for many white Americans at the time, to become white."[17]

Nonetheless, while southern efforts to curtail the consequences created by a literate slave population were generally successful, enough exceptions to the rule existed to suggest that the African's innate move toward literacy existed before the Civil War and dramatically during Reconstruction. Accordingly, for the Freedmen, being literate and having a strong ability to verbalize what was read, through oration, or to provide credible verbal testimony of their experiences was an important accomplishment, and one that provided them not only with a sense of importance but a deeper comprehension of those political exigencies surrounding them.[18] For that reason, their scrutinizing of newspapers became a popular and deliberate activity as well as a communal exercise. Information gleaned from one newspaper was verbally transferred from household to field, from porter to carriage driver, from village to village, and in many instances from state to state, thereby binding the individually enslaved into an informed community of communicators. Though this information network increased the importance of being literate among the Freedmen, it also explicates the serious confusion and threat felt by most southern whites.[19]

Freedmen literacy was directly connected with community organizing primarily around issues such as voting and armed resistance to night-riding gangs. Whereas many rural blacks generally understood that "voters who could not read letters well knew how to read men" was critical for physical survival, equally important was an ability to organize in a manner that ensured a level of protection while attempting to both vote and become literate.[20] With the emergence of black political clubs throughout the south in the early spring of 1867, a level of militancy that transcended oratory challenges to southern conservatives appeared. Though more will said about this development in a later chapter, it is important to note that the correlation between the Freedmen's ability to "read men" and "read letters" was strengthened by their involvement in political clubs, associations and armed militia-type bodies, which effectively provided them with a sense of community responsibility and pride. For example, in late November a group of veterans of black Civil War regiments from South and North Carolina bonded together as a result of being jailed in Charleston for petty crimes against property. Known as the Tigers Zouaves no. 12, they patterned themselves "under the same rules as the Union Leagues" and appealed to their jailers for the right to "get out of jail to try to be as a man."[21] As innocuous as the Zouaves appeared in 1867, throughout the south neighborhood bodies of Freedmen began to loosely patterned themselves on the model of a military regimental company and began to assume responsibility for organized and regulated public affairs.[22] This development was quickly followed an assumed air of responsibility by Freedmen that even "suffrage rights forged in Congress would encounter a rural activism that had germinated without authorization in the shape of political life."[23] These inklings of Freedmen militancy were not without precedent. Almost a year earlier in Charleston, northern military officials were not very supportive or sympathetic to the militant expressions by Freedmen as was reported in the conservative *Charleston Daily Courier*:

Yesterday a number of Freedmen, who had formed themselves into a Zouave organization, made their appearance on our streets in full Zouave uniform, red cap, blue jacket, red breeches, white legging and low quarter shoes. The officers wore Zouave shoulder straps and side arms.[24]

The combination of fancy colors presented such a strong contrast as to excite considerable curiosity and remark. It was generally believed, however by the uninitiated of our citizens that they belonged to some company of United States colored soldiers recently arrived at this post.

After assembling about seventy in number, they marched to the Citadel, where some of their colored female friends were in waiting to present them with a beautiful banner. An officer at headquarters had been requested to act as spokesman. On the arrival of the procession they were received by an officer with an order from General Scott for the arrest of those wearing shoulder-straps and side-arms, in violation of General Orders of the Department, which prohibit military organizations of any kind in this State.

The officers of the Association were then escorted into the parade ground, where they were deprived of all their illegal military insignia, and were allowed to retire when the company was dismissed.[25]

About the same time in the Barnwell District of South Carolina, reports of armed marching groups began to circulate throughout the countryside. In August 1866, one white planter became so terrified that only when his anonymity was assured did he agree to relate the following account to a fellow planter, J.D. Palmer:

Military companies formed on the Santee, would, on the night of Sunday the 2nd September next, march under the lead of the lead of the said Johnson, for Barnwell Court House, cross the Edisto river at Orangeburg C[ourt] H[ouse], and then devide the force into two bodies, one taking the Cannon's Bride, and the other the Bennakers Bridge Road, and unite again in Barnwell District — the Volunteers from each section, joining them at various points on the march: ... It was intended to kill every white man they could find, and take what they wanted.[26]

For southern secessionist-minded white Americans, a literate, articulate, politically aware and armed black populace was an anathema. As a result, shifting post–Civil War political arrangements designed to improve the economic status of the Freedmen and poor whites did in fact establish fertile ground for southern white political protagonist to begin championing for a resurrection of their displaced social order, that is, a southern white past. Establishing extralegal associations known as Regulators, highly mobile gangs of white men began exercising violent control over a vulnerable populace of ex-enslaved blacks and pro–Republican whites while propagating a racist pro–Democratic political agenda. In the course of examining these developments what is often ignored (or at best minimized) are verbal and nonverbal interactions that ensued between raiders and their intended victims. Interactions that often revealed shared levels of hatred, fear and paranoia between raiders and their victims.

For example, after the Civil War, it was those intended and nonintended communicative moments between blacks and whites that gave their reality a level of punctuated importance. By assiduously exploring these various interactions and the varying social frames in which interpersonal communication could and did occur, one can begin to assess levels of intimidation, fear, deceit, gesturing, role-playing, lying and misrepresentations that occurred particularly during raids by formalized armed terror groups, such as the Ku Klux.

That is to say, although violent attacks by the Ku Klux generally inflicted havoc among unarmed rural Freedmen, individual occurrences of armed resistance to these attacks as well as by organized groups also occurred. It is surprising to know that due to the scarcity of published data on Freedmen resistance to terror attacks by the Ku Klux, fixed notions of who were victims and victimizers have emerged from this era. Understandably, hostile racial contacts became institutionalized into folkloric tales of conflict between good and evil, while perennial victim roles were transformed into truths about reality and convoluted social relationships.

Herein existed a major problem for historians; by assigning "traditional" roles to groups such as the Ku Klux and Freedmen during Reconstruction, a number of false and misleading generalities begin to appear, such as verifiable accounts and testimonies that questioned Ku Klux *effectiveness* against the Freedmen.[27] Imbalances in data collection and a tendency to ignore one side in a dyadic (albeit violent) social relationship has led to a preponderance of skewed information that over the years inaccurately attributed credibility to Ku Klux terrorism where ineptitude and fear existed. As a result, a grievous historical inaccuracy persist in numerous assessments of Reconstruction, in part because a total submission to Ku Klux attacks has been assigned to southern blacks when successful resistance was more often than not conspicuous.

Within post–Civil War South Carolina, pressure was exerted on both blacks and whites to withdraw support for the Republican Party. In fact, any allegiance with northern unionists immediately following the war was generally viewed by secessionist whites as traitorous and a direct threat to values that for over 200 years defined empowerment primarily in terms of race. As one writer noted, "quite apart from the considerations of race and class, the elements in a community that have long exercised exclusive control of government do not generally relinquish that control without a struggle. The contest in the south, however was inevitably embittered by the difference in race and culture."[28] For that reason, impoverished nonelite southern whites easily concluded that if political empowerment, social privilege and grace was to befall them, it would naturally have to occur at the expense of the ex-slave. They understood that though *their* Confederacy was destroyed by war, American law and social practice still characterized their once chattel property as cultural and political enigmas whose subordination was essentially guaranteed by the Constitution. Correspondingly, if *extralegal* actions were needed to ensure that the newly created Freedmen would be eliminated as economic and political competitor, then so be it. Resulting political agreements throughout the south forged the beginning of numerous paramilitary secret societies or regulators, such as the Knights of the White Camellia, the White Brotherhood, the Pale Faces, the Red Shirts, and the Ku Klux, who took it on themselves to wage terrorist attacks and in some cases continuous low-intensity warfare against southern blacks and white Republicans. It became a struggle that many southern and northern whites agreed was a dirty but necessary war to maintain both social and political domination over blacks.[29]

Books, articles and even films extolling the effectiveness of Ku Klux terror campaigns, particularly the reputed night raids that purportedly frightened the Freedmen into total submission, have generally been accepted as a valid part of American history and even folklore. Although this material generally insist that black victimization was analogous with their total submission to white authority, documented evidence of blacks' successful resistance and armed retribution, though not popularly known exist, challenges the impression of Ku Klux omnipotence during the post–Civil War era.

As a result of a paucity of examples in American literature praising or even recognizing examples of blacks' successful resistance to Ku Klux violence, most Americans, regardless of racial background, find it difficult to envision courageous armed blacks fighting night-riding terrorist groups after the Civil War. More popular are images of frighten, befuddled blacks who in acknowledging their inferiority, survived only as noble pariahs waiting for either their eventual demise or deliverance by some benevolent outsiders! Even the famed Buffalo Soldiers of the 1870s are portrayed in contemporary western literature as men fighting to make the western frontier safe for white settlers while relinquishing their own worth as citizens in the ignominious role of armed second-class citizen soldiers![30]

Secessionist Propaganda: Problems in Establishing the Myth of Pax Democratica

After the American Civil War, the problem facing recalcitrant secessionist-minded southerners was how to fashion a political mindset that juxtaposed a growing fear that all was lost, with one that converted racial sentiments into an institutionalized struggle between white benevolence and black evilness. If successfully accomplished, southern white leadership presupposed that they could declare that a calming rather than disruptive social environment was reestablished throughout the land.

In keeping with these sentiments, one aspirant for governor of South Carolina, R. B. Carpenter told investigators in the 1871 congressional committee on Ku Klux Klan activities that the best political characteristics he found in southern blacks was that they were childish and as such were being led astray by northern carpetbaggers and southern scalawags:

> They believed anything they are told, not matter how ridiculous. As an instance of that I will say that two of the most serious charges made against me by the colored population when I was a candidate for Governor were, first, that if I was elected I would reduce them to slavery; an second, failing to do that, I would not allow their wives and daughters to wear hoop-skirts![31]

Though Carpenter declared that such notions by Freedmen bordered on the absurd, he also suggested that their "ridiculous attitude" was matched only by a credulous personality that allowed white Republicans to exert, even after slavery, "absolute control over them as any slaveholder."[32] Through such deceitful and hypocritical methods, he proposed, individuals hostile to a "pax Democratica" successfully gained legislative control of the state by assuring the ex-slave, "we are your friends; we are going into this thing and have you educate your children, and make everything better for you."[33] Actually, Governor Carpenter feared what most whites dreaded about the Freedmen: once having gained self-confidence and an understanding of the political process, they would become an anathema to southern whites' interest.

Surmising that preservation of conservative whites' racial interest was sacrosanct and congruous for full economic recovery of the south, Carpenter argued that such feelings did little to abate southern whites' deep-seated anxieties concerning carpetbaggers and scalawags successfully influencing southern blacks. Attached to his concerns was a belief that Republicans had convinced the Freedmen that southern planters should forfeit control over the vast plantations and that those lands properly belonged to those who labored on them, not to their former masters![34] Undoubtedly, many northerners also speculated on the economic repercussions of liberating 4 million stateless Africans within the territorial bounds of their ex-masters.

By June 1865, both southern conservatives and northern liberals were aware that the other southerner, the liberated African, was very much aware of his own refugee status, as well as the existence of "fatal cracks in a moribund social order" that portended either a race or class war on the political horizon. From this perspective, a series of ultimately dangerous and frightening issues forced many (but not all) southern whites to confront the possibility of outright physical attack by former slaves, as well as the torching of planters' dwellings, gin houses (cotton barns), and crops, slaughtering of livestock, rendering useless of any equipment required to run an efficient farm and an ultimate demand for reparations would be part of the Freedmen's arsenal in their struggle for the land.[35]

Examples of this were not difficult to find, particularly when organized bands of Freedmen successfully challenged terrorist threats from Ku Kluxers and similar type groups during the terror campaigns of 1870. Accounts of armed Freedmen enlisting in clubs such as the Union Leagues, Loyal Leagues and Grant Ranger Clubs suggest that some level of success was achieved in protecting black voters during the 1870 municipal elections.[36] In Georgia during the same period some 150 armed black men rallied to protect the militant Reverend Henry M. Turner against white terrorist threats; another 1,000 armed men assembled in 15 minutes to guard a Florida state senator, Robert Meacham, from assassination.[37] So fervent were the feelings of many Freedmen in protecting their newly gained constitutional rights that individuals such as Henry Lipscomb, a Spartanburg, South Carolina, farmer, declared that "at the start" black people were not afraid of Klan terror. They were at the least determined to demonstrate their will to vote; "they went up and voted, every one of them, and some swam the river in order to, and some waded"[38] Illustrating this resolve, Edward Magdol the following incident:

> Richard Burke of Gainesville, Alabama, a former slave, was by 1870 a Baptist preacher and the representative in the state legislature for Sumter County. He had a reputation or being a peaceful man. Nevertheless, in August 1870, he was shot to death in a riot in the town of Livingston. The shooting occurred at a political rally when some white men attempted to break up the meeting and in the course of the ensuing fracas opened fire on the assembled blacks, some of whom fled because they were unarmed. Burke met them at the edge of town an denounced them as "cowardly sons-of-bitches; You go back and shoot out your last load of ammunition, and then club your guns and fight to the last." This was the Nat Turner side of the peaceable former slave.[39]

Additional evidence supporting Carpenter's apprehensions were quickly validated when one impassioned black South Carolina Congressman, Beverly Nash, advised his constituents in 1866:

> The Reformers complain of taxes being too high. I tell you that they are not high enough. I want them (whites) taxed until they put these lands back where they belong, into the hands of those who worked for them. You toiled for them, you labored for them and were sold to pay for them, and you ought to have them.[40]

Irrespective of Nash's charge, Carpenter was not prepared to claim that there was a concerted attempt by blacks to wage a race war or that one was imminent. Neither was he willing to acknowledge that black political assertiveness had extended beyond rhetoric and was beginning to result in a great many white-owned cotton gin houses and dwelling being torched. To do otherwise would be to admit the existence of a direct political and military threat to white hegemony and by implication recognize the capability and determination of an alleged pariah race! Instead, the Carpenters of the south choose to deduce that it was expected that "uncultivated wild men," such as South Carolina's "coloreds," would be subject to very strong passions and impressions if they felt they have "been particularly ill-treated or anything of the sort," and that they are therefore very capable of "fearful revenge."[41] Selecting a gruesome incident as an example, and one that he knew would arouse white Carolinians' deepest anxieties about black violence, Carpenter recalled that when he was a judge:

> In several cases of murder that came before me, sometimes the man would have twenty bullet wounds. In one case in particular, not only was his head cut off, but he had four or five stabs in his right breast; his heart was literally pierced four or five times, stabbed through and through, and then he was disemboweled. They are a very peaceable people naturally, and if let alone they want to do right; but when their passions overcome them and they commit crimes they do it with a vengeance.[42]

However the threat of violence was only one aspect of racial relationships that appeared as a plague to southern whites. A more critical if not deeply embedded problem was envisioning blacks with any passion for life beyond that of childlike imitation of whites! Two hundred and fifty years of southern history had not prepared them for enhanced social or political relationship with the ex-slave. Accordingly, attempts by Freedmen to obtain economic independence through land ownership, local businesses, as skilled workers, or to participate in the social cultural realm of society beyond that as subordinates was regarded by patronizing whites as a dangerous and aberrant occurrence. Any achievement that contravened centuries of paternalistic repression was deemed unacceptable, thereby requiring immediate suppression. Agreeing as much, Carpenter's condescending response to congressional investigators implying that blacks have a "peculiar disposition" and an enormous "ability to be misled," was not surprising:

> Yes sir. Still there is a great deal of kind feeling toward them on the part of white people, and a great deal of kind feeling towards whites from a large class of the colored people. The colored men who are not either local or State politicians, who have any intelligence generally feel very kind to the whites, and come to them if they want any help about anything-if they want to borrow any money or get any help of the sort. A great many of them have very excellent credit and are of good character.[43]

Paternalistic concerns put aside, by the late 1860s it was becoming difficult for Southern white laborers to accept the fact that only a veneer of racial dominance separated them from significant social economic challenges by Freedmen. Accepting this as a social truth meant conceding that within a few years of their emancipation an enslaved race of blacks were becoming their economic equals and, given time, would surely seek if not proclaim social equality. Such an eventuality also inferred that the past was premised on an untruth, a deception, a lie that now in a devastating manner insinuated that throughout slavery, blacks alleged faithfulness and subordination to their white masters was primarily an orchestrated, highly manipulative and largely cunning and successful strategy for survival! It was in fact their war of deception and intrigue against a dominate group. Nevertheless even more devastating was the implication that God's sanctioning of slavery, and therefore Amer-

A man from the Freedmen's Bureau stands between armed Afro-Americans and Euro-Americans. *Harper's Weekly*, July 25, 1868. LIBRARY OF CONGRESS PRINTS AND PHOTOGRAPHS DIVISION, WASHINGTON, D.C.

ican economic ascendancy, as a sort of sacred trust was now questionable, particularly if the compliance of the slave was generally a subterfuge.

Throughout the post–Civil War period the notion of racial dominance both psychological and physical became handmaidens to American nationalism. And while the idea of "exuberant nationalism" or "manifest destiny" continued to define political and economic progress in racial terms, by deduction it legitimized progress in as an ever on-going violent struggle against nonwhites.[44] In such an evolving social process, southern whites ascribed social and political positioning to themselves, and by doing so envisioned political growth throughout the south as that which required their direct involvement for the sake of the nation's economic health. In fact, few other choices for a displaced white aristocracy or laboring class were available. In doing so, their choices were unambiguous. They either accepted the fact that an extra exertion of force was needed to obtain their former dominance, or accepted blacks' assertive economic and numerical challenge was a political fait accompli. For the Carpenters of the south and other remnants of a failed Confederacy, facing such alternative implied there were no alternatives or viable options, only a reliance on a past that proclaimed for almost three centuries: An ignoble race shall not be guaranteed a status of social grace and economic opportunity equal to that of an exalted race. This they could not reject. To do otherwise would be to accept life's vicissitudes, something that most conservative whites, north or south, were unprepared to brave.

For those who were now ready to confront the reality that an unending new insurgent-like civil war must now be fought, the specter of fighting throughout numerous southern hamlets and townships for the minds and souls of two irreconcilable but bound extremes was both appealing and frightening. On one side there were millions of ex-slaves seeking political and economic empowerment, and on the other, an even greater number of whites endeavoring to retain control over both. This irreconcilable dichotomy provoked one Boston journalist traveling throughout the south to remark, "Let conversations begin where it will, it ends with Sambo." In similar fashion, an Ohio schoolteacher arriving in Mississippi discovered that whether one was in hotels, railroads, or riverboats, "The nigger is the everlasting theme and the general complaint is they won't work."[45] Still others in delusional fashion hoped that massive hunger and disease among the black population would eventually bring on the specter of a "vanishing Negro," and "like the red man of the forest, the Freedmen will follow the tide of destiny to utter extinction."[46]

Though the possible extinction of the ex-slave as a "troublesome artifact of a past era" dominated the pages of many northern and southern newspapers, their growing resistance was also discussed, pondered and not always dismissed as unlikely. In the spring of 1866 a correspondent for the *Nation* magazine reported on such a discussion while traveling by carriage from Newberry, South Carolina, to the state capital in Columbia. Describing his fellow travelers—a Charleston merchant, a judge, a rich planter, a doctor of divinity and a wounded Confederate war veteran—the author wrote the following:

> All of my fellow travelers were young men and had been Confederate soldiers, and the night was chiefly spent in talking about their campaigns and companions in arms. In the midst of a story about old Jubal, who "certainly could just exactly swear," and who, if he believed there was a Providence, could never have expected to win a fight, the driver suddenly Interrupted the narrator by stopping the mules and asking us in a low tone if we were armed. It happened that there was not a weapon in the carriage. "That's bad," he said; "however, gentlemen, never mind; when I begin to talk about my pistols you must all say something similar. We're coming to a pretty bad place here. On the next plantation the niggers are a very unruly set, and some of them have guns. We must look sharp," One of our company had several thousand dollars about his person, and having a very bad opinion of free negroes, he evinced a good deal of anxiety and trepidation. It was to him, therefore, that we left the duty of responding to the driver.
>
> Soon the conversation between them began, the driver directing his voice Towards the right-hand side of the road and the passenger towards the left.
>
> "Yes, it's the prettiest rifle powder you ever saw. I wouldn't take any money for it if I couldn't get any more."
>
> "I prefer the cartridges: they're so much handier. A cartridge is always sitting up."
>
> "Oh, well, I always can have twelve shots, you know, and there are always pistols in the coach."
>
> "A man would be a fool to travel these times without his pistols."
>
> "Shouldn't think of it."
>
> "I say, driver, I would like very much to see any six men attack this coach tonight."
>
> "Well, now, they would have a very sorry time of it, sir. But there's no trouble of that kind on this road."
>
> By-and-bye we were informed that the danger was past, and then for awhile the negro was the theme of discourse. My three companions and the driver represented four districts, and each reported it as an undoubted fact that the Freedmen were forming themselves into companies and holding meetings at night for the purpose of drill. I enquired if many of them had arms, and was told that every nigger had a gun. The niggers around the driver's house couldn't get ahead of him, for he had two that told him everything.[47]

After hearing similar rumors of drilling Freedmen, the *Nation* correspondent made inquiries of General Ralph Ely who was the Acting Assistant Commissioner of the Freedmen's Bureau for fifteen districts in northern and western South Carolina. Ely asserted that

In one instance, the assertions were so positive and seemed so well supported that he rode out himself to [a] plantation in order to make an investigation on the spot. Having been posted where he could see and not be seen, he was an eye-witness of the whole parade. Negroes to the number of thirty or forty men, women, and children had gathered themselves together near their cabins and were drawn up in line. Some shouldered sticks, some had gun-stocks, some gun barrels, some guns, and some were empty handed. They marched and counter-marched and halted, and marched again in straight lines and curves for nearly half an hour, their evolutions being interspersed with dancing and rough play and accompanied by much laughter and noise. When he had witnessed these maneuvers for some time, the general went out and had an interview with the people. They said they were only having a frolic imitating the soldiers. None of the firearms were serviceable. In several instances he had made an examination of the facts and had found them similar to these stories about Negroes drilling are not worthy of serious consideration.[48]

The irony of these accounts is that in the former instance, ex–Confederate sympathizers were attempting to bluff their way through an assumed danger by alluding to nonexistent weaponry, and in the latter situation, drilling Freedmen did so without the necessary ammunition or serviceable arms to conduct a military action if they so desired. In both occasions, symbolic gesturing, though harmless, conveyed a level of deadly seriousness in motivation if not intent. While the coach riders took care not to reveal their vulnerable status to local Freedmen, the likelihood that frolicking drilling Freedmen would acknowledge the serious of any future intent to a white military officer was contextually absurd for a number of reasons.

Returning federal soldiers to the south, many of whom were ex-slaves, quickly discovered that local Republican activists were attempting to organize rural blacks into disciplined structures that would give meaning to their lives, such as the Union Leagues. Though these emerging social structures focused on alleviating the Freedmen from the horrors of postwar America, they also provide a framework for self-organization.[49] Companies styled after the military, "visibly reshaped public space to accommodate a working class male structure of social authority, independent of the old regime's obligations." In this respect, what worried General Ely and others was the Freedmen's development of a collective consciousness as a result of continued military held by political clubs that eventually would spill over into increased demands for fair contracts between planters and sharecropping families. For the even less critical Republican mind, the notion that drills of this sort were establishing the early sinews of an armed political formation that on the grassroots level would eventually become the backbone of an active resistance campaign against terrorism was not envisioned or suspected.

Imperatives for Struggle

Many unforeseen problems occurred throughout postbellum America, as time-honored practices seemed no longer applicable. Attempts to render clarity to familiar exigencies were now complicated by a growing network of informational sources that added additional perspectives and social remedies. A multitude of rumors, hearsay, innuendos, speculation and conjectures found their way into print and for many became truth. Ascertaining what was germane and plausible became difficult as new values were created and old mores were modified or disregarded. However, increasingly southern white nationalists, propagandizing the issue of racial domination refined customs from what were once natural into what was now essential if power was to be retained. As one observer put it: "The Propagandist naturally cannot reveal the true intentions of the principle for whom he acts ... that would be to submit the projects to public discussion, to the scrutiny of public opinion, and thus to prevent their success ... propaganda must serve instead as a veil for such projects, masking true intention."[50]

In this regard efforts to define blacks as a pariah race necessitated visible proof that as a group they fulfilled all of the necessary criteria. For some, this was not a difficult process, for once separated from official enslavement in 1865 blacks were a disruptive influence within the traditional social structure of Old Dixie. In South Carolina, the Freedmen's threat to white domination was not only numerical but if allowed to mature into an effective political entity, would easily become the engine for black domination throughout the state.

For example, the struggle for land and enfranchisement during the postbellum period was so intense that in the fall of 1865, an article in the *New Orleans Tribune* noted that a black woman in South Carolina who thought "out loud" about owning land almost had her house burned to the ground by the Ku Klux. Identifying South Carolina's planter class as the "stumbling block," "a great obstacle to peace" and a class that resisted "public security, union and harmony" throughout the state, the author asserted that South Carolina was in the midst of an agrarian class war over land and that in such a struggle most if not all planters would resist any attempt to expropriate their property even if it took subverting the political machinery of the state. By doing so, all attempts to share the land with "a new class of man," primarily the African, were frustrated.[51]

This development was further complicated by President Andrew Johnson's inclination to award leniency for those who supported the Confederate cause. In doing so, he turned a deaf ear to complaints by black farmers whose lands were systematically expropriated by terrorist gangs who were marginally employed by the planter class. As a result, the federal government's plan to distribute land in an equitable manner under a program called the Southern Homestead Act of 1866 in theory provided a basis for regularizing property ownership on a more equitable racial basis. In practice this initiative was falling apart under the weight of southern states who pursued a policy of white racial preference and terror through a legal device know as the Black Codes.[52]

> Planters not only prohibited black landownership they enacted extreme measures of social control that virtually restored slavery. The Black Codes struck directly at Freedmen striving to escape subordination and to obtain their communities. It was class and race legislation. But Planters escalated the struggle on the political plane by pressing President Johnson to curb the redistribution of lands to Freedman. Simultaneously, they demanded that the results of the war be set aside by their insistent demand for restoration of their lands. The President responded with alacrity during the second half of 1865 and until his impeachment.[53]

Southern planters' fear of black domination was so absolute that as they began relinquishing their antebellum "capitalistic identities," retribution was sought against the new social order by first attacking the general black populace and then those agencies that supported the Freedmen's political and economic franchise.[54] Among those agencies to be attacked was the federal government's program, the Bureau of Refugees, Freedmen, and Abandoned Lands, also known as the Freedmen's Bureau. The bureau not only assisted blacks in obtaining farming land but also provided an infrastructure for further development in the areas of voting, education, banking and political representation. Undoubtedly, it was hoped that with the insertion of Republican-styled institutions and the spreading of their philosophical agendas throughout the old Confederacy, a new class of black southerners and enlightened whites would begin to push their way into the halls of political and economic power to first challenge then displace the former racial status quo. As one observer noted:

> There was the nub of the matter — the struggle over the land in the summer and fall of 1865 was an agrarian class conflict. The planters resisting expropriation used the machinery of state....
>
> At the same time it should be realized that former Confederate planters hoped to prevent their displacement as a ruling class by the so-called carpetbagger or northern entrepreneur and planter. This much may be conceded to their paternalistic self-conscious assertion of hegemony.[55]

However, this situation was further exacerbated by a pronounced economic weakness of the newly freed populace, and the sheer massive scale and economic implications of emancipating over four million people whose previous and present labor is critically tied to the nation's economy. Southern planters and northern investors acutely aware of the importance of this labor force in restructuring the south sensed an immediate threat to their interest. Speaking to this point, one planter's letter to the *New York Times* succinctly expressed the feelings of undoubtedly countless others when he addressed the issue of possible labor scarcity and its remedy:

Four years ago I purchased a plantation near Charleston, S.C., which at the time was settled by the hands of the former owner. These Freedmen had during the war been planting on their own account on Edisto and other islands in the vicinity, but at the end of the war all had returned to the plantation, on which they were born and had labored for many years. As they had planted a crop of corn and cotton, I agreed to receive one-third of the cotton for the rent of the land for that year. I have reason to believe that they gave me nearly my share. The following year, 1867, I endeavored to hire these hands, offering to give them liberal wages by the year, feed them, give them houses and gardens, and as much land as they want to plant in corn and potatoes. They refused the offer, but proposed to remain and cultivate the land on the same terms as the previous year. This I declined, and they left to a man and woman to plantations in the vicinity where they would work on the share system. Their efforts that year were ill repaid, partly owning to the wet season. The next year they continued planting on the share system. That year, 1868, proved still more disastrous to them, and on the 1st of January, 1869, they came back to their old home and begged to be employed on my terms. I engaged some fifty men and women — all that I could employ. The rest returned to their precarious cultivation with great reluctance. Thus far, (and my crop is "laid by,") these hands have performed their contract faithfully and done their work well; so well that old planters say "the work is done as well as in old times," — before the war [see Appendix A for more text from this letter].[56]

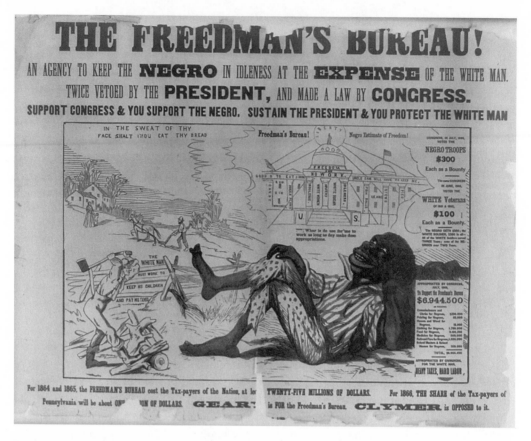

Racist poster attacking radical Republicans and the Freedmen's Bureau ("Freedman's" in head-line is an error). Poster depicting blacks idle at the expense of whites. The conservative poster advocates the election of Hiester Clymer who ran for governor on a white-supremacy platform, supporting President Andrew Johnson's anti–Reconstruction policies. LIBRARY OF CONGRESS RARE BOOK AND SPECIAL COLLECTIONS DIVISION, WASHINGTON, D.C.

For many planters, this newly found economic truth underscored their demands for a reconstituted labor system. Though it proposed the restructuring of cherished social values, it also proposed the development of a wage labor system permeated with the dynamics of the previous slave society and the social etiquette of a plantation culture. Secure in the belief that they knew their negroes and the time-tested ways of handling them, most planters belittled any suggestion that laborers would continually assert independent thought in defiance of their previous owners. Nor did most planters feel a need to elaborate on what for most was the economic racial truth of the day: Blacks were best controlled for their own benefit by a systematic form of steady labor.

Within this racially stratified and polarized environment, a major contradiction unfolded as many economically displaced southern whites became obsessed with the possibility of reclaiming what they perceived was lost during the Civil War. Emanating from a culture entrenched with racial entitlement, on both a personal and organizational level they clashed with Freedmen who sensed and grabbed at every opportunity to strip away those residual quasi-legal bonds of subordination and implicit dependency that persisted despite the abolishment of slavery by the Thirteenth Amendment to the Constitution.[57] Both racial groups now judged and tested the prospects of open competition and with expectations as great as their fears, were now determined that this moment should not pass without a struggle.

The moment that would not pass was steeled in four years of civil war and centuries of passive resistance by blacks. With the insertion of black federal soldiers throughout the five military districts of the south and the creation of almost one million new voters as a result of the Reconstruction Act of 1867, the enhanced social placement of blacks on paper singularly threatening the racial status quo throughout the south.[58] The actual attempt to implement the new racial alignment predictably raised the level of violence to new heights and consequently ushered in what was "one of the bloodiest eras in American history."[59]

Notwithstanding the immense racial enmity that existed immediately following the Civil War, subsequent dynamics of assumed racial entitlement by white Americans united the nations southern and northern financial sectors into an interminable violent battle against black empowerment, wherever it existed. Between 1867 and 1871, this fact precipitated the murder of some 20,000 people at the hands of Ku Klux terrorists, while the cream of southern society, its planters, doctors and lawyers denied the very existence of the Klan or their connection to these crimes.[60] However, two factors emerged from this cauldron of terrorism; first, conservative southerners insistence for total political and economic domination regardless of the cost in lives to achieve this goal. Second, their incapacity to accommodate or comprehend the Freedmen's phenomenal surge toward economic self-determination. In a sense, the demise of slavery created social engineering problems for an American economy and political structure that was resisting the full and equal participation of its ex-enslaved class in the demands of free market economy.

For example, though southern blacks enjoyed a clear numerical advantage in at least four southern states by 1870, this was not the case in the north, where whites agreed that maintaining blacks "minority" status was beneficial for all.[61] However, though racial disparity throughout the northern states lessened perceptions of blacks as a potential threat, their high visibility coupled with an assertive desire for social uplift made them barely acceptable to a native whites or an increased numbers of European immigrants.

Similarly, northern blacks, lacking numerical advantage or economic parity, increasingly found themselves continually socially transfigured or politically diminished either by law or custom. They were a tolerated deviation from the norm and though often empathized with, floundered in a sea of infinite social hostility.

Relentlessly newspapers such as *The New National Era* pointed out those "numerical" characteristics in specific southern states (states shown in boldface in Table 1, page 30) and the implicit political threat posed if blacks were to gain numerical superiority in specific northern states.

Nonetheless, one obviously cautious African American commented:

> As a Negro's color carries with it the presumption of loyalty, nothing but ingratitude can open our ranks to the enemy, and nothing but disloyalty will attempt the corruption of our people.
>
> Let us be on our guard. If with godly showing as to numbers we allow either a white rebel or a colored renegade to demoralize our ranks, it will not be our misfortune and disgrace, but the step will doubtless involve evil irreparable.
>
> We have a balance of power that may be wielded for good or evil. If we keep true, natural and earnest, our alliances will be where they always have been, with party with which it

TABLE 1. COMPARATIVE RACIAL POPULATION NUMBERS FOR 22 STATES (1870)

	White	Colored
Alabama	526,271	437,770
Arkansas	324,143	111,259
California	358,143	4,259
Connecticut	457,504	8,627
Delaware	90,989	21,627
Florida	**77,747**	**82,677**
Georgia	591,550	465,698
Indiana	1,338,710	11,428
Kentucky	919,484	236,167
Louisiana	**357,456**	**358,073**
Maryland	515, 918	171,131
Mississippi	**353,899**	**437,131**
Missouri	1,063,489	118,503
New Jersey	646,699	25,336
New York	3,831,590	40,005
North Carolina	629,942	361,522
Ohio	2,302,808	36,673
Pennsylvania	2,849,259	56,949
South Carolina	**291,300**	**412,320**
Tennessee	820,722	283,019
Texas	420,891	183,921
Virginia/W.Va.	1,047,299	548,907

Source: Census data extracted from *The New National Era* newspaper, 12 May 1870.

is "possible" for us to form alliances. But if we become political tricksters, we have the power of damning our race in its political infancy.[62]

Having a clear majority in four southern states (Florida, Louisiana, Mississippi and South Carolina) and imminent numerical parity in Alabama and Georgia, southern blacks intuitively expressed a positive political and social attitude about the future. By the fall of 1868, southern whites viewed this kind of expressed assertiveness as "arrogant" and "impudent"! White America was further shocked when an article in the *New York Times* titled "Address of the Negroes to the native Whites" proclaimed that blacks would no longer accept their pariah social status as a permanent social arrangement:

Fellow-citizens: We the colored citizens of Charleston, address you, in answer to two very remarkable addresses which you have of late issued in this city respecting us and our race in this city and state, and in fact to the whole world, in which you have been pleased to allude to our race in such a manner, and in such terms, as to place us in a false light before all mankind, attributing to us motives and designs, aims and determinations of revenge, raping, arson, murder, pillage and violence such as we never entertained for a moment, nor had any reason to perform or attempt; you have in that special address to the whites of this state, and to the whole country charged us with seeking to destroy your property, to bring on a war of races, and thus inaugurate a reign of terror, such as did prevail here during the late unhappy war, which attempt we emphatically deny as groundless....

We wish to see our agriculture, mechanical and mercantile resources developed, and we desire to see the thousands of poor people on homesteads of their own, contributing their share in paying the taxes of our State; and we are willing to join hands and heart with you in forwarding all of those interest, But we cannot surrender the great palladium of our liberties—the ballot box—for any consideration whatever. And if we are to be massacred because we refuse to vote the Democratic ticket; if we are to be murdered, then let it come—we can die but once; and if, as you state, thirty millions of white men are going to fall upon four millions because they are black, and will not vote for Horatio Seymour and F.P. Blair for President and Vice President of the United States, both of whom have declared that the Negroes have no right to vote, then we are prepared to die, but not to vote to be killed.

With a strong faith in God, and eternal justice, we wait the decision of high heaven. If our cause be just, god will now suffer us to fall with a firm faith in the right. We ask nothing at the hands of our fellow-man but a fair chance in the race of life, and equal opportunities for ourselves, our wives and our children. We ask no more.[63]

Understanding the immensity of those social and political problems at hand, neither unreconstructed southern white Democrats or northern Republican who favored reconstructing the south were blinded by the racial and political implications of this letter. Few had any false illusions about the struggle that would ensue around issue of transforming the ex slave into full citizenship and the concomitant financial impact this would have on an already devastated southern economy, as portrayed in Table 2.

TABLE 2. ASSESSED VALUE OF SEVEN EX-CONFEDERATE STATES, 1860–1870

North Carolina	$292,297,602	$132,046,391
Louisiana	$434,787,265	$350,588,810
Kentucky	$528,212,265	$423,776,099
Florida	$68,929,685	$31,167,468
Mississippi	$529,479,912	$154,685,527
Georgia	$618,232,387	$202,565,557
VA & W.VA	$657,821,339	$458,821,967
Total	$3,129,760,455	$1,753,651,809
Decreased	$1,377,108,646	

Source: *The New National Era.* 11 May 1871, p. 2, col. 3. Note: totals for 1860 and 1870 are miscalculated in original source, for example, total for 1860 was listed as $3,209,935,880 and total for 1870 was listed as $1,455, 782, 515. Similarly, decreased amount in original source is $1,754,153,365. Corrected totals are used within the text.

Though four years of civil war severely crippled the south's economy, hard-line southern Democratic whites made it plain that they would rather plunge the region into further chaos than accept the ascension of black political or economic parity. As one observer of recalcitrant whites commented in the *New National Era:* "To people of any practical common sense, the figures we present would prove an argument against all future rebellion that would render them impossible; *but* they seem incapable of comprehending such an argument, and lack the ability rather than the disposition to plunge into another insurrection."

By 1870, the newly ratified fourteenth and fifteenth Amendments to the U.S. Constitution naturalized the nations black population and in theory proclaimed that "the vote shall not be denied or abridged by the United States or by any State on account of race, color, or previous condition of servitude."[64] Given that political interest inside and outside the Freedmen's community assumed that *inclusion* within America's political system was the desire if not stated goal, only in a few instances was self-government advanced as an alternative goal.[65] Though few examples of self-government existed, social historian W.E.B. DuBois noted that "the chief witness of Reconstruction, the emancipated slave himself, has been almost barred from [the] court," of public opinion on this issue.[66] This observation by DuBois underscored a divergent aspect of an emerging black leadership that on one hand envisioned itself as being nonrural, well-educated, conservative and acculturated to middle-class American ideals and objectives. However, there also existed a rural, upcountry, village leadership who viewed land acquisition, self-sufficiency and armed defense as the all-important issue and goal of the day.[67] Ironically when these polarized political elements within the Freedmen populace clashed, it occurred in conjunction with conservative whites obstruction of black Republican demonstrations.

In summer 1867 Major General W. Martin, commander of the Tennessee Military District, sent a letter to the Commissioner of the Bureau of Refugees, Freedmen and Abandoned Lands Bureau, General O. O. Howard, calling attention to the widening philosophical rupture between Freedmen on the issue of self-reliance and armed self-defense. Citing an incident that occurred on July 6, 1867, Martin's letter reveals the building up of explosive tensions that were beginning to explode all throughout the south as blacks rejected the notion of being passive actors in the structuring of their destiny:

General:

I have the honor to submit the following report on the affray that occurred at Franklin, Williamson County, on the 6th inst. between the colored Loyal League on the one part, a body of Conservatives composed principally of ex-rebel soldiers & Negroes on the other. For a correct understanding of the causes which culminated in riot and bloodshed on the 6th at 8 o'clock p.m. it is proper to refer to a series of occurrences which took place a few days previously.

The Colored League had recently procured drums and a fife, and had been marching about the outskirts of the town after supper for several nights without disturbing anyone. On different occasions they were interrupted by colored Conservatives (Dick Crutcher and A. J. Gadsey passing through their column while marching, firing shots &c). In consequence of this interference some members of the League consulted a lawyer and prominent citizens to ascertain if any legal steps could be taken to protect themselves against thee disturbances. Finding that there was no legal remedy the League armed some of its members for protection. They were again disturbed and fired on, and returned the fire without injury to anyone. The occurrence taking place out of town was perhaps not known to many citizens.

A general feeling of insecurity seemed to seize upon the members of the League and the idea prevailed that their procession and marching were objected to by many persons and fears were entertained that attempts might be made to prevent their continuances. There is no doubt that the conservatives viewed the marching and displays of the League as a military demonstration and feared that it might result strife. Impudent remarks and foolish boasts were made by individuals of both parties, and each had come to regard the other with a jealous eye.

On the 6th instant there was a political meeting which was addressed by Mr. John Trimble & Mr. Elliott, Republican candidate for Congress & State Legislature respectively.

This meeting passed off quietly & amicably. In the afternoon a colored Conservative named John Williams passed through the town and was prevailed upon to return & speak. After he had spoken a short time, the Radicals became dissatisfied with his style & attempted to withdraw from the meeting. A Mr. J. C. Bliss a member of the League, was assailed by Col. John House & a party of armed men who seemed to be acting under his orders. He was struck by this Col. House & assaulted by abusive epithets. Mr. Bliss them went among the members of the League in a very excited condition & their attempted to get a pistol with which to defend himself or to attack Col. House. This altercation between Bliss & House & the efforts of the Conservatives to prevent the Radicals from leaving the meeting created great excitement among the members of the League. They were marched away there from the point where the speaking occurred & fired a few shots in the air as they moved off as a salute as they claim. Their white friends urged them to disperse & go to their homes, which they seemed unwilling to do, feeling that their liberties were infringed upon; however they were prevailed upon to march out of town to a grove where they were addressed for an hour & a half by Mr. Elliott & Mr. Clifton, both of whom again urged them to disperse & go to their homes. They seemed to object to this for two reasons—the first was that the Conservatives would attribute their retirement to cowardice; the second that they had planned a torchlight procession for the evening which they were unwilling to abandon, but they finally decided to march into the public square & there break ranks & disperse to their homes, giving up the plan of a torchlight procession. This was about half past eight o'clock in the evening. In the meantime it was manifest that a collision was expected — and the Conservatives were preparing for it by gathering arms and ammunition into the store of Col. John House —& perhaps other places around the square. During the afternoon also the number of arms seemed to have increased among the members of the Loyal League, numbering perhaps ten muskets & a few pistols, the number not known. At half past eight, the League marched towards the public square and the party of Conservatives estimated at from 25 to 30, apparently under the command of Col. House, formerly of the Rebel Army, took position under corner of the wall of House's store facing the square.

Just at this time any efficient officer of the law could have interfered and prevented bloodshed, all that was necessary was for either party to disperse and go to their homes or to refrain from firing. The acting Mayor of this city was well aware that a conflict was imminent, in fact he stated to me that he knew it would take place, but made no effort to prevent the outbreak. There was no police force in the town, no indication whatever of the presence of a civil government. It seems that the town had been given up willingly to the mob.

The colored League seemed fully to expect a conflict on reaching House's store, they had probably been informed of the assembling of the armed party of Conservatives. They marched on, however, past this party of Conservatives at House's corner with perhaps ten armed men at the head of the procession. In the meantime Col. House & his party had been notified by a N. A. O. Williams, a prominent member of the Colored League, that they were merely marching into the square for the purpose of breaking ranks & dispersing to their homes.

When the rear of the procession had come about opposite the left flank of House's party a white man advanced from the Conservatives Party ten or fifteen steps toward the Colored League and fired two pistol shots towards the league. There is now a conflict of testimony as to the party which fired the first volley succeeding these pistol shots. Many witnesses testified that these pistol shots were followed by a volley from the entire Conservative party, and that that was returned by the armed men of the Colored League, while others testify that immediately on the firing of the pistol shots the armed men of the

Colored League faced about & fired a volley, killing Michl. H. Cody Jr. and wounding six white & several black Conservatives.

No doubt that the firing of the Colored League was very deliberate & very accurate as nearly as many Conservatives were killed or wounded as there were arms in the hands of the colored men and it was evident that none of the arms were reloaded and fired a second time. It is worthy of remark that the 27 colored men whose wounds were dressed by Dr. D. B. Cliff of Franklin were all wounded in the back or in the back part of the limbs sowing clearly that they were fired upon from the rear & flank by the Conservative Party while marching in procession, or after they had broken ranks and were running away from the conservative mob.[68]

It is extremely important to note that in those instances when Freedmen were adequately armed, self-defense was deliberate, accurate and substantial enough to parley those brutalities generally associated with southern conservative terrorist attacking unarmed blacks. Yet as the above conflict dramatically illustrates, allied associations between conservative whites and blacks to block economic and political parity of the ex-slaves was not unknown, and in fact often accentuated the viciousness, fear and political duplicity of a racist ideology propagated through terrorism. Though it is not clear what General Martin's views were as to the likelihood of Freedmen in Tennessee securing their constitutional rights in the state that spawned the Ku Klux in the previous year, he did however close this letter by stating

> On the 8th inst. I visited Franklin and found the town quiet and the people apparently very sorry that the affray had occurred. All parties, especially the white conservatives, seemed very solicitous that the company of U.S. troops sent there by Genl. Duncan on the 7th should remain. The Circuit Court met on the 8th at 10 o'clock and there was consequently an occasion for the Military Authorities to interfere further than to prevent another outbreak. The courts of Williamson County have heretofore been noted for their impartial administration of justice where colored people were concerned.[69]

Racial conflict of this type did not occur in a political vacuum. As the brand of Freedmen leadership that choose resistance rather than complicity with racial terrorism grew, southern Democratic conservative whites, be they planters, small farm owners or returning Confederate soldiers, instinctively sensed that the Freedmen's franchise was an obtrusive and dangerous development that had to be curtailed as quickly as possible and at any cost. From fall 1866, the assertive leadership by the Freedmen particularly as demonstrated in Franklin, Tennessee, was viewed by southern white planters and small farm owners as an obtrusive social development. To support their contentions, angry southern conservatives simply had to look at the growing numbers of Freedmen farms beginning to appear in the rich agricultural areas of Florida, Georgia, South Carolina and Louisiana and the economic support they were receiving from government institutions such as the national Freedmen's Savings Bank and Trust Company.[70]

According to the Memphis city council's census, whites returning to Memphis after the war discovered that the black population had increased threefold from 3,882 to 10,995.[71] An even more significant realization for whites was the federal government's structuring of a more comprehensive program for the ex slaves development within society, one that was coordinated by the newly conceived Bureau of Refugees, Freedmen, and Abandoned Lands, better known as the Freedmen's Bureau.[72] Supervised by Republican officials throughout southern cities, this federally sponsored bureau had as its multifaceted mandate the supplying of medical supplies, educational materials, construction of Freedmen schools, supervision over contracts between the Freedmen and their new employers, managing confiscated land from "unreconstructed" Confederate acolytes, instituting a land lease program, and when necessary acting as an agency to investigate registered abuse charges from Freedmen.[73]

In August 1865, the Freedmen's Bureau in Memphis conducted a census that concluded out of 27,703 residents, 16,509 were black.[74] With nearly 60 percent of the total population black, of which a large number were skilled laborers, the yearning to publicly establish their economic acuity was ever present. This development not only signaled an economic threat to white laborers but also suggested that a political challenge to the racial status quo would not be far behind.

Once the Memphis's Freedmen's Savings Bank and Trust Company was established in 1865, locally skilled blacks such as Buck Fuller, a drayman, Henry Gerry, a painter, Julius Nelson, a laborer, and Turner Hunt, a carpenter, could now open up their first saving accounts, thereby creating a basis for new personal and community wealth.[75] Needless to say, the response by Memphis whites to blunt these efforts and thwart this emerging entrepreneurial spirit was swift. By January 1866, newly elected governor William G. Brownlow pushed through the Tennessee state legislature a bill that eventually became law clarifying any "misunderstanding" some might have entertained about the Freedmen's *true* status, notwithstanding the Thirteenth Amendment. His bill proclaimed:

> That persons of African and Indian descent are hereby declared to be competent witnesses in all the courts of this state, in as full a manner as such persons are by an act of Congress competent witnesses in all the courts of the United States, excluding such persons from competency are hereby repealed: *Provided, however,* That this act shall not be so construed as to give colored persons the right to vote, hold office, or sit on juries in this State; and that this provision is inserted by virtue of the provision of the 9th Section of the amended constitution, ratified February 22 1865.[76]

In the state that produced the Ku Klux, racism was so widespread that it was popularly known that "East Tennesseans, though opposed to slavery and secession, do not like 'niggers.'" Writing some seventy years later in 1935, noted scholar DuBois noted that more prejudice against color existed among the middle and poor classes, than among the planters who owned slaves by scores and hundreds.[77] For many secessionist-minded southerners, particularly those who would have to compete daily with assertive blacks, a kind of virulent racism was fundamental and undying. It tugged at the very essence of what it meant for many to be a white, southern and an American:

> The designs of the great secession [a] majority of Tennessee may have been changed by the events of the war, and so may have been their opinions of their own strength and of the strength of the government, but unless your memorialist greatly misunderstand them, their sentiments, sympathies, and passions remain unchanged. They welcome peace because they are disabled from making war; they submit because they can no longer resist; they accept results they cannot reject, and profess loyalty because they have a halter around their necks. They recognize the abolition of slavery because they see it before them as a fact; but they say it was accomplished by gross violations of the constitution, that the Negro is free only in fact, but not in law or of right.[78]

Exasperated by apparent disregard by blacks for their previously assigned racial status, white officials in Memphis began arresting specific blacks on the claim that they were in violation of the newly instated "Black Codes." Nonetheless, in 1866 these state-enforced codes became illegal, at least on paper, particularly after the federal Supreme Court decision in *Church v. State of Tennessee* that ruled the legal grounds for these codes were themselves null and void.[79] Codes or no codes, white Tennesseans suffered a severe psychological jolt when within a few years, the race that was viewed intellectually inferior, irresponsible and childish now appeared to be advancing faster toward economic viability than were whites.

Tennessee whites in particular had much to worry about, for just eighteen months after the war's end and despite bloody terrorist attacks Memphis blacks, an emerging class of Freedmen had accumulated 8 churches, 500 owned hacks, 8 stores, several saloons, 2 fruit stands, 2 furniture stores, 4 lunchrooms, and enough barbershops to organize the Memphis Colored Barber's Association. Census data from 1865 also indicates that while 300 blacks had property and money valued from $100 to $500, eighteen blacks had a worth of $500 to $1000, four blacks were worth $2000 or more, and three blacks had a worth of $5000 or more.[80]

For returning Confederate veterans and thousands of displaced white Memphis laborers, this sudden and phenomenal development was not only startling but a tormenting fact that contradicted every standard and known law of nature and God that they had been nurtured to believe since birth. Consequently, Freedmen who were able to amass capital and tried to purchase land were now threatened with expulsion. More to the point, to be black and a farm or landowner was in itself becoming a suspicious or criminal offense. In this regard, former Union Army General Fisk reported in 1866:

> I have today received the statement of two very respectable colored men who went into northern Mississippi from Nashville and rented plantations. Both were men of means, and one a *reputed* son of Isham G Harris, a former Governor of Tennessee. Both were very intelligent colored men that have been driven out and warned not to put their feet within the state again.[81]

Their intimidation, as reported in the *New York Herald*, came from individual's known as "regulators," who as in other southern states were "ex–Confederate cavaliers of the country," who had as their mission, "to visit summary justice upon any offenders against the public peace." The *Herald* also noted that,

> It is needless to say that their attention is largely directed to maintaining quiet and submission among the blacks. *The shooting or stringing up of some obstreperous "nigger" by the "regulators" is so common an occurrence as to excite little remark. Nor is the work of proscription confined to the freedman only.* The "regulators" go to the bottom of the matter, and strive to make it uncomfortably warm for any new settler with demoralizing innovations of wages for "niggers."[82]

Unquestionably for whites, particularly those who secessionist dreams were destroyed in the Civil War, the possible loss of racial privilege, preference or advantage was a psychological burden that cut across intraracial class lines throughout the south as well as most of America. However, to the degree that their efforts in suppressing challenges from the Freedmen class were successful while simultaneously criminalizing their efforts to succeed in an environment that marginalized their every movement is critical to this study. From this perspective, a content analysis of offenses committed by Freedmen and whites during this period and how they were adjudicated is instructive on how the law functioned in support of white conservative ideals.

The law in action on southern streets was generally skewed, biased and impatient with the notion of armed self-defense by blacks. For example, from 1865 to mid–1866, Memphis became a center for increased violent conflict between the races. In Collierville, a small town just east of Memphis, white citizens on August 24 forced two black soldiers off a passenger train and then lynched one of them for shooting a white man in self-defense who had pulled a gun on them while demanding a seat![83] In fact daily racial confrontations in Memphis became so endemic that one simply had to review the Memphis police records to ascertain the racialist nature of criminal arrest as blacks made up 49 percent of daily arrest.[84] In Charleston, South Carolina, the level of daily interpersonal violence and social disorder was rampant for both races, though in categories that were dichotomous and reflective of extreme polarized economic and social statuses. For instance, from February 1869 to January 1870 the Charleston Police Department affected some 3115 arrest in which blacks were charged with 79 percent of all larceny, 67 percent disorderly conduct, 85 percent vagrancy, 78 percent trespass, 68 percent safe keeping and 92 percent of burglary offenses.[85] However, during this same period, police records indicated that white Charlestonians predominated in the following categories, 70 percent for drunk & lying-down, 67 percent for drunk and disorderly conduct, 94 percent for selling liquor on Sunday, 69 percent for interfering with police, 74 percent for violation of a city ordinance and one person for desertion from a ship![86]

Statistics indicating the seemingly mild criminal behavior of Charleston whites as opposed to the social deviancy of Freedmen mask the troublesome post–Civil War reality of a racially promiscuous society, in which the transfer of political power and the changing social status of society's pariah race are in direct conflict with recalcitrant racial precepts of the past. In such a context, violent, forceful, challenging acts by an ex-enslaved race were penalized in a variety of punitive ways while antisocial activities such as whipping, raping, lynching and other similar terrorist activities by whites were generally ignored or reclassified under the rubric disorderly conduct, drunkenness or uncontrollable outrages. It would take a congressional investigation to even approach any semblance of judicial control when it came to whites murdering of blacks. Ironically, statistics indicating the Freedmen's criminality as listed above actually camouflaged acts of resistance to racism by a class of blacks who fervently rejected conservative southern white edicts about social ranking, culture and race. This extremely frustrating situation was further underscored by racial discrepancies in sentencing.

Of the 3,115 arrests in the Charleston judicial system, only some 350 prisoners were "delivered to magistrate" for sentencing, of which 255 were black and 95 were white. However data indicates that while 1047 prisoners were adjudicated by the Charleston court, 614 (59 percent) whites as opposed to 433 (41 percent) blacks were discharged. This could be explained partially by the fact that 77 percent of whites as opposed to 23 percent of blacks were able to pay their fines. Consequently out of 615 prisoners sent to the "House of Correction," 29 percent were white, 71 percent were black![87] Clearly rising levels of anti social behavior of Freedmen directly after the Civil War was fueled by a growing conflict over which race would enjoy the spoils of war and who would be deemed the political proprietor in the south.[88] The intensity of this struggle was discernible in almost every venue of southern life. For example, without exploring the conditions or abuses incurred during incarceration by Freedmen in Charleston jails, one can speculate about the following 1868 article in the conservative pro–Democratic *Charleston Daily Courier*:

> *Shameful.*—Complaints have been made of the appearance in the street of a Negro man almost in a state of nudity. When questioned, he stated that he had just been released from the Penitentiary, meaning thereby the House of Correction. This should not be allowed—when prisoners have served their time they should not be sent in the streets in a nude state; it becomes an offence against decency.[89]

In a bolder display of Freedmen antisocial behavior the *Courier* could not resist publishing the following incident:

> On Monday night a gentleman residing in Queen street, saw a Negro leaping his fence, and suspecting that he was intent upon stealing, he pursued and overtook this would be robber. When questioned as to his business he gave evasive answers and resisted the attempt made to Arrest him. Upon being threatened however, he signified his willingness to accompany the gentleman to the guard house. On the way to that place, at the corner of King and Queen streets, the thief knocked down His captor, while off his guard, and stabbed him in the breast, after which he made his escape. The wounded man was taken to his house and upon examination proved not dangerously injured, but the thief escaped and has not since been heard of. He will gets his desserts though one of these days.[90]

A few weeks later the same newspaper reported on a direct assault against local police authority:

> *Brutal Assault on a Policeman*: Yesterday, a short time after the accident at the corner of King and Queen streets, a crowd of excited colored men passed near the spot and made an assault upon a policeman who was standing by. The policeman had said nothing to any of the crowd, and the assault was without provocation and most brutal in its nature. After beating him they left him and passed on down the street with a shout for Pillsbury [Gilbert Pillsbury, first president of the Union League in South Carolina].[91]

Earlier that same day, another reported fight ensued between a "white and colored man" in downtown Charleston:

> Yesterday about one o'clock, a white and colored man became engaged in an altercation in Meeting street. The crowd of Negroes near soon rushed in and commenced a vigorous assault upon the three white men who were in company. In the fight Mr. Duncan Cameron was cut in the back of his neck by a knife in the hands of some person unknown. The wounded man was taken to his home where his wounds which fortunately were not of a serious character, received the proper attention. The party who inflicted the wound is not known.[92]

Indicative of heightened racial tensions, these daily encounters also represented the bottom tier of a social pyramid that was replete with racial skirmishes that reflected both inter- and intragroup dynamics. As such, class interest again masked in political rhetoric and racial symbolism structured an arena for both armed attack, resistance and retaliation between the races. For example, in an article titled "More bloodshed," it was reported:

Passengers by the Greenville Rail Road, Monday, report that a white man, whose name they did not know, but who was a Democrat, was shot through the thigh by a negro on Saturday night; and on Sunday night, Lee Nance, a colored man, but a Conservative from Newberry, and who was thought to be at the head of the party who fired on the white man was shot through the breast and it is thought mortally wounded.[93]

Yet near the same Greenville district, a local newspaper, *The Phoenix*, in a veiled warning to its "colored citizens" reported that

Yesterday, we learn that James Minor, a colored man who has been stumping the upper districts in the interest of the Democratic party, and was to return home Monday, a number of his political opponents proceeded to the Greenville depot, prepared, it is reported, to give him a *warmer* reception than he anticipated.

On this subject the *Phoenix* says: The killing of Randolph, and the lawless feeling apparently existing in portions of the up-country, is deeply deplored and deprecated by the better class of the community: and we sincerely hope that our colored citizens, who have been heretofore noted for their excellent behavior and praiseworthy conduct, will not be led astray by the excitement or the advice of bad men, and attempt to retaliate upon innocent individuals for the guilt of others, and by so doing estrange their white friends. If there is any law in the land, punishment will be meted out to law-breakers.[94]

Developing economic exigencies between the races was articulated not only in newspapers of the day but in personal journals and diaries. For example, the diary of Ella Gertrude Thomas, the wife of a successful antebellum South Carolina planter succinctly reveals a mindset shared by many of her class, particularly on the issue of slavery and the loss of accustomed economic and social advantage:

Sunday, October 8 1865: We owned more than 90 Negroes with a prospect of inheriting many more from Pa's estate. By the surrender of the southern army, slavery became a thing of the past and we were reduced from a state of affluence to comparative poverty. So far as I individually am concerned to utter beggary for the thirty thousand dollars Pa gave me when I was married was invested in Negroes alone. [Gertrude's father's will stated that she would receive $25,000 in property (mostly enslaved blacks) at the time of her marriage. Jefferson Thomas, her husband, was given $5,000 in his own right. There were additional bequests by the liberal father who left each of his seven children the equivalent of $45,000 in property and/or cash, with the prospect that they would inherit more when his estate was finally settled.]

This view of the case I did not at first take and it is difficult now to realize it. But "each heart knoweth its own bitterness" and I alone know the effect abolition of slavery has had upon me. I did not know until how intimately my faith in relations and my faith in the institution of slavery had been woven together. True, I had seen the evil of the latter but if the *Bible* was right then slavery *must be.*

Slavery was done away with and my faith in God's Holy Book was terribly shaken. For a time I doubted God. The truth of revelations, all, everything. I no longer took interest in the service of the church. From May until July [1865] I lived a sad life. Lived with a prospect of again becoming a mother and yet felt no longings, no desire for increased spiritual faith. When I prayed my voice appeared to rise no higher than my head. When I opened the Bible the numerous allusions to slavery mocked me. Our cause was lost. Good men had faith in that cause. Earnest prayers had ascended from honest hearts. Was so much faith to be lost? I was bewildered. I felt all this and could not see God's hand.[95]

Three years later, in 1868, Ella Thomas's attitude was mirrored by southern white state legislatures who in opposing federally supported institutions such as the Freedmen's Savings Bank and Trust Company argued that such institutions placed economic control in the hands of Republican federal authorities rather than the state Democratic party and their local political functionaries. This sentiment was accentuated by a general attitude among farm owners large and small that the real purpose of the Freedmen's Bank was to abrogate their traditional hold on the land by providing blacks with access to capital. This they claimed constituted an unfair arrangement between the federal government and local black leadership. As a result, everything possible was done to curtail the bank's growth, including threatening anyone who supported it. For example, black Virginians "depositing a reported $12,000 during the first weeks of operation," and were the Freedmen's Bank most important if not sole depositors; however, the bank refused to hire blacks as clerks![96] One Norfolk newspaper espousing a nineteenth-century version of anti-affirmative sentiment even exclaimed white Virginians must "rid the State of an element [blacks] that will hinder its prosperity, ... an element that would tax the property of others to relieve themselves of [the] obligation to educate their children and care for their paupers."[97]

Regardless of its detractors, annual reports from Freedmen's Bank indicated that from 1866 to 1870 there was a steady increase of depositors (Table 3, page 42). Once these reports were published in black-owned newspapers, there was little doubt about the determined and thus far successful efforts of Freedmen to establish an economic base throughout the south just five years after the abolition of slavery. Even far more foreboding for southern white Democrats was that given blacks rate of economic growth and political awakening in 1870, it was apparent for even the most skeptical observer that black Americans would become an economic and political force in the south as well the rest of the country within the foreseeable future.

Reflecting on a plethora of schemes that eventually fostered the demise of the Freedmen's Bank, DuBois asserted that there was a perception, albeit false, that the Freedmen's Bank was more a philanthropic effort by northern liberal whites than an institution founded on sound economic efforts emanating from within the black community:

Before 1871, there had been errors in the conduct of the bank and disregard of law. Indeed, it is not clear whether in the original charter the bank had any right to establish branches outside of the District of Columbia. Soon the speculators of Washington were attracted by the assets of the bank and discovered how they were growing. The assets were, however, amply protected by provisions requiring investment mainly in government bonds. An amendment to the charter was introduced into congress in 1870 which provided that one half of the deposits invested in United States bonds might be invested in other notes and bonds secured by real estate mortgages. Immediately the pennies of poor black laborers were replaced by worthless notes. Money was loaned recklessly to the speculators in the District of Columbia. Jay Cooke and Company, the great bankers, borrowed half a million dollars, and this company and the First National Bank of Washington controlled the Freedman's Bank between 1870 and 1873. Runs were started on the bank and then an effort was made to unload the whole thing on Frederick Douglass as a representative Negro. This was useless and the bank finally closed in June 1874. The *Commission of*

Three which liquidated the Freedmen's Savings Bank paid depositors 30 percent [of their deposits] and charged for their services, $318,753.

At the date of closing, so far as is known, there was due to depositors, $2,993,790.68 in 61,144 accounts; this was never paid. The assets amounted to $32,089.35. The rest was represented by personal loans and loans on real estate which were practically uncollectible.

The total business transaction by the Freedmen's Bank was extraordinary, considering that the bulk of its clientele had just emerged from enslavement; its total deposits at one time reached $57,000,000.[98]

The psychological significance of this loss was profound for an aspiring black middle class and struggling black farmers whose sense of political and economic emancipation was partially contingent on this bank's success. Frederick Douglass, who was appointed bank president a few months before its collapse in 1873, confided in a letter to his longtime abolitionist friend Gerrit Smith: "Despite my efforts to uphold the Freedmen's Savings and Trust Company, it has fallen. It has been the black man's cow, but the white man's milk. Bad loans and bad management have been the death of it. I was ignorant of its real condition till elected as its president."[99]

In fall 1874, Douglass further lamented how the Freedmen's Bank and the moral atmosphere of America had become so "tainted" that part of the problem was blacks' inability to gain an economic foothold as free men in a national environment of "avarice, duplicity, falsehood, corruption, servility, fawning and trickery of all kinds, which confront us at ever turn."[100]

Undoubtedly the bank's failure was a bitter experience that would haunt him for the rest of his life. Yet his dismay about America's lack of moral commitment to the Freedmen's development simply but tragically underscored a more fundamental social political contradiction between displaced white working class, its despondent but conniving "aristocracy," and the threats presented by an aspiring competitive black entrepreneurial class bent on empowerment after centuries of enslavement. Within this explosive milieu, Republican liberals and blacks such as Douglass who continued to maintain hopeful aspirations about America's expanding democratic processes found themselves politically marginalized and socially doomed to suffer the consequences of extreme political naiveté as white America conducted genocidal policies against its indigenous population while terrorizing the black American.

In this era of hope, black businessmen, laborers and political office seekers believed that with support from a federally supported banking institution and other governmental agencies, centuries of abuse, exploitation and murder could be remedied, thereby opening an unobstructed path toward their empowerment! What was lacking however, was an indepth organized political commitment to the principle of racial survival. A commitment that transcended, not simply emulated, the values of white America. Nonetheless, misdirected efforts by a small but energetic class of educators, preachers and entrepreneurs consciously allowed the machinery of white American ethnocentrism to prosper within its own ranks! More important, black entrepreneurs needed institutions that would collate, articulate and convert the economic potential of their farmers and skilled city laborers into a viable political power base. Lacking this philosophical orientation and coordinated thrust, an entrenched Euro-American business ethos, both north and south simply waited, conspired and exploited blunders made by these new competitors!

TABLE 3. RELATIVE BUSINESS OF THE FREEDMEN'S BANK, 1866–1870

Years Annum	Total Amount Deposits	Total Amount Drafts	Net Deposits	Inc. %
1866	$305,167.00	$105,883.58	$199,283.42	—
1867	1,624,853.33	1,258,515.00	366,338.33	84
1868	3,582,378.36	2,944,079.36	638,299.00	74
1869	7,257,798.63	6,184,833.32	1,073,465.31	70
1870	12,605,781.95	10,948,776.20	1,657,006.75	65

The gain for the past year is $583,541.44. The average increase on *one year on another* is 73 percent. The amount, *now* on deposit is EIGHT DOLLARS FOR EVERY DOLLAR, March 1 1866. The Company has paid in cash interest to its deposits as follows

For the year ending	Jan. 1, 1867	$1,985.47
" " " "	Jan. 1, 1868	9,521.60
" " " "	Nov. 1, 1868	24,544.08
" " " "	Nov. 1, 1869	43,896.98
Total		79,948.13

The great success which has attended the operations of the company encourages the Board to hope they have, as yet, only seen the beginning of the work of economy among the people of color. Instead of thirty thousand depositors, there would be three hundred thousand. If the people of color had the same ratio on deposit with their banks of that state, our net deposits would reach two hundred millions. Though so much has been done in a short time, much remains to be done (*The New National Era*, March 30, 1870, p. 3).

Source: Abstract of the Fifth Annual Report of the National Freedmen's Saving and Trust Company, made to the Board of Trustees at Washington, DC, on the 10th of March 1870.

The problem simply stated was not easily resolved for a race emerging from centuries of physical cultural dislocation and enslavement. Addressing this era, one historian noted that

African American nation building between 1865 and 1899 was intended to be a part of a new nation coming together out of the national fragmentation that characterized the antebellum period. Reconstruction and its aftermath destroyed that goal. African Americans found themselves confronting not full citizenship after 1865 and 1877, but the need to find alternatives to the emerging problems of second class citizenship. African American leadership, according to historian Vincent P. Franklin, has, at times, been closely aligned with the African American masses. At other instances that leadership lacked consistency.[101]

Espousing the virtues of self-reliance and assimilation while proselytizing variations of Christianity, an increased number of freed blacks embraced the outward manifestations of Americanism, though secretly acknowledging numerous imposed social limitations. As a consequence, for many southern blacks, economic and political parity with whites was primarily limited to ostentatious displays of cultural conversion. Pronounced displays and or apprehension about one's public appearance, dress, speech, worship, recreation, industriousness or support for popular causes became indicative of social progress despite white America's rejection of them as full-fledged citizens. It was exactly these and other acculturating factors that pressured some blacks to depreciate the importance of racial associative collaboration in farming, small businesses, political affiliations, lodges and banking. Eventually by relinquishing this kind of collective racial support, the possibility of black political or economic domination where numerically possible deteriorated quickly as propaganda threats and antiblack terrorist attacks increased. Yet in those instances where black resistance to terrorist attacks prevailed, strong collective bonds between black farmers, laborers and an intellectual class also existed.[102]

Nevertheless every constitutional ideal that the Freedmen assumed they were entitled to was positioned at the very core of racial conflict. In fact, their nascent advance toward political parity simply provided "unreconstructed" southern propagandist with "evidence" that blacks' continued progress if left unchecked assured the demise of white racial privilege. This, secessionists argued, was not only unacceptable and offensive but un–American. As one white southerner noted, the Confederacy "represented all that remained between anarchy and constitutional law and conservatism in America."[103]

Fear of the Freedmen's economic, political and possible armed capabilities beyond that which many southern whites felt was proscribed by tradition and law forced many Americans to come face to face with an array of deadly political circumstances. Of paramount importance to many southern whites was the question: to what degree should the Freedmen participate in American society beyond that of a pariah class? The answer to this political conundrum was clearly multifaceted.

(1) While franchise and suffrage rights, at least on paper, created the potential for sharing political influence between the races; it did not address the culturally destructive aspects of enslavement or the psychological terror of potential economic dependency that threaten every single person of African heritage.

(2) Freedmen civil rights functioned only when federal troops were available, *or* willing to enforce those rights, or when the Freedmen used or threaten the use of armed force, rather than by the willing consent of a southern secessionist minded white populace.

(3) National commitment to the Freedmen's equal participation in the affairs of state were at best cynical and deceitful. The conferring of political rights via the thirteenth, fourteenth and fifteenth Amendments was premised on the government's need to exercise political direction on ex-slaves who might otherwise seek to decentralize political power under their own aegis. It was an effective use of political initiatives by the federal government to parley any further demands by the blacks. While the amendments and a series of civil rights acts from 1866 to 1875 conferred on paper specific benefits, by implication, they signified that only white Americans had the power to bestow rights on a questionable segment of its general population. In this regard, the ex-enslaved population was never offered an opportunity to decide either by plebiscite whether they desired union with, separation from or the establishment of a separate political apart from that of the federal government.

(4) After their military defeat, supporters of the Confederate States of America found themselves physically, psychologically and politically defeated, yet tentatively in possession of large segments of land with an unemployed white laboring class. Susceptible to northern capital and southern guile, this class of whites were summoned to impede then destroy their immediate economic competitor, the ex-enslaved African. Easily convinced by centuries of social practice that race predominates in all human affairs, they accepted all of the myths, parables, allegories and fables that could be devised to elevate their diminished notions of self after the fall of their political aspirations.

However, for embittered conservative whites the problem was painfully clear: To accept blacks on any level beyond what 250 years of southern history and tradition defined meant acquiescing to their demands for equal access to the nations resources. It also meant acknowledging that the past was "a creation based on superstition, ... an irrational belief in the ominous significance of a particular thing or circumstance," in this case, the African.[104] However, no matter how intelligent and efficient some blacks appeared, most whites agreed that power sharing with a subordinated race was not an option to be seriously considered.[105]

In what was reasoned to be capitalism's fait accompli, southern whites and complying Republicans recognized that eventually deception and brute force would be needed to manage black development, not because they had been disappointed by the Freedmen's failure but due to their astonishing success and promise of even greater success![106] Even more so, poor farm-based whites and embittered Confederate veterans dreaded any proposition that placed them in competition with a labor force that they risked their lives in the war to keep enslaved. Accordingly by fall 1865 black political development and economic growth became a serious social menace for southern columnists, newspaper editors, and apologists for the Confederacy. One leader making a clarion attack against Freedmen was *New York Times* columnist James Pike, who emotionally and fearfully claimed,

> Southern thinking minds have always been deeply exercised over the problem of the Black population, from Mr. Jefferson down. They strive to master it. They try hard to elucidate it. They have an unconquerable desire to find holding ground for their speculations. They look backward, and around them, and forward to the future, to try and discover a philosophy and a theory which shall explain the various and curious facts brought to their knowledge, and guide them out of the smokey labyrinth wherein they grope. But that full solution they so much desire always eludes their grasp. Africa rises always to their view. There the Negro has had sway through unnumbered entries. There he is a barbarian still. Give him sway elsewhere, will his condition be different? What ground is there for the supposition? When the white element exists in him, it modifies but does not improve him[107] [see Appendix B for more from James Pike].

Aligned to wash away the fears and frustration of Confederate defeat, propagandists such as Pike continually ruminated about the spiritually defeated southern whites who were quite capable of intense, violent, psychotic reactions against what they deemed as their self-interest. Recognizing that many southern whites were suffering a feeling of betrayal, low self-esteem and political bankruptcy, Pike appealed to the base instincts of human behavior when he encouraged his readers to gain membership in associations, clubs and secret societies, and thereby acquire a sense of racial identification that would hopefully mollify political efforts of the "barbarian" in those states were they where the numerical majority.

This sort of racial thinking was not confined to the general southern white population. Resistance to black political expressions on any level was also widespread among occupying northern soldiers. In fact, while various southern governors expressed concern for the plight of the Freedmen as an important labor source, the attitudes of occupying northern soldiers was often ambiguous in this regard. And though it is was no secret that federal officers in Mississippi consistently displayed little compassion in their dealings with Freedmen, their underlings often expressed an even greater dislike. Expectedly, this was not necessarily the case with Union soldiers, many of whom were combat veterans from

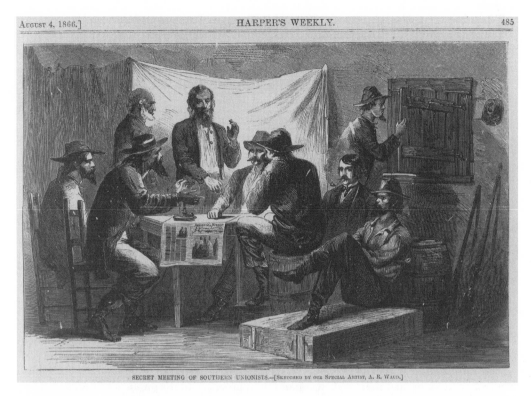

SECRET MEETING OF SOUTHERN UNIONISTS.—[Sketched by our Special Artist, A. R. Waud.]

"Secret Meeting of Southern Unionists," *Harper's Weekly*, August 4, 1866, p. 485, by artist Alfred Rudolph Waud. Library of Congress Prints and Photographs Division, Washington, D.C.

the war. Not only were Freedmen impacted by seeing blacks in military roles, they used these military images as role models and paradigms to reorganize their own defense against Ku Klux–like gangs.

As early as August 1865 examples of military bearing and political organizing among the ex-slaves could be identified. Historian J. Saville even asserts that "small work groups experimenting with precision marches in several areas of Barnwell District" zealously followed behind the nearby 35th Colored Infantry and the 54th Massachusetts Colored Volunteer Infantry units.[108] Furthermore, as a result of their experience in fighting Confederate forces, many of the black soldiers were not reluctant in displaying assertive (if not aggressive) attitudes toward whites, and in doing so influenced many Freedmen citizen to do so in kind, which caused many to observe, "there was more social criticism than imitation underlying popular adaptation by blacks of military form."[109] Imitation or not, the presence of black soldiers in their midst was an affront Confederate sympathizers and nationalists were not willing to accept.

Part of the problem was that many northern white soldiers were themselves conscripts who came from poor families, and as such didn't agree that ex-slaves were their equal as citizens or potential economic competitors. Consequently racial enmity, outright hostility and rancor were not unknown as many northern soldiers reflected strong southern sympathies.[110] In this regard, northern compliance to southern realities was particularly evident in Mississippi, where one observer noted:

While in the excitement of the elections of 1867 and 1868, the troops were often "a restraint curbing" to the turbulence of the negroes, they were never so regarded by the whites. There was some misuse of them while [Adelbert] Ames was military governor. But as a rule, if not invariably, the sentiment of the troops, and especially the non-commissioned officers and privates were hostile to the Negro.[111]

One English traveler in 1868 heard similar sentiments as he made his way throughout the south. When he reportedly asked northern troops what their mission was in the ex–Confederate states, for the most part they responded, "shoot radicals and niggers,"[112] General Pennypacker, who was second in command in Mississippi and reputedly sympathetic to southern Democrats, is reported to have continually alerted Ku Klux terrorists of impending raids by northern soldiers.[113]

The editor of the *Natchez Tri Weekly* even went so far as to warn Freedmen who persisted in their demands for equality, that history teaches no two dissimilar races can live together on a basis of equality, and if the situation presents itself to the contrary, "one *must* be superior — one *must* be dominant. If the Negro should be the master, the whites must either abandon the territory, or there would be another civil war in the south, a war of the races, the whites against the black, and the war should be a war of extermination."[114]

Among thousands of tragic testimonies of personal terror, a daughter's unhappy struggle to protect her father, Nelson Fitzhugh, illustrates the cauldron of psychological terror experienced by just about every black person in postbellum Mississippi. In a brief local newspaper commentary, there is mention of Fitzhugh's daughter's public plea for her father's life, underscored by the tragic ironies, complexities and social incongruities of being black in Mississippi. The commentary explains:

> Fitzhugh, freed long before the war, and possessed of some education, had gained modest success in the community, having been a *slaveholder* and manager of a mercantile establishment. Like William Johnson, the barber, and Robert McCary, the Negro meteorologist, he had been considered a good Confederate, and had been held in high esteem by his white neighbors. Then, in 1866 someone discovered in the Philadelphia *Christian Recorder* a letter from Fitzhugh which indicated that he had been selling subscriptions for that Journal. The writer [Fitzhugh] went on to say that the *Natchez Courier* was full of lies, and that he hoped the *Recorder* would make some effort to prevent the kidnapping of Negroes for subsequent sale in Cuba. That was all, but it was enough. The editor of the *Courier* immediately leaped to the attack: "This man Nelson Fitzhugh had been wearing a mask. He is full of deceit and hypocrisy.... He has been a systematic hypocrite all his life.... Cloaked under the garb of religion, sanctimonious as a pilgrim, seemingly honest and honorable, still kept in kindly remembrance for past offices, be they well meant or hypocrisies, Nelson Fitzhugh is still a part of this community.... He is now a Radical agent and a colporteur among us, and disseminates poisons of the literary kind, stirring up bad blood among people kindly disposed towards each other...."
>
> A few days later the paper reported that numerous letters, attacking Fitzhugh as a "turn coat" and a "snake in the grass," had been received from white citizens. There was also a letter from the Negro's daughter, in which she prayed that the condemnation of Fitzhugh not be extended to other members of his family: "And now, my dear Southern friends, for the sake of a family who are Southern in sentiment and principle, I hope you will look over my father's indiscretion, for he is old and childish. I really do not believe that he meant what he said, for I never heard him utter a word against the South in all my life. I

will now close by asking you to give this to your readers, that they may not hold the family responsible for what my father may have said."[115]

Methods utilized in a struggle for survival are often costly and rarely made without consequences. This was certainly true in Mississippi, as it was in South Carolina where the specter of black economic growth generally evoked from whites sworn allegiances to "stop the nigger!" Surrounded by a crumbling way of life in 1867, campaigns initiated to persuade whites to believe that their lowered social condition was the result of irresponsible Republican strategies was fully under way. Central to this argument was the idea that Republicans in their desire for national power were willing to promote the unnatural uplifting of Africans to accomplish that end. Eagerly heralding in this new round of political struggle, educators such as John A. Leland, president of the Laurensville Female College, South Carolina, proclaimed the need to reestablish economic control throughout the south, regardless of the military surrender at Appomattox. In his book *A Voice from South Carolina,* Leland adamantly proclaimed political redemption and economic restoration for white South Carolinians while envisioning himself as a southern American patriot. Ruminating on the evils of Republicanism and Reconstruction, Leland expressed a deep apprehension and fear of "the fanatical faith of the whole African race" that was deaf to all appeals and arguments from their former master[116]:

He [the slave] was not safe from the vengeance of his own race if he continued outside the League [Union], and once in, his identity was lost, and he became a mere pawn on the political chessboard, to be moved by a higher intelligence. This accounts for the apparent anomaly that, when he gets into straits or troubles, or needs advice about his business, he will come to his former owner with all the humility and confidence of the olden time; he will work for him, and with him, as cheerfully, if not as faithfully, for wages, as he ever did under the former system; but as soon as the subject of politics is broached, he becomes as silent and solemn as a tombstone. *That* is a subject with which "Old Massa" has nothing to do; It is sacred between him and his God — but through the Radical [Republican] party.[117]

With this as his political and social context, Leland viewed the postbellum new Negro as a social aberration that had to be rationalized away by racially centered propaganda and then systematically removed from positions of influence through acts of terror. Aware that throughout the south there existed displaced planter aristocracy who cynically concluded (as did many northern investors) that their financial interest was best served by maintaining and enhancing at any cost both an economic and social void between the races. In this respect, testimonies in the form of diaries written by the wives of southern planters are particularly interesting and insightful in their description of these turbulent times.

Evidence of such is an engrossing diary entry written one month after Robert E. Lee's April 9, 1865, surrender at Appomattox. Ella Gertrude Clanton Thomas, wife of a Georgia plantation and slave owner, scrutinized a number of dilemmas that were intruding on her family's lifestyle. No longer was Ella Thomas assured the class status that she was born and married into; only her racial background afforded some protection from the swirling exigencies that threaten to engulf her family and destroy the void between the races that she was accustomed to. With the military destruction of the Confederacy came the family's loss in property, both human and otherwise. This factor alone made Ella's future appear to be difficult, confusing and eminently dangerous. In a deeply personal testimony composed on three separate dates in May 1865, she succinctly described her confusion and anger about the changing social order:

May 1, 1865

Today I have witnessed what I am sorry shall prove our last experience as a confederate nation. A riot has taken place in Augusta, an event often dreaded but never experienced before! Soon after breakfast I heard that the soldiers were breaking open the stores on Broadstreet and helping themselves immediately after I saw numbers of men walking rapidly, some running with large bags, bundles and etc., upon their shoulders. The bell just now tolls for one o'clock. When another 1st of May rolls around, the bell which for so long a time has tolled to remind us to pray for the soldiers and alas by so many of us has been neglected, will toll no more. God help us.

As an independent nation we will not exist. The bright dream of Southern independence has not been realized. The war is over and again we become a part of the United States, how united will depend alone upon treatment we receive from the hand of the North. It will prove to their interest to be very discreet for the South will prove a smoldering volcano requiring but little to again burst forth. Treated members of one family, a band of brothers, *in time* we may have a common interest, but pressed too hard upon, our property taken from us, a desperate people having nothing to lose, the South may again revolt and speaking of revolts reminds me of the riot of today which I had commenced to notice....

The war is over and I am glad of it. What terms of agreement may be decided I cannot say but if *anything* is left us, if we can count with certainty upon enough to raise and educate our children, I shall be grateful. It is humiliating, very indeed to be a conquered people but the sky is so bright, the air so pure, the aspect of nature so lovely that I can but be encouraged, and hope for something which will benefit us. Upon only one point am I settled in my opinion, that of Slavery but more of that hereafter.... It is rumored that two thousand Yankee soldiers will arrive in town this afternoon. I hope I will not see them. When I learn the terms of treaty offered and accepted I can better endeavor to cultivate friendly feelings. "If despite is on me thrown I've a soul as hard as Iron." I haven't quoted that right but the feeling is the same.

Sunday, May 7, 1865

This morning a large force of Yankees came marching into Augusta, the drums beating & colours flying, surrounded by a large crowd of Negroes. We did not get up until late and did not see the first company of them. Patsy said there were 800 of them. After breakfast a number of them marched by here on the other side of street, two officers riding on Horseback in front. I felt no particular emotion as I looked at them through the closed blinds but when I read the morning paper and saw the reward of $100,000 dollars in gold offered for Jeff Davis [president of the Confederate States of America] with a promise of the money for the captors which the President was said to have with him, *then* I felt that the Philistines were amongst us. Immediately after, I read the General order issued by Gen. Smith for the Carolina planters having reverence to free labor.

Tonight the impression is general that *slavery* is *abolished*, that *the Negroes are free*, that is at liberty, the greater portion of them to plunder and starve. It does not surprise me as much as I expected but I will write again in the morning.

Monday, May 8, 1865

The news was just communicated to us by Pinck as Mr. Thomas and I were out a buggy overtook us an enquired if we had seen the order from Gen. Smith with regard to free labor vis: that the Negroes were to be subsisted, paid six month wages in advance an half

Four black youths sit among the devastation of the badly damaged Circular Church in Charleston, South Carolina, on the eve of the Confederacy's capitulation, April 1865. SELECTED CIVIL WAR PHOTOGRAPHS, 1861–1865, COMPILED BY HIRST D. MILHOLLEN AND DONALD H. MUGRIDGE, LIBRARY OF CONGRESS PRINTS AND PHOTOGRAPHS DIVISION, WASHINGTON, D.C.

the crop made to be divided among them. Contracts to [be] made between Negro and Planter — there I have followed the Yankee fashion of naming the Negro first and the Master last. A failure to plant will cause the land to be confiscated ...

As to the emancipation of the Negroes, while there is of course a natural dislike to the loss of so much property, in my inmost soul, I cannot regret it. I always felt that there [this] was a great responsibility. It is in some degree a great relief to have this feeling removed. For the Negroes I know that I have the kindest possible feeling. For the Yankees who deprive us of them, I have no use whatever. I only hope I shall see very little of them. Yesterday Mr. Thomas unfastened Turner's Battle Flag from the staff and I will put it away as a memento of the time when he was a marker in the Wheeler Dragoons. Who knows, perhaps someday it may be used again. Oh a free people may be won but not crushed.[118]

Freedmen family near a canal in Richmond, Virginia, the former capital of the Confederacy, April 1865. BRADY CIVIL WAR PHOTOGRAPH COLLECTION, LIBRARY OF CONGRESS PRINTS AND PHOTOGRAPHS DIVISION, WASHINGTON, D.C.

The views of emotionally and materially displaced whites, such as Ella Thomas, however subtle, replicate a particular historical analysis that positioned blame for their fallen status solely on the arrival of new political force, one that they naturally contended was corrupt, incompetent and ruthless. Most however ironically feared that with the collapse of a Confederacy that promised security, prestige and power, the only friendship they might secure was that of the ex-slave, but at the price of social equality. For many this was intolerable and unbearable. However, for those who were literate and understood the importance of change, the following verse by William Yeats was most appropriate:

> Things fall apart, the center cannot hold;
> mere anarchy is loosed upon the world ...
> the best lack all conviction, while the worst
> are full of passionate intensity.[119]

2

The Interminable Conflict

They are distributing arms, Winchester rifles, all through the south,
and it is their intention to put a rifle into the hands of every white
man who is a Democrat, and to carry the election in South Carolina
in 1872 by the bullet and the dagger of the assassin.
—*New National Era,* February 9, 1871

Abiding Honor, Myth and Fear

Social fantasy emanating from angry, acrimonious and embittered southern whites
was entwined with many aspects of Ku Klux propaganda during the Reconstruction years
of 1867 to 1877. Hateful accusatory language gave succor to the south's most economic,
degenerate and base elements as well as to those with material assets and intellect. Attempts
at reconciling four years of horrific warfare however now fell on deaf ears, as a depraved
catharsis of regional bloodletting and terror embraced the consciousness of most southern
whites. With "obnoxious" blacks as the expected sacrificial lambs, *purification* processes were
established to politically and ethnically *sanitize* the south of its military defeat.[1]

Functioning in alliance with organizations such as the Ku Klux, southern Democrats
attacked any Republican–inspired agency that displayed any support for the ex-slave. One
such supportive agency was the Union Leagues of America. The league and smaller organizations such as the Lincoln Brotherhood and the Red Strings functioned as political con-
duits for the Republican Party throughout the south.[2] Though the political beginnings of
these clubs were the result of northern abolitionist sentiments before and during the Civil
War, its membership ironically appealed first to southern Republican whites.[3] However by
1867 the Union League was preparing the Freedmen for greater civic participation, all of
which southern Democrats attacked as both illegal and immoral attempts by the federal
government to exploit an economic vacuum left over from the Civil War. Though later more
will be discussed about the Union League's impact on black resistance to Ku Klux and similar groups, it is apparent that some historians viewed the league as an organization whose

primary function was political education and the protection of the Freedmen's economic interest. Few however have delved into their more assertive actions in response to Ku Klux–like provocations.[4] Accordingly, an 1868 published statement from the league stating that "The country is full of secret societies of a bad and treasonable nature; this fact also make it the more necessary for loyal men to have secret societies," is more a warning to Freedmen to prepare themselves for difficult and vicious struggle than a plea for southern conservative tolerance.[5]

Sensing a dangerous precedent, southern political pundits deliberating on the deposed Confederacy also vilified blacks, southern Republican whites and so-called carpetbaggers with unabashed fervor and intensity. Even more astute observers cautioned against the existence of racially disruptive "elements" who if not monitored would effect *dangerous* economic collaboration between poor farmers and laborers of both races while establishing an armed political presence. To forestall any interracial collusion of this sort, white mercantilist and planters employed night-riding terror squads against those who would effect such a meaningful change.[6] Known as regulators, recalling an earlier eighteenth-century period of American resistance to British colonialism, these groups began to popularize the idea that resistance to the federal government in deference to state's rights was not only a political necessity but a honorable duty to one's race and country.[7]

Citing a U.S. government investigation reports on election fraud in South Carolina, and the role regulators played in these activities, W. E. B. DuBois noted that in Edgefield and Laurens Counties, South Carolina, armed organized bands of regulators, continually traversed these counties maltreating Negroes without any avowed definite purpose in view. They treat Negroes, in many instances, in the most horrible and atrocious manner, even to maiming them, cutting their ears off, and so on. In one case, two citizens of one of these counties testified against these parties and were instantly compelled to leave the county, barely escaping with their lives. The citizens (white) are bound in honor, by an understanding or compact among them, not to testify against the regulators; so that it is impossible to get evidence against them unless the Negro gives it.[8] Accordingly, these extralegal forces were fashioned to ensure a social policy that mandated, regardless of the Civil War's outcome, one's primary social status is unalterably wedded to one's skin.

America's Mother Lode of Terrorism

Part of America's post–Civil War bloody history began during the early summer of 1865 with the return of Confederate soldiers to small southern towns and hamlets such as Pulaski, Tennessee, the county seat for Giles County. Exhausted by years of brutal combat and marching across countless miles of war-torn countryside, returning veterans of a defeated Confederate army were confronted with the fact that at least on paper, the slave was no more. Predictably, resistance to this was swift and deadly. By December 1865, a group of six individuals, Captain John C. Lester, Major James R. Crowe, John B. Kennedy, Calvin Jones, Richard R. Reed, and Frank O. McCord, came together in the backroom office of a local judge, Thomas M. Jones (the father of Calvin Jones), to discuss and sort out their young lives. They called themselves the "Ku Klux." Myth and legend have mired these early beginnings in intrigue and error.[9]

On the side of an old office building in downtown Pulaski, a sign asserted: "Ku Klux

Klan, Organized in this, the Law Office of Judge Thomas M. Jones, December 24th 1865."[10] However, some historians have submitted that "the Klan has almost as many birthday's as historians."[11] For example, though Stanley Horn's often cited book, *Invisible Empire* places the date of their beginning on "a late evening in December 1865," the *New York Herald* in April 1868 reported that a person claiming to have "expert knowledge on this matter" placed the origins and beginning dates for the Klan in Giles County, Tennessee, August 1866![12] There are still other versions that maintain the best evidence for its birthday rest with the Klan's first anniversary parade in Pulaski on June 5, 1867.[13] Though these dates and others are debated, the essential fact is that, sometime in mid–1866,

> An organization with no very definite aims was effected; and at a second meeting, a week later, names were proposed and discussed. Some one pronounced the Greek word, "Kuklos," meaning a circle. From "Kuklos" to "Ku Klux" was an easy transition — whoever consults a glossary of college boy's slang will not find it strange — and "Klan" followed "Ku Klux" as naturally as "dumpty" follows "humpty." That the name meant nothing whatever was a recommendation; and one can fancy what sort of badinage would have greeted a suggestion that in six years a committee of Congress would devote thirteen volumes to the history of the movement that began in a Pulaski law office, and migrated later to a deserted and half-ruined house on the outskirts of the village.[14]

While the auspicious beginning of the Ku Klux went unnoticed, the first initiates were by no means unaware of its intended secretive nature, ominous ciphering, by-laws, constitution and rituals. In fact, throughout mid–nineteenth-century America, Greek mythology in the form of fraternities and sororities was very much the fad for organizations seeking a distinctive notoriety, on and off college campuses.

> In the south perhaps the most familiar of these organizations was the social fraternity, Kuklos Adelphon or "old Kappa Alpha," founded at the University of North Carolina in 1812. By mid-century it had spread throughout the south, not only to college campuses but to cities and towns where there were college alumni to keep it up. The society began to dissolve in the 1850's and disappeared altogether after the Civil War, but most educated Southerners in 1866 were familiar with it, including surely the founders of the Ku Klux Klan. One of the founders indicated that the Klan's ritual, at least, was closely patterned after that of a widespread college fraternity, and Kuklos Adelphon most certainly provided the model.[15]

Similar to other social fraternities, the founders of the Ku Klux agreed that future recruits would be held to an oath of secrecy, silence, obedience and responsibility particularly about its initiation rituals. Innocent as this may have seemed to outsiders, the Ku Klux emerged within the context of a post–Civil War environment were lawlessness throughout many areas of the southern states had become a way of life for thousands of war veterans, the unemployed, the ex-slave, poor white farmers and restless youth whose fortunes were yet to be made or lost. As one historian put it, "Southerners could scarcely be expected to repudiate cheerfully the doctrines for which they had fought and died. Neither could they be expected to welcome as an equal, the ex slave, or the Yankee who came to teach him." However it was apparent that while some accepted their situation, northern and southern definitions of "the situation" did not coincide, notably in the matter of elected public officials. Conservative southern whites to a man turned to their old leaders, former Confederates. To victorious northerners, such choices demonstrated an unrepentant spirit.[16]

This was no more apparent than in the mountains of south central Tennessee where early initiates of the Ku Klux, some of whom were ex–Confederate soldiers, joined the new order out of need to have a sense of security in a society now crippled by war but also saturated by the ruminations of what could have been. Their response to Republican presumptions about a postwar south and the Freedmen's assertion of equality was surprising only to those who presupposed that a fantasy no matter how deadly could be eliminated simply by war. Not surprisingly, on July 12, 1866, the *Nashville Press and Times* reported that

> In some portions of West Tennessee the rebels have formed a secret association the object of which is to prevent the employment or patronage of Unionist in any capacity whatever, whether as day-laborers, clerks, book-keepers, teachers, physicians, lawyers or mechanics. In all cases rebels are to be employed, as the members of the association pledge themselves to starve out or drive out every Union man from that part of the country.[17]

Needless to say, these "rebels" or self-appointed regulators gave little credence to the idea that with the war's end, the ex-slave's involvement in a competitive job market was now assured. For example, when a Negro saloonkeeper in the increasingly lawless town of Pulaski hung out a sign in front of his establishment bearing the name *Equal Rights*, it was hauled down the same day, "by request of some of our young friends from the country," according to newspaper editor Frank McCord, who would later become the Grand Cyclops of the Ku Klux Klan.[18]

Ensnared in an endemic wave of violence that was spreading throughout the south, a Pulaski newspaper editor in 1867 reported that "Chronic drunkenness and debauchery had become so common that he was becoming weary of reporting on it." He also noted that mixed crowds of blacks and whites whooped, yelled and shot off pistols on the streets from eight to twelve on Friday nights in one large "riotous drunken jubilee."[19] Robbery and assault was so common in Pulaski that U.S. Army Captain George E. Judd who was attached to the local Freedmen's Bureau observed that

> especially at night, that no man was safe on the streets alone after dark. The town was the scene of repeated rowdyism and shooting sprees on the part of young bloods who crowded the saloons. "Roughs collect in Pulaski from this and adjoining counties." They have their own way here, threaten to kill and drag out all who disagree with them.[20]

As the year progressed, increasing levels of daily violence parodied an already horrendous relationship between blacks and whites. Intensified economic competitiveness and political activity from blacks who just a year earlier were slaves created a social climate that challenged the very basis of traditional southern mores. Whereas little in southern social or legal associations with slaves or quasi-free blacks prepared them to deal with the reality that previous held human property now demanded parity with their ex-masters, astute members of the ex-slaveholding class recognized that such a social development would indeed have dangerous ramifications for traditional economic and political interest in the north as well as in the south.

Traditional American ethos that demanded whether you were poor or rich, recent immigrant or not, being white denoted equity in one's own whiteness! It functioned as a physiological and psychological shield against the iniquities of enslavement and blackness! It was patently clear by the fall of 1865 that any social, political or cultural advancement by blacks that threaten to exposed the spuriousness of this racial paradigm had to be viewed as a direct threat to the concept of a southern pax Americana.

On the question of race itself, self-delusion quickly became an integral part of a southern psychic shield against an imagined physical onslaught of blacks. Nor was it too surprising for many southern whites at the August 11, 1867, Democratic Party convention in Brownsville, Tennessee, to hear candidate for Congress and founding member of the Ku Klux, Nathan Bedford Forrest pledge that he would resist to the point of civil war any effort by Republican Governor Brownlow to neutralize the Ku Klux. The ex–Confederate General now asserted:

> I can assure you, fellow-citizens, that I for one do not want any more war ... nor do I want to see Negroes armed to shoot down white men. If they bring this war upon us, there is one thing I will tell you: that I shall not shoot any negroes so long as I can see a white radical to shoot, for it is the radicals who will be to blame for bringing on this war ...
>
> I can assure you, fellow-citizens, that I shall at all times be ready to go forward and assist the sheriff or any other officer in carrying out the laws of the state, and in order to assist him thoroughly, I will get as many of my old soldiers as possible to go with me. But if they send the black men to hunt those confederate soldiers whom they call Ku Klux, then I say to you, "go out and shoot the radicals." If they do want to inaugurate civil war, the sooner it comes the better, that we may know what to do. [Applause.] I do not wish it understood that I am inciting you to war ... I wish you to exhaust all honorable means before you do anything, and I would prefer that you should suffer before I should see civil war inaugurated in this country....
>
> I now want to say a few words to the black men who are here before me ... to ask them to stand by the men who raised you, who nursed you when you were sick, and who took care of you when you were little children. I say stand by those who are your real friends, and leave your loyal leagues, where you are taught to refuse the franchise to those who have always proved your friends. I tell you that if you will only stand by us that we will always stand by you, and do as much for you as any white man can do for you. You can have no interest with any scalawags and carpet-baggers.... I feel to-day that Gov. Brownlow is one of that class. [Hisses.] He has escaped to this time because he has been with sickness and weakness, and is considered crazy, but if he inaugurates civil war in this state, then I tell him he must suffer the consequences. [Cheers.][21]

The Mind of a Ku Klux Terrorist

Up until the first disbanding of the Ku Klux in 1871, similar types of associations sustained an unremitting propaganda crusade to exhort public opinion against black enfranchisement and their armed clubs such as the Union League. Success in implementing a policy of terror by propaganda against the Freedmen depended on a centralized command structure that on the one hand demanded adherence to policy from its peripheral chapters yet allowed for innovative approaches to resolve local situations. The relative success of this type of structure was founded on unique partisan military tactics developed by Confederate cavalry units during the Civil War under the command of individuals such as John Singleton Mosby and John Hunt Morgan.[22] Though both Mosby's and Morgan's raiders were often brutally effective in their ability to strike suddenly and with extreme violence, they also fostered a mystique about the raider, who though outnumbered, continued fighting on for a noble cause![23] Accordingly, after the war, the philosophy that "it is just as legiti-mate to fight an enemy in the rear as in the front. The only differences is in the danger," was clearly understood by Klansmen, who wasted little time in applying this axiom to their interminable enemy, the Freedmen.[24] The Ku Klux's rapid growth during the postbellum period also made it appear for the unwary that Klansmen were everywhere, and that every southern white was a member, if not sympathizer.[25] Though varying levels of efficiency existed from chapter to chapter, and intimate knowledge of the brutal methods utilized by Ku Kluxers was generally unknown, the mystical notion of night riders seeking justice for the abused and downtrodden southern whites became both their mantra and mythologi-cal burden.

Armed with the invective "keep the nigger down," Pulaski Ku Kluxers initiated two committees to establish rules and rituals for future members. Names, duties and areas of influence were soon established and cloaked in linguistic subterfuge with a kind of mythol-ogy meant to mystify the skeptic. Initiation procedures and grandiose hierarchical titles soon appeared such as, "Grand Wizard of the Empire," "Grand Dragon and his Eight Hydras," "Grand Titan of the Dominion and His Six Furies," and so on.[26] At the Ku Klux's initial meeting it was agreed that future recruits would be held to an oath of secrecy as was their initiation ritual that emphasized a code of silence and strict personal responsibility. In these early days, evidence of terrorist tendencies had not yet appeared as an organized part of the Ku Klux strategy or tactics though their ranks were quickly filling up with frus-trated, unemployed and disillusioned war veterans seeking material or psychological resti-tution for what they perceived was a social system turned upside down.

In August 1866 a sympathetic agent for the Freedmen's Bureau in Tennessee, Captain George E. Judd, noted that blacks in Pulaski fared poorly compared to other towns, and everything possible was done to degrade them and keep down to what they (whites) saw fit as their proper place:

> The consequence is that the negroes do not do as well as they do in other places where I have been. A great many of them are indolent and vicious. They become so by having to fight their way against the abuse of whites and from being cheated out of the proceeds of their labor. The idea of negroes getting justice before the magistrates of this county is per-fectly absurd. They will hear the testimony of the blacks, but will give it no weight unless it happens to suit their purpose.[27]

However the inability of this federal agent to affect a change in the manner Freedmen were characterized or treated by southerners without the terms such as "indolent" and "vicious" is indicative of the deep seated viciousness of the time and those social personal-ities that are formed by the experience. For while losing control over four million Africans had a direct impact on the social expectations of individual southern whites who more often than not had never owned slaves, they continued to draw psychological and material sus-tenance from what they saw as the interminable struggle to maintain core values from a preordained institution, but what others defined as really a peculiar institution.[28] As such, their social personality, self-esteem, their personal relationships, family connections, the very meaning of life itself, separate and apart from the military defeat of the Confederacy, rested primarily on the fact that they weren't "niggers." These emotions were not simplis-tic abstractions but social reflections premised on deeply felt personal experiences that were closely associated with embedded relationships premised on land and property ownership.

Reflecting on this, sociologist Lonnie Athens proposed that "significant social experiences are consequential and unforgettable. They have a lasting impact upon peoples' lives and are remembered weeks, months, and years after the experience was undergone." Even more interesting, Athens notes that those "social experiences" that push people toward violent dangerous actions "are the significant experiences" of their lives rather than the trivial ones.[29] In this regard, one can speculate on a seemingly isolated but reportedly violent clash between an unidentified Freedman and one Thomas Tyler in Orangeburg, South Carolina:

Bloody fight on Dean Swamp: We learn that on Monday, the 21st inst. house of Mr. Thos. B. Tyler Jr. was broken open and a large amount of clothing taken out. Mr. Tyler who had been at a spring about 100 yards from his house, saw the rogue making his escape. He [brought] up his gun and pursued, overtook the negro and ordered him to halt. The negro drew a revolver and threatened to kill Tyler if he followed him. Tyler fired at him about 40 yards off and thinks he hit him. Two of Tyler's dogs coming up brought the Negro to bay, whereupon Tyler rushed up to him (the negro continuing to snap his pistol at Tyler,) and a blow over the head with his gun brought him to his knees. The negro, however being much the strongest man, got the gun from Tyler and jumped on him, striking him with his pistol on the breast and head. In the scuffle Tyler got out his knife and stabbed the Negro in the bowels, whereupon he jumped off and ran away in to Dean Swamp. The ground was covered with blood where they fought, and the Negro must be badly hurt. No clue to the name of the rogue has been obtained.[30]

In line with Athens's observations, post–Civil War resurrection of the African, though traumatic and distressing for southern whites, was also harrowing, problematic and dangerous for southern blacks regardless of their class background or region of birth. For instance, when a black attorney's professionalism was excoriated in the conservative *Courier,* and then same charges were dismissed by a federal district court, only the paper's own conservative accusations now needed to be examined:

The Negro Lawyer Bradley — His Releases from Arrest: The negro Bradley, who has been stirring up strife on the islands below Savannah, is thus referred to be the Boston correspondent of the Springfield *Republican*, under date of the 31st ultimo:

"Aaron Bradley, the colored lawyer from Boston who has been stirring up mischief among the Negroes down near Savannah, is well known here. He was dismissed from the bar several years ago for malpractice, which consisted in forgery or some such peccadillo, but under the veil of time and the tenderness of the new bureau for the colored man, he tried a year or so ago to get reinstated and this time was put on examination before two prominent lawyers as to his acquirements. The result was a ridiculous exhibition of ignorance and charlatanry, which made an amusing chapter in the local law literature, but was fatal to his professional ambition in this latitude. And so he natural took his cheap wares and his gross impudence to another market. His stirring among his more ignorant and more honest brethren in the south is quite in keeping with previous character here. Bradley knows just enough to be a mischief-maker, and it would be a useful service doubtless to the Negroes and to good morals, to subject him to a trifle of old fashioned plantation discipline.[31]

Bradley's "detention and imprisonment by the Military authorities of the United States," and his subsequent discharge from jail by the authority of Honorable Judge Erskine from the U.S. District Court for the Southern District of Georgia are important and politically significant when we read Attorney General Fitch's statement that

Bradley had been arrested upon the application of Capt. Brandt, Sub-Assistant commissioner of the Freedmen's Bureau and Abandoned Lands for the State of South Carolina, and was predicated on an order issued from Brevt. Major-General Robert K. Scott, Assistant Commissioner B. R. F. and A. L., Directed to Brevt. Lieutenant Col. R. E. A. Crofton, commanding the port of Savannah. The "return" concluded by stating that Bradley was a prisoner in consequence of "counseling and inciting certain colored people to resist the authority of the United States, thereby causing great injury to the colored as well as the white population, and to prevent insurrection on the coast": and that his arrest was based upon the provisions of the 14th section of the Act of Congress of July 16th, 1866.

The Court decided that after carefully read the petition and the other papers In the case, it could see no cause for Bradley's detention; that there was nothing In the act cited to change its mind in that respect; that the Court was unobstructed in the full plenitude of its powers by civil or military authority in the State.[32]

It appears that among many of the struggles that Freedmen had to wage was validating themselves in a world that they neither created nor controlled. The fact that attorney Aaron Bradley could be a nuisance and a mischief-maker that required special handling on the part of the federal government forced many Freedmen to realize that future battles will not necessarily be terminated in a judicial setting. Furthermore, concluding remarks by the liberal Boston correspondent implying that Bradley needed some "old fashion plantation discipline" was not lost on the Freedmen. The winds of a second civil war were well on their way.

In a classic study of the Ku Klux, historian Allen Trelease declared that the concept of a hooded force, riding around the countryside, inciting fear into a presumed inferior evolved from an earlier period when blacks, having a pariah status in American society were continually susceptible to whites' "practical jokes" and harassment:

Bullying Negroes was an established pastime with a sizable portion of Southern white manhood, and the inclination increased with Emancipation. It is also true that many Negroes took their new freedom literally and began to act more like white people; choosing their own employers, working or not working as the spirit moved them, expressing their opinions more freely, and not always giving up the sidewalk. Not only were they less servile, but many of them, poverty stricken to the last degree and victims of generations of exploitation, engaged in petty thievery at the expense of those more favored than they. White men confronted by these trials had the precedent of the antebellum slave patrol before them. This institution was no longer possible on an open or official basis, but the need for it was apparently greater than ever. Thus duty and inclination combined to produce bands of postwar regulators or vigilantes throughout the South.[33]

For white South Carolinians who found glory even in a failed attempt at secession, armed night riders or regulators were an important component in attempts to retain some control over social cues that were at least two centuries old. Adherences to correct racial etiquettes to the point of unconscious obedience were the cornerstone of southern whites' notions of innate power. From this perspective, publicly and privately shared fountainheads of privilege gushed forth to prescribe a specific way of life. Denoting violence, both symbolic and direct racial mores became the social highway for the pursuit and maintenance of racial privilege both spiritually and politically. It therefore seemed rational for many that if the use of violence, particularly in retaliation to a loss of racial privilege helped clarify *who* the enemy was while nullifying the disastrous conclusion of the past war, then any action taken of this sort was acceptable. Conversely resistance or retaliation by their adversary was unthinkable, for by resisting the role of victim is rejected.

Early attempts at cajoling the local populace along this line of thought was documented by John Lester, an original member of the Ku Klux. In a lesson-like fashion Lester described a July 4, 1865, rally in Pulaski where explicit propaganda techniques were utilized by Klansmen in an attempt to evoke a reverence like response from observers, both black and white:

> Henceforth they courted publicity as assiduously as they had formerly seem to shun it. They appeared at different points at the same time, and always when and where they were the least expected. Devices were multiplied to deceive people in regard to their numbers and everything else, and to play upon the fears of the superstitious.
>
> As it was now the policy of the Klan to appear in public, an order was issued by the Grand Dragon of the realm of Tennessee to the Grand giants of the Provinces for a general parade in the capital town of each Province on the 4th of July, 1867....
>
> > On the morning of the 4th of July, 1867, the citizens of Pulaski found the sidewalks thickly strewn with slips of paper bearing the printed words: "The Ku Klux will parade the streets to-night." This announcement created great excitement. The people supposed that their curiosity, so long baffled, would now be gratified. They were confident that this parade would at least afford them the opportunity to find out who were the Ku Klux. Soon after nightfall the streets were lined with an expectant and excited throng of people. Many came from the country. The members of the Klan in the county left their homes in the afternoon and traveled alone or in squads of two or three, with their paraphernalia carefully concealed. If questioned, they answered that they were going to Pulaski to see the Ku Klux parade. After nightfall they assembled at designated points near the four main leading into town. Here they donned their robes and disguises and put covers of gaudy material on their horses. A skyrocket sent up from some point in the town was the signal to mount and move. The different companies met and passed each other on the public square in perfect silence; the discipline appeared to be admirable. Notices were posted in every public place, and even pasted on the backs of hogs and cows running loose in the street.
> >
> > Not a word was spoken. Necessary orders were given by means of the whistles. In single file, in death-like stillness, with funeral slowness, they marched and counter-marched throughout the town. While the column was headed North on one street it was going South on another. By crossing over in opposite directions the lines were kept up in almost unbroken continuity. The effect was to create the impression of vast numbers. This marching and counter-marching was kept up for about two hours, and the Klan departed as noiselessly as they came. The public were more than even mystified ...
> >
> > Curiosity had not been satisfied, as it was expected it would be. The efforts of the most curious and cunning to find out who were Ku Klux failed. One gentleman from the country, a great lover of horses, who claimed to know every horse in the county, was confident that he would be able to identify the riders by the horses. With this purpose in view, he remained in town to witness the parade. But, as we have said, the horses were disguised as well as the riders.
> >
> > Determined not to be baffled, during a halt of the column, he lifted the cover of a horse that was near him — the rider offering no objection — and recognized his own steed and saddle upon which he had ridden into town. The town people were on the alert also to see who of the young men of the town would be with the Ku Klux. All of them, almost

without exception, were marked, mingling freely and conspicuously with the spectators. Those of them who were members of the Klan did not go into the parade.

This demonstration had the effect for which it was designed. Perhaps the greatest illusion produced by it was in regard to the numbers participating in it, reputable citizens— men of cool and accurate judgment — were confident that the number was not less than three thousand. Others, who imaginations were more easily wrought upon, were quite certain there were ten thousand. The truth is, that the number of Ku Klux in the parade did not exceed four hundred. This delusion in regard to numbers prevailed wherever the Ku Klux appeared. It illustrates how little the testimony of even an eyewitness is worth in regard to anything which makes a deep impression on him by reason of its mysteriousness.

The Klan had a large membership; it exerted a vast, terrifying and wholesome power; but its influence was never at any time dependent on, or proportioned to, its membership. It was in the mystery in which the comparatively few enshrouded themselves. However, most members of the Klan had been Confederate soldiers and were familiar with military drill and discipline. Gen. (Bedford) Forrest, before the investigating Committee, placed the number of Ku Klux in Tennessee at 40,000, and in the entire south at 550,000.[34] This was with him only a guessing estimate. [Nathan Bedford Forrest denied that he had made such an estimate. There were many other organizations similar to the Ku Klux, thus combined the total membership was probably about half million throughout the south.]

Those dark days of the Reconstruction period rapidly followed the horrors of civil war, and the reign of the carpetbagger began, goading the people (to) desperation. For their protection the younger and more reckless men of the community now formed a secret society, which masqueraded at night in grotesque and gruesome character called the Ku Klux Klan. Always silent and mysterious mounted on horses, they swept noiselessly by in the darkness with gleaming death's heads of the evil-doer, while the peaceful citizens knew a faithful patrol had guarded his premises while he slept....

At the parade in Pulaski while the procession was passing a corner on which a negro man standing, a tall horseman in hideous garb turned aside from the line, dismounted, and stretched out his bridle rein toward the negro, as if he desired him to hold his horse. Not daring to refuse, the frightened negro extended his hand to grasp the rein. As he did so the Ku Klux took his own head from his shoulders and offered to place that also in the outstretched hand. The negro stood not upon the order of his going, but departed with a yell of terror. To this day he will tell you: "He done it, suah, boss. I see him do it." The gown was fastened by a drawstring over the top of the wearer's head. Over this was worn an artificial skull made of a large gourd or of pasteboard. This with the hat could be readily removed, and the man would then appear to be headless. Such tricks gave rise to the belief — still prevalent among the Negroes — that the Ku Klux could take themselves all to pieces whenever they wanted to.

Some of the Ku Klux carried skeleton hands. These were made of bone or wood with a handle long enough to be held in the hand, which was the concealed by the gown sleeve. The possessor of one of these was invariably of a friendly turn and offered to shake hands with all he met with what effect may be readily imagined. A trick of frequent perpetration in the country was for a horseman, spectral and ghostly looking, to stop before the cabin of some negro needing a wholesome impression and call for a bucket of water. If a dipper or gourd was brought it was declined, and the bucket full of water demanded. As if consumed by raging thirst the horsemen grasped it and pressed it to his lips. He held it there till every drop of the water was poured into a gum or oiled sack concealed beneath the Ku Klux robe. Then the empty bucket was returned to the amazed negro with the remark:

"That is good. It is the first drink of water I have had since I was killed at Shiloh." Then a few words of counsel as to future behavior made an impression not easily forgotten or likely to be disregarded.

Under ordinary circumstances such devices are unjustifiable. But in the peculiar state of things then existing they serve a good purpose. It was not only better to deter the Negroes from theft and other lawlessness in this way than to put them in the penitentiary; but it was the only way, at this time, by which they could be controlled. The jails would not contain them.[35]

Though Lester's analysis of this parade placed emphasis on Klansmen as "regulators" correcting the *evils* of Reconstruction, assumptions about human nature were also revealed. In fact, Ku Klux chapters in South Carolina, Georgia, Tennessee, Mississippi, Alabama and Florida considered public display rallies not only effective but essential in creating and maintaining and elitist status. In addition, the idea of social regulators, albeit Ku Kluxers operating beyond the established constraints of the law while claiming the right to function in behalf of those encumbered by the mundane activities of daily life, helped facilitate an emotional safety net for those whites who measured the quality of their lives in terms of their relative social distance from the Freedmen. Finding solace within a Christian philosophy that clearly separated evil from good, Ku Kluxers functioning as high priests also envisioned themselves as Christian warriors carrying forth the work of the Lord! Often bordering on pure fantasy, their actions were now aimed at cultivating a highly fundamentalist response from devotees.

Feeling responsible to uphold Christian precepts of sacrifice and glory, the second Imperial Wizard of the Ku Klux envisioned that the south would eventually be delivered from its tragic state of affairs by godly forces that would distinguish good from evil, right from wrong, white from black, man from nigger. This, he assured devotees, would occur when:

From over the mysterious borderland, from the Empire of the Soul, the Ku Klux Klan came. Out of the sable shadows of the darkest night that ever afflicted any people they rode with a determined purpose; pure, as typified by the snowy white of their ghostly garments; hearts loyal as ever pulsated, as typified by the cross on the crimson shield worn upon their manly breast; and a sacred devotion that laughed at death and faltered not at danger, as typified by the sacrificial cross of Christ.[36]

Given that a recurring theme that typified nineteenth-century Ku Klux Klan propaganda was the notion of Christian fortitude confronting evil in the name of a white Protestant God, they attempted to become an abiding reminder of the Puritan's vision of sacrifice, pain and resistance in the face of the devil's temptations.[37] Such a notion proclaimed that those who would envision a new future must also exhibit a forceful and if need be violent posture in defense of specific ideals, as when South Carolinian educator John Leland evoked a biblical depiction of King Solomon's determination and alleged wisdom: "If thy people go out to battle against their enemies, by whatever way thou shalt send them, and they pray to thee toward this city which thou hast chosen and the house which I have built for thy name, then hear thou from heaven their prayer and their supplication, and maintain their cause" (11 Chron 6:34).

By asserting religious doctrine to support a southern secessionist vision of the world, propagandists such as Leland viewed themselves as being in the midst of a religious, albeit violent crusade. Accordingly biblical texts emphasizing the solemn nature of their cause were meant to foster a deep fervor about the burden that history has placed on their backs. In line with this thinking, sworn allegiances of resistance were not lost on southern whites when evoked from the pulpit by sardonic clergymen in countless towns, villages and hamlets throughout the south:

> Hear my prayer, O Lord:
>   Give ear to my supplications!
> In thy faithfulness answer me, in thy
>   righteousness!
> Enter not into judgment with thy servant
> for no man living is righteous before thee
> for the enemy has pursued me;
> he has crushed my life to the ground;
> he has made me sit in darkness life
>   Those long dead.
> Therefore my spirit faints within me;
>   my heart within me is appalled
> I remember the days of old,
>   I mediate on all that thou hast done;
>   I must on what thy hands have wrought.
> I stretch out my hands to thee;
>   my soul thirsts for thee like a parched land [Psalms 143:1–6].

It was not difficult for anti–Republican secessionist propagandist such as Lester and Leland to expand on one of America's most dramatic nineteenth-century shibboleths, Manifest Destiny.[38] Armed with what they assumed was sufficient evidence of their ultimate righteousness, the forces of good who were subjugating the heathen native population by force of arms, now targeted *'the nigger'* for the right to control southern lands. Ku Kluxers armed with the following pledge, swore that this would be fulfilled on the graves of dead comrades, south and north[39]:

I do solemnly swear that I will support and defend the Invisible circle; that I will defend our families, our wives, our children, and brethren; That I will assist a brother in distress to the best of my ability; That I will never reveal the secrets of this order or anything in regard to it that may come to my knowledge, and if I do may I meet a traitor's doom, which is death, death, death: so help me God, and so punish me my brethren.[40]

In his own fashion, John Leland, "the reputed Ku Klux" expressed similar sentiments to his colleague, Simon Pearson:

> My dear friend Simeon,
>   I have the opinion,
> Your motto is now grown bigger;
>   "Whatever is, is right!"
> "Let it come day or night
> From heaven, earth or hell,
>   man or nigger."[41]

In spite of Democratic southern propagandist obstinate political and spiritual rhetoric, by 1868 southern conservative newspaper articles continually warned their readers of increasing resistance by Freedmen to daily white racism or more organized attacks by Ku Klux–type gangs. As white-owned farms continually burned and pro–Democratic conservative blacks increasingly became targets of Republican-oriented blacks, Union League chapters heighten their own rhetoric of resistance to terrorist gangs. For example, as the summer months arrived, from Wilmington, North Carolina, reports of "incendiarism" were easily found in newspapers:

> A difficulty occurred in Wilson County on Saturday between a white and colored man, in which the latter was shot and slightly wounded in the leg. The former as immediately arrested and bound over to appear at the Superior Court. Afterwards a Negro President of the Union League made an incendiary harangue in which he advised the Negroes to burn the houses and kill the white people. About eleven o'clock that night the barn of Green, the man bound over, was discovered on fire, but he and his family could not go out of the house for fear of being shot. A negro was seen near the barn just before the fire, and was arrested, tried before a Magistrate, his guilt established, and in default of $300 security, sent to jail. Much excitement prevails but is hoped that no further disturbance will occur.[42]

Some southern newspapers, such as *The Winnsboro News* in South Carolina, used the term "incendiarism" to define what they considered inflammatory speech by Freedmen at local meeting. However, in the following article titled, "Incendiarism in Fairfield — a Fact for the North," the reporters on conclusions about the meeting are themselves indicative of a deep-seated antipathy toward sentiments expressed:

> At a meeting of at least a thousand blacks, held at Blackstock last Saturday week and attended by Loyal Leagues from Chester and elsewhere, and which perhaps was the largest meeting of blacks ever held in Fiarfield District, a gentleman informs us that he heard the most popular of their speakers us the following language:
>
> "Now, my friends, you hear the white people make a good deal of talk about their heavy losses by black men stealing. But do they lose anything by it? No, they don't; for you work for them, and they get it back in your labor. Suppose it's something to eat that a black man steals, it makes him stronger, and the white people get it back in his labor. Suppose he sells what he steals, and buys clothing, don't he work for the white people, and don't they get back what he stole to buy clothes with his labor?" [Immediate applause.]
>
> Is comment necessary? We tell the people of the North, that the patience and forbearance of Southern men towards these foolish semi-barbarians, temporarily converted into our rulers, finds no parallel in history. Through large tracts of country, nine tenths of the stock has been killed, and small depredations without number are committed daily which would long since have exasperated any set of Northern farmers to an uncontrollable pitch of fury and vengeance.[43]

During this period, attacks and counterattacks in Charleston, South Carolina, by blacks and whites in a number of social venues was not unusual. On November 14 the *Courier* reported that

> A distinguished officer of the United States Army who witnessed the disgraceful conduct of the Negro mob at the polling precinct of Ward 2 during he recent elections, and their outrages during the next day, remarked that did he not know the contrary to be true, he would be induced to believe the white people of Charleston the most arrant cowards. It

is needless to say that it was the forbearance of the white and colored conservative citizens of Charleston, under the insults and outrages committed upon them, that caused this remark.[44]

And then as a warning, the author concludes, "they have ever desired to sustain the reputation of our city as a law abiding community, and a desire to do this kept them silent under insults they never would have otherwise borne. Of this we are glad; but we trust, for the sake of law and order, that our forbearance will not soon be tested."[45]

Without question, the battle between the races was mirrored by intraracial struggles between Democratic and Republican whites and blacks. For example, in one particular street confrontation,

James Bails, a colored man met Frank Oliver, another colored man in Church-Street, and accosted him with abusive language, threatening to kill him because he Oliver, voted the "Democratic ticket." Oliver immediately proceeded to a Magistrate and having made the necessary affidavit, Bails was arrested and bound over to keep the peace. Upon the arrival of the officer to execute the warrant, a large crowd of colored men assembled in the vicinity, but we learned of no resistance to the policeman.[46]

In a more violent confrontation that appeared to have suggested both the intraracial political motivations of the fight as well as a growing proficiency among armed blacks, *The Washington Republic* in Walterboro, South Carolina, reported that

A private letter received lasts evening from Brevet Lieutenant-Colonel Welsh, Fortieth United States Infantry, Commanding Post of Walterboro, South Carolina, states that while engaging in rescuing a colored man from an armed band of Negroes on the 24th of August, ultimo, the Colonel's force of twenty men was attacked by the mob and a skirmish of several hours duration ensued. The troops were first fired on, and the Colonel thinks would have been defeated, so great was the disparity of numbers, but for the superiority of their arms (breechloaders.) ... The Colonel gave no particulars being engaged in making his final report, but states the fight was a hot one.[47]

Though incidents as described tend to emphasize the daily context in which racial conflict occurred during the latter years of the 1860s, they also illustrated a coalescing of racialist values by southern whites *without* the ritualistic garb worn by the Ku Klux. One writer even noted that "the racial and social objects of the Klan were in perfect harmony with the objects of the white community, and it was hardly necessary for white males to swear solemn oaths, perform rituals and wear costumes to pursue the same end. There was a unity of feeling and action in the white community which rendered forms unimportant."[48]

Sowing the Seeds of a Deadly Fantasy

By 1867, comparable terrorist organizations to the Ku Klux were forming, such as the Pale Faces in Tennessee; the White Brotherhood; the Constitutional Union Guard, and the Invisible Empire in North Carolina; Knights of the Black Cross; the Heggie' Scouts; the Washington Brothers in Mississippi; the Knights of the White Carnation in Alabama; the Knights of the Rising Sun and the Ku Klux Rangers in Texas.[49] One Louisiana organization, the Knights of the White Camellia formed in the fall of 1867 was extremely active and successful in resisting black Republicanism in the major port city of New Orleans. Covertly propagating messages, strategies and tactics advocating white racial supremacy, this highly secretive association eventually expanded throughout other southern states such as Texas, Georgia, and the Carolinas. Their constitution, adopted in June 1868, provided for the development of an elaborate structure in state counties and local communities, while its regional affairs "office" functioned as a supreme council in the major cities, such as New Orleans.[50]

Only white men, eighteen years of age or older were recruited as initiates, and even then only when they "promised not merely to be secret and obedient, but to maintain and defend the social and political superiority of the white race on this continent."[51] Once inducted they were charged with orders that proclaimed:

> The fundamental object is the MAINTENANCE OF THE SUPREMACY OF THE WHITE RACE in this Republic. History and physiology teach us that we belong to a race which nature had endowed with an evident superiority over all other races, and that the Maker, in this elevating us above the common standard of human creation, has intended to give us over inferior races, a dominion from which no human laws can permanently derogate ... and it is a remarkable fact that as a race of men is more remote from the Caucasian and approaches nearer to the black African, the more fatally that stamp of inferiority is affixed to its sons, and irrevocably dooms them to eternal imperfectability and degradation.[52]

Not surprisingly, the single-mindedness of this order relied heavily on its members' adherence to an exacting form of personal discipline and racial ideals. With alleged unwavering vision, the well-armed Knights of the White Camellia were extremely effective in demanding and receiving obedience from its members, however they were not directly associated with ex–Confederate General Nathan Bedford Forrest's Ku Klux organization in Tennessee though its "cause" was one that many southern white males identified with. With a membership composed primarily of businessmen and professionals who felt they could benefit from an association with the other "best citizens" of Louisiana, their influence and presence was felt more than actually seen. Though they were not above "night riding" when ordered to do so, considering their general social background, such activities when engaged in appealed more to a need to feel powerful and in control, rather than a desire to associate with lower-class "night riding" whites who they otherwise abhorred.[53]

In the fall of 1868, the Knights of the White Camellia membership numbered about 15,000 with New Orleans being its major stronghold. This is significant when one considers that the adult white male population at that time was about 32,000.[54] Pitted against this armed and well-organized population of Democrat whites were politically assertive black Republican clubs and Loyal Leagues, none of which were as well armed or organized. Recognizing a violent racial struggle for political control of New Orleans was unavoidable, elements of the Knights established armed ten-man patrols that met nightly and prepared strategies on how to crush any insurgency by black Republicans or Loyal League clubs throughout the city.

Buttressed by a special committee's donation of $500 for guns and ammunition, New Orleans's mostly antiblack street vendors were also organized into armed units known as the Innocents. Having anticipated the end of slavery and the economic development of Freedmen as a direct threat to their already marginal economic existence, by the spring of

LEADERS
OF THE
DEMOCRATIC PARTY.

THE RIOTER SEYMOUR.

" Remember this, that the bloody and treasonable and revolutionary doctrine of public *accusli
can* be proclaimed by a mobun well as by a Government."—*Seymour's Speech at New-York, July 4, 1865.*

"Let to also see, if successful exertion by the North is less revolutionary than successful secession by the South.] Shall we compromise after war, or compromise without war?"—*Seymour's Speech at Tweddle Hall, Albany, January 31, 1861.*

"MY FRIENDS : Let me assure you that I am your friend. [Uproarious cheering.] You have been my friends. ['Yes, yes, that's so. We are and will be again.'] I wish to inform you that I have sent my Adjutant-General to Washington to have this draft suspended and stopped."—*Seymour's Speech to the Rioters at New-York, July 14, 1863.*

" The war is a failure. Let hostilities cease."—*Seymour's Plank in the Chicago Platform of 1864.*

THE BUTCHER FORREST.

" Forrest says : 'No quarter! no quarter! Kill 'em! kill 'em! damn 'em!' That's Forrest's orders, not to leave one alive."—*Map's Official Report.*

"In closing my report, I desire to acknowledge the prompt action of Brigadier-General Chalmers, commanding the forces around Fort Pillow. His faithful execution of all movements necessary to the successful accomplishment of the objects of the expedition, entitles him to special mention. HE HAS REASON TO BE PROUD OF THE CONDUCT OF THE OFFICERS AND MEN OF HIS COMMAND."—*Forrest's Official Report of the Fort Pillow Massacre.*

THE PIRATE SEMMES.

" Captain Semmes ordered the captains of both ships on board the Alabama, examined their papers, and allowing them to take a small quantity of clothing, burned their ships, and sent them adrift in their boats without any water or provisions."—*Report of the burning of the American ships Semens and Highlander, near Singapore, East Indies.*

"I drew my sword against the old flag—the old flag which no longer represented those principles. It was not the flag of 1776 against which I drew my sword, but the flag which had become 'a flaunting lie,' moulded by prominent politicians of the North. But now, in spite of the efforts of those politicians, who endeavored to strangle the old Democratic party by seeting in its stead a new Conservative party : a sort of conglomerated party—which was to comprise politicians of every shade of opinion, the grand old Democratic party has risen from the long slumber in which it has indulged, and now gives signs of new life and vitality ; and I have come here tonight from the country to ratify and rejoice with you in the nomination of Seymour and Blair."—*Semens' Speech at Mobile, Alabama, July, 1868.*

THE HANGMAN HAMPTON.

"Colonel Hampton seized a rifle and said : 'Watch me, boys ; do as I do.' He then shot down successively several Federal officers."—*Richmond Whig, July 24, 1861.*

" Hampton and Pickett will hang, shoot, or quarter all the Yankee foragers they catch, and it is just what they deserve."—*Floridian, Dec. 10, 1864.*

"When the resolution offered by the Senator from Maryland, which declared that the rights of suffrage belonged to the political powers of a State, were being considered, I begged to add a few simple words. They agreed ; and I took the resolutions, which you will find embodied in the platform, and added to them, 'And we declare that the reconstruction acts of Congress are unconstitutional, revolutionary, and void.' (cheers.) That was my plank in the platform. I wanted nothing else ; for when the great Democratic party had pledged themselves to that, when they had declared that these acts were 'unconstitutional, revolutionary, and void,' I was willing to wait in patience until that party would be triumphant, and apply the remedy."—*Wade Hampton at the Charleston Ratification Meeting.*

1868 this strata of the white laborers became, as one Democrat described them in a letter to his mother, the most violent and ruthless segment of "cut throats, thugs, assassins and the vilest characters in the city."[55] More will be said later about this group.

As a result, segments of New Orleans' white population and those living in the surrounding parishes organized and armed themselves to confront what was envisioned as an increasingly assertive black population. Even a prearranged signal of church bells was to be rung throughout the city when a crisis arose; one, and then two rapid taps, and then one more tap indicating that armed forces must be mobilized at specific points throughout the city and the nearby parishes to confront an armed challenge by blacks and their Republican allies.[56]

The dissemination of inflammatory literature further heightened anxieties in New Orleans, as newspapers supporting either Republican or Democratic philosophies carried daily reports of armed clashes and mayhem. However, the Knights of Camellia viewed these newspaper accounts as an essential aspect of their strategy in preparing whites for what was assumed would be a bloody racial struggle. They didn't have to wait long for this struggle.

In the early summer of 1868, the *New Orleans Republican* reported that a Catholic priest asserted, if Louisiana Republicans had any idea of what he knew, "their hair would turn gray." The priest went on to warn, "ten thousand men can be drawn together at the tap, of a bell, ... men organized in secret for [the] purpose of assassination and murder, whose places of rendezvous are in all parts of the city, and whose plans are terrible."[57] In August, another newspaper account revealed that a priest knew that Democrats were planning the massacre of radical Republican leaders in a few weeks, and would actually stage a fight among blacks to act as the impetus to attack.[58] Rumors as such, though having some basis in reality, once published took on a level of veracity that functioned to propagate an image of impending violence and disaster. Another paper, *The Iliad*, even asked its readers and any public official who would listen: "Why were such activities tolerated? Will anyone point out to us a white Union man or a Freedmen who has harmed or offered violence to anyone?"[59]

Opposite: A searing 1868 election year poster depicts four prominent figures in the Democratic Party, three of them former Confederate officers. Former New York governor and Democratic presidential nominee Horatio Seymour is portrayed as a rioter. Standing in a burning city, he waves his hat in the air while he steps on the back of a crawling figure. In the background a corpse hangs from a lamppost. Between 1862 and 1864 Seymour had opposed Lincoln's war policies, and he was branded an instigator of the 1863 New York Draft riots. Below the portrait are inflammatory passages from his speeches. Tennessee general Nathan Bedford Forrest, one of the founders of the Ku Klux Klan, and infamous for his role in the massacre of surrendered Union troops at Pillow, is called "The Butcher Forrest." He waves a flag labeled "No quarter" and fires a pistol. Extracts from reports of the Pillow massacre are given below his picture. Confederate admiral Raphael Semmes is portrayed as a pirate, wielding a knife in one hand and holding aloft a flaming torch in the other. Behind him flies a flag with a skull and crossbones. To the right a family cowers in fright. Semmes was the scourge of Union shipping during the Civil War. Under his command the *Alabama*, a British-built ship, captured sixty-two merchant vessels, most of which were burned. An excerpt from Semmes's July 1868 speech at Mobile, Alabama, appears below his image. Confederate cavalry officer Wade Hampton appears as a hangman. He holds his plumed hat at his side and wears a uniform embossed with a skull and crossbones and a belt inscribed "C.S.A." (Confederate States of America). In the distance three Yankee soldiers hang from a gallows. Broadside Collection, portfolio 236, no. 27. Library of Congress Rare Book Special Collections Division, Washington, D.C.

"Shall we call home our troops? We intend to beat the Negro in the battle of life, and defeat means one thing—EXTERMINATION," *Harper's Weekly,* January 9, 1875. LIBRARY OF CONGRESS PRINTS AND PHOTOGRAPHS DIVISION, WASHINGTON, D.C.

By the fall of 1868, passive inquires such as the above began to fall on deaf ears throughout the south. In Louisiana, a black state senator, P.B.S. Pinchback, responded to personal attacks from conservative newspapers by asserting, "The next outrage of the kind which they [white Democrats] commit will be the signal for the dawn of retribution, of which they have not yet dreamed — a signal that will cause ten thousand torches to be applied to this city; for patience will then have ceased to be a virtue and this city will be reduced to ashes."[60] While Pinchback's "warning" of ten thousand incendiaries did not emerge, violent clashes between two contending racial and political groups did erupt and eventually raged throughout New Orleans from September to the presidential elections in November 1868. Unchecked killings, beatings, rapes and robberies soon spread to neighboring parishes of Algiers, Jefferson, St. Bernard and the suburban town of Gretna.

On October 24, political clubs in New Orleans, both Democratic and Republican, were marching, organizing, preparing their constituents for the November 3 elections. On the evening of the 24th a group of Democrat clubs marched down to Canal Street and finished their speech making in front of a Republican club. A lively debate and name calling ensued. Ending peacefully, the two groups proceeded down further down Canal Street, essentially side by side with only a tree-lined divider separating them. Within minutes, "a small number of men and boys jumped from what was known as the neutral ground (the tree lined divider in the center of the street) and fired into the Republican procession."[61] After the surprising attack, many blacks fled Canal Street, returning to their homes; armed themselves with guns, axes and knives; and returned to the streets. Approximately 11:30 that evening they were attacking whites all along Dauphine Street in downtown New Orleans. In one incident, a streetcar was attacked,

> J.R. Smalls was severely injured by a blow from an axe, and a number of other whites were shot or stabbed. Patrick Brady, a white carriage maker was hacked to death by hatchets. In still another attack a former Confederate officer who served as a member of the New Orleans Police department until he resigned when the first blacks were appointed to the force, was shot to death.[62]

Two days later, the street fighting raged back and forth between Republicans and Democrats, but more significantly between the races. Even Republican state governor Henry Clay Warmoth "incapable of maintaining order" was rumored to be "fleeing the State."[63] Black police who consisted of one-third of the Metropolitan Police Force and were three of the five commissioners who were alleged to be actually Warmoth's private "state militia" were reported to be largely ineffective and in effect did not report to duty at the height of the riot.[64] Whether they were in the street fighting against Democratic mobs is open to speculation.

Three days later in the late evening of October 26, white mobs, now extremely well armed, began attacking black business establishments, homes and essentially any unarmed blacks found within known Republican wards and radical club headquarters, such as the Seventh Ward Republican Club and the Cofax Legion.[65] With mounting casualties on both sides and after intense house-to-house fighting there appeared to be no tapering in the fighting around the French Market and Treme Market areas or locations further removed from the Mississippi levee.[66] After severe bloody encounters, armed mobs of whites with the assistance of the Knights of the White Camellia, were slowly able to drive resisting blacks out of black-dominated ward areas into the surrounding swamps while searching for guns,

536 HARPER'S WEEKLY. [AUGUST 25, 1866.

THE RIOT IN NEW ORLEANS—THE FREEDMEN'S PROCESSION MARCHING TO THE INSTITUTE—THE STRUGGLE FOR THE FLAG.
[Sketched by Theodore R. Davis.]

THE RIOT IN NEW ORLEANS—SIEGE AND ASSAULT OF THE CONVENTION BY THE POLICE AND CITIZENS.—Sketched by Theodore R. Davis.
[See Page 535.]

ammunition, money and anything of value that they could strip from those fleeing or killed. Even a company of white-led black U.S. Infantry troops sent to maintain order proved to be ineffective, though evidence exist that they may have been purposefully incompetently led.[67]

The Knights' infiltration, influence, and control of the New Orleans Metropolitan Police force's leadership was so extensive that they were able to control how this force functioned during the fighting. About 10 p.m. the Innocents were again marching, this time carrying trophies from the previous street brawls, such as a captured black Republican banner and caps worn by Republicans. Numbering three hundred marchers and dressed in their traditional red shirt with a cap bearing their name, they also carried a distinguishable banner, "which portrayed a black on the ground about to be stabbed with a knife."[68] They stormed into a ward heavily populated by blacks and immediately found themselves targeted by sharpshooters. In the initial clash, Edward Malone, a thirty-six-year-old native of Ireland and a member of the Innocents, was killed by gunfire. This kind of expert sniping by black sharpshooters continued on until Wednesday morning October 28.[69] At once point in the fighting, the Knights Council itself detailed twenty men for patrol duty in Jefferson Parish until the armed conflict phase of the disturbances with the Republican factions in the metropolitan police was finally over.[70]

By November, a report from a congressional elections committee indicated that an estimated 1,081 persons were killed, 131 shot and some 507 other persons were "outraged" in Louisiana between April and November 1868. Freedmen's Bureau chief George Edward Hatch reported that as appalling as these figures were, they did not include other victims of violent clashes throughout the state, as "hundreds of instances are not reported and a great many never will be."[71]

While black Republican political interest suffered a damaging physical and psychological blow as a result of continued armed attacks by the Knights of the White Camellia, Innocents, and Klansmen, an interesting if not significant revelation occurred as a result of blacks resistance. Voting figures for 1868 indicated that in upstate Louisiana parishes, where little or no violence occurred, the state election results of April and the November presidential election were relatively the same. However, elsewhere in seven parishes that had earlier supported Republican Governor Warmoth with some 4,707 votes, no votes were given to Republican presidential candidate Ulysses S. Grant during the fall elections![72] Eight other parishes that in April had a Republican vote of 5,520 now gave 10 votes to Grant in November! Twenty-one parishes cast 26,814 votes for Warmoth and only 501 for Grant. Only 276 votes for Grant came from New Orleans, though the entire state in April consigned some 61,152 votes for the Republicans in April 1868, by November that number was down to 34,659. The impact of terrorist propaganda, coupled with violent raids by Klansmen or their sympathizers throughout the countryside and increasing violent clashes between Republicans and Democrats in New Orleans clearly had an effect when considering that in April the Democrats received 43,739 votes, but in the presidential elections in November, 88,225![73]

Though these figures indicated to southern Democrats that strategies aimed at curtail-

Opposite, top: "The Riot in New Orleans — The Freedmen's Procession Marching to the Institute — The Struggle for the Flag" and, **bottom,** "The Riot in New Orleans — Siege and Assault of the Convention by the Police and Citizens," both *Harper's Weekly,* August 25, 1866. LIBRARY OF CONGRESS PRINTS AND PHOTOGRAPHS DIVISION, WASHINGTON, D.C.

ing blacks' participation in the voting process would continue to be successful if enough armed pressure was available, they concomitantly suggested to Freedmen that immediate improvements in the following areas were needed if they were to survive.

(a) An inability to obtain sufficient weaponry to defend their homes and hamlets often left blacks in the dubious position of having to depend on often an apathetic northern military force or an inadequately trained or apathetic police force.

(b) Once violent pressure from white terror groups increased, alliances with northern liberal organizations would undoubtedly collapse under threats of violence from white extremist groups. Their survival depended primarily on self-sustaining abilities to either deflect aggressive attacks by subterfuge or amass enough fire power to fraught any direct attacks.[74]

Targeting Klansmen

As racist metaphors systematically shaped the norms and values of southern society by socially compressing blacks into simplistic stereotypical categories, a pernicious and ritualistic kind of social reductionism emerged to encourage the perception of an *evil external forces* waiting to strike down the unwary southern white. Ku Klux racist liturgy and ritual worked feverishly to further polarize white communities into bastions of fear as if every semblance of public order was in danger of being destroyed. As part of this fabrication, Ku Kluxers wearing long monk-like robes with pointed or otherwise oddly shaped head masks, displaying whips and propagating their own reputed activities as "night riders" quickly became powerful visual metaphors for many southerner Ku Klux sympathizers of an envisioned mythological warrior clan seeking retribution for past wrongs. Embodied with symbolic authority, night riders and others became the cathartic emotional release for thousands of psychologically displaced whites. To be a member of this supposedly secretive clan, to know someone who was suspected as being a member, to feel pride in their resistance and mistreatment of "the nigger" was for many to be in effect, a Klansmen.

However, contrary to the beliefs of many southern whites, visits by night-riding Klansmen were often viewed by Freedmen as rambling, comical discursive characters that impeded neither their personal discernment of southern whites nor a desire to defend themselves. Assertive demands by Freedmen for civil rights generally differed with what was commonly believed to be their stereotypical response to white aggression. For example, when blacks violently resisted abuse or terror it was psychologically more convenient for southern whites to rationalize these responses as "criminal behavior," a social aberration, or some form of lunacy![75]

Conversely, some northern Republicans refused to characterize southern whites as overt sympathizers of Klan terrorism, but instead argued that there were enough good people in the south to allow the eventual triumph of justice. For them, the struggle in the south was essentially a *moral* struggle! Not surprisingly, by 1869, southern newspaper editors who published this sort of liberal analysis risked public censure by being labeled northern sympathizers, scalawags and "nigger lovers."

In the early spring of 1871 the conservative *Kentucky Statesman* newspaper hazarded being labeled a southern traitor when it published an article in which the writer tangentially attacked "respectable outlaws" by stating:

Silly people sometimes asks us, with an air of sever censure, why is it that you are opposing your own race, and defending the negroes? The only possible answer to such people is,
that they are born fools, and, we fear, will die fools. We have such a high opinion of the
white race, that we have believed that they could be persuaded to do the negro justice —
that they would give him his liberty, protect him in his civil rights, make his life, labor
and property secure, and allow him to enjoy his political privileges in peace. What has the
white man to gain by persecuting or injuring, or allowing the negro to be maltreated?
Nothing whatever. If their humanity is not touched by the condition of these people, their
justice ought not to follow them to be wronged.

Now there are mean men, with narrow minds, and hearts full of prejudice, that consider it a degradation to do the Negro either a kindness or justice. To such men it is useless to say anything. They will soon die, and we will be rid of them, and blessed in their
departure. But why should men, who claim to be human gentlemen and Christians,
countenance violence or injustice towards this lowly people, once their slaves, still our
wards, it is to say, hard to comprehend.

Let us say to some people who professed respectability, and are yet leaders and encour-
agers in schemes of violence towards this race that neither their money nor their fine
clothes make them gentlemen; though the doors of genteel society are thrown open to
them, and they are permitted to approach better people, yet they are nothing more nor
less than bullies and outlaws, and richly deserve to be hung by their neck until they are
dead.

Their big farms and fine houses may save them while they muster gangs of bad men to
maltreat these poor negroes; but those possessions cannot protect them from the [...] of all
good people; and the hour will come when the better men who now wink at their evil
doings will openly execrate their names, and point out their children as those of an
outlaw.

Happily but very few of these men are enabled to gain riches and respectability. We
would hope that good men and women everywhere would execrate this bad treatment of
those poor Negroes. In the name of our common creator, Ruler and Judge, let them alone;
and let us all help them to be intelligent, industrious and orderly. The great enemies of
every community are those who take the law into their own hands. Those people ought
to be driven from the community.[76]

In similar fashion the editor of the *New Era,* an outwardly liberal but clearly more cautious southern Republican newspaper, republished an article critical of Ku Klux terrorism,
though conveniently forgetting the specific name of its source:

Men are waylaid and shot, or taken by bands of disguised rebels, hung up to trees and
whipped to death and the most diabolical cruelties perpetrated upon them. Neither respect
nor mercy is shown to women or children who fall into the hands of the ruthless
"avengers" as they call themselves. A reign of terror prevails in many sections, and families
are fleeing out of the country to save their lives.

The worst phase of the whole matter is that these outrages are either perpetrated or
countenance by southerners who rank according to their own showing among the "first
families." We are glad to observe that vigorous steps have been taken to bring these
scoundrels to justice. Advice from Raleigh represent a terrible state of affairs in some of
the interior counties, and a dispatch from Richmond of Wednesday says that, "Colonel
Kirk has arrested about seventy more prominent citizens of Caswell county, N.C., some of
whom resisted and were badly maltreated. There is great excitement in the county.

We want to see these "prominent citizens" taken care of, and if guilty, made to answer with their lives for the murders they have done or instigated. some parts of the south, especially the more isolated portions, are as venomously rebel in sentiment to-day as they were during the war, and "prominent citizens" are as cruel and treacherous as they were when they crowded our poor boys like sheep into the filthy prison pens of Andersonville, Belle Isle and Millen, and starve them to death on corn cob meal, or shot them down like dogs when in their insane moments, mad with thirst and hunger, they crawled too near the fated "deadline." Many of the human fiends who committed the outrages live and feed their selfish passions on the blood of unoffending Negroes or hard working migrants from the north, murdering and maltreating with impunity under the black disguise of the Ku Klux Klan.

The halter is too good for these ghouls and we hope the authority of the Government will be exercised in the murder cursed region of the south with the utmost rigor. Or else let us admit at once that "constitutional guaranties" of protection to all peaceful citizens in every part of our national domain are but the shallowest twaddle.[77]

Interestingly, just a few months earlier and in this same newspaper another republished article from the *Chicago Republican*, commented on a number of intriguing political scenarios being enacted in North Carolina where armed whites, blacks and Indian guerrillas were pitted in a low-level guerrilla war against both Klan militia units and federal troops.[78] However, while reporting on the fighting, the editorial policy of the *Chicago Republican* appeared to be reluctant to want law and order restored through a Republican administration! The paper noted that while North Carolina's Republican governor William Holden was under a lot of pressure to proclaim martial law, a "prominent citizen" in possibly a conspiratorial-minded manner was "silly enough to go all the way to Washington, DC to try induce newly elected President Grant to interfere in the internal affairs of the State [North Carolina] without any demands being made upon him, by the State authorities for that purpose!" The *Republican* went on to suggest that this citizen really "sought the Federal governments violation of the fundamental law of the Republic in the interest of assassination!"[79] Whose assassination, however, was left open to speculation. The paper also proclaimed that while such a request was actually beyond the authority of the President Grant to entertain, in any event, on receipt of such a request, the state would first have to demonstrate its inability to control or suppress insurrection or domestic violence within its own borders, particularly by blacks or Indians. Governor Holden eventually sent the state militia in pursuit of the Ku Klux; however, rather than curtailing the activities of terrorism, the effect of this effort actually facilitated the growth of Klan membership in ten counties that in turn ensured a Democratic Party victory in the 1870 legislative elections and removed Holden from office.[80]

Though testimony received by the U.S. congressional subcommittee on Ku Klux Klan terrorist activities was voluminous and brimming with unspeakable brutality against blacks, it also contained poignant evidence revealing significant levels of "feigned innocence" by Klansmen.[81] And while excerpts depicting "Klan outrages" provided the public with some understanding of the organization's violent nature, it also concomitantly legitimized the organization's existence in an era where as conservatives lamented, there appeared to be no end to blacks' lawlessness and interracial strife. Moreover, by 1870 as many white Americans were tiring of a seemingly unending southern racial problem, they were quite prepared to accept high levels of violence against those social elements that were prohibiting the expansion of American manifest destiny and racial hegemony westward, be the obstacles "red skins" or "niggers."[82] As a consequence, many antebellum abolitionists readily became postbellum conservatives and in many instances Klansmen in spirit or fact.[83] This was decidedly the case when promises of greater personal and national economic stability enabled many to conclude that little economic and social value could be derived from conducting another civil war. Accordingly, finding a solution to the "interminable nigger problem" simply underscored the pathetic drama of American political expediency and racism cloaked within the haunting robes of democracy. As one south Carolina Chester County planter put it, "the K. K.s are an excellent institution if kept in proper bounds. They have been of immense benefit in our county." Another white farmer in Spartanburg expressing the attitude of many small white farmers was hopeful that the Klan would frighten "Negro legislators that they would resign and prevent his [farm] being 'sold out for taxes in a year or to more.'" He further proudly noted, "there is a new sort of beings got up call K Ks that has a powerful show. These K Ks whip and kill as they pleas."[84]

How American racial policies functioned on the day-to-day level of human interaction is instructive particularly as to an understanding of what it meant to be a southern white or an emancipated black during the latter years of the 1860s. With each in fear of the other, they both were tied to the question of who would dominate that which was significant to all southerners, the land.[85] Yet a significant difference existed between these two combatants in that they were not equally armed in this deadly struggle. Southern whites certainly had sufficient access to those implements of war to propagate outlandish fears and mythological constructs on blacks as well as hesitant whites. In doing so, they functioned partially through the aegis of terror gangs who fashioned a political rational for violence that elevated racial and caste differences into an overwhelming carnal desire for violent, vicious confrontation. Feeding from the gory trough that was the Civil War, organized rebel bodies persistently addressed "the deeper revolution wrought by the war and oath: the creation of an explosive culture of hatred, personal firearms, and political alienation."[86] Unfortunately however, for many of these self-proclaimed beleaguered southerners, cathartic release seemed only possible with the spawning a new phoenix like persona, the Klansmen.[87]

Testimony from Klansmen before congressional investigators revealed that though many recruits entered the Ku Klux as a result of intimidation, for others more subtle factors were at work. For instance, previous friendships and the desirability for a new status based on common experiences played a major role in attracting Klan initiates.[88] Membership was also enhanced by the likelihood that for the first time in the initiate's life they would be empowered by their peer group, not some distant impersonal political body, to fulfill a worthy mission. As such, a sense of conformity and valued membership in the Ku Klux, as with other secret societies theoretically cemented social relationships while enhancing the notion of valued goals, regardless of one's class status. To the extent this actually blurred other ascribed characteristics is questionable, yet factors such as enhanced self-esteem and group membership, particularly for the unemployed and landless, were important inducements to join this alleged covert organization. And while many inductees certainly speculated on the risk and demands they might be expected to comply with, the need for a valued association was irresistible. Similarly, the more highly esteemed the organization became, such as the White Knights of Camellia, the greater were those satisfactions derived from adopting the organization's values. In a sense, these extralegal groups became a refuge for those who perceived the world as an increasing hostile environment. A world where group loyalty and an adherence to traditional norms and opinions were now being challenged.[89]

Congressional testimonies exposing the deadly fantasy of innate racial superiority also revealed that Ku Klux members were vigorously controlled by the double-edged sword of fear and intimidation, not to mention the knowledge that dire consequences existed for any who resisted induction.[90] While concerns for the sanctity of a victim's life were minimized during raids, an emotional deferential reaction to Klan threats and violence was expected from all victims. This functioned to such an extent that Ku Klux raiders' programmed expectation of fearful reactions by their intended victims functioned as a dependent variable on which Klan social fantasy and mythology activated on the raider's own psyche! As a result, an ultimately destructive and often internalized psychological *dependency* was forged between terrorizing Ku Kluxers' need to cruelly denigrate their victim's social worth and a concomitant desire to appear loyal to mythological constructs of their purportedly implacable moralistic organization. In this regard DuBois observed: "Back of the writhing, yelling, cruel-eyed demons who break, destroy, maim and lynch and burn at the stake is a knot, large or small, of normal human beings and these human beings at heart are desperately afraid of something."[91]

Testimonies from the 1871–1872 congressional investigations into Klan activity in South Carolina are instructive on this point. Utilizing first the Enforcement Act of 1870 that outlawed disguises and masks and protected the civil rights of citizens, a Republican strong Congress legislatively supported an increasing beleaguered black population's ability to vote.[92] One year later this was followed by the Ku Klux Act of 1871 that essentially outlawed Klan-like activity and laid the basis for indictments and trials of Klansmen when necessary.[93] Supporting these developments, Congressmen Joseph Rainey summed up the sentiments of most but not all black Republicans when he proclaimed, "I desire that so broad and liberal a construction be placed on its [the Constitution] provisions, as will insure protection to the humblest citizen. Tell me nothing of a Constitution which fails to shelter beneath its rightful power the people of a country."[94]

Rainey's statement unmistakably pointed to not only the growing threat of white terrorist organizations but more pointedly to an increasing violent response by whites to the specter of armed black militias throughout the south. In fact, a major subtext for the congressional hearings into Ku Klux activities was whether black militia units were providing effective protection to the ex-slave and their ability to ensure the safety of Republican political interest. As one south Carolinian political activist stated in 1870, "I will carry the election here with the militia, ... I am giving out ammunition all the time." Similarly in Mississippi, a letter from a Yazoo city resident to a friend claimed, "it is with Pleasure I write you this to inform U of some Politocal newse. They are preparing for the election very fast ... [and] are buying ammunition. The colored folks have got 1600 Army guns. All prepared for business."[95]

Evidence of armed organized bands of Freedmen roaming the countryside after the Civil War are documented by an affidavit produced by J. D. Palmer, dated August 25, 1866, where he asserts that a veteran named "Johnson" of the 55th Massachusetts Volunteer Infantry Regiment was organizing Freedmen into "companies" to aid other "military companies" formed by blacks near the Santee River, South Carolina.[96] However, in this regard it is important to know that support for state controlled armed militia units who would curtail or fight organized bands of Ku Klux raiders and similar type gangs did not officially begin until July 25, 1868, when Senate Bill 648 proposed to repeal an earlier law that prohibited the use of militias in those states that supported the southern confederacy. Though this bill did not become law until July 15, 1870, a number of states, acting illegally, organized militia units that included a variety of activities from guerrilla campaigns, naval engagement, diplomatic activities and even full-scaled pitched battles complete with artillery, cavalry and the deployment of troops.[97] Undoubtedly "Johnson's" efforts were not isolated, but enjoyed some official support.

In Tennessee, the birthplace of the Ku Klux, black militias were used a early as 1867 to offset politically destabilizing efforts by the Klan. In fact, realization by conservative whites that the growing formations of black militias were separate and apart from the regular black federal military companies raised anxiety levels of many southern whites that their worst fears had become a reality. What was at first viewed as a novel development — that is to say, blacks mimicking federal soldiers — was now interpreted as an unbelievable and explosive degradation of their own sensibilities. One *New York Herald* correspondent in the fall of 1868 echoed the sentiment of many southern and northern white conservatives when he concluded, "The fact is inevitable that bloodshed will follow. Reconstructed governments are bad enough with negro legislators, negro magistrates, negro police, and negro Commissioners of Education and other matters; but when armed negroes appear as military forces to keep white men in order ... the spirit ... must revolt."[98]

An almost contrite Governor Robert K. Scott of South Carolina told an audience in Washington, D.C., that he was convinced the only law South Carolinians understood was the Winchester rifle.[99] Even Republican Governor William Brown running for re-election in Tennessee expressed similar sentiments when pleading to voters, "Send up a legislature to reorganize the militia," while promising to put an end to the Democratic supported violence which was sweeping over the very state that in 1866 spawned the Ku Klux Klan.[100] However, Governor Scott's pleas were not idle threats or warnings, It went without saying that in his state, attacks on Freedmen increased in those counties where actively worked to arm themselves against what many perceived would be an onslaught of attacks.[101] Though Scott actually had enough arms for a tenth of the militias statewide, the Laurens County militia had "620 breech-loading rifled muskets, 50 Winchesters rifles, and 18,000 rounds of ammunition, that is, roughly 10 percent of the total distributed."[102] It is not surprising to learn that as more weaponry was sent to counties such as Spartanburg, Newberry, Union, Chester, York, Fairfield, Kershaw, Edgefield and Laurens, South Carolina, racial attacks and counterattacks increased.[103] However in Oconee, Pickens and Greenville counties, where the white population numerically dominated, no arms were sent! Moreover in Anderson and Abbeville where only ninety-six muskets were sent, no major violent outbreaks occurred.[104] It can be surmised that a major catalyst for interracial violence during this pre-election period was the attempt by southern white vigilantes to disarm black militias or individual Freedmen who may have possessed anything from a naval colt pistol to a Winchester rifle. In this regard, the attacks in 1870 by white rioters and vigilantes in the town of Laurens, South Carolina, was primarily focused on stealing arms from the town's armory that were stored there for use by Republican militias. This will be further discussed later, but the central motivating fear of white Democratic party conservatives was that any successful *armed* expression by Freedmen particularly during the coming state and federal elections could easily be parlayed into political and economic parity if not domination. On this point, historian Franklin Frazier once observed that "the very fact that the Negro wore a uniform and thereby enjoyed certain rights was an affront to most southern whites."[105] If so, conjecture would suggest that while the sight of Freedmen in military uniform was generally enough to enrage most southern whites, the possibility that a collusion on the part of conservative Republicans and Democrats to illegally transfer rifles and other weaponry earmarked for black militias to southern white vigilantes by attacking an armory was certainly not beyond the realm of possibility.[106]

Even more indicative of Freedmen assertiveness was the militant organizing of black males (of whom many were nonliterate) into military formations to assist other Freedmen in the voting process. Whether it was the state or federal elections of 1868 and 1879, Union League officials and self-appointed workers proceeded in military fashion to "get out the vote."[107] Impressing both black and white with their military maneuvers, "drill societies mounted demonstrations whose participants numbered in the thousands in Union County (South Carolina) and even broader region appearances in Sumter and Fairfield."[108]

In late July 1870, an ex-slaveowner, Lalla Pelot, described one of these political demonstrations and their various contingents as "quite a show ... when our darkies (from Laurensville) were dressed in black coats & white pantaloons those from Crosshill in red coats & white pants — Clinton men in yellow coats & white pants."[109] Colorful or not, many of these black Republicans saw their work and Republicanism in general as "standing upon the Lord's side."[110] Notwithstanding regional differences, many Freedmen saw the Lord's work as being their functioning as a special oversight committee for local Republican sheriffs, magistrates and even county juries. In this sense, Union League members were often forced to exercise the powers of posse comitatus, thereby claiming authority to arrest suspected violators of the peace when necessary.[111]

For example, in April 1867 report to the 2nd Military District, South Carolina, a Union League official ex-slave Ebby Johnson was asked by members of the Dimery family to complain for them about abuses they suffered at the hands of their white employer, W.Z. Wingate. Believing threats from Wingate that he would kill them if they complained directly to "civil authorities," the family complained to Johnson and his committee regarding the landowner's assault on one of the female children. After assembling a committee of fifteen men, Johnson inspected their weapons and then proceeded to locate Wingate. They found him riding in his buggy, whereupon he was arrested and after some pressure convinced to "cross out a disputed plantation account against members of the Dimery family!" It was later reported that Wingate was humbled to the point that he "invited Johnson into another room and treated him to liquor."[112] It is important to note that attempts by Freedmen to exercise authority over their own lives was occurring at a time when extralegal gangs were selectively applying violent tactics on unprepared, untrained and for the most part unarmed blacks. Understanding this, historian Julie Saville noted that various chapters of the Union League from 1868 to 1870 began to incorporate a number of philosophical and practical approaches to the problem of combating terrorism:

(1) League members were determined to engage civil institutions in their popular arrest and detentions, thereby distinguishing the ex-slaves' forms of popular justice from the summary acts of Ku Klux Klan–style vigilante bands.

(2) Leagues challenged the alleged discretion of conservative sheriffs and local magistrates to exclude club members from local procedures pertaining to the governance of a community or county.

(3) League members were adamant that neighborhood law officials acknowledge account-
ability to a superior authority, the Federal government, and that the leagues had
derived authority from Washington to "power to protect the place."

(4) They would assume supervision of local officeholders with a vigilance that martial law
had actually placed at the disposal of an occupying army.

(5) They served warrants on parties local authorities were slow to apprehend.

(6) They investigated Ku Klux raids that local officers claimed ignorance.

(7) They viewed law enforcement as central to Union League's mobilization.[113]

As a response to inquiries alluding to the league's increasing militancy and if it was a
military organization, one Union League neighborhood president, Clark Cleveland Sr. shrewdly
responded, it was "a kind of semblance of such a thing, ... the main now is to abide by the
laws, and to learn us how to know about the law."[114] With responses such as the above by Clarke
Cleveland and the apparent organized militancy within Freedmen communities, Klansmen
and similarly constructed groups knew that a reordering of society was at hand, and that only
the gun and faggot could possibly stop, slow or arrest this changing order of life.

The hundreds of subsequent indictments that were drawn up were aimed at those
individuals or groups who violated the constitutional rights of others either by intimidation, physical injury or murder and where it could be shown that a citizen's right to bear
arms was violated.[115] Under the prosecutorial leadership of U.S. Attorney D.T. Corbin and
his assisting special counsel Attorney General Daniel H. Chamberlain, who later became
governor of South Carolina (1874–1877), trials of reputed Ku Klux Klansmen began in
November 1870. However, in York County alone out of 220 persons indicted during its court
term, only 58 were brought to trial! And though some 53 individuals pled guilty, only five
went to trial and were eventually found guilty.[116]

Standing before presiding judges Hugh L. Bond and associate judge George S. Bryan,
defendants with varying degrees of articulation and levels of remorse described their vio-
lence-filled lives as Klansmen.[117] At times, the court as well as members of the defense
appeared to be as shocked at some of the defendants' confessions. Shocked or not, some
committee members found the uncomplicatedness, seemingly natural recollections on terrorism difficult to comprehend, while others knew that these testimonies were apart of
America's deeply ingrained but deadly fantasy on race. Yet Ku Klux sympathizing newspapers such as Georgia's Rome *Courier* complained that "and now the young men who so
thoughtlessly engaged in that unfortunate frolic, will [now] have to be outcasts and fugi-
tives in a strange land, or brave the horrors of a Northern prison."[118] Still other southerners viewed Judge Bond as an unfortunate autocrat presiding over "the Spanish Inquisition
or Judge Jeffries and the Bloody Assizes of King James II."[119]

As testimony from Ku Klux trials in states such as South Carolina suggest, Klansmen
consigning themselves to the mercy of the court received reduced or circumvented sentences while unwittingly provided useful evidence pertaining to a number of motivations
in their ongoing armed struggle against the African. What wasn't expected to emerge from
these trials were the paradoxical realities in which Ku Klux raids occurred and the threatening dynamics that were set in motion. For example, in an early twentieth-century analysis of Reconstruction in South Carolina, historian J. Reynolds called attention to a thesis
seldom emphasized: The Ku Klux Klan during Reconstruction "was a self-defense force
designed to protect whites from armed black militiamen." As such, "the specter of black

political authority enforced at gunpoint seemed sufficiently threatening that the Klan acted preemptively to secure the rights of white South Carolina."[120] This astonishing analysis places a terrorist organization such as the Ku Klux in a defensive political stance responding the aggressive actions of Freedmen!

Though somewhat problematic in that this analysis minimizes the racial cultural conflict while emphasizing the political challenges, it does coincide with a more contemporary view by historian Joel Williamson that black militias were not only effective "in forging black pride but that they stirred deep concern in the white community" because of the pride now being instituted in the Freedmen communities.[121] Envisioning a connective thread of armed militancy from John Brown's raid at Harpers Ferry a decade earlier, Williamson further asserts that the Ku Klux riots of 1870 and 1871 occurred not because the Freedmen were organized in militia companies but that these black militias were heavily armed and highly effective in specific areas of South Carolina and were inspiring local unorganized blacks to become more assertive in defense of their own lives and property.[122] One can also conclude that the battle for armed supremacy between the races had as much to do with the Freedmen's physical and economic survival as it did with the Second and the Fourth Amendments to the Constitution, which proclaimed the "right of the people to keep and bear arms" and their concomitant right to be secure from unlawful search and seizures, particularly from extralegal groups such as the Ku Klux Klan.[123]

Accordingly the following assertions of remorse and confessions related to terrorist activities are examples of psychic confusion that existed at least among one class of Klansmen in South Carolina during early Reconstruction:

Confessions of Stephen B. Splawn

I suppose I belong to the order, though I was never sworn into it; there were some people of our place down a Limestone, and they brought up word about this organization, and they brought up an oath, or what they called the platform. I told them I did not see anything wrong in it; it seemed to me like a vigilance committee, and they were getting them up in all the different neighborhoods, and I said I thought it would be very well for us to have one to protect our neighborhood, for there were some depredations committed around. I had nothing to do with getting up the organization; there were some eight or ten joined before I knew anything about it. One day they met, and after a good deal of caviling they settled that I should be their leader; we kept hearing of these offenses that had been committed in York and Union [towns in north western South Carolina]. I attended a meeting of the Klan at Limestone, and I there found out that the Grand Klan had given orders for whipping men that didn't comply with their notions. When I returned home I had a meeting, and I told them what I had found out, and we just disbanded, and said we would have no more to do with it. The object of the Grand Klan was to interfere with voting. I don't know that there was anything said about voting, but that was the way I took it. I never was on any raid, but I just met one. I did not think it was right to do what they were doing, and anything that was contrary to law I was opposed to.[124]

Confession of Lewis Henderson

I lived in Spartanburgh district. I have only been on one raid, but never whipped a Negro in my life. I didn't know anything about the raid until they were going on it. (*Court's Note: this prisoner was so ignorant that he seemed incapable of understanding the simplest English or of expressing himself with any coherence.*)

   Judge Bond

   The sentence of the court is that you be imprisoned three months.[125]

Confession of Charles Tait

I belong to the Horse Creek Klan. I've been on five raids or six raids, as well as I recollect. I was on the raid that went on the McKinney Negroes. They didn't whip them, but they took their shot-guns. About a week after they were ordered to go back, and then they whipped Reuben McKinney, Wash McKinney, and Henry Scruggs. Then I was on the John Harris raid, and the Rutherford raid, Jonah Vassey commanded that raid. Then I was on the Sam Gaffney raid. That was commanded by a man named Russell. The reason I joined the order was that they told me it was a good thing to be in it, and that if I didn't join I would be very likely to be driven from the country. I can't either read or write.

(*Court's Note: Mr. Corbin, on being appealed to be the court, said he knew nothing favorable of the prisoner.*)

Judge Bond

The sentence of the court is that you be imprisoned for eighteen months.[126]

Confession of Andrew Cudd

I am twenty-two years old. I can't read or write. I have been on two raids. On the raid that I went on we whipped Jimmie Gaffner and Matt Scruggs. The Chief of the Klan was Jonas Vassey. I shouldn't have joined the Klan, but they threatened to whip me, and they abused my folks right smart, and threatened to kill the girl that lived with me. They said if I didn't vote the Democratic ticket they'd give me five hundred lashes. One of my friends advised me to join it, for he said they would be sure to whip me if I didn't. I might have left but I was so fixed that I could not get away. I had a family, and so had to stay with them.[127]

William Self's confession is particularly significant as he tries to articulate his feelings on what appeared to be increased psychological pressure to be a Klansmen. Indicating some level of contrition, he was asked to explain how he became a member of the order, and he responded,

The way I came to join the order was that a couple of friends kept at me, wanting me to join, and I kept qizzening them to know something about it, and at last he just up and told me just as it was, and said I would have to join it now or else they'd whip me or kill me, or I'd have to leave. On them conditions I joined the order. I was only in the order a short time and then I quit, and wouldn't have anything at all more to do with it. I guess I've been on three raids. The first [raid] was on Ben Phillips. We struck them three licks apiece.

When asked if there were men or women who were whipped, Self replied, "Well, they was a mixtry. There was two women and one man. The next was on Mr. Roberts, and we went on [raided] him. He had a grocery and had whiskey to sell. He was selling whisky on the days off the church. We went to tell him to stop." Curious about this issue of drinking, selling or making of whiskey, one panelist asked him, "Where all your Klan members of the Temperance Society?" "I don't understand," responded Self. Appearing to not understand the question when repeated a few times, he was finally asked, "Do you know what a temperance society is?" "No sir." Again he was asked, "Were they all opposed to drinking whisky?" Responding vaguely, he said, "Well, I was myself. There was nothing said to the niggers we whipped about politics. We next went on a man named Johnnie Green. We didn't do anything to him."

Somewhat frustrated at the witness, Judge Bryan asked Self if he felt ashamed of his actions, whereupon the witness stated, "Well sir, I know I done wrong." "Yes," responded the judge, "but didn't you know you were doing wrong at the time?" "Well sir, I was ordered to do it by the Klan. Of course I didn't feel it was right." Explaining that he wore a disguise on his raids, and that he was illiterate, Self also volunteered that he was a Christian and that he had never heard the preacher say anything about whipping "niggers" being wrong! When asked if there was any talk in his church about "these things," he responded, "No sir. I never heard anything about what happened. They talked about what happened eighteen hundred years ago." He finally made it be known that he was a farmer, and that "I wasn't arrested, but I came here [to the court] without any warrant at all."

Taking into account the discomfort Self experienced as a member of the Klan, a compassionate Judge Bryan in passing sentence stated that "We trust you realize how unmanly your conduct has been. You seem to show signs of contrition for your conduct, and as you say you were forced into the matter, the judgment of the court is that you be imprisoned three months, including the imprisonment you have already suffered."[128]

Though some Klansmen claimed that they were forced to comply with the dictates of the Ku Klux, and that it was this compliance that facilitated their violent behaviors, missing were remorseful expressions over their actions or any feelings of guilty about their debasement of their victims. And while in some cases defendants standing before the court appeared to be suffering role confusion and appeared apprehensive about their fate at the hands of a Republican-dominated investigation body, their overall disposition suggested a belief that there wasn't a court in the land that would convict them, or render any serious penalty for killing or brutalizing "a nigger" or white Republican.[129]

Not all Ku Klux raiders were remorseful about their actions. Stephen Splawn, as we read, appeared to support Ku Klux philosophy when he forthrightly explained to Judge Bond that he didn't see anything essentially wrong with their purpose or ideas.[130] For Splawn, having a "vigilance committee" patrolling black communities and reducing if not eliminating "depredations" is especially poignant since it was predicated on at least two centuries of slave patrolling. It was the customary thing to do. While Splawn never testified to a more meaningful comprehension of what his social experiences told him what was correct, he might have agreed with the following hypothetical reasoning:

> why should things be different, even if our niggers are supposedly free? Has their personality or mine changed overnight? Ain't I still the master? Don't these niggers still refer to me as "boss," "Massa," Cap'n. 'Sah, and me to them as "boy," "nigger" or what ever comes to mind, ... though they are supposedly free? Are these niggers any freer or stronger today than they were yesterday? I don't think so. Look how they jump when I demand obedience, there're still my niggers! Are you saying that I must now refer to them as "sir" or "Madam," when yesterday I wouldn't have thought about addressing them at all! No, there are some things that haven't changed as a result of the war, nor should they, for I am a white man, therefore my family and my grand children are deemed by natural law to be ruler and master, not servant and lackey.

For Klansmen such as Stephen Splawn, the need for direct action against blacks was further spurred on by the existence of armed Republican Union Leagues and black self-defense clubs. *These* were the depredations that needed regulation. However, even a Splawn-like reasoning was laden with contradictions, in that while agreeing that the white community's protection was primary, he also felt a need to denounce the Grand Klan's order to whip those who didn't comply with their notion of law! The question of course is *whose* sense of order and law did Splawn really feel compelled to honor — that of the deposed

Confederate States or the federal government? Was it that he approved of the forceful disarming and general abuse of blacks as did his fellow raider Charles Tait, but disapproved of whippings, particularly when it involved recalcitrant whites? Or was his confession simply an attempt to lessen the consequences of his Klan activities?

Very little, if anything in Tait's brief admission suggest regret for his activities as a night rider, yet his description of Reuben and Wash McKinney as "McKinney Negroes" does acknowledge a conviction that most southern whites held dearly: a legal and moral sanctity in the ownership of blacks as property. Not only in a vernacular sense but as an integral functional part of society. As a result, Tait's view of "McKinney Negroes" as property belonging to a white male is not unusual. For him there was no other descriptive term for them. Even if the blacks working for McKinney now envisioned themselves as Freedmen, for Tait they were "McKinney Negroes." His social experiences inundated him as it certainly did the black populace with implacable social cues that ignorance of (either pretended or not) would have been a dangerous challenging thrust at the social order.

As a philosophical concept, property in humans or the promise of such was still a vivid psychic concern for would-be or actual Klansmen. Its assumed naturalness and unquestioned acceptance of a southern reality was critical during this postwar era. Though the general population was quite cognizant that slavery as an institution was dead, they were not ready to give up the notion of property in their own whiteness. It was the one raison d'être that generations of southerners regardless of class background assumed. It represented a social political rational steeped in the agricultural milieu of America; a golden promise that proclaimed that with force of arms, a new and continual rebirth was possible for even the most obtuse migrating European. It assumed a correctness in the forced removal of millions of people for the attainment of a more productive and free society. It announced to others that their presence had little social value except that which an interloping European conferred on them. Embracing this as reality, it was difficult for white Americans to conceive of blacks as true Americans having concerns that were not contingent on Euro American values or expectations. *Blackness* itself became a monolithic nonvarying entity whose perceived impenetrability had to be either contained, controlled or destroyed. From this perspective, any idea that purported the ex-slave having a sense of property or ownership in their own labor was unacceptable, threatening and for some a violation of the nation's Constitution.[131]

Accordingly, the disarming of the black community became an indispensable political priority if southern whites were to regain a sense of validation and empowerment. It was a process that literally and symbolically had black political and social emasculation as its primary goal. In this respect, Charles Tait's recollection of his commander's advice that the Ku Klux was "a good thing to be in" was not an empty analysis, but a statement premised on an expected threat from armed southern blacks. Any questioning or outright rejection of this "advice" was also viewed as a threat to the social order by suggesting a disinclination to accept Ku Klux mythology as truth. In this manner, Klansmen were created.

3

Dialogues on
Human Rights Abuses

"Do We Look Like Gentlemen?"

Both the Enforcement Act of 1870 and the Ku Klux Act in April 1871 were conceived to aid nearly four million ex-enslaved southern blacks to live their lives free from political terrorism. Being too little and too late, both acts failed miserably when one considers the incalculable social depth of nineteenth-century American institutional racism. A major impediment in the process was getting white southerners similar to Cudd, Henderson, and Self to envision any relationship between their lives and that of the ex-slave beyond that of master and slave. This difficulty was further complicated by their admitted personal and social illiteracy. On the other hand if the claims of these three admitted terrorists are accurate, and their illiteracy was limited to an inability to read and write, but not a misunderstanding of their immediate social environment, then assessing their use or misuse of violence as a communicative tool for personal empowerment is critical in evaluating the effectiveness of their roles as Ku Klux raiders. For example, Ku Klux raiders generally emerged from a southern agricultural environment that communicated primarily through institutionalized symbols of violence, force, privilege and patronage. Recognizing this helps us comprehend how verbal and nonverbal cues among Klansmen during a raid functioned to determine the parameters of violent interaction with Freedmen, and how the use of threat both explicit and implicit became an effective and in some instances the ultimate tool to communicate terror. With compliance as the goal of most threats, raiders also relied on both victims and victimizers to make a correct assessment of their situation through verbal and nonverbal cues during raids.

Invariably personal testimonies by raid victims also revealed an intense willingness on the part of the raiders to inflict punishment in a manner choreographed to dehumanize their targets. There appeared to be an agreement that it was not enough to administer a brutal whipping, but instead the victim had to be frightened into a confession of guilt, thereby demonstrating remorse before a superior morality. This supposed demonstration of contrition by the victim as a result of a painful experience functioned as a redemptive spiritual cleansing for the victim. However, given the hostile conditions in which "confessions" were generally elicited, a victim's knowledge of penalties that might be incurred if their confession exhibited less than stellar levels of contrition is critical, particular when attempting to ascertain the validity or relative truth and sincerity of their confession! In this respect truth shaped by language was largely a metaphorical phenomenon. It constructed as it deconstructed. It created possibilities for action where none existed moments earlier. It was a veil for thoughts better left unsaid, and for actions better restrained than performed. As social psychologist Erik Erickson asserted, "the truth in any given encounter is linked with a persons development and the historical situation of their group: together they help to determine the actuality, i.e., the potential for unifying action at a given moment."[1]

For this reason, a key factor in understanding verbalized moments of truth, particularly when Klansmen confronted their intended victim, is primarily appreciating the emotional intensity of these interactions. Though violent encounters between combatants can appear to be moments of truth, it was incumbent on skilled Ku Klux propagandists to connect these moments into a seemingly seamless succession of coherent truths, so that when presented publicly they appear as a contiguous display of actualities, i.e., an accepted reality. This was apparent when levels of violence against blacks became so common that reporting on these attacks began to take on a normative persona, as evidenced in an 1871 *New York Times* article titled "More Ku Klux"[2]:

How They Act in South Carolina — County Officers to Resign

By a gentleman from Union we learn of the further perpetration of outrages in that county, counting among them the killing of three men, one on Friday night, and two on Sunday night. Also, that the Ku Klux have posted notices on the bulletin board at the courthouse, to the effect that the county Commissioners, the School Commissioner, and the members of the Legislature, must resign their positions by the 27th inst. It is understood that the Sheriff and School Commissioner have tendered their resignations under pressure of the circumstances, It is also asserted that other officers will resign, rather than subject themselves to the indignities of the midnight marauders, known as Ku Klux. The following is handed to us as the document found posted in Union a few days since:

K.K.K.
Head-Quarters Ninth Division, S.C.,
Special Orders No. 3, K.K.K.
"Ignorance is the curse of God."

For this reason, we are determined that members of the Legislature, the School Commissioner and the County Commissioner of Union shall no longer officiate. Fifteen (15) days' notice from this date is therefore given, and if they, *one and all* do not *at once and forever resign* their present inhuman, disgraceful and outrageous rule, then retributive justice will as surely be used as night follows day.

Also.— An honest man is the noblest work of god. For this reason, if the Clerk of the said Board of County Commissioners and School Commissioner does not *immediately* renounce and relinquish his present position, then harsher measures than this will most assuredly and *certainly* be used. For confirmation, reference to the orders heretofore published in the Union *Weekly Times,* and Yorkville *Enquirer* will more fully and completely show our intention. By order Grand Chief.

    March 9, A.D. 1871   A.O. Grand Secretary

From this perspective, the actions of participants in these bloody dramas were reported in a fashion that reflected a highly parochial understanding of truth, personal anger and social discord. However in time, continued reports on violent interactions between night-riding white raiders and blacks became repetitively filled narrative truths that were actually concocted social constructions of reality.[3]

Metaphoric examples of Ku Klux mythology that by themselves were ineffective, now when reported and detailed seemingly became powerful, effective, mythic demonstrations of social and political control! As one historian put it, "Mythology requires effort. Achilles and King Arthur may have begun as men of flesh and blood, but Homer and Sir Thomas Malory labored hard to make them the figures we remember."[4] Black insolence, real or imagined in the face of white intimidation defined the limitations by which a nonviolent propaganda campaign could be effective. This was particularly true for local white professionals and planter elites who viewed any exercising of political influence by blacks as a threat to rearrange their agricultural system. In similar fashion, poorer whites resented the Freedmen's apparent involvement with armed militia groups such as the Union Leagues. Political expediency, it was argued, demanded the curtailing of these leagues through the forceful interdiction of southern white "extra legal groups."[5]

Despite the fact that Negro testimony describing the horror and brutality of Ku Klux terror gangs were more a symptomatic demonstration of a violent postwar America, they provide us with examples of southern whites' fear of violent retribution and black political ascendancy. However, it is also essential to recognize that though these accounts illuminate and evaluate the effectiveness in Ku Klux raids and their attendant propaganda, these testimonies are not necessarily representative of all raid victims. However, they do infer that time-honored suppositions about southern blacks' passivity and alleged total deference in the face of Ku Klux terror are erroneous. In addition, close examination of congressional testimony illuminating Klan "outrages" in states such as South Carolina in the late 1860s indicate that black Americans' innovative resistance and survival techniques against terrorist gangs were not only often conspicuously successful, but uncompromisingly passionate in a desire not to exist as whites' enduring victim. The 1871 congressional testimony of Elias Thomson is an example.

Testimony of Elias Thomson

On July 7, 1871, in the town of Spartanburg, South Carolina, a congressional subcommittee investigating abuses and outrages against southern blacks and Republicans received fascinating testimony from Elias Thomson, a witness and victim of Ku Klux Klan terror. Thomson was born in slavery on a plantation owned by a well-known local doctor. His experiences were of interest to the committee, particularly as then related to injuries he received as a result of a nocturnal visit by Klansmen.

There came a parcel of gentlemen to my house one night. They went to the door and ran against it. My wife was sick. I was lying on a pallet with my feet to the door. They ran against it and hallooed to me, "Open the door, quick, quick, quick." I threw the door open immediately — right wide open. Two little children were lying with me. I said, "Come in gentlemen." One of them says, "*Do we look like gentlemen?*" I says, "You look like men of some description; walk in." One says, "Come out here; are you ready to die? I told him I was not prepared to die. "Well." Said he, "Your time is short, commence praying." I told him I was not a praying man much, and hardly ever prayed, only a very few times, never did pray much. He says, "you ought to pray, your time is short, and now commence to pray." I told him I was not a praying man. One of them held a pistol to my head and said, "Get down and pray." I was on the steps, with one foot on the ground. They led me off to a prune tree. There was three or four of them behind me. And it appeared, one on each side, and one in front. The gentleman who questioned me was the only man I could see. All the time I could not see the others. Every time I could get to look around they would touch me with a pistol on the other side. They would just touch me on the side of the head with a pistol, so I had to keep my head square in front[6] [see Appendix C for the continuation of Thomson's testimony].

When queried by the committee chairman to describe these raiders, Thomson responded that, there were about fifteen of them with a variety of disguises. They generally wore something that resembled "speckled Calico" over their faces, and this was tied about the neck. "They had very long white gowns, white as sheets that came down until I could just see their feet." In response to the question, "Did they come on horseback?" Thomson stated that "they came to the bars" (bars were horizontal railings used to secure horses in front of most homes or stores).[7]

Acknowledging that he didn't know any of them, but suggesting that in better light he might have recognized one or more of them, Thomson noted that other blacks in the area were also whipped during visits by Klansmen. Though many of the victims were so traumatized by the experience that for weeks fearing another visit slept outside their cabins, others were frightened into not reporting their assaults. However, some victims found strategies to partially diffuse what could otherwise have been both an emotionally and physiologically destructive experience.

QUESTION: Did you make a complaint of this matter to anybody after it happened?
ANSWER: No sir, I will tell you how I did. They told me not to say anything about it. I never said a word. I said to my family, "let me tell you, don't open your mouth. If anybody ask you if the Ku Klux had been here, you tell them no." My wife was in bed sick, and said, "don't you have anything to do with it, none of you."

QUESTION: How did it get out then?
ANSWER: That is what I am going to say. This was on Friday, the first Friday night in May, ... and by 10 o'clock on Saturday, it was all over the settlement. The boys, a good many of them went to meeting on Sunday, about four miles from my house. Several came up by my house. They had it that the Ku Klux had killed or beaten me pretty near to death, and some of them said, "that's not so, for we came by his house this morning."

QUESTION: Did the circulation of these reports cause alarm among the colored people?
ANSWER: Yes sir, That evening a number came by my house from church to know this matter. I laughed it off. Says I, "Boys, you see I am not injured much. I don't look like a man that is most dead." Says I, "hold on for a while. Somebody knows more about it than I do, you can learn it from them. I have nothing to say about it."[8]

Exhibiting humor, Thomson gambled that he could mollify his attackers' attitude to think that he was simply a misguided Negro buffoon. At some point he realized that some of the raiders suspected they might have been recognized. However, when it was apparent that he was not going to point them out, these individuals curtailed the level of violence against him. A sort of nonverbal agreement between victim and victimizer emerged.

Assessing if Thomson was indeed successful in aligning his adversaries' actions, thereby tempering a potentially life-threatening experience, is important in evaluating the effectiveness of this raid. Of interest is also Thomson's apparent disdain for his attackers and their mythological rambling: "Old man, we are just from hell," and "have you heard a wild goose holler lately ... that is one of us coming over and looking down to see what you have been doing this time."[9]

In effect two significant reactions occurred in this attack. One, by faithfully not indulging himself in the Ku Klux's assigned social script, Thomson's actions suggested that only through the use of violence could he be forced to verbally comply with his attackers wishes. Second, once Klansmen sensed that their credibility was threatened if not outright rejected by a noncomplying victim, only whipping would restore what was considered to be the proper social interaction between themselves and Thomson.

The history of violent attempts at subjugation by Ku Klux raiders also suggest that once the raider "senses his notoriety and the social trepidation which it brings and then feels for perhaps the first time personal potency, it makes him very resistant to reassessing the meaning of his newly discovered violent notoriety" other than being a raider.[10] As self-perceptions become totally dependent on those social experiences that have enhanced rather than distracted from his violent role, little reflective thought is given to the proposition that "while fame may be morally superior to infamy, their impact may be remarkably similar."[11] In this regard, the very instruments of violent subjugation and terror such as the whip can themselves become symbols of a failed or successful social policy.

The whip as a physical weapon and metaphor for terror was unparallel within western slave societies. Throughout American slavery and after it was both a tool for punishment and a symbol of institutional coercion and repression. Having no other equal in southern American lore, its use represented not just authority and one's right to use force to control another being, beast or human. When used effectively, whipping functioned as a means by which the very essence of a person's resolve could be compromised by painfully curtailing their ability to control personal actions and dispositions. Used on humans, the whip became the initiator and maintainer of social and cultural practices that were premised on the physiological abuse. However, after the Civil War when this weapon seemed ineffective in controlling "unruly" blacks, other tactics such as drowning, mutilation, castration, rape and lynching existed as alternatives, or as one witness recalled, "De Ku Klux uster stick de niggers head on er stake alongside de Cadiz road en dar buzzards would eat them till nuthin' was left but de bones. Dar was a sign on dis stake dat said, 'Look out Nigger You are next.'"[12]

Resistance to whippings was itself a serious offense. It represented a direct rejection of white authority over blacks' physical existence, and as such was viewed as a denial of whites' use of black bodies, either for pleasure or pain. To witness a whipping became a battle, an internalized struggle in deciding if now was the most opportune time to strike back. Similarly, many southern whites believed that any indication of resistance, large or small, if remained unchecked would not only establish a dangerous and defiant precedent but endanger lower-class nonslaveowning whites' presumptions that power and authority was also *their* racial birthright. Frederick Law Olmsted, a northern traveler passing through Mississippi in the mid–1800s recalled an incident where the whip was significant as a symbol of authority for the lowly plantation overseers:

> Southern whites also believed that African Americans would not work unless they were threatened with beatings. Olmsted reported that in Mississippi he had observed young girl subjected to "the severest corporal punishment" he had ever seen. The white overseer, who had administered the flogging with a raw-hide whip "across her naked loins and thighs," told Olmsted that the girl had been shirking her duties. He claimed that "if I hadn't [punished her so hard] she would have done the same thing again tomorrow, and half the people on the plantation would have followed her example. Oh, you've no idea how lazy these niggers are.... They'd never do any work at all if they were not afraid of being whipped."[13]

As a consequence, the whip, even for the downtrodden economically degraded whites or in a few instances designate blacks, regardless of age or gender, became the euphoric symbol of white empowerment and authority. With this said, the physical presence of a whip or one's knowledge of a recent whipping did not always translate into social obedience to the will of white terrorist, as we saw with Elias Thomson. This was partially true do to a commonly held belief among Freedmen that those who during slavery submitted easily to this kind of abuse were more than likely to be targets of further white rage. Drawing from his own experience as a slave, Frederick Douglass also acknowledged what many slaves knew from experience: "overseers prefer to whip those who are most easily whipped."[14] Further congressional testimony from Pinckney Dodd and his neighbors confirms this point.

Testimony of Pinckney Dodd

On July 7, 1871, Pinckney Dodd, a resident of Spartanburg, South Carolina, became another victim of Ku Klux violence. His experiences underscored Douglass's remarks on whippings as well as the importance of torture in shaping the dialogue between victim and victimizer. Recalling his painful experiences from the night of May 1, 1871, Dodd remembered that his attackers were dressed in an assorted array of "disguises" when they arrived at his one horse farm:

> I heard them come and frighten the dog, and I heard them at the door cursing, and they told me to get up, and before I got up and got there they had the door burst open. When I got there, he told me to stop, and kept cursing me. He said, "What are you doing in there?" He asked if I had heard of the Ku Klux? I said I had. He said, "do you know them?" I said, "No." He said, "Is there anybody else in there? Tell him to come out damned quick, or we will help him out, damned quick. Did not you promise," he said. "to help the Ku Klux out, if they came here?" I said, "No, I didn't say so." He says, "Never mind, God damn you, we can prove it to you. Shut up, don't talk so damned big. Tell that other fellow to come out." I called him — he was lying on the bed, not asleep. I told him to put on his clothes. He says, "Never mind to put on your clothes, but come out." But he got on his clothes and came out — just outside of the door. There was another fellow living on the place, named Spencer. They brought him down there, so they say. He was standing there outside of the gate. They had some pistols, and they said they had come from hell

"Visit of the Ku-Klux," *Harper's Weekly*, February 24, 1872. LIBRARY OF CONGRESS PRINTS AND PHO-
TOGRAPHS DIVISION, WASHINGTON, D.C.

that night. I went to the gate. There they had another fellow from that other house that
night.

Wanting clarification, committee member Philadelphia Van Trump from Ohio asked
Dodd, "You and another fellow were at your own house, and Spencer was at the gate and
another colored man, four of you. Is that it?" "Yes," Dodd answered. He continued:

They told this fellow with Spencer to pull of his shirt. They asked him who he voted for.
He said, "For Scott." They said, "What did you do that for?" He says, "They told me that
was best." "Who told you so?" says he. "What people was it told you so?" He had on two
shirts, and when he went to pull them off, the man said, "You were fixed for it — you knew
the Ku Klux were coming." He says, "I always wear two shirts in the winter time." The
man says, "What is your name?" When he pulled off his shirt, he said, Number one," and
"Hit him thirty." He commenced counting one, two, three, four, five and when he got to
five — he counted aloud so that I could not hear him count after that.

After a while he told him to stop, and he stopped hitting, and he asked him, "do you
think you will ever vote again?" He said, "I don't know." He said, "do you think you will
ever vote for Scott again?" He said, "I don't know as I will." He says, "Number two, hit
him five." Then number two, another fellow stepped up and hit him. I suppose he hit him
five. He says, "Do you think you will vote for Scott?" "I don't think I will," says he. He
says, "Don't you know?" "I reckon so," he says. "Don't you know it?" "No sir, I never will
vote for him again," say he. Then he told him to get up.

Another fellow, named Lewis, was there — the same fellow I was going to tell you about.

I can't think of his full name. He ran off, they didn't get to whip him. When he started, some one said, "shoot him," and they fired. Some said three shots, but I didn't hear but two pistols. They told me to get down. They said, "who did you vote for, and be sure you don't tell me a damned lie." I said, "I voted the democratic ticket." He said, "Be sure you don't tell me a lie, ... take off your shirt." I did not tell him true, but I had to do that. That said, "Pull off your shirt," and he said, "Hit him five, number one," and they hit me I don't know how many times, and then number two hit. He said, "Do you think you will vote for Scott again? Be sure you don't tell me a lie." Another one says, "He said he didn't vote for Scott." Then he says, "I think I didn't give you enough, but just a caution." They asked another fellow to get down, and they asked how did he vote. He said, "I didn't vote at all — I was too young," and he said he come down to the meeting on Saturday. They said, "What were you there for?" and then one of them said, "What sort of a thing is that? What in hell is a meeting? Take off your shirt, and get down here." He got down and took his shirt off, and they began to beat him — I don't remember how much. They didn't say. Number one beat him, and then this other one said, "number two." Number two came around and gave him some.

Raiding Klansmen always forcefully searched for firearms, and this occasion was no exception.

They asked me if I had a gun. I told them I had an old gun that I had bursted on Christmas, and made a sort of pistol of it. They said, "Where is it?" I told them, "In the house." They went in and I got it for them. They said, "Is it loaded?" "No," I said, "it is not loaded." "let me see it," said he, then he looked at it. I told him I had that shot-gun. He asked me if I had a pistol. I said, "No, I never had but one in my life." Says he, "Are you certain?" "Yes Sir," I says. He took the old gun down from over the door, and one told the other to take it out and mash it up to pieces. They looked at it a while, and another said, "lay it back up there." The other one, the first one I told you about, took it away and broke it all to pieces.[15]

After congressional investigators heard hundreds of testimonies detailing attacks, assaults, and murders by Klansmen, federal grand juries in South Carolina began issuing warrants and subpoenas throughout the state. In order to maintain a level of secrecy in their efforts to apprehend the more vicious suspects, habeas corpus was suspended on October 17, 1871, in South Carolina counties of Spartanburg, York, Marion, Chester, Laurens, Newberry, Fairfield, Lancaster, and Chesterfield. They became the only southern legislative areas where habeas corpus had to be suspended, and even then, many who were indicted for murder fled the state. For example, in York County, about "200 members (Klansmen) fled the state, including the highest leaders," some of whom went to Canada.[16]

Nevertheless, by December 1871, there were "195 persons imprisoned in York County alone for serious crimes" in violation of the antiterrorist Ku Klux Act enacted earlier in April.[17] The effect of this campaign was similar to a latter-day Truth and Reconciliation Commission in contemporary South Africa. As it wasn't expected that hardened racist supporters of apartheid would accept any rapprochement with victorious black militants, so it was in South Carolina. While reconciliation between the races or southern Democrats and radical Republicans was *not* an expected outcome of these investigations and trials, neither was the release of some 500 indicted individuals who had voluntarily surrendered, given depositions and been released![18] This was the case for the thirteen-year-old son of a Klan leader who was arrested, but later released after it was learned that he was initiated into the order and taken on a raid.[19] Within this context, the experiences of terror raids on Harriet Postle and her children were simply the tepid contaminated backwash of southern justice.

Harriet Postle

The full impact of Ku Klux Klan raids are difficult to comprehend unless one places themselves psychologically in a postbellum rural peasant community that is saturated with the living remnants of a deposed landowning planter class, dependent white wage-earning labors or employed and Freedmen. This was the social context that a rural black south Carolinian family was living in during the spring of 1871 when Ku Klux raiders forced themselves into the Postle's homesite. Comprised of farmers, the unemployed and at least one night-riding physician, these raiders cared little about the sanctity of their victim's home, and even less about the implications their actions would have on any children witnessing the attack. Testimony by Harriet Postle before the congressional committee on December 30, 1871, focused attention on the more troubling psychological aspects of Ku Klux raids had on children who were traumatized by or after witnessing their parents being brutally assaulted. While certainly presumptions of civil or human rights by unarmed black rural folk was generally present, it was largely discounted by whites because it was unenforceable. However for Freedmen living within a cauldron of terror, the will to survive and an ability to possibly outwit their attackers was often the only recourse for survival. In this respect, Harriet Postle explained:

> I live in the eastern part of York County, about four miles from Rock Hill, on Mr. James Smith's plantation. I am about thirty years old. My husband is a preacher. I have a family of six children. The oldest is about fourteen. The Ku Klux visited me last spring. It was some time in March, I was asleep when they came. They made a great noise and wake me up and called out for Postle. My husband heard them and jumped up, and I thought he was putting on his clothes, but when I got up I found he was gone. They kept on hallooing for Postle and knocking at the door. I was trying to get on my clothes but I was so frightened I did not get on my clothes at all. I looked like they were going to knock the door down, then the rest of them began to come into the house, and my oldest child got out and ran under the bed. One of them saw him and said, "there he is," and with that three of them pointed their pistols under the bed. I then cried out: "It is my child," they told him to come out. When my child came out from under he bed, one of them said: "put it on his neck," and the child commenced hallooing and crying, and I begged them not to hurt my child. The man did not hurt it, but one of them ran the child back against the wall, and ground a piece of skin off as big as my hand.
>
> I then took a chair and set it back upon a loose plank, and sat down on it. One of the men stepped up. Seeing the plank loose, he jerked the chair and threw me over while my babe was in my arms, and I fell with my babe to the floor. When one of them clapped his foot upon the child and another had his foot on me. I begged him, for the Lord's sake to save my child. I went and picked up my babe, and when I opened the door and looked I saw they had formed a line. They asked me if Postle was there. I said no. They told me to make a light, but I was so frightened I could not do it well, and asked my child to make it for me. Then they asked me where my husband was. I told them he was gone. They said: "He is here, somewhere." I told them he was gone for some meal. They said he was there, somewhere, and they called me a damned liar. One of them said: "He is under the house."

Then one of them comes to me and says: "I am going to have the truth to-night, you are a damned, lying bitch, and you are telling a lie." He had a line and commenced putting it over my neck, saying: "I want you tell where your husband is," and said he, "the truth I've got to have." I commenced hallooing, and says he: "We are men of peace, but you are telling me a damned lie, and you are not tell me any lies to-night." The one who had his foot on my body mashed me badly, but not so badly as he might have done, for I was some seven or eight months in travail [pregnant]. Then I got outside of the house, and called the little ones to me for they were all dreadfully frightened.

They said my husband was there, and they would shoot into every crack — and they did shoot all over the place — and there are bullet holes there, and bullet marks on the hearth yet. At this time there were some in the house and some outside. They said to me, "We are going to have the truth out of you, you damned lying bitch. He is somewhere about here." I said, "He is gone." With that he clapped his hands on my neck, and says again, "Were going to have the truth out of you, you bitch damned bitch," and with that he beat my head against the side of the house till I had no sense hardly left, ... but I still had hold of my babe.

There was a moment of silence as Ms. Postle gathered her thoughts. She was then asked if she recognized any of the raiders.

Yes, sir, I did. I recognized the first man that came into the house, it was Doctor Avery [pointing to the accused]. I recognized him by his performance and when he was entangling the line round my neck. As I lifted my hand to keep the rope off my neck. I caught his lame hand, ... it was his left hand that I caught — his crippled hand. I felt it in my hand. I said to myself right then, "I know you,"... I knew Joe Castle and Jas Mathews, the old man's son. I didn't know anyone else. I suppose there was about a dozen altogether there. Dr. Avery had on a red gown with a blue face, with red about his mouth, and he had two horns on his cap about a foot long. The line that he tried to put over my neck was a buggy line, not quite so wide as three fingers, but wider than two. They said to me that they rode thirty-eight miles that night to see old Abe Brumfield and preacher Postle. They said that they had heard that Preacher Postle had been preaching up fire and corruption. They afterward found my husband under the house, but I had gone to the big house with my children to take out of the cold. I did not see them pull him out from the house.

The center of Ku Klux Klan activity and deprivation in South Carolina was York County. In the latter part of the 1860s its major mill town was Rock Hill, which was about eighteen miles east of the state capital at Columbia. Though this was a stronghold of Republicanism and most of the white population and virtually all of the Freedmen were illiterate, the Republicans held the balance of political power whenever there was a "full and free election."[20] All of this changed rapidly by the fall of 1870 when black South Carolinians began responding to the voting rights guarantees of the newly ratified Fifteenth Amendment to the Constitution.

Thomas Morehead

Black Americans' human and civil rights were continually challenged on many levels throughout the Reconstruction era of 1867 to 1877. However, in the area of voting, resistance by whites became acutely identified with the south's overall opposition to black enfranchisement. In this regard, the testimony of Thomas Morehead, a witness for the prosecution during the congressional trials, illuminated the immense pressure that blacks weathered at the height of Ku Klux raids. Questioned primarily by United States prosecuting attorney for South Carolina, D. T. Corbin, Morehead who was a captain of H Company in the local black militia stated that he lived for five years in Rock Hill.[21] When he went to nearby Columbia to vote in the November 1868 presidential elections, he found that white mobs were attempting to "crowd away" blacks from voting polls. Assuming that because he was now an American citizen due to the recent ratification of the Fourteenth Amendment, "I thought I could go there and vote on my oath." This indeed was a major presumption on his part. When he approached the polling booth window, "they objected to my vote," and forced him away from the poll. Morehead recalls that

> the window was a narrow one, and the white men just stood in a ring right around the window. Dr. Avery was standing right [there] with his hand on the window, and tested every vote that was given. Voting was a new thing to the colored people, and they were nearly afraid anyhow to exercise the privilege of voting. This crowd being there prevented a great many from voting at that election.[22]

Morehead who was eventually forced to leave Rock Hill after repeated threats by the Ku Klux, told prosecutor Corbin that in the fall of 1868 a gang of whites had assaulted one of his militiamen and then later when confronted violently resisted arrest.

> After they refused to be arrested, and armed themselves, and went off from there leaving threats to the Trial Justice if he sent any force of militia, or any force whatever they intended to shoot as long as they had balls to shoot, and wouldn't be arrested and be brought before a damned nigger Trial Justice, that was Squire Davis. After they made their escape, Squire Davis then asked me to assist him in making the arrests with a small force of militia. I went along with them, and we met the party. They had been to Squire Crook's and got the business fixed there. Then we left them alone and came back to Rock Hill. Early the next morning, Charley Cobb, met me, and says: "If we had known last night which way you was going, we would have given you a hell of a battle in the road." I told him I was prepared, and he says, "well, we will give you hell anyhow, in the rounds." Then after that, they sent a dispatch to the governor, about the niggers turning up the country generally, running women and children out of the houses, and they were all frightened. I went there to Rock Hill that day, with twelve men, but I didn't see any alarm. Governor Scott called in the arms (rifles), and they were given up on the governors orders, and put in the Depot, and in a few days after that, there was a notice put up. It had Squire Davis' name and my name at the head, and Denny S Steele's and Jim Bynam's. Bynam was a white man, a member from our League — he was Secretary, and I suppose they found it out.[23]

Corbin's inquiry into the content of the posted notices indicates that the Ku Klux had at this point also established an armed propaganda unit that aided their efforts to neutralize contentious forces, black or Republican.

> They marked on top of the paper, as well as I can recollect, "K.K.K." No name signed to it. On the face of it was, "Oh, ye blind and foolish parties, stop! stop! and study before you further go!" and at the bottom of it, they had a grave and coffin, and straps down in the coffin, and the lid off one side. It says, "We won't stop, we have guns and bayonets. We have bowie-knives and pistols. We have held out our hand to you, and if you won't accept it. We have offered and you won't accept, and it you won't now, stop before you further

go, and listen and sympathize with us." Then he says, "Your voices shall be shut up in a lonesome valley where they will never be heard no more." I don't remember it all. There was about twenty or thirty pages of it. A long concern. Jones tore it down, and said he expected the Ku Klux would come after him, but he would just as soon die one way as another — damned niggers would kill him any how.[24]

However, it was not Ku Klux propaganda, armed or otherwise, that chased, neutralized or physically eliminated some blacks from effectively defending themselves against armed attacks, but rather the complicit actions of local government figures to ensure that these terrorist groups *were* armed and that their intended victims were *disarmed*! Morehead explained that while the militias arms were deposited in the armory by Governor Scott's direct order, "the first guns were taken out on the 19th of February 1868 by 'unknown parties.' After the first ones were taken I began to get a little dubious. I didn't know but that I might be killed some night, or might be shot coming home. I lived about a mile from Rock Hill."[25]

At this point in the trial, the attorney asked Morehead if he knew another Militia Company leader, Jim Williams, and the circumstances around his murder? He responded "yes" and that Williams was killed the very next Monday after he fled York County.[26] What Morehead did not elaborate on were the details surrounding Williams's brutal murder, the almost daily attacks on black communities throughout York County, and the tragic conspiracy to curtail the ability of black federal troops to root out Ku Klux terrorism.

Operating under controls that limited what they could investigate, apprehend or shoot, black soldiers led by their white officers were in many instances helpless to assist Freedmen who fell victim to Ku Klux attacks. Terror cells eventually became so emboldened by restrictive conspiratorial covenants established by conservative Democrats and Republicans that Klansmen were able to function as an extralegal system that killed at will and punished on whim and fancy. The murdering of blacks became so common that both northern and southern newspapers began to delete the terms *killing* and *rape* from their headlines and replace it with a more innocuous term, *outrages*. Such was the case in the spring of 1868 when a frustrated Jim Williams was alleged to have issued a proclamation stating that Klansmen and conservatives, a pseudonym for Democrats, must be "killed from the cradle up."[27]

As a result of Williams's persistent appeals for support in the fight against terrorism he was murdered after a gang of forty to fifty Klansmen led by physician J. Rufus Braxton raided his home at night. They dismounted some distance from Williams's home and proceeded secretly on foot to surprise him. After bursting into his home they took him outside and hung him from a nearby tree, then placed a sign on his body stating, "Capt. Jim Williams on his big muster."[28]

Threats from the black communities to retaliate by descending on Yorkville did not materialize; however, once a series of arson attacks on cotton gins, barns filled with corn, wheat and other crops occurred, an immediate call for moderation was heard throughout some sectors of the white community. The editor of the Yorkville *Enquirer*, the county's only newspaper, even accused the black-dominated Union Leagues for advocating violence and arson. However, as the burning of farmhouses increased, and fields of burning crops turned the night sky into a reddish hue, the *Enquirer* urged older whites to tell "younger men *not* to engage in whipping and murdering the colored people."[29] For a brief period, some semblance of order was reached when on February 11 a biracial public meeting was held in the Clay Hill region of the county, where white's whipping of blacks and black's burnings of white owned farms had been common. Those attending the meeting recognized that Ku Klux "outrages" had preceded Negro arson (a rare concession), and consequently they condemned both. Moreover, some of the whites promised to protect "Negroes" from further outrage in return for a pledge not to hold any more secret nocturnal meetings of the Union League, which they were convinced had organized "Negroes" into bands of arsonist.[30]

Needless to say, some blacks, such as Amzi Rainey in York County, learned a painful but valuable lesson about the relationship between violence, economics and the price one must pay for civil or human justice.

Amzi Rainey

Some Freedmen undoubtedly believed that to be vulnerable to the caprices of another human being, and still be considered a dangerous enemy, a feared competitor, a vile serpent of evil *was* in itself to have attained a measure of self-empowerment. They believed such an unfortunate convoluted social relationship actually validated their existence in the mind of a tormentor. Their persecutors' compulsion to control them, they hoped, would lead to frustration and eventual defeat. The psychic implications of this however could be devastating if one's tormentor is continually viewed as a point of self-reference.

The testimony of Amzi Rainey illustrates this murderous almost Freudian-like relationship between the controlled victim's id and an omnipresent victimizer's superego. Attacked on the very farm of his birth by twenty-five masked Ku Klux terrorists dressed in white and red gowns because he was black and voted for a Republican, he experienced the quintessential civil and human rights abuse. This horrendous act was surpassed only by Rainey's inability to protect either his wife or child from assault. Rainey testified before the court that

> It was about the last of March, as near as I can recollect. I was laying down. I laid down at the first dark by the fire. The rest done been abed, and about ten o'clock my little daughter called me, and said: "Pappy, it is time we are going to bed, get up." Just as I got up, and turned around I looked out of the window and I see some four or five disguised men coming up, and I ran up in the loft. They came to the door and when they came to the door they commenced beating and knocking. "God damn you, open the door! Open the door! Open the door!" and commenced beating at each side. There is two doors, and they commenced beating both door and my wife run to one of the doors. They knocked the top hinges off of the first, and she run across the house to the other. And again that time they got the two hinges knocked off the other door, and the bolt held the door from falling, and she got it open. She pulled the bolt back and throwed it down and when they come in, they struck her four or five licks before they said a word.
>
> They asked her who lived here? She said, "Rainey — Amzi Rainey." "What Amzi Rainey? What Amzi Rainey? And she said, "Amzi Rainey," and he struck her Another lick, and says: "Where is he? God damn him, where is he?" And she says: "I don't know." And one said: "O, I smell him, god damn him, he has gone up in the loft." He says: "We'll kill him too," and they come up then. This Sam Good, they made him light a light [Sam Good lived on the same farm, and was forced to accompany the terrorist]. He [Sam] lit the light, and they made him and my wife go up before, and he followed them up there. I was in a box, and they said: "Oh, he is in this box, God damn him, I smell him. We'll kill him!"

The other says: "don't kill him yet," and they took me down. This man that struck my wife first, ran back to her and says: "God damn her, I will kill her now, I will kill her out." The one that went after me says, "don't kill her," and he commenced beating her then, ... struck her some four or five more licks and then run back and struck me. He then ran back to her, drew his pistol and says: "Now, I am going to blow your damn brains out." The one by me threw the pistol up and says: "don't kill her." He aimed to strike me over the head and struck me over the back and sunk me right down. Then, after he had done that my little daughter, she was back in the room with the other little children, he says: "I am going to kill him." She run out of the room, and says, "don't kill my pappy, please don't kill my pappy!" He shoved her back, and says, "You go back in the room, you god damned little bitch, I will blow your brains out!" He then fired and shot her, sure enough. The ball glanced off from her head. Then they took me right off ... up the road about a hundred and fifty yards.

They wanted to kill me up there and one said, "No, don't kill him, let's talk a little to him first." He asked me which way did I vote. I told him I voted the Radical ticket. "Well," he says, "Now you raised your hand and swear that you will never vote another Radical ticket, and I will not let them kill you." He made me stand and raise my hand before him and my god, that I never would vote another Radical ticket, against my principle ... I did raise my hand and swear. Then he took me out among the rest of them, and wouldn't let them shoot me, and told me to go back home.[31]

One of the prosecutors asked Rainey a difficult question about his daughter's treatment. "Do you know what they did to your daughter in the other room?" A long pause occurred, and then he replied, "I didn't see it, ... I have only her word for it." The prosecutor indicated that he would not press the issue, whereupon Rainey again stated in what must have been a painful moment, "I didn't see that, I didn't see that."[32]

After twenty-nine days of proceedings that were full of confessions, pleas and alleged remorse from defendants, this nineteenth-century truth and reconciliation commission found a number of individuals guilty of heinous crimes. In spite of this, many southern newspapers found the congressional investigations to be similar to the Spanish Inquisition, and as historian Allen Trelease noted in *White Terror*, some whites compared presiding Judge Hugh Bond to "Judge Jeffries and the Bloody Assizes of King James II."[33] Not to be distracted from his task, though maligned by most southern newspapers throughout the hearings, Judge Bond finally addressed the court in Columbia with the following remarks on terrorism and its effects on the practitioner of terror.

You have pleaded guilty to an indictment which charges you with conspiring with other men throughout this state to intimidate a certain class of voters by means of threats, beating, and even killing, because that class of citizens were opposed to the conspirators in political opinion.

We acknowledge great perplexity in determining what punishment shall be meted out to you. We have no words strong enough to signify our horror at the means employed to carry out the purpose of the Klans. Our difficulty is personal to you.

You have, as it appears from your statements to the court, been brought up in the most deplorable ignorance. At the age of manhood, but one or two of you can either read or write, and you have lived in a community where the evidence seems to establish the fact that the men of prominence and education — those who, by their superiority in these respects, establish and control public opinion — were for the most part participants in the conspiracy, or so much in terror of it that you could obtain from them neither protection or advice, had you sought it....

You and your confederates must make up your minds either to resist the Ku Klux conspiracy or the laws of the United States. They both cannot exist together; and it only needs a little manliness and courage on the part of you ignorant dupes of designing men to give supremacy to the law. Be assured it will not be taken as an excuse in your case or in any other to hear it said, "I slew this man because the chief ordered it, and I was afraid," and "brushed and raped these others because I dreaded to be whipped if I did not"[34] [see Appendix D for continuation of Judge Bond's remarks].

Harper's Weekly said it well when they commented on a similar racial struggle in Louisiana, where

the reports of the Ku Klux Committee for 1871–1872 show how successful the White Leaguers [terrorist group] of four or five years ago overawed or ill-treated their miserable fellow-citizens; how in 1868 scarcely a Republican ventured to vote in many parishes, and what perpetual bankruptcy and poverty ruled in the small community. Two thousand persons were murdered by these Klan-like "White Leaguers" in a population not much larger than that of Brooklyn.[35]

Armed Propaganda Masked as Social Etiquette

An examination of Ku Klux terrorism during Reconstruction indicates that a priority was placed on creating a plausible scenario that would transcend any doubt as to the organizations effectiveness and its all-knowing abilities. In this respect, three significant questions are raised:

(1) To what extent were Ku Klux communiqués before an attack salient enough to have influenced verbal and nonverbal communication between victims and victimizers during a raid?

(2) To what extent were propagandists committed solely to the use of nonviolent fear appeals?

(3) To what extent were fear appeals effective in disciplining whites to accept Ku Klux precepts?

To properly address these questions one must reexamine early research on fear appeals by social scientists such as Irving Janis who suggested that while fear arousal appeals have a point of diminishing return, their use can also facilitate a reduction in attitude change inversely to time.[36] This indicates that when two or more groups are in contention for power, extended dominance will more likely occur when two conditions are also established:

(1) One group is able to impose its will by demonstrating sufficient ability to control the *interactive* process over an extended period of time.

(2) The same group is capable of employing explicit imagery that will demand of others an understanding of what is expected of them.[37]

However Janis's research also specifies that any slacking of vigilance as with southern whites in implementing the above approaches would invariably allow a reversal in the expected submissive attitude of their intended victims, thereby facilitating a sense of hope from the victims that their treatment or social status could be ameliorated. Janis also observed that "hyper-vigilance" on the part of socially defined victims, in this case south-ern blacks, interfered with their receptivity of Ku Klux fear appeals via communiqués! It also seems that these fear appeals actually *minimized* the worst aspects of impending vio-lence by allowing their victims time to psychologically prepare and thereby deflect the worst aspects of Ku Klux violence by feigning compliance! If Janis's suppositions are correct, then significant portions of testimony during the congressional hearings on Ku Klux violence, though replete with "residual emotional tension," were also fraught with levels of insin-cere recollections and subterfuge.[38]

Though testimonies can be a rich source of "affirmation of fact or truth, such as that given before a court," they are extremely subjective and therefore interpretations of what is assumed to be reality.[39] In addition other sources of historical data, such as diaries and journals, can provide the researcher with narrative depictions of events that may or may not be accurate, and they do assist in understanding how people portray their own social experiences. With this said, corrections, deletions, adjustments, cloak-ing and camouflaging of events become important indicators of their subjective inter-pretation of the surrounding social context and the role each participant fulfills. To this extent, diaries of ex-slaveowning southerners during Reconstruction are often important repositories of what would otherwise appear to be innocuous data, as one frustrated white South Carolinian diarist intimated just three months after the confederate surrender in 1865:

> The Negroes are acting foolishly, running to the Yankees. Judge Tholson's whole crowd started, but before they got to Columbus he compromised with them and they returned home and are to get a part of the crop for their service.[40]

Reflecting deeply felt feelings of anxiety about the changing social relationships between a deposed social class and the ex-slave, southern whites who earlier never considered the social worth of blacks now found themselves engulfed by a growing assertive black citi-zenry. Another diarist from North Carolina tallied up his human assets while pondering over his role as a slaveowner:

> This day all persons of African descent, heretofore acknowledged as slaves are acknowl-edged to be *free*. Estimated by the Census of 1860 to be about four millions of souls, of those about 100, besides those I advanced as my children belong to me. I count from memory 98 —&— think I omit some of the small ones. Although the pecuniary loss is great, I feel no regrets that the result is so. For the institution, I never had a fondness, nor could I advocate it on any other grounds than that slavery was the best state for them. We shall see whether I was correct in this.
>
> I found the institution here when I came upon the stage of life. I have brought many & sold few; never bought but that I thought I bettered his or her condition & most of those I bought I done so at their own request.
>
> May they do better for themselves is the only wish I have, but fear the result.[41]

The wife of a South Carolina plantation owner, Ella Gertrude Clanton Thomas kept a diary that provides us with an example of one whose feigned detachment from a chang-ing world was continually challenged by an unyielding desire to set things *right* through a southern white ethnocentric value system that she knew was correct. Expressing suppressed concerns of many southern whites who realizing that their idealized world was crumbling and spiraling into an abyss of political irrelevancy, Ella counseled in her diary three years after the Civil War that "dark days are gathering," and "with most of us the present duty — the duty of the hour is to provide sustenance for our family's and avoid politics. The South has a *glorious record*. Let us not dim her glory by senseless humiliation. Let us retain our dignity. Zenobia in chains was still a queen."[42] Ella's concerns for the south's "glorious record" no doubt reverberated throughout the ranks of thousands of vicious regulators and highwaymen. And while a large number of southern whites were economically far removed from the Thomas family, they too were adamant about relinquishing any privileges that might result in the social upgrading of blacks. For lower placed southern whites, publicly disassociating themselves from any recognition of blacks' as social equals became a necessary and unequivocal political ritual that sanctioned a racist fantasy: The only factor protecting them from economic challenge and psychological obscurity was color! Some even rationalized that it was prudent to either excuse or ignore excesses committed by groups such as the Ku Klux, and if necessary publicly deny any affiliation with their tactics or goals.

This was evident in Ella Thomas's diary when, forced to recognize dramatic changing social relationships between blacks and whites, she nostalgically reflected on her husband's background as a slaveowning South Carolina planter. Acutely aware that any loss of land property was a loss in human property, social arrangements that once provided the glue for obtaining this kind of material wealth was now a problem for the "new south."

For example, in an April 1871 diary entry, Ella's rendering of surrounding social changes revealed a pampered personality whose responses to a diminished social status were subjectively interpreted as threats to her "southern nature." By totally discounting the African's "southern nature," and their own arousal by the promise of enfranchisement and not the values of their former owners, Ella wrapped herself in the saturated cloak of secessionist etiquette and lamented:

> I stopped writing this afternoon to go up stairs and select some summer clothing for the children to have done up. While I was up stairs Turner [her son] returned from Augusta on Horseback to spend the night, as Mr. Thomas [her husband] is in Columbia having left home this morning. Calling to one of the servants to ask some questions, I heard him reply, "Yes" in reply. I looked out. "Who was that answered you then Turner," said I? "Henry," was his reply. "Henry" said I, "When you reply to Turner you must be more respectful." To this he replied that he was willing to say yes sir to *Mr. Thomas* but not to boys of his size.
>
> I came down stairs and told Henry that I was very well pleased with him, but that there was a distinction to be made between Turner and Charley Hall [one of the servants on the farm] and it must be made. He replied that he could leave and continued talking in this way for a while. "Henry" said I, "You have said enough and you must stop. I repeat to you that while you are in our employment you must reply respectfully to Turner or leave. You can do as you please, but I should tell you the same if you were the only servant to be hired in the state." I told him this and came in. I do not know whether he will go or stay. I should prefer his remaining for hands are scarce but respect is a quality I demand from servants even more than obedience. I can over look neglected work but cannot tolerate disrespect....
>
> The servants are very tenacious of their honor. They all call Turner "Buddy," the old name every one of our own servants have addressed him by ever since his birth. They are willing to compromise by calling him "buddy" and Mary Belle [Ella's daughter] "Sissy," to

avoid speaking as Master Turner or Miss Mary Belle, for that would be too submissive to please them.[43]

Social assessments by families such as the Thomases generally concurred that Ku Klux activities were a necessary evil if order and fearful obedience could not be maintained by traditional norms. By allegedly not being concerned with the intricacies of how the Ku Klux established a synthesis between terror and social order, the unsavory aspects of Klansmen was relegated to mythology. Few wanted to know the gory details of social control that filled congressional reports such as:

> Dead bodies of murdered Negroes were found on and near the highways by-paths. Grue-some reports came from the hospitals— reports of colored men and women whose ears had been cut off, whose skulls had been broken by blows, whose bodies had been slashed by knives or lacerated by scourges.[44]

While night raids were often bloody sorties against an unarmed enemy, they required from both victimizer and victim a degree of acquiescence that ensured a level of physical if not psychic survival for all participants desiring as much. From the raiders' perspective, it was surmised that with enough physical pressure black farmers and southern Republicans would capitulate and follow the southern Democratic political line! Though not an unreasonable assumption, this type of analysis erroneously assumed that increased Ku Klux forays, intimidation, terror and fear were salient enough factors that would ensure success during Klan forays.

Strategist favoring this approach tended to overestimate the impact of these tactics by erroneously viewing raids as one-dimensional interactions between the victimizer and the victim. By disregarding the likelihood that *all* participants in a raid would be emotionally affected by its violent interactive aspects, emotional factors impacting on the raiders such as anxiety, stress and fear were generally ignored or at the very least minimized.[45]

Fear is not necessarily a strong motivator for compliance, and in some instances its use may evoke an opposite response, one that many Klansmen soon became aware of. In fact, congressional testimony strongly suggest that it was when relative low fear arousal appeals were enacted, optimal levels of compliance from the targeted black populace were obtained.[46] Conversely, increased whippings, shootings, beatings, rapes and killings of blacks simply produced a high level of false compliance that in effect transferred the victims suffering into cunning defensive avoidance tactics! As a result, any social cue by blacks that could be interpreted by whites as an assertive challenging gesture was now masked by the victim in a fog of subterfuge and simulated compliance. Similarly, in many instances violent attacks by white gangs or ruffians were often ameliorated in such a manner that the victims developed a greater degree of psychic resistance, and in many instances, control of the interaction.[47]

Additional studies examining stressful situations such as those that might be found during Ku Klux raids also imply that personality responses such as hypervigilance, actu-ally reduced mental efficiency that might otherwise significantly shape the outcome of highly intense interactive situation.[48] If so, determining the extent in which this is manifested during a raid and by whom is important.

It appears that for southern whites, a sense of hypervigilance against an envisioned onslaught of blacks may have been the most provoking impetus for what was reasoned as a need for preventive violence, i.e., have first strike capabilities against a socially defined enemy. If so, then southern whites' perceptions of blacks' political and economic assertiveness and uplift from enslavement was certainly defensively defined as provocative and obnoxiousness. Psychologists J. Dollard and N.E. Miller observed that such social attitudes are largely learned and supported by effective myth making propaganda campaigns that can effectuate a number of responses: "When fear is learned as response to a new situation, it serves as a drive to motivate trial-and-error behavior. A reduction in the strength of the fear reinforces the learning of any new response that accompanies it."[49]

Ironically, congressional testimony from Ku Klux marauders in South Carolina not only inadvertently called attention to the victims' comprehension of which social-political mores were violated, but most importantly their understanding that they needed to suppress this awareness when confronted by raiders. Accordingly, Klan forays quickly turned violent when it was apparent that verbal appeals failed to elicit a proper response from their victims. Within this violent context, the extent by which victims successfully masked their feelings through subterfuge is indicative of a much larger failure in the Ku Klux terror campaigns.

Communicative modes or interactions after slavery between southern blacks and whites did not radically change overnight, especially when the social economic arrangements and political institution remained essentially intact. With that said, while most blacks by 1866 were cognizant that slavery as defined by law had indeed been terminated, they were also very much aware that political and economic relationships were another matter. As an allied insurgency of Klansmen and their acolytes converted the south into a testing ground between the former order and an emerging challenger, blacks' internalized rage was often converted into cynical statements and derision aimed at their tormentor, rather than an outright physical confrontation.

As acts of terror by night-riding Klansmen and similarly constituted groups increased from 1868 to 1871, southern whites' general sense of their own empowerment, retribution and social control returned! Defining the ills of the postwar period as Republican attempts at Reconstruction, armed raiders became the sinew of hope and a metaphor that pulled fractured segments of the old Confederacy around the concept of whiteness. They united landless poor whites and a struggling landowning planter class into a political accord aimed at stopping the Freedmen at all cost. This was evidenced by Ella Thomas's diary entry that suggested while in the past her status as wife of a plantation owner did not require her to interact with the family's slaves on a daily basis, during Reconstruction her frustrations, economic stresses and resulting anger with the loss of servants could easily be interpreted as "Ku Klux in nature."[50] Socially constructed symmetries of this kind among southern whites, particularly on the question of what to do with the Negro were common and easily found solace and sympathy in organized white resistance. Accordingly, as Ku Klux fear appeals increased in strength, their purpose evolved from warnings to threats, and eventually resulted in outright violence. Conversely, blacks' ability to communicate or verbalize any form of compromise with their tormentors diminished.[51]

It was during daily interactions between blacks and whites that indications of resistance appeared. Though some instances were blatant and others more subtle, clearly these indicators of changing social relationships were apparent. For example in one issue of a 1867 New York Times, two separate clashes over streetcar use in Charleston, South Carolina, underscored the rising social tensions on race and place.

On Tuesday afternoon, March 27th after the adjournment of the Freedmen's mass meeting in Charleston, S.C. an attempt was made by some of them to test their right to ride in the street car which is denied them by the rules of the Company. One of them entered a car, and declined to leave it when requested to do so by the conductor, who at the same time informed him of the Company's rules. The conductor, however insisted that he should at least leave the inside of the car, and finally his friends who found he was liable to be forcibly ejected if resistance was offered, persuaded him to yield.

On its return trip the car was filled at the same place by a crowd of negroes, who rushed into it to the great discomfort of the white passengers and although remonstrated with and appealed to by the conductor declined to go out. The driver then attempted by direction of the conductor to throw his car from the track, and failing in this, unhitched his horses and [...]. The negroes threatened personal violence to the conductor, but the arrival of the police and detachments of soldiers caused the Negroes to disperse. Other cars were in the meantime entered to interrupt the travel of the cars by placing stones on the track. The Charleston *Courier,* from which we gather the above details of the occurrence, say that the community is greatly indebted to the military authorities for their prompt assistance, and particularly to Gen. Clitz, who repaired to the scene and successfully employed his efforts to prevent what promised at one time to be a serious if not bloody affair.[52]

A few days later on April 1, an additional disturbance was described in the *Times*:

Another street-car difficulty occurred this afternoon. Two negroes got inside a street-car and refusing to leave were ejected by the Police. They forcibly resisted, but were overcome and lodged in the station-house; thereupon the Negroes outside became disorderly, using brickbats and threatened to rescue them. In the melee several parties were injured. Information was promptly sent to headquarters and a squad of regulars interfered and took charge of five of the ringleaders. The matter will be investigated before the Provost court tomorrow.[53]

Actions taken to resolve the social disjunction of civil law and human rights are not easily taken and when they are, often evolve into a conflict between terrorism and resistance. In a June 1870 issue of the liberal *New Era*, the following article bridges the gap between these two alternatives and invites its readers to resolve the issue:

More Shootings. From a letter written from Columbus, (Ga.) we learn that a scion of chivalry by the name of Halstead, who has something to do with a livery stable there, in the most deliberate manner shot a colored man who was employed in the stable. Just like a cowardly rebel, he set up the plea that the Negro threw a brick at him, and the Ku Klux police, ready to seize any excuse to justify such outrages, arrested the wounded and bleeding Negro and put him in the calaboose. And yet we are told with the greatest coolness that these fiends are the negro's best friends. Some Negroes are found who are shallow enough to swallow this oft-repeated absurdity and publicly announce themselves as "Democrats." Well, time will show them what asses they are making of themselves. If the Negroes of Columbus would only organize, and since there is no protection for them before the courts, retaliate for these horrible outrages against them, rebels would soon learn to have respect for them. The more they submit to being killed, the more they will be killed, and the more they ought to be killed.[54]

Though inbred southern social attitudes that gave rise to the above incidences were generally applicable in most violent confrontational situations between the races, these attacks were also symptomatic of a deeper social malaise. For conservative whites, daily altercations, armed or otherwise, functioned as a physic release that while helping ease the specter of military and social defeat, reinforced the idea that their values and traditions could still be enforced and honored. However, for many Freedmen these violent confrontations facilitated a sense of dominion over self, while assuring them that they would not longer be confined to social or political obscurity. Interestingly enough, continuous day-to-day violence as described above also helped define Ku Klux Klan rhetoric and its accompanying mythology on race by anesthetizing southern white economist, politicians, agricultrialist, nascent industrialist, shopkeepers, farm-workers, skill or unskilled laborers, young girls, aspiring students, ex–Confederate soldiers and dirt poor journeymen from the infinitely harsher social dilemma of intraracial class conflict.

In demeaning fashion a newly enfranchised black population now willing to brave their former masters was now ridiculed as a credible source of social power or political influence. Arguments from all sectors of southern white society purported that the Freedmen's power base was neither entrenched in numerical strength or along traditional economic lines, but instead a creation of white Republican intrigue aimed ultimately at undercutting planters' control of the nation's southern agricultural base. Any political articulation of blacks to the contrary was deemed unthinkable, politically foolish and socially unwise by most whites, particular in South Carolina. Thus an early twentieth-century novel by Albion Tourgee, *A Fool's Errand, by One of the Fools,* the essence of white conservatism was captured by the following statement: "The spirit of the dead Confederacy was stronger than the mandate of the nation to which it had succumbed in battle."[55]

Nonetheless, in South Carolina blacks *were a threat* to white domination! The threat, first perceived by whites as numerical was by the late 1860s understood as to be economic, political and social. Exploiting this challenge, Ku Klux propagandists curtailed any perception of the Freedmen as being competent, responsible, creative, productive members of society or a military threat. Instead they labored to concoct an image of childish blacks imitating southern whites' worse traits as when one writer in the *Richmond Virginia Examiner* visualized the Freedmen as a paranoid race and a people susceptible to the travails of life who would forever require whites parental guidance. He then opined:

> How easily the Negro Dies: In statistics recently complied and published it is plainly shown that the Negro is not equal to the burdens of freedom, and that when he puts on a uniform he has almost surely enshrouded himself for burial. Bullets do not kill him, but disease claims him for its own, and perishes suddenly. Only 2,997 dies in action and of wounds, while 26,301 fell victim to disease. Here is a huge disproportion. The deaths in action and by wounds stand to those by disease in the ratio of one to eight.
>
> Among whites the ratio is only one to two. This shows that the Negroes are not of that "perdurable stuff" of which freemen should be made. Not only in war does he show his incapacity to meet and endure the harassing responsibilities of life, but in peace he sinks beneath the ordinary trials of this uncertain and soul-trying world. As children need parents, so do negroes need master. The world will recognize the fact one day, but too late.[56]

Similar analysis could be found in northern newspapers and journals. *Harper's Weekly*, a widely read and reportedly liberal newspaper, was one such journal. Known for its illustrated versions of historical and contemporary events in an era when photographs were not a part of a newspapers format, the widely read journal periodically published images and stories on race that projected blacks as helpless, politically dependent victims of racism. In a December 1864 edition a Christmas toy was advertised as "Santa Claus Automation Negro Dancer" that "imitates the motions of a living negro, affording infinite amusement to both old and young—price $2."[57] This advertisement, however, was complete with an illustration of a black male in rags, dancing barefoot "for the amusement of young and old." A few years later after the enactment of Reconstruction in 1876, *Harper's* had a dramatic illustration of a black male lying flat on his back, blood running from his head, appearing to be dead amidst the ruins of destroyed southern city. A poster was on a nearby wall which stated "negro killed" and the scribbled letters of K.K. Under this depiction were the words, "One Vote Less—Richmond Whig."[58] An even more dramatic depiction of the ensuing warfare raging throughout the country's southern landscape occurred in October 1874 when *Harper's Weekly* published an illustration of two Freedmen, male and female on their knees, head bowed while holding a baby in their arms. Standing over them are two white males, one has a book in his pocket labeled "White League," and the other is dressed in a white hooded robe with the letters K.K. on it. Each is well armed with daggers, pistols and rifles while holding a human skull over the head of the Freedman. Surrounding this entire scene are the words, "Worse Than Slavery," "The Union as It Was" and "The Lost Cause."[59]

Though depictions as with other newspapers were alleged attempts to clarify critical issues of the day, they were replete with racial duplicity. Repetitious depictions and suppositions of Freedmen as incompetent citizens who were incapable of finding necessary resources to protect themselves against assertive southern white Democrats simply strengthened racial stereotyping of blacks. It fed into an analysis that inferred; any resolution of critical social issues were far beyond the political control or mental resources of southern blacks. Not surprisingly, when a columnist in the *Richmond Virginia Examiner* opined that "as children need parents, so do negroes need masters" many northern liberals also concurred that blacks as a dependent race required *their* protection and guidance for proper management and exploitation.[60]

The Ordered Society

Ku Klux propaganda was replete with various descriptive inquiries into the Africans' alleged mental and physical ineptitude. As a result, it was believed by many southern whites that for the benefit of the nation, as in slavery, a state of economic and political dependency had to be enforced over the ex-slave. Planters asserted, without this, blacks' notions of racial equality would destroy the very fabric of an agrarian system that for centuries was premised on the supposition that subordination of its laboring force was a social truth! Others even claimed that to ignore the importance of white hegemony as the driving force for a stable and productive southern economy would instantly foster the harbinger of an unwanted evil—black social political ascendancy.[61]

In 1868, one unidentified white South Carolinian succinctly verbalize his fear of being socially displaced by blacks when he claimed:

> Intelligence, virtue, and patriotism are to give place, in all elections, to ignorance, stupidity and vice. The superior race is to be made subservient to the inferior.... They who own property are to levy taxes and make all appropriations.... The consequences will be in effect, confiscation. The appropriations to support free schools for the education of the

Negro children, for the support of old Negroes in the poor-houses, and the vicious in jail and penitentiary, together with a standing army of Negro soldiers [the Militia], will be crushing and utterly ruinous to the State. Every man's property will have to be sold to pay his taxes ... The white people of our State will never quietly submit to Negro rule.... By moral agencies, by political organizations, by every peaceful means left us, We will keep up this contest until we have regained the heritage of political control handed down to us by honored ancestry. That is a duty we own to the land that is ours, to the graves that it contains, and to the race of which you and we are alike members— the proud Caucasian race, whose sovereignty on earth God has ordained.[62]

A drawing of the line attitude by southern white Americans accentuated the capability of metaphorical language to create a world full of villains, heroes, saints and enemies. In this historical context, one's birth into an alleged band of Confederate brothers helped alleviate a sense of powerlessness in the face of an immediate threat. It inoculated the weak against their own fears while empowering them with a passion to fight against the dragons of the world.

Ku Klux use of symbols such as white robes and gourds with horns have often been interpreted as efforts at scaring or intimidating rural blacks with visions of vengeful night-riding dead Confederate soldiers. However, sociologically speaking, these customs and ornaments functioned more to unify Klansmen around a central philosophical concept, albeit a community that claimed for themselves the role of combatants for southern white justice.[63] Though years later additional Ku Klux icons emerged, such as a burning cross, the sense of spiritual self-righteousness and white racial awakening remained a central issue in Ku Klux terrorism. Understandably volatile racial clashes were immediately refashioned and politically skewed for public consumption through books, newspapers and the sworn testimony of witnesses. In this manner, myth for many southern whites was far more than a product of fantasy, legend or fable, it was a formula for action.[64]

For Klansmen and other devotees of racial supremacy, acts of violence against psychic black dragons may have fostered in their psyche verifiable truths about reality and the importance of battling evil! Viewed within a social framework already replete with cultural stereotypes, one is reminded of psychologist Robert Bales's observation that within such a violent milieu, some participants will be horrified, while many will be enthralled, committed, exalted and impelled to perform. Such passions when fused with Klan imagery and paraphernalia tended to spirit up deep-seated emotions that escorted the unwary into a fantasy world of terror.[65]

Research by psychologist Silvan Tomkins on the psychology of commitment and its associative relationship to violence and suffering recognized that resonance, i.e., attempts by individuals or group to find their place in the order of events, was a critical factor in obtaining shared commitments to a cause, regardless of its practically.[66] Tomkins further explained that

By resonance we mean the engagement of feeling and thought by any organized ideology or social movement. The fit between the individual's own loosely organized ideas and feelings ... and the more tightly organized ideology or social movement need not be a very close one to resonance.[67]

If it is resonance rather than the existence of psychological demons that were a primary element in the development of social movements, such as the Ku Klux Klan, it may

"'VERDICT', HANG THE D— YANKEE AND NIGGER".

"Verdict, Hang the D — Yankee and Nigger." LIBRARY OF CONGRESS PRINTS AND PHOTOGRAPHS DIVISION, WASHINGTON, D.C.

be reasonable to accept that the level of resonance in a social movement will be indicative of the group's commitment to stated ideals. The irony however is that a continual resonating and propagating of racial supremacist dogma as if it were a static phenomenon assumes that targeted audiences, in this case disenchanted whites, had to be continually persuaded that their world was indeed in disarray. That being the case, only by involving themselves in direct action could any sense of normalcy and order be established, or as one southern conservative propagandist concluded, "society as a whole may be lacking in sanity."[68]

For Klansmen and sympathetic whites, the desire for social order was an attempt to reconstruct the present in a manner consistent with their notions of the ordered society. It is society religiously founded on what they assumed were unshakable mores steeped in the righteousness of their causes, the validity of their philosophy, and the goodness of their goals. Commitments of this type obliged them to insist on a special status within society, no matter how fallacious it seemed to others.[69]

Similarly, idealism of this sought converted Klan propaganda into a prescription for vicious acts that enhanced the likelihood that brute force would be used to seize social control over nonwhites, even with the possibility of racial genocide. As the editor of a Mississippi paper, *The Meridian,* stated after blacks and Republicans were defeated in the 1868 statewide elections:

> Thank god, we can announce that it is over, the election, the most disgusting, disgraceful and degrading thing ever devised by the malice of man. Thank God it is over!, and pray His holy name to remove the sin creating thing, negro suffrage, the most abominable of all abominations....
> The first preparations for the great work before us is, to shape and temper our firm resolves till they be hard as adamant and true as steel. Then, with the skull an cross bones of the "Lost Cause" before us, we will swear that *This* is a White man's government; and trusting in our firm purpose our good right arms and God of Right, we will maintain it so![70]

Mounting notions of racial dominance were accordingly geared to essentially inhibit any economic or political thrust by blacks to alter their "traditional" role as America's pariah race. This too was a part of the ordered society. Elaborating on this point, DuBois in *Black Reconstruction* noted that options for the ex-slave were painfully limited: either destroy the old economic order and its cultural antecedents, or suffer social marginality. In this respect, DuBois opined, there was no choice:

> The unrest and bitterness of post-war lawlessness were gradually transmuted into economic pressure. Systematic effort was made by the owners to put the Negro to work, and equally determined effort by whites to keep him from work which competed with them or threatened their future work and income. Cotton and other crops were in price, and hard work would soon restore something of the losses of war. The planters offered the ex-slave, therefore, a labor contract, and were surprised when he refused. He had to refuse. The plantation laborer, under the conditions offered, would still be a slave with small chance to rise to the position of independent farmer, or even of free modern laborer.[71]

Interestingly enough, *The Charleston Leader,* a Republican newspaper published an article in 1868 titled "Loyalty and the Planter" in which planters throughout the state presented eight resolutions concerning their economic and political interest in the Marlboro District of South Carolina. Conceived by a committee calling themselves the Guardians of the Public Safety, these resolutions, reading more like demands, were published in most of the leading Democratic and Republican papers of the day. In extremely succinct language, ex-slaveowning planters suggested a way of resolving the economic quagmire and cyclical violence that was beginning to entrap southern economy by declared their own version of the ordered society:

Ku-Klux Mode of Torture.

A Ku Klux mode of torture. LIBRARY OF CONGRESS PRINTS AND PHOTOGRAPHS DIVISION, WASHINGTON, D.C.

That the withdrawal of the military from the state, at the earliest possible period, is the best measure to secure, on a lasting basis, sure, and satisfactory to both Freedmen and planters, the relations existing between them.

... That such a measure would be accompanied with less confusion and difficulty than any other, and that, having pledged ourselves by the oath of allegiance to recognize the existing state of things, we do not hesitate to say that it is our honest purposes to abide thereby.

... That, if inconsistent with the views of the authorities to remove the military, we express the opinion that the plan of the military to compel the freedman to contract with his former owner, when desired by the latter, is wise, prudent, and absolutely necessary.

... That we, the planters of the District, pledge ourselves not to contract with any freedman unless he can produce a certificate of regular discharge from his former owner.

... That, under no circumstances whatsoever will we rent land to any Freedmen, nor will we permit them to live on our premises as employees.

... That no system can be devised for the present which can secure success, where the discipline and management of the Freedmen is entirely taken out of the hands of the planters; and we invoke the authorities to recognize this fact, which cannot but be apparent to them.

... That we request the military to cease the habit of making negroes act as couriers, sheriffs, and constables, to serve writs and notices upon planters—a system so destructive to good order and discipline.

   ... That we call on our young men to fill up the military companies now organized in the district, not only to preserve order and quiet, the lives of the weak and unprotected, seriously threatened under the existing state of affairs.

   ... That these proceedings be published in the papers of Charleston: that a copy be sent to our members of the legislature, and one to Col. Murray, Commandant at Chersaw.[72]

Implementation of these resolutions by so-called guardians of public safety attempted to create a supplicated force of black laborers who would survive only at the mercy of a racially ordered economic system.[73] To ensure that this was the case, planters developed a system of armed patrols to enforce supportive local ordinances. Simultaneously, an appeal was made to disenfranchised whites to demonstrate their loyalty to race and Christian principles by participating in the enforcement of these antiblack regulatory actions. As could be expected, conservative northern investors in southern plantations feigned ignorance or plainly ignored the racist repercussions of this form of economic terrorism. They were not, however, reticent of the fact that while the Civil War destroyed southerners' hope for a separate nation, the beginnings of a centralized and industrialized southern economy with northern finance were now a possibility. In fact, an increasing number of Americans, particularly Republicans, now believed that an expanded southern economy with the help of an increased railroad system would stimulate postwar employment and generate prosperity.[74] However, southern Democrats argued, yes, but not at the cost of bringing white labor, both native and immigrant, into wage competition with skilled black labor. This they asserted was too high a social cost to pay for economic development. Another arrangement would have to be formulated.

4

Themes on Racial Conflict

One feature that distinguishes the process of reactionary terror is
the fact that deadly violence is usually an early response to perceived
threat rather than the culmination of a long process of radicalization.
A related feature is the existence of a tradition of violent resistance in
the affected community, which is more or less quickly activated by
externally imposed change.[1]

Propagating Economic Terrorism

Though postbellum census data indicates that a little over 4 million Africans populated the United States from 1840 to 1880, during this same period, nearly 8 million Europeans immigrated to America armed with agricultural and laboring skills required for the
country's expansion westward.[2] These skills, along with brute strength in the areas of mining, construction and manufacturing, placed immigrant labor in direct competition with
the skilled and now emancipated African laborer.

Commenting on this development, social scientist Stephen Steinberg opined that
"indeed if slavery is to be credited with laying the foundation for the nation's industrial
development, then it was foreign labor that finally erected the industrial edifice itself!"[3]
Steinberg's exaggerated if not inaccurate conclusions should have parenthetically added
that "foreign labor" was able to contribute to the country's growth only as a result of a sanctioned and savage assault on African *Americans* civil and human rights.

For example, an early 1900s labor report on immigration from the 1880s indicated
that of twenty major mining and manufacturing centers, 58 percent of the workers
were foreign born![4] Moreover, it was precisely in the skilled areas of road construction,
tanning, rubber factories, steel mills etc., where skilled but enslaved labor excelled for
two and a half centuries that were now the protected occupational havens for immigrating
Europeans.

Coal mines	48 percent immigrant labor
Iron mines	67 percent immigrant labor
Clothing factories	76 percent immigrant labor
Slaughter & packing houses	46 percent immigrant labor
Tanneries	53 percent immigrant labor
Steel mills	51 percent immigrant labor
Rubber factories	41 percent immigrant labor
Textile mills	49 percent immigrant labor
Road construction	46 percent immigrant labor

Source: Compiled by the author from The Ethnic Myth: Race, Ethnicity, and Class in America, by Stephen Steinberg, p. 38.

Interestingly, Steinberg's omission doesn't mention the impact that cheap immigrant labor had on the murder of thousands of African American laborers when he noted that:

> To be sure, the nation's expanding industries needed labor, but even more than that, they needed cheap labor. For labor to be cheap, it had to exceed demand even at a time when demand was accelerating rapidly. A tight labor market not only would have constricted economic growth, but also would have resulted in an upward pressure on wages as industries competed for scarce labor. The existence of a labor surplus had the opposite effect. It exerted pressure on workers to accept long hours, poor conditions, and low wages. The real function of the liberal immigration policies of the period, therefore, was to flood the labor market in order to keep labor, abundant and cheap. Without this contrived surplus of immigrant labor, the costs of economic growth would have been immeasurably greater, thereby shrinking the capital base that was essential for economic growth.[5]

As a result of this process, several factors emerged:

(1) While thousands of black laborers could have easily fulfilled the burgeoning labor needs of a post war southern economy, racist proclivities favored the importation of a more economic compliant European labor force. Furthermore, by anticipating that racial hegemony over blacks could be maintained by tolerating culturally similar European immigrants, southern planters, manufacturers, distributors and general merchants were able to maintained exploitative wages for immigrants and a pariah status for blacks.

(2) With the reality that southern blacks outnumbering whites in at least three States, South Carolina, Louisiana and Mississippi, and their having near parity in three others, Alabama, Florida and Georgia, the potentiality that African Americans could dominate if not control the state legislative assemblies raised the volatile question, who will rule?[6]

Native-born white Americans well as for European immigrants, regardless of the numerical ratio, made certain assumptions about their place and order in society. Part of the Americanization process for immigrants was coming to a realization that after three centuries of European explorations and domination in the "new" world, governing the indigenous and imported blacks in almost every segment of public life was natural and expected. They had no frame of reference to envision otherwise. However with the passage of Civil Rights Acts from 1866 to 1875 and implementation of the thirteenth, fourteenth and fifteenth Amendments to the Constitution, the African American was becoming extremely reluctant to have these legislated rights trampled on without a struggle. Accordingly, DuBois claimed that it was not a question of whether a reconstructed south could prosper under black political and economic rule, it was essentially *whose* interest would be served under their political leadership: "It was not, then that the post-bellum south could not produce wealth with free labor; it was the far more fundamental question as to whom this wealth was to belong to and for whose interest laborers were to work."[7]

The ensuing struggle for jobs and wages was further complicated by the practice of barring nonwhites from membership in craft unions or associations established for the protection of workers' rights. This prompted DuBois to claim that

> it [the south] is for the most part against unions and the labor movement, because there can be no real labor movement in the South; their laboring class is cut in two and the white laborers must be ranged upon the side of their own exploiters by persistent propaganda and police force. Labor can gain in the South no class-consciousness. Strikes cannot be effective because the white striker can be threaten with the colored "scab" and the colored striker can be clapped in jail.[8]

Justifications for these racist attitudes were also gleaned from emerging academic disciplines of such as biology, sociology and anthropology. Among many noted scholars of the day who forged constructs on race was Herbert Spencer. Advocating that Charles Darwin's evolutionary theory, *Origins of the Species,* should be reinterpreted into a construct known as "social Darwinism," theorist such as Spencer coined the phrase, "the survival of the fittest," and with that formulated human behavior as a sociobiological construct.[9]

By the late nineteenth century (1896), Spencer's social Darwinism engendered very succinct ideas about the superior and inferior nature of cultures, particularly when he opined that black children would not be able to keep pace intellectually with whites due to biological limitations, i.e., "their intellect being apparently incapable of being cultured beyond a certain point."[10] With scientific thinking of this sort emerging as evidence of European biological superiority, black social equality, particularly in labor relationships, was unthinkable and seemingly unnatural to many white Americans. To argue against this evidence was to risk arguing against science, cultural tradition and most important, the birthright of every European immigrant for a second chance at material gain, regardless of the misfortunes of black Americans.

Unfortunately, many southern newspaper editors, both black and white, maintained an editorials policy that simply replicated the violent rhetoric they received for their letters to the editor column. These letters in turn became testimonials to an openly contentious and highly competitive labor market. In addition, for many whites the issue was not about racial prerogatives, for this they assumed for themselves! More troubling was the presence of a skilled black laboring class who were insistent on being involved in all things economic and political. The reality of this challenge forced many whites to find some rational to explain *their* economic predicament, such as one worker who in the fall of 1868 expressed his patronizing concerns in a sympathetic journal, the *Workingman's Advocate:*

> We all know that the negro is a free man, never again to be bought and sold, and who does not feet thankful that the greatest stain on the fair issue of our country is removed by the act of emancipation, now seeing they are as free as all God's creatures are by nature, and should be by practices. Such being the case, the question then arises, what are the duties of a free man in a country? It is an easy matter to solve by each person seeking

himself the question. Then what you claim for your self you should willingly grant to others, and that is in this country a voice in making the laws we live under, and in whose eye all should be on an equality, all receive alike the same protection.

Now sir, you will see by my sentiments that I consider that although that Colored cooper is not as yet my political equal in this state he should be. But you say political equality to the negro will be political enmity to labor, because the white laborer refuses to place himself on a social platform with the Negro laborer, and I must confess, honestly, that I have not the slightest ambition to work with a Negro, to meet him in our trade unions, or do anything that would have a tendency to break down the demarcations of race that God has seen fir to ordain, and for those reasons, I know that no sensible negro will be my political opponent, and furthermore, no sensible negro will demand such concessions, for it takes them out of their element. I am sure that a poor colored cooper, surrounded by thirty white men, just felt as I would feel surrounded by a like number of blacks, and I am sure I have not the least wish to realize the feeling. The old saying, birds of a feather flock together, has always proved true in the past, and will I feel persuaded, in the future, ... And I think that the lines of demarcation between the races will be more closely drawn in the future than they were in the past. My reasons for thinking so are these:

First, Freedom leaves the negro at liberty to turn their faces in any direction they wish.

Secondly, A growth in intelligence consequent upon their changed relations in life, will enable them to see that they are contending against odds in competing with a superior and more enterprising race.

Thirdly, Self-preservation will cause them to draw from the unequal contest and colonize by themselves, and it is my serious impression that if such a course should not be pursued they will the sooner disappear before the coward march of the white race, which is destined, I believe, at no very remote date to supplant all the races of the globe.

As regards their political action, in that I see nothing to fear. Some, like the minority of our own race will have minds of their own, and act with us and for us, while the mass like the many of our own race, will be the puppets of political gamblers. I have now come to the pleasing contrast, and I must say that I cannot see the parallel between the societies. The society you have branded as false, is a protective society composed of men of the same race who assemble at these meetings on a social, not a political equality, and only separate to commingle more closely. The true society is a speculating enterprise, where one person's money is as good as another's, and when they separate they may not meet again until the next meeting.

I remain, yours truly,

John Hewitt, Member of United Coopers' No. 4, New York[11]

In Boston, a city known for its raucous racial relationships, ethnocentrism and class interest among workers, especially Irish construction workers and hod carriers (men who carried on their shoulders a portable trough used for carrying mortar, bricks, etc.) was contentious and more often violent than in other northern cities. A few months after the abolition of slavery in January 1865, a number of tersely written articles in the *Boston Daily Evening Voice* expressed a multitude of economic fears held mostly by Irish workers. Propagating that a fundamental competitive and often violent relationship existed between the races and in particular between the newly freed slaves and European immigrants, these articles advised that the sooner white workers became cognizant of this "fact," a proper racial and class relationship with blacks would be established![12]

This kind of insipid fear precipitated by northern white newspapers provided a basis for a level of anxiety that complimented southern whites' reasoning that only direct terror could stem the economic and political insurgency of blacks. The fact is that by the late 1860s, in cities like Boston, the African American community, albeit slowly, was establishing itself as a small but viable economic entity. Many of its most notable residents were well known as black abolitionists before the Civil War and as soldiers during the war, while others had local stores or were meaningfully employed. As their population increasingly became literate and informed about its tenuous economic and dubious political status, articles appearing in conservative Republican newspapers began complaining that blacks were becoming an insufferable, intolerable and socially offensive threat! The problem succinctly was that the relative growth of the black population away from the chains of enslavement and 250 years of stateless status was too phenomenal a development for most white Americans or immigrants to understand or accept, particularly in the area of labor. It challenged their assumption that America was not only the land of opportunity, but a place where they were assured that their status could never fall below the level of the country's official pariah race and class, the blacks. This conscious acceptance of racial preferential status, in effect allowed major employers and controllers of industry the ability to essentially kill two birds with one stone; exploit existing racial and class antagonisms while curtailing any nascent development of workers' unions.

Even before the onset of Reconstruction in 1867, white workers, particularly the Irish, were cognizant of the economic vise unfolding around them, as one white worker explained in the *Boston Daily Evening Voice* why the hod carriers went out on strike in 1865:

> It is said that a party of hod-carriers, who have been receiving two and a half dollars a day, have demanded an advance; that the employer refused to accede and employed a party of negroes; that the police were ready to put down any attempt on the part of the white hod-carriers to molest the negroes, — which is not objected to, if the same police are ready to put down an attempt on the part of the capitalist, sitting in their bank parlors and counting-rooms, and contractors sitting in the mechanics' exchange, concerting plans to compel workingmen to work at the prices dictated by the nabobs who have the control of money, and through this control can say to the laboring man, work at our price or starve.

> Why is it more cruel for the hod-carrier to fight against his competitor than for the capitalist to say to him, we will starve your wife and children unless you conform to our demand? Both are wrong, entirely wrong, and need reform. But is there not reason to fear that some police officers perform with alacrity the duty (as they call it) of mauling a hod-carrier, while they are little skittish when called upon to protect the hod-carrier form the oppression of capital? Now the question is asked, why should the negro be willing to carry a hod carrier than anybody else? Why should he be induced to do so? Why should not the hod-carrier be as well paid as the contractor? And why should not the contractor be as well paid as the merchant, or moneylender? Indeed it might be asked, why should the money-lender be paid at all, seeing that money is a creature of the government, created for the common good at the common expense, and should not be tampered with. At any rate, keep the moneylender at six percent. If this will not support him, let him go to work or retrench his expenses. Do not let him take advantage of the demand for money which himself and the other bank directors have created, and say to the contractor, take the extra interest out of the hod carriers' and other laborers' wages; and say to the merchant, change to the consumer. Why should not the hours of the hod-carrier furnish him with as much money as the hours in any other indispensable vocation?

When will workingmen learn that competition among themselves to get employment from the capitalist is suicide?; that this competition is just what keeps the workingman under the thumb of capital?; and this is the face of the fact that all of what is called capital is the result of labor performed by workingmen. The result of the hod carrier strike proves that workingmen should feel that the successful management of the boss and capitalist in this case is a blow at all labor; and harder blows are yet to be delivered, unless all work-ingmen are as willing and able to combine as the capitalist. One of two things should be done — either repeal all the legislation in favor of capital and against labor, or else enact laws which shall protect labor as well as capital.

If the negro hod-carrier will underbid the white hod-carrier because the negro can live cheaper, soon the white will underbid the black, because he has learned to live still cheaper, and then again the black and then the white, until the lowest rate is obtained; and so it will be as long as it is necessary that every laborer shall change his labor into money and a few banks or a combination of banks can control the money.

Many capitalist and opponents of the eight-hour law and other labor reforms, look upon the contest between black and white as a good joke. Pity it is so, but so it is. Are we to have a "poor white trash"?[13]

Essential questions pertaining to an eight-hour day and the use of black laborers to break union-called strikes continually placed black and white workers on a collision course. One newspaper account in the *Workingman's Advocate* underscored the tensions in the nations capital by quoting one laborers observation that

The white Irish workmen engaged in clearing out the canal which runs through Washing-ton, who have been working on the eight-hour plan, and who are expected to vote for the re-election of Mayor Wallack, struck today for higher pay. A gang of colored men promptly took their places, but the white men refused to permit them to work and began to pelt them with stones. The police came, arrested the ringleaders and locked them up, after which the colored men shoveled away unmolested.

We don't like that, — the most of it, perhaps none of it. We believe eight are enough hours per day for any man to work at clearing the filth from a canal; and if the workmen were getting insufficient wages they were justified in striking. But we don't like the idea of other laborers, white or colored, taking their places after they had struck, and we don't like the pelting measure. The strike was badly managed. Henceforth let there be an under-standing between all laborers, white and black, that the employer cannot play off the one class against the other. This will be much more for the interest of both classes than either underworking or pelting each other.

The eight hour men of Washington have nominated H. N. Easby as their Candidate for Mayor. We wish every laborer man in the city could have the privilege of voting for him.[14]

Noting that striking Irish workers held little sympathy for blacks laborers who were will-ing to replace them on job sites, one recalled:

We should judge by the appearance of the blacks now on the work that some of them were recently arrived from the south, and rather green at Northern work. The boss builder told us he paid them the same as he had paid the white men, and to our question whether they proved as capable hands he said he could not tell without further trial; but he should give them a pretty thorough trial before he hired Irishmen again. Irishmen should make dis-passionate note of this, and learn that when they strike against colored men, they do not hurt the colored men, but themselves only.[15]

In the spring of 1868, the editor of pro-labor *Workingman's Advocate* newspaper was reminded that

Now that slavery is abolished that fruitful source of agitation has become extinct, and in its place that ghastly shadow of negro labor is looming up in the distance. To those who are satisfied with a glance at the surface of things, negro labor may have a terrible significance, and it may scare the timid into the contemplation of some terrible things for this unfortunate race. But I cannot see what direful consequences are to result from free negro labor. By emancipation the relation only of the slave to the master was changed and *not the nature* of the negro; the masters of the Negro remains the same whether in the condition of freedom or slavery....

But by far the most important feature in the consideration of this matter is the probable existence of the Negro race on this continent. The Negro is naturally improvident, he is lacking in parental affection and that care which is a prerequisite to the preservation of a race is not a quality of his nature.... In their condition of slavery there was an interest, and a great interest too, in preserving the race and in bringing it to as high a state of perfection as was possible, and under such a regime, and the accessions made to it by the slave trade, the Negro population of the south increased, while that of the north decreased. But now things are changed; the Negro is no longer a slave; the relation between master and slave is destroyed. The incentives to the care and preservation of the race by the Caucasian south no longer exist; the place of the Negro can be supplied by the German and Irish emigrant, and the necessity for negro labor will with time pass away. Thus the Negro, naturally improvident and indolent, will be reduced to pauperism, and the extinction of the race becomes a question of time and not of fact.

It is true this will not take place in a day, a month, nor a year; but every decade of time, as it rolls around, will make it, to those who choose to observe it, more perceptible, and the unfortunate Negro, like the poor Indian, will have to move out of the path of the over-conquering Caucasian. Why then should the white man fear his competition? To do so is a weakness incompatible with his nature. Leave the Negro to work out his own salvation, extending to him all rights and privileges to which his nature, relation, and condition entitles him. Let us study and understand ourselves, and closely scrutinize the motives of men, particularly political leaders and demagogues, and the ghost of Negro competition need no longer haunt the mind of the white workingman.

Veritas, Baltimore[16]

Black women shared no less grief in the struggle against economic terrorism. For example, one laborer signing her name, "a colored woman" replied to an earlier editorial in the *Philadelphia Morning Post* by remonstrating about the welfare of the poor in the coming winter of 1871 and "the prevailing caste spirit in our midst, depriving deserving, respectable colored people in all our large cities from obtaining employment"[17]:

When respectable women of color answer an advertisement for a dressmaker, either in families or a dressmaker, they are invariably refused, or offered a place to cook or scrub, or to do housework; and when application is made at manufactories immediately after having seen an advertisement for operators or finishers, they meet with the same reply, sometimes modified by bidding you "call again," "just suited," "will want more hands in the course of a few weeks," etc. There are many respectable workmen of color competent to fill any of the above named positions, and who make out a scanty livelihood sewing at home, who would gladly take permanent situations, to sew, operate or finish; and some have advertised to that effect, making their color known, and received no answers.[18]

After the Confederacy's surrender in 1865, economic competition would have its pound of flesh from those blacks who would not adjust to whites insistence of a priori rights in everything economic, political or social. For the maladjusted Freedmen, or those who whites defined as "idle Negroes," employment opportunities ranged between peonage and the chain gang, as suggested by the following newspapers articles:

Black Wages

The Richmond Republic reports that a meeting of the farmers representing seven counties in Virginia, held to consider the question of the wages of negro labor, after due deliberation, fixed the hire of field hands at five dollars a month, the hand to clothe himself and pay his own in harvest was fixed upon. The Republic supposes this will fix the wages throughout Virginia and the south.

These wages for first class hands, subject to the usual contingencies of sickness and seasons, will prevent the liberty of the blacks from being made dangerous by riches. We suppose that if the blacks of the aforesaid counties should hold a meeting to deliberate on the subject of wages for labor, and should fix the rate without which they would not work, it would be regarded as proof that the negro would not work in a state of freedom, and that slavery was the only condition he is fit for.[19]

And on June 24, 1866, the New Orleans Daily Tribune's headlines reported

Chain Gang for Idle Negroes

Preparations have now been completed to have a chain-gang of the idle negroes found in Columbus (Ga.). All colored people, who have no visible means of support, are to have a ball and chain attached to them, and set to work at leveling the fortifications around the city, the city to feed them the while. It is the determination of both the civil and the military authorities that no idlers, who can only exist by pilfering and robbery, will be allowed to remain in the city, unless they can be put to work this morning.[20]

An early spring 1866 edition of the National Anti-Slavery Standard exposed a deeper well of hatred and anger which planters held for the Freedmen. By resolving to institutionalized a series of labor regulations or black codes, planters took steps to resume the same authority and control mechanism's that existed before the abolition of slavery. Refusing to relinquish any of their previous assumed authority, social control was refined to heighten a sense of terror in every aspect of the black laborer's life. Part of this plan, as discussed in a meeting of planters in Cumberland County, Virginia, was to implement wage scale regulations for all black laborers. Second, to regulate those civil rights that the Freedmen thought they were entitled to as a result of the thirteenth Amendment, such as the right of free movement, free choice of an employer and the ability to converse with other workers!

Appalled by the blatant civil as well as human rights abuses now being enacted, one writer commenting on the planter's plans began an article in the National Anti-Slavery Standard by emphasizing:

The mere publication of these proceedings, without a word of comment, would be sufficient for the intelligent reader, and were it not said by commenting upon them, we can thereby answer some of our contemporaries' outrageous falsehoods respecting colored laborers, we should not bear a single word to either prefer or append to this most infamous schedule of prices.[21]

Proceeding to the heart of the matter, the *Standard* reporter elaborated on how easily economic terrorism when *legislated* by anointed economic interest, transcends protective but fibrous barriers of civil and human rights. When this occurs, personal liberties are abridged, appropriated and eventually vanquished. In a meeting held on November 27, 1866, in a small Cumberland County courthouse, he reported on how easily nonlegislators but landowning heir apparent whites shaped public policy:

The meeting was for the purpose of adopting some regulations between the farmers and the negroes. The meeting adopted resolutions expressing kind feeling toward the Negroes, but asserting that up to this time, they had, too generally, been guilty of idleness, insubordination, vagrancy and theft. The following scale of prices for the ensuing year was adopted:

> For men, strictly No.1 in every respect, $6 per month.
> For next class, $50 per year.
> For ordinary men, $40 per year.
> For boys between fifteen and twenty, from $25 to $40 per year.
> For strictly No.1 house women, cooks or washers, $60 per year.
> For strictly No.2 house women, cooks or washers, $40 per year.
> For No. 3 house women and field hands, from $20 to $30 per year.
> For girls from fifteen to twenty, from $10 to $30 per year.
> For boys and girls under fifteen, food.

On half the annual pay is to be paid in July — the other half in January. The men will not be allowed to converse during working hours; they will not be allowed to raise stock or fowls for their own use; they will be charged with all the property, stock or fruit on the farm that may be lost or stolen; they will have 30 minutes for breakfast, and 45 minutes for dinner; they will be fined one dollar for quarreling, fighting, or willful disobedience.

The above may be taken as a fair specimen of the prevailing ideas of justice and fair dealing among many of the planters in different sections of our own and neighboring States. We presume this action of the planters in Cumberland county, to be one link in the solution of the all-absorbing question, "Will the negro work?" Should the Freedmen of said county find that, during the months of July and August, they have no clothes to wear, no money to pay doctor's bills, or to meet the thousand other incidental wants of their families, and should, in consequence thereof, express the slightest word of dissatisfaction or discontent, the self-appointed regulators of capital and labor will undoubtedly consider the great problem solved, and will exhibit to the world new and conclusive proof that the "Negroes are inclined to idleness, insubordination, vagrancy and theft."

The most infamous portion of the rules laid down for the government of the colored laborers, is that relating to their *personal liberty*. They are not allowed "to converse during working hours." Even the small enjoyment of enlivening the weary hours of toil with "small talk" is denied them, and their mouths are locked in silence. The birds chatter while building their nests; the industrious bee hums while storing his hive, and a republic of busy ants hold converse with each other while laying up their winter food, but a community of human beings, endowed with reason and intellect, must transform themselves into dumb oxen, and work. Again, they will not be allowed "to raise stock or fowls for their own use." Here we have "Shylock" with a vengeance. The planter, in substance, says, "your labor is mine, and I will exact all, even to the last quiver of a muscle." Again we see cropping out that same disposition to discourage industry and enterprise among the Freedmen. They must do nothing, be nothing, say nothing except what will profit their *masters*, alias employers. They are to be charged with everything "that may be stolen or lost." They will be "allowed 30 minutes for breakfast and 45 minutes for dinner." "They will be fined one dollar for each time that are impudent." These are the enactments of professedly Christian planters, in a civilized land in the nineteenth century.[22]

Oblivious to any charge of hypocrisy and unconcerned about the personal liberties of blacks, self-proclaimed "Christian planters in a civilized land" succumbed to an insatiable greed for economic gain and the requisite force needed to accomplish this end. The desire for control, even beyond that required for profit in itself became a form of intense psychic terrorism, causing many Freedmen to concluded that their life might have been better during enslavement than what now existed in freedom!

Mary Anderson's Testimony

Such was the reasoning for Mary Anderson, whose recollections of enslavement on a Wake County, North Carolina, plantation hinged primarily on a close working relationship, physical subservience, economic dependency and deference to the concerns of her owners. Mary's frame of reference, like millions of similarly enslaved blacks contained few personal rights beyond that which any white person might confer on her. In this regard, the abolition of slavery neither freed southern blacks like Mary from a feeling of benign benevolence, nor did it conferred on her a sense of empowerment. Instead, Mary's perceptions of freedom similar to thousands of other refugees were very much contingent on a previous adaptive social attitude of deference toward their ex-masters and whites in general. With this mind, the degree to which Mary's recollections are an accurate assessment of a lifelong traumatic experience that appeared to have resulted in her overidentification with the source of an oppressive lifestyle is crucial in understanding the cost some pay for survival.

> The war begun and there were stories of fights and freedom. The news went from plantation to plantation and while the slaves acted natural and some even more polite than usual, they prayed for freedom. Then one day I heard something that sounded like thunder and missus and master began to walk around and act queer. The grown slaves were whispering to each other. Sometimes they gathered in little gangs in the grove. Next day I heard it again, boom, boom, boom. I went and asked missus "is it going to rain?" She said, "Mary go to the ice house and bring me some pickles and preserves." I went and got them. She ate a little and gave me some. Then she said, "You run along and play." In a day or two everybody on the plantation seemed to be disturbed and master and missus were crying. Master ordered all the slaves to come to the house at nine o'clock. Nobody was working and slaves were saling over the grove in every direction. At nine o'clock all the slaves gathered at the great house and master and missus came out on the porch and stood side by side. You could hear a pin drop, everything was so quiet. The master said, "good morning," and missus said, "good morning, children." They were both crying. Then master said, "Men, women and children, you are free. You are no longer my slaves. The Yankees will soon be here"... I think slavery was a might good thing for mother, father, me and the other members of the family, and I cannot say anything but good for my old master and missus, but I can only speak for those whose conditions I have known during slavery and since. For myself and them, I will say again, slavery was a might good thing[23] [see Appendix E for more from Mary Anderson's oral history].

The psychic brutalizing of black labor was not lost on conservative whites, who quickly understood that any forced subservience of the black population not only curbed a challenge to their hegemony in the job market, but it also inhibited blacks' political growth. Accordingly, penalizing black workers for being impudent had as much to do with a continuation of southern etiquette as it did with chastising and penalizing a perceived subservient class. Given that context, while most blacks after the Civil War would have found it difficult to publicly utter Mary Anderson's sentiments, few had any illusions about the their actual social status. For example, in a grammatically flawed letter to the authorities of a Richmond and Manchester, Virginia, tobacco factory mechanics indicated that their wages had actually decreased after the Civil War:

Dear Sirs, we the tobacco mechanicks of this city and Manchester is worked to great disadvantages. In 1858 and 1859 our masters hired us to the Tobacconist at a prices ranging from $150 to $180. The Tobacconist furnished us lodging food and clothing. They gave us tasks to performe. All we made over this ask they payed us for. We worked faithful and they paid us faithful. They then gave us $2 to 2.50 cts, and we made double the amount we now make. The Tobacconist held a meeting, and resolved not give more than $1.50 cts per hundred, which is about one days work in a week we make 600 pounds apece with a stemer. The weeks work then at $1.50 amounts to $9 — the stemers about one half what we made when slaves. Now to Rent two small rooms we have to pay from $18 to 20. We see $4.50 cents or 5 will not more them pay Rent say nothing about food clothing medicin Doctor Bills. They say we will starve through laziness that is not so. But it is true we will starve at our present wages. They way we will steal we can say for ourselves we had rather work for our living. Give us a chance. We are compeled to work for them at low wages and pay high Rents and make $5 per week and sometimes less. And paying $18 or 20 per month rent. It is impossible to feed ourselves and family — starvation is Cirten unless a change is brought about.[24]

After the Civil War, economic tensions and conflict between the races was not limited to recalcitrant southern white workers or employers who feared blacks as economic competitors. Though southern whites were generally labeled by northerners as unforgiving racists and secessionists, many northerners were very cognizant that their albeit recent history of abolitionist fervor was comforted by the fact that Reconstruction's exigencies were hundreds if not over a thousand miles away. As such, northern racist sentiments were subsumed under financial investment concerns and not the daily confrontations between the vanquished slave and the reconstituted planter class. During this postbellum period, the notion that government sponsored social development programs for the Freedmen could occur with an emphasis on "political rights and functional economic program's ignored southern whites insistence for a separate and unequal existence" in spite of a growing and massive resistance by southern whites of various class backgrounds. Similarly, in spite of Republican efforts to ensure a determined growth among the ex-enslaved populace, "one may conclude that the grand design was incomplete assimilation which would enhance emotionalism and perpetuate a dangerous sub-culture" of Freedmen.[25] Moreover, another potentially explosive problem lay with white abolitionist woman who, witnessing the emancipation of the African, now sought full franchise for themselves.

Among those who now had to face the changing racial and political landscape were leading white female abolitionists, such as Elizabeth Cady Stanton and Susan B. Anthony.

I Sell the Shadow to Support the Substance.

SOJOURNER TRUTH.

Though both were outspoken supporters of Abraham Lincoln's wartime Emancipation Proclamation, they now became critical of Freedmen and Republicans who supported the Fourteenth Amendment to the Constitution in 1868 that gave black *men* and not women the vote. Both Stanton and Anthony argued that with the introduction of the word *male* into the Constitution, "the basis of representation therein shall be reduced in the proportion which the number of such male citizens shall bear to the whole number of male citizens twenty-one years of age in such State."[26]

Women were institutionally relegated to second-class citizenship if not sacrificed for the benefit of black male rights. More significantly they asserted that the concept of "universal rights" for all citizens was now abandoned.[27]

Sojourner Truth, another well-known abolitionist, ex-slave and in her own right an imposing articulate spokesperson for the Freedmen, defended the concept of political rights for black men at this time. Truth exhorted that the black women's struggle to survive in a racist society was a reality not necessarily understood by white women! She explained that the consolidation of the black family was a primary and critical issue, and that her experiences and those of countless thousands of black women were shaped by the fact that, "we came from another field — the country of the slave ... and in the field, washing is about as high as a colored women gets."[28] Her point was that the growth of the black family was contingent on many factors, and the implementation of the Fourteenth Amendment, albeit skewed toward males, was simply another forward step for all blacks, regardless of gender.

Responding to challenges by Stanton and Anthony, black newspaper publisher Charles Lenox Remond patronizingly proclaimed for his wife and sister all that he claimed for himself, and by deduction, refused to argue against the rights of women in his family![29] As the debate developed, Truth riled against the issue of racial economic disparities, yet let it be known that while she was not oblivious to the gender issue,

> I have done a great deal of work; as much as a man, but did not get as much pay. I used to work in the field and bind grain, keeping up with the cradler; but men doing no more, got twice as much pay; so with the German women. They work in the field and do as much work, but do not get the pay. We do as much, we eat as much, we want a much.[30]

Truth was not alone in trying explicate the relationship of civil rights, gender and equal pay. Three years earlier in 1866, a petition by the Colored Washerwomen of Jackson, Mississippi, to its mayor emphasized the same point. Announcing that this was the first collective action taken by the Black Women Workers of Mississippi, they wrote:

Mayor Barrows, Dear Sir:

  At a meeting of the colored Washerwomen of this city, on the evening of the 18th of June, the subject of raising the wages was considered, and owing to many circumstances, the following preamble and resolution were unanimously adopted:

  Whereas, under the influence of the present high prices of all the necessaries of life, and the attendant high rates of rent, while our wages remain very much reduced, we, the washerwomen of the city of Jackson, State of Mississippi, thinking it impossible to live uprightly and honestly in laboring for the present daily and monthly recompense, and

Opposite: "**I Sell the Shadow to Support the Substance**," 1864. GLADSTONE COLLECTION, LIBRARY OF CONGRESS PRINTS AND PHOTOGRAPHS DIVISION, WASHINGTON, D.C.

hoping to meet with the support of all good citizens, join in adopting unanimously the following resolution:

Be it resolved by the washerwomen of this city and county, that on and after the foregoing date, we join in charging a uniform rate for our labor, that rate being an advance over the original price by the month or day the statement of said price to be made public by printing the same, and any one belonging to the class of washerwomen, violating this, shall be liable to a fine *regulated by the class.*

We do not wish in the least to charge exorbitant prices, but desire to be able to live comfortably if possible from the fruits of our labor.

We present the matter to your honor, and hope you will not reject it as the condition of prices call on us to raise our wages. The prices charged are:

$1.50 per day for washing
$15.00 per month for family washing
$10.00 per month for single individuals

We ask you to consider the matter in our behalf, and should you deem it just and right, your sanction of the movement will be gratefully received.

Yours, very truly,
THE WASHERWOMEN OF JACKSON[31]

Apparently deciding not to directly attack an organized attempt by black women to petition for economic rights, Stanton in an astounding manner rebuked black men for being Unionist "apostles" of Republicans, who did not have their interests totally at heart! Though Stanton was most likely correct in this analysis, her patronizing attitude became problematic for many blacks. For example, at a meeting of the Equal Rights Association in Washington, DC, one year before the adoption of the Fourteenth Amendment, George T. Downing, a strong supporter of the amendment and leading citizen of Newport, Rhode Island, asked Stanton if she would oppose the enfranchisement of black men if women did not get the vote at the same time? Stanton responded that she would not trust the black man to make laws for her because "degraded oppressed himself, he would be more despotic with the governing power that ever our Saxon rulers are!"[32] Her preferences were that educated people must first be placed in power, for "this incoming tide of ignorance, poverty and vice" must not be empowered![33] Envisioning herself in a position to speak for millions of women, she claimed that without woman suffrage, only the "highest type of manhood" should vote and hold office.[34] Stanton obviously believed that the Freedmen lacked both the political experience and intelligence to govern over whites, nor did they possess a true understanding or appreciation of the franchise! Her statement also implied that educated whites somehow rise above racist attitudes and proclivities and therefore should be given the opportunity to govern.

Sentiments such as these, openly expressed and defiantly made in the press and during public forums by former white abolitionists, continually stigmatized blacks' ability to function effectively in a society dominated by whites! By the fall of 1868, Stanton felt confident enough to scold black men when she asserted:

If colored men had been as wide awake as women, instead of idly waiting for republican abolitionist, now melted into one apostle, Wendell Phillips (having announced his adhesion in last week's *Standard*), they would have had their Labor Unions, and their delegates to this "National Labor Congress." Such representative men as John L. Langston, Robert Purvis, and Frederick Douglass, would have been readily admitted, and would not only

Elizabeth Cady Stanton (seated) and Susan B. Anthony. LIBRARY OF CONGRESS PRINTS AND PHO-TOGRAPHS DIVISION, WASHINGTON, D.C.

"Colored Citizens Paying Their Respects to Marshal Frederick Douglass, in His Office at the City Hall" (Washington), in *Frank Leslie's Illustrated Newspaper*, April 7, 1877. LIBRARY OF CONGRESS PRINTS AND PHOTOGRAPHS DIVISION, WASHINGTON, D.C.

have dignified Their race, but by their learning, eloquence, and power have added to the ability and interest of the union. We urge the colored men of the nation to remember that "they who would be free themselves must strike the blow"; hence, if they are not represented in the next National Labor Congress to be held in Pittsburgh, Penn., August, 1869, it is their own fault. You see, friends, so soon as we women get a foothold among the "white males," instead of selfishly rejoicing in our own good fortune, forgetting all that are behind, we turn to help our colored brother up to the same platform. The world never hears us say, "this is the women's hour," for in the world of work, as in politics, we demand the equal recognition of the whole people.

One thing was clearly understood in the Convention — that the workingmen would no longer be led by the nose by politicians, as they proposed to have a People's party in '72. They feel that it is a matter of no consequence which party succeeds in the coming election, as their condition will be precisely the same in the success of either Grant or Seymour. As to all the talk about a country, with Grant we shall have peace, and with Seymour war, so long as neither party proposes Universal Suffrage, or a sound monetary system, it makes no difference to the masses which succeeds; or, whether they are made slaves by brute force or cunning legislation.[35]

At the 1869 Equal Rights Association meeting in Washington, DC, Stanton opined that the concept of universal suffrage was now such an "appalling question," that one wonders how this society could, "make their wives and mothers the political inferiors of unlettered and unwashed ditch-diggers, boot blacks, butchers, and barbers, fresh from the slave plantations of the south, and the effete civilizations of the old World?"[36] Stanton's apparent class biases, separate from her feminist advocacy, undoubtedly found some level of sympathy among southern and northern whites who regardless of their varying political affiliations or concerns about white women's equality, were more distressed about their possible economic and social displacement, as was Stanton by those who were "fresh from the slave plantations of the south."[37] While Stanton's opinions were not purposefully expressed to evoke an atmosphere of subliminal terrorism and intolerance, alleged ignorance of resulting terrorist implications, either purposeful or not, added to the country's growing racial divide.

However, some post–Civil War critics such as William Sylvis suggested that the problem of social equality extended far beyond the question of blacks or gender:

> Whatever our opinions may be as to immediate causes of the war, we can all agree that human slavery (property in man) was the first great cause; and from the day that the first gun was fired, it was my earnest hope that the war might not end until slavery ended it. No man in America rejoiced more than I at the downfall of Negro slavery. But when the shackles fell from the limbs of those four millions of blacks, it did not make them *free* men; it simply transferred them from one condition of slavery to another; it placed them upon the platform of the white working men, and made all slaves together. I do not mean that freeing the negro enslaved the white; I mean that we were slaves before; always have been, and that the abolition of the right of property in man added four millions of black slaves to the white slaves of the country. We are now all one family of slaves together, and the labor reform movement is a second emancipation proclamation.[38]

While sentiment in some quarters of both the black and white working class recognized that both races increasingly shared similar exigencies, there were also attendant reminders of an underlining class struggle within America's multiracial populace. Increased instances of social conflict illustrated that both race and class would function as definers of the American reality throughout the rest of the nineteenth century. Accordingly, a call for a second emancipation by some whites hinted at a growing belief among some sectors of the white working class that while enormous forces were now shaping the nation's postwar economy, it was the black workers who were the immediate threat! Accepting this analysis, one white worker even qualified the distinctions between black laborers and tradesmen:

> As a rule the Negro does not take kindly to steady labor. He can be made to work, it is true; but left to his own guidance, he would be content with little pay provided he was liable to illegible work. Give him his choice between a shilling an hour and a dollar a day, he would accept the former, and with great industry earn the first three or four shillings, then he would weary of his task, throw it up in disgust, and devote the balance of the day to lounging or to playing policy. To this statement there are, of course exceptions. Not a few Negroes labor zealously all day, doing a full white man's work, and we doubt not if more opportunity was afforded, the number of these Negroes would be found to increase. But after all, our general rate applies.[39]

Continuing on, the writer reasoned that when you are working with black tradesmen, one learns that

> Negroes sometimes make capital carpenters. Edward Latham in Chrystie street, is said to be an illustration of this statement. Colored blacksmiths are also found to be good workmen oftimes. As tailors, the Negroes are known to be comparatively skilful ... as

barbers, Negroes have a few equal among the Caucasians. As whitewashers, they "defy competition," while as caters they are inimitable. With equal chances, one half the male blacks in New York would rival Delmonicos or Martinez. Almost all the rich Negroes of the Metropolis have made their pile as caterers.[40]

Ironically, throughout much of this period it was the competency of black laborers in a number of occupations throughout the southern states that set the stage for an intense antiblack sentiment! Such was the case with black tailors in Charleston. Angered by low wages, one hundred black tailors and three whites bonded together in a strike to force salaries upward. At the time this labor action was reported in the *Charleston Daily Courier*, "not a stitch of work has been done in any of the shops in the city."[41] Following the example of black longshoremen who struck earlier in the year, they also hoped to gain financial and local support. However this was not forthcoming from Charleston's relatively large conservative black and white leadership as reported in a cynical *Courier* article:

Imitating the example set by the Longshoremen, the colored tailors have gotten up a strike for their own special benefit. Hurrah! we say. Let the colored workers being more white labor to this city by their exorbitant demands. The more white men come, the better for the prosperity of the community, and white men will come when they can get better wages and cheaper living here than in the North. There are always a number of such persons out of employment in all the Northern cities, who will be glad to get permanent employment at remunerative wages, while these colored men led on by demagogues are deluding themselves with the idea that they are a necessity to the community. No man is a necessity to any community. The greatest of all men die, and he is missed but for a moment; but of all men, the one who is least needed is a colored tailor. If he must strike for the purpose of asserting his independence, he can do so to his heart's content. The master tailors have only to publish the fact, and their places will be supplied by others, who do not feel that a strike is a necessary part of a freeman's or Freedmen's existence.

We are glad to know that the master tailors have taken the same view of the question. The prices which they now offer will pay a industrious and capable man from $25 to $30 a week — wages high enough to tempt the best Northern white labor. For these prices the colored tailors were unwilling to work up to a late hour last night. If they continue to refuse what is offered, the master tailors will send an agent North at once to engage and bring out thirty-five journeymen tailors, and the colored strikers, without any work at all may then practice their antics elsewhere.[42]

However, the above tensions between a skilled black labor force and recalcitrant whites was not necessarily the case in the liberal bastions of the north. In fact, a New York City 1867 survey of twenty-five selected occupations indicated that blacks were generally restricted from the merchant or manufacturing sectors of the most commercial ward of the city, the Eighth Ward. Those services which they were allowed to function in were designated service occupations. For instance, the data (table below) indicates that "waiters, cooks and caterers," followed closely by "laundresses" and "coachmen" were their dominant occupations. However this survey also indicates that if the number of "thieves (male and female)" and "prostitutes" were combined, they would constitute the third largest Negro occupation in that ward! With a relative paucity of black merchants, longshoremen and tailors, but an overabundance of blacks categorized as servants and whitewashers throughout the eighth, political, economic and social marginalizing of blacks in the city's most prosperous commercial ward was assured.[43]

Again, the specter of terrorism raised its ugly face in the paychecks and failed aspirations of a marginalized and socially castigated citizenry.

TABLE 4. ESTIMATED NUMBER OF NEGROES IN SELECTED OCCUPATIONS
IN NEW YORK CITY, 1867, BASED ON THE EIGHTH WARD

Occupations	Number
Schoolteachers (male and female)	50
Thieves (male and female)	250
Cartdrivers	50
Shoemakers	20
Barbers	60
Longshoremen	20
Writers, editors	10
Caterers	300
Saloon-keepers and employees (male and female)	90
Mechanics	30
Professional musicians	25
Merchants	2
Professional orators	6
Tailors	30
Laundresses	500
Prostitutes	200
Nurses	100
Waiters and cooks (public and private)	2,000
Whitewashers	400
Notary publics	2
Ministers	20
Doctors and druggists	20
Bootblacks and chimney sweeps	100
Coachmen	500
Fortune tellers	20

Source: *New York World*, March 16, 1867.

Attempts by blacks to function outside these occupational categories in cities such as New York were perceived by whites as an immediate challenge to an economic prerogative they assumed was theirs to dominate. Endeavors to broaden their professional aspirations into areas such as longshoremen, mercantile agents, doctors, druggists and carpenters were immediately countered by both violent and psychological resistance. Viewed as usurpers attempting to do "white men's work," those blacks who were able to secured professional employment did so at the lowest wages available. Within this social framework, it was generally agreed that blacks who somehow managed to succeed did so either because of their perniciousness as thieves or as a result of their God-given talent as whitewashers or barbers! Equally, those who failed did so due to innate indolence!

Such was the political climate of post–Civil War America where race for many whites was a major and necessary tool for social political exclusion. It explained away previous African enslavement while rationalizing their present economic subordination as an indispensable social truth. A reporter from Newberry, South Carolina, stressed this point when he characterized the economic battle between German immigrants and Freedmen as a contest between "Hans and Cuffee" when he wrote:

> The contest is pretty sharp between these two elements—the German and the Negro. Cuffee is afraid that Hans will make things uncomfortable for him, and therefore he opposes immigration. But Hans is a very imperious gentleman. Instead of fighting these things, and plunging into political hot water, he quietly and doggedly goes to work, and soon vindicates his superior claims.[44]

The writer then shrewdly posits any Freedmen's resistance to de facto racism as a prime example why immigrant whites must eventually develop their own "protective societies."[45] Predictably, social attitudes as expressed in the *Courier* simply indicated that after four years of war, the battle for one's economic and political racial place in society was not resolved: The attempt will occur with the enactment of stringent labor and social laws aimed at providing preferable access for social development to southern whites at the expense of the Freedmen.

Terror and the Black Codes

Once slavery was terminated by the Thirteenth Amendment to the Constitution and more significantly with the ending of the Civil War, a sharp competitive edge of societal racism and xenophobia surfaced not only throughout the southern agricultural belt but in northern urban centers that were being inundated by European immigrants. For the Freedmen, this problem was exacerbated by what many of them perceived was a southern confederacy that was militarily but not necessarily psychologically defeated who were also determined to ignore any discussion on economic compensation for the Freedmen or agree to a plebiscite to ascertain if the political desires of its noncitizen ex-slave population were being addressed.[46]

In 1870 two major political realities influenced the new post–Civil War battlefield. The first was a national census that indicated a little over 4 million people of African heritage lived within the United States, most of whom lived in the southern states. Their presence immediately raised questions for southern Democrats about this population's absorption into a post–plantation style southern economy. Second was Congress's adoption of the Fifteenth Amendment to the Constitution that at least on paper brought male Freedmen into the voting process as fully enfranchised individuals. Both of these events evoked violence and contention from southern whites who maintained that in the case of the amendment, its adoption was being forced on southern whites under military coercion and the Reconstruction Acts and that its implementation was unnecessary![47] In addition, an amazing editorial in the *Charleston Daily Courier* also purported that "the rights of all classes, irrespective of previous conditions, are secure, and everywhere acknowledged. All allegations to the contrary are more delusive utterances for the purpose of covering up the designs of centralization and power."[48] In essence, it took just a few years after the Civil War for the struggle over who would control an emerging population of 4 million Freedmen both economically and politically to escalate into an organized institutional violent struggle over power. The contentious nature of enumerated state rights versus assumed federal power particularly in the area of the Freedmen's civil rights was now at the center of the struggle. However, for many southern whites it was all very clear: "The proposed amendment is not the friend of liberty; it is its enemy: it can accomplish no other purpose than that of making Congress supreme over all States and people. If left to the voluntary and unbiased action of the American people, it would not stand the ghost of a chance."[49]

However the above two social factors were severely moderated by other demographic realities that indicated from 1840 to 1880, nearly 8 million Europeans immigrated to America, and this wave was simply the first wave of 2 million who arrived between 1880 and 1930.[50] While some of these migrants were industrial workers and skilled craftsmen, an overwhelming number were farm laborers who, possessing brute strength, found employment in mining, construction and manufacturing sectors of society. It was specifically these skills that placed their arrival in direct competition with the recently emancipated and now franchised African American laborers and craftsmen.

After the assassination of Abraham Lincoln on April 14, 1865, a newly installed President Andrew Johnson made several highly controversial decisions that had devastating repercussions on the nation's economy and the Negroes' place in post–Civil War America. A key element in Johnson's strategy was his May 29 Proclamation of Amnesty and Pardon that outlined terms for the "restoration" of all ex–Confederate States into the Union. This presidential order conferred amnesty on all ex–Confederate soldiers and sympathizers, with the exception of those who either held high office, had property in excess of $20,000 or who mistreated Union prisoners of war.[51] However, within a few months, even individuals such as Confederate terrorists and bushwhackers were pardoned. And while many Republicans viewed southern Democrats as traitors, not to mention directly responsible for the killing of over 600,000 soldiers and over a million wounded during the Civil War, Johnson maintained that these national crimes had to be pardoned if the country was to ever unite.[52]

Johnson's second proclamation (announced on the same day) established conditions for reorganizing the south. Under this scheme, former Confederate States would be allowed reentry into the Union once they officially recognized the abolition of slavery (Mississippi did not ratify the Thirteenth Amendment until February 1995), authorize nullification of the ordinance of secession and repudiate the Confederate debt.[53] To assist the "reconstruction" of the south, he selected seven southern conservatives in June and July to be provisional governors for North and South Carolina, Georgia, Florida, Alabama, Mississippi and Texas.[54]

By the spring of 1866, President Johnson's attempt at restoration was dramatically more pro-southern than what many northern Republicans could tolerate. More troubling however was his February 22, 1866, speech where within a year of Lincoln's assassination, he blind-sided Republican critics by accusing *them* of successfully conspiring to assassinate Abraham Lincoln! He then revealed his deeply felt southern sympathies by vetoing the Freedmen's Bureau Bill (Bureau of Refugees, Freedmen and Abandoned Lands) and the March 13 Civil Rights Bill that nullified the *Dred Scott* decision of 1857. These presidential decisions thereby decisively indicated his intentions to support southern whites whose interest would be directly threatened by any congressional acts supporting the Freedmen's enfranchisement. Johnson made it clear that he was very much a Tennessee conservative, who though often at odds with southern planters as a class, supported their traditional southern values on race and power.[55]

England's minister to the United States, Sir Frederick Bruce, an interested observer of the American south, noted in his report to his government that President Johnson not only ignored any serious role for Freedmen in American society, but that Johnson was convinced that their sudden emancipation by Lincoln was detrimental to blacks' best interest and if left to their own devices they would become "idle, thievish and dissipated."[56] More directly, the British minister claimed that Johnson was convinced that the ex-slave would be better served if they relied on the "interest" of southern planters (the same planter class that he personally abhorred) than on "ignorant Northern sentimentalist" and their "Radical majority in congress" who manipulated freed blacks as a device to "prolong their tenure of power."[57]

Despite his apparent conservative disposition and his beliefs in the utility of "natural laws," curiously President Johnson decided to investigate the tendency of ex–Confederate States to impose a series of labor restrictions on their black population.[58] He asked statesmen and journalist Carl Schurz to conduct a tour of southern states to assess this development. Traveling through Mississippi and Alabama, Schurz verified that indeed whites were imposing a number of economic and political regulations, know as black codes on their black population. Noting that these codes were imposed to clearly redirect the social and economic of southern blacks and curtail their participation in southern politics, he reported:

> That the Negro exists for the special object of raising cotton, rice, and sugar *for the whites,* and that it is illegitimate for him to indulge, like other people, in the pursuit of his own happiness in his own way. Although it is admitted that he has ceased to be the property of a master, ... it is indeed, not probable that a general attempt will be made to restore slavery in its old form ... but there are systems intermediate between slavery as it formerly existed, and free labor as it existed in the north, but more nearly related to the former than the latter, *the introduction of which will be attempted.*[59]

Though these outrageous slave-like codes were quite acceptable for most southern whites, it literally enraged blacks as an editorial in Georgia's *Macon Daily Telegraph* explained:

> There is such a radical difference in the mental and moral constitution of the white and the black race, that it would be impossible to secure order in a mixed community by the same legal sanction. A short confinement in jail as punishment for petty theft might deter a white man, but not a black. The stocks or hiring out for labor were the only punishments that could possibly keep the penitentiary from being inundated. To make policy on the basis of absurd theoretical notions of legal equality would be to abandon common sense and self-respect and administer our internal affairs on the fanatical notions of Thaddeus Stevens and Charles Summer.[60]

Emerging southern white legislation that supported these codes and restricted essential aspects of the federal Constitution from the black population also functioned as a criminal code that criminalized every aspect of a black persons life. In doing so, criminal and labor law was fashioned into one synonymous with racially prejudicial legal strategy. By definition the Freedman was suspect, a potential criminal. Under this rubric their ability to migrate was severely curtailed, while employment regulations resembled enslavement. Political and social activity if allowed had to comply with the dictates of the southern Democratic Party. The right to bear arms in all but a few cases was eliminated, the right to purchase or sell property or enter into contract was severely limited, and living areas were restricted by law.[61] With forced abjuration of their constitutional rights by multiple aspects of the black codes, particularly the right to bear arms in one's defense, those Freedmen who choose to obey such restrictions though living in a social environment replete with personal weaponry were themselves vulnerable to the brutal violent caprice of others. The following two reported incidents in the *Loyal Georgian* from Augusta underscore not only the vulnerable dangers of not defending oneself but the barrenness of liberal sympathy unsupported by force. In the first incident it was reported:

> We are informed that a most fiendish outrage was committed near Hamburg, South Carolina, one night last week by five *white* men, disguised with masks. They went to the house of Chandler Garrot, a *colored* man, and each violated the person of his wife, a *colored* woman. They then went to the shop of Wesley Brooks, a poor colored man, and robbed him of sixty dollars nearly all the money he possessed.
>
> Comment upon the conduct of these men is unnecessary. Why do not our city dailies mention some of the outrages committed daily and nightly by white men against Freedmen? If a freedman commits an offense against a *white* man it is immediately heralded, but when the Freedmen suffer, the world seldom bears of it. Christian men of Georgia and South Carolina we appeal to you, will you not help to put a stop to these outrages? For the sake of humanity help these poor creatures.[62]

The second article not only delineates what kind of personality formations can occur under sever oppressive psychological conditioning such as slavery or institutionalized racism but the insensitivity of those who alleged understanding and compassion:

> A most brutal outrage was committed in Warren county a few days since. Lewis and Green Rhodes—Freedmen—with their wives, were at work for Mr. John E. Spinks. After they had worked a month, some difficulty arose and Mr. Spinks gave one of the women a hundred lashes. The case was reported to Mr. Jones, Agent of the Freedman's Bureau at Crawfordsville, Taliaero county—but he failed to settle the difficulty. The parties returned to Warren County, and another difficulty arose. Mr. Spinks put a chain around the neck of each of the men and with a pad-lock fastened them to the floor; one in the smoke house and the other in the kitchen. They managed to break their chains, and with them yet around the neck commenced their escape. Mr. Spinks fired at them severely wounding one of the men. In the meantime he gave one of their wives another hundred lashes. They went to Crawfordsville, reporting the case to Mr. Jones; failing to receive justice from him, they upon the advice of Hon. A. H. Stevens came to this city. Such are the facts as reported to the officers of the Bureau in this city. The men when they arrived here had the chains around their necks, and the ball was yet in the body of the wounded man.
>
> Can any reasonable person wonder that "niggers" will not work, when they receive such treatment? Is it surprising that Freedmen dread to go into the Country to work, and lounge around our cities? We know that many stay in the cities who would rather live in the country because they are afraid. We call upon the good men of Georgia to help punish the villains who thus maltreat Freedmen.[63]

When southern whites felt threatened by the rising expectations of the Freedmen, all sorts of codes, regulations and formulations were devised to reinstate a sense of "mutual obligations and duties of the servant and master."[64] Published before the congressional elections of October and November 1865, state-supported black codes throughout the south were vilified by northern newspapermen such as Horace Greeley of the *New York Tribune*, yet praised by southern papers like the *Charleston Daily Courier*. Defining supporters of the codes as "disloyal men ... and unrepentant secessionists," Greeley viewed southern Democratic legislators as congressional assassins who with baited breath waited with "daggers in hand ready to strike down the goddess of Liberty."[65] The *Newark Daily Advertiser* stated clearly that the election of former Confederates to Congress such as Alexander H. Stephens simply demonstrated that throughout the south a "reptile spirit of secession is still alive and ready to display its fangs at any moment."[66] Recently installed conservative white legislators now characterized blacks as the south's ever present, dependent servant-like caste, the perennial nigger.

Reflecting on those circumstances that led to secessionist Stephens entry into Congress, DuBois pointed out that for four months Stephens was a prisoner of war at Fort Wagner. However once he was pardoned by President Johnson's liberal policies, Stephens waited not a moment too long to repent and return to Georgia. Applying for permission to enter public office in the very same country that just a few months earlier he tried to destroy, Stephens was quickly elected to the Senate by the same constituency who supported the Confederacy! DuBois also noted that the December 1865 Congress was so infamous that at its opening session, the former "Vice President of the Confederacy, four Confederate Generals, five Confederate Colonels, six Confederate Cabinet Officers, and fifty-eight Confederate Congressmen," were present to take seats as representatives, "none of whom was able to take the oath of allegiance."[67]

The succession of social-economic codes developed by planters and other business interests to restrict the black populace within the economic boundaries of a southern agricultural economy simply reflected as to the extent southern economic interest was willing to subvert federal law in order to dominate the land. Though many of these codes were not fully implemented, they fashioned an atmosphere of fear, apprehension and terror among blacks and whites that in fact wrecked any possibility of terminating 250 years of racial terror.

For example, after the Civil War the question of interstate black migration was problematic particularly in South Carolina where state restrictions regulated blacks immigration by declaring: "No person of color shall migrate into or reside in this State, unless within twenty days after his arrival within the same state, he shall enter a bond, with two freeholders assureties ... in a penalty of one thousand dollars, conditioned for his good behavior."[68]

Furthermore law and custom demanded that Freedmen "must be especially licensed" if they were to seek any employment outside of being a farmer or servant. Those licensed must prove their fitness, as well as pay an annual tax that ranged from $10 to $100. Under no circumstances could the black worker legally produce or sell liquor, and licenses for work were to be granted by a judge and were revocable upon any complaint. Violation of these restrictions resulted in a fine double the amount of the license, one-half of which went to the informer.[69]

Mississippi as the first of the southern states to establish black codes, and as one writer in the *New York Times* observed, did so by furnishing "a great deal of the propaganda material for northern liberals. First of all, Mississippi's legislature body was apparently dominated by 'narrow-minded men from the rural districts' who were determined to drive blacks back to the land and compel them to work in slave like conditions."[70] As such, these codes monitored the ex-slave population by proclaiming, every freedman, free Negro, and mulatto shall on the second Monday of January, one thousand eight hundred and sixty six, and annually thereafter, have a lawful home or employment, and shall have written evidence thereof ... from the mayor ... or from a member of the board of police ... which licenses may be revoked for cause at any time by the authority granting the same.[71]

In Louisiana, a 1865 law required all "agricultural" workers to have a contract in writing within the first ten days of January. In addition, each laborer after choosing an employer:

Shall not be allowed to leave his place of employment until the fulfillment of his contract, unless by consent on the part of the employer; and if they do so leave, without cause or permission, they shall forfeit all wages earned to the time of abandonment.

In the case of sickness of the laborer, wages for the time lost shall be deducted, and where the sickness is feigned for purposes of idleness, ... and also should refusal to work be continued beyond three days, the offender shall be reported to a justice of the peace, and shall be forced to labor on roads, levees, and other public works, without pay, until the offender consents to return to his labor.

When in health, the laborer shall work ten hours during the day in summer, and nine hours during the day in winter, unless otherwise stipulated in the labor contract; he shall obey all proper orders of his employer or his agent; take proper of his work mules, horses, oxen, stock; also of all agricultural implements; and employers shall have the right to make a reasonable deduction from the laborer's wages or injuries done to animals or agricultural implements committed to his care or for bad or negligent work. Bad work shall not be allowed.[72]

A more insidious nature of the codes was their fundamental social principle; southern whites had a God-given and political right to intrude in the personal lives of blacks. Therefore, continual efforts to solidify control of the ex-slaves' physical and psychic aspirations became a major preoccupation of southern Democrats, as when Louisiana's codes exhorted:

Failing to obey reasonable orders, neglect of duty and leaving home without permission, will be deemed disobedience; for all absences from home without leave, the laborer will be fined at the rate of two dollars per day; laborers shall not receive visitors during work hours; all difficulties arising between the employers and laborers, under this section, shall be settled, and all fines be imposed, by the former; if not satisfactory to the laborers, an appeal may be had to the nearest justice of the peace and two freeholders, citizens, one of said citizens to be selected by the employer and the other by the laborer.[73]

In South Carolina, the codes were simply a continuation of enslavement. As DuBois explained, "elaborate provisions were made for contracting colored *servants* for white *masters.*" In states such as Kentucky, Florida and Mississippi, written contracts by Freedmen had to be attested to by a white person and a judge to approve it. If the person stopped working, his wages for a year were to be forfeited. In Alabama,

when any laborer or servant having contracted as provided in the first section of this act, shall afterward to be found, before the termination of said contract, in the service of employment of another, that fact shall be *prima facie* evidence that such person is guilty of violation of this act, particularly if he fails and refuses to forthwith discharge the said laborer or servant, after being notified and informed of such former contract and empowerment.[74]

Masters were given the right to "moderately" whip servants under the age of eighteen, while others were to be whipped on authority of judicial officers. These officers were also given authority to return runaway servants to their masters. On the other hand, servants were given certain limited rights; their wages and period of service had to be specified in writing and they were supposedly protected from unauthorized attacks on their persons, inadequate food, and laboring Sundays and at night.[75] However, it is also important to note that emerging out of this, a significant aspect of the codes was the presumption that any employed black was automatically considered a servant and any white a master! The relationship between these two statuses, i.e., master and servant, as prescribed by law was accompanied by severe penalties and regulations for all who violated this arrangement.[76] In addition, those blacks who failed to acquire a written contract were committing not only a misdemeanor punishable by a fine of $5 to $50, but more significantly were jeopardizing an expectation that they would labor from sunup to sundown with set breaks for meals, and if beckoned come to the aid of their master in defense of his person, family or property![77]

Though the 1857 *Dred Scott* decision was rendered null and void by the March 1866 Civil Rights Act, most southern state laws were steeped in the spirit of Supreme Court Judge Roger B. Taney's majority opinion that essentially proclaimed that "Africans" had no presumption of rights that white Americans were constitutionally bound to respect.[78] Predictably, Mississippi legislators in the fall of 1865 adopted a provision that mimicked *Dred Scott* when they declared that

> Every civil officer shall, and every person may, arrest and carry back to his or her legal employer any freedman, free Negro, or mulatto who shall have quit the service of his or her employer before the expiration of his or her term of service without good cause; and said officer and person shall be entitled to receive for aforesaid the sum of five dollars, and ten cents per mile from the place or arrest to the place of delivery, and the same shall be paid by the employer and held as a set-off for so much against the wages of said deserting employee.[79]

In South Carolina, the law also stated that any white person, regardless of their status in life, witnessing a misdemeanor committed by a person of color

> may arrest the offender and take him before a magistrate, to be dealt with as the case may require. In case of a misdemeanor committed by a white person towards a person of color, any person may complain to a magistrate, who shall cause the offender to be arrested, and, according to the nature of the case, to be brought before himself, or be taken for trial in the district court.[80]

Though a preponderance of black legislators existed in South Carolina during the middle years of Reconstruction, the above provision pertaining to a "misdemeanor committed by a white person," while law, remained unenforceable. With the exception of Louisiana, this provision couldn't even be mentioned in any other southern state legislature without it being considered a self-imposed death sentence at the hands of regulators.[81] Mississippian law specifically stated that:

> where any white person has been arrested and brought to trial, by virtue of the provisions of the tenth section of the above recited act, in any court in this State, upon sufficient proof being made to the court or jury, upon the trial before said court, that any freedman,

free negro or mulatto has falsely and maliciously caused the arrest and trial of said white person or persons, the court shall render up a judgment against said freedman, free negro or mulatto for all cost of the case, and impose a fine not to exceed fifty dollars, and imprisonment in the county jail not to exceed twenty days; and for a failure of said freedman, free negro or mulatto to pay, or cause to be paid, all costs fines and jail fees, the sheriff of the county is hereby authorized and required, after ten days' public notice, to proceed to hire out at public outcry at the court-house of the county, said Freedmen, free negro or mulatto, for the shortest time to raise the amount necessary to discharge said freedman, free negro or mulatto from all cost, fines, and jail fees aforesaid.[82]

While controlling "Freedmen, free negroes, or mulattoes" became a southern priority of the black codes, it was also understood that

Any freedman, free negro, or mulatto committing riots, routs, trespasses, malicious mischief and cruel treatment to animals, seditious speeches, insulting gestures, language or acts, or assaults on any person, disturbance of the peace, exercising the functions of a minister of the gospel without a license from some regularly organized church, vending spirituous or intoxicating liquors, or committing any other misdemeanor, the punishment of which is not specifically provided for by law, shall, upon conviction thereof, in the county court, be fined not less than t en dollars, and not more than one hundred dollars, and may be imprisoned, at the discretion of the court, not exceeding thirty days.[83]

In Florida, "coloreds" and white persons never had to nor were they expected to function equally within the same social arena. Consequently, by law the races were "forbidden from intruding upon each other's public assemblies, religious or other, or public vehicle set apart for their exclusive use, under punishment of pillory or stripes, or both."[84] And though these regulations help establish an atmosphere for exploitation and social abuse, it was a series of vagrancy codes that personified the brutality of the postbellum American south. In this regard, Carl Schurz noted that

Wherever I go, the street, the shop, the house, the hotel, or the steamboat, I hear the people talk in such a way ass to indicate that they are yet unable To conceive of the Negro as possessing any rights at all. Men who are honorable in their dealing with their white neighbors, will cheat a Negro without feeling a single twinge of their honor. To kill a Negro, they do not deem murder; to debauch a Negro woman, they do not think fornication; to take the property away from a Negro, they do not consider robbery. The people boast that when they get Freedmen's affairs in their hands, to use their own expression, "the nigger will catch hell."

The reason of all this is simple and manifest. The whites esteem the blacks as property by natural right, and however much they admit that the individual relations of masters and slaves have been destroyed by the war and by the President's emancipation proclamation, they still have an ingrained feeling that the blacks at large belong to the whites at large.[85]

Corroborating Schurz's observations, one Freedman recollected:

There was a distinct tendency toward compulsion, toward reestablished slavery under another name. Negroes coming into Yorktown from regions of Virginia and thereabout, said that they had worked all year and received no pay and were driven off the first of January. The owners sold their crops and told them they had no further use for them and that they might go to the Yankees, or the slaveholders offered to take them back but refused to pay any wages. A few dollars a month and clothing and food. They were not willing to pay anything for work.[86]

Those Freedmen who could not secure work were immediately endangered by the peculiarities of the vagrancy code in states such as Virginia where it was avowed:

Any justice of the peace upon the complaint of any one of certain officers therein named, may issue his warrant for the apprehension of any person alleged to be a vagrant and cause such person to be apprehended and brought before him; and that if upon due examination said justice of the peace shall find that such person is a vagrant within the definition of vagrancy contained in said statute, he shall issue his warrant, directing such person to be employed for a term not exceeding three months, and by any constable of the county wherein the proceedings are had, be hired out for the best wages which can be procured, his wages to be applied to the support of himself and his family.[87]

For those Freedmen who absolutely refused to work under these conditions and choose instead to find another employer or even leave the county or state, Virginia law was un-equivocal:

That in case any vagrant so hired shall, during his term of service, run away from his employer without sufficient cause, he shall be apprehended on the warrant of a justice of the peace and returned to the custody of his employer, who shall then have one month in addition to the original term of hiring, and that the employer shall then have power, if authorized by a justice of the peace, to work such vagrant with ball and chain. The said statute specified the persons who shall be considered vagrants and liable to the penalties imposed by it. Among those declared to be vagrants are all persons who, not having the wherewith to support their families, live idly and without employment, and refuse to work for the usual and common wages given to other laborers in the like work in the place where they are.[88]

Implementing and enforcing the black codes required the establishment of special courts. In South Carolina, these courts employed a six-man segregated "petit jury" system. An appointed local white magistrate was charged "with the supervision of persons of color in his neighborhood, their protection, and the prevention of misconduct." To ensure that his will was enforced, a militia force of forty-five or more regiments was organized.[89] Unfortunately capital punishment in the violent world of postbellum South Carolina, capital punishment was not an option for "surly blacks," it was mandated.

For instance, capital punishment when mandated for blacks generally evolved directly from the social and economic environment in which they were forced to live. More often than not, capital punishment, legally instituted or otherwise, as in lynching, functioned for white South Carolinians as an instrument for the social control of surly blacks. Consequently, it was mandated for "colored persons" who were

Guilty of willful homicide, assault upon a white woman, impersonating her husband for carnal purposes, raising an insurrection, stealing a horse, a mule, or baled cotton, and house-breaking. For crimes not demanding death, Negroes might be confined at hard labor, whipped, or transported; but punishment more degrading than imprisonment shall not be imposed upon a white person for a crime not infamous.[90]

Though capital punishment was generally viewed as being solely a legitimate function of government, it was often systematically administered by southern states through their minions. This development, augmented by individuals, groups, clubs and terrorist gangs who functioned as part of an unofficial scheme to control blacks and Republicans by use of the rope and fagot, did succeed in creating a social atmosphere of fear and political anarchy. However it is here where the presence of terror, implied or explicit, can be assessed as a factor that not only shaped daily personal relationships between southerners of varying racial and class backgrounds, but accentuated the phenomena of *race watching*. That is to say, the imperative of predicting the personality, characteristics and actions of others in dominate and subordinate relationships was developed as a protective social function throughout America's institutionalized slave system. In the postbellum and Reconstruction era, race watching posited the notion that successful adaptation to one's environs was predicated on an ability to read, to understand, to even feel the intentions of others. Understandably after 250 years of slavery, race watching in the south became an art form for blacks as well as whites. Though it warned of surprised attack, it more often than not increased a sense of paranoia. Similarly, it forced the unprepared to quickly develop adaptive social personalities based on what they perceived were the characteristics of an attacker. However, race watching invariably revealed the depths of a shared personal and social fears between dominant and subordinate groups.

Brawley Gilmore of Spartanburg, South Carolina, dramatically alluded to this fact when he described how he recognized one night-riding terrorist from another:

> We lived in a log house during the Ku Klux days. Dey would watch you just like a chicken rooster watching fer a worm. At night, we was skeered to have a light. Dey would come around wid de "dough faces" and peer in de winders and open de do.' Iffen you didn't look out, dey would skeer you half to death. John good, a darkey blacksmith, used to shoe de horses fer de Ku Klux. He would mark de horse shoes with a bent nail or something like that; then atter a raid, he could go out in the road and see if a certain horse had been rode; so he began to tell on de Ku Klux. As soon as de Ku Klux found out dey was being give away, dey suspicioned John. Dey went to him and made him tell how he knew who dey was. Dey kept him in hiding, and when he told his tricks, dey killed him.[91]

Lynching as Scheduled Terror

Scheduled executions of "Freedmen, free Negroes or mulattoes," as opposed to a spontaneous lynching were never attended even in "the remotest South Carolinian county seat, by less than six or seven thousand people."[92] A major factor at these executions was their ritualistic procedures and the communal ecstatic reaction of a witnessing crowd. One eyewitness account of an official execution recalled that only after the condemned individual received a week of religious service was he then led to the gallows at an appointed time and day. Once within the arena-like atmosphere, the victim was again afforded prayers on the scaffold, which extracted groans of assent from the concourse who were now frenzied by the speech of the usually repentant and confessing criminal.

Hymns were then sung, giving the spectators a sense of participating in sacred drama; this was broken by the falling of the drop as the doomed person was launched into eternity. At this instant a piercing and universal shriek, followed by the wildest religious mania seizes on the crowd, they surge to and fro, sang, and "raise the holy dance." The scene was described by many as shocking above description.[93]

Often a portion of the crowd at these public executions were black, particularly if the victim was also black! This of course raises the question, why in the midst of racial hostility, brutality and murder would blacks attend a hanging when certainly emotions by armed whites could quickly result in an unscheduled lynching? This is possibly answered by understanding the level of social intimidation that existed at this time. Undoubtedly after a life of enslavement and now questionable freedom a number of Freedmen were compelled to attend these executions on demand by whites. For them, capital punishment by the mob was not an exception to the rule, but an ongoing expression of southern whites' control over their lives! Armed resistance by this segment of the black population was out of the question. For them, physical as well as psychological degradation existed as a tolerable price to pay for being black in a white man's world. Yet successful resistance certainly occurred within this violent context and though many must have willfully choose not to attend these demonstrations of white power, there existed an intense overpowering fearful expectation that willful rejection to attend a lynching might very well be interpreted as a form of resistance! The important factor being that the nexus of thought control laid with the desires of a white mob bent rather than with those who may have been racially akin to the victim.

Although "official" state-sponsored capital punishment existed as an ongoing illustration of institutionalized cruelty, the brutalizing of black people more often than not occurred as an "unofficial" event known as lynching. The significant difference between the two being that "unofficial" lynching usually occurred on the whim of a mob of irate whites who for a number of highly personalized reasons decided to murder blacks. It was the seeming arbitrariness of the act that invariably had negative affects on the psychic health of many southern blacks. Needless to say, indirect and direct state collaboration in this form of murder shaped tense social relationships between the races into bloody arenas of conflict, fear, competition, stress and anticipated brutality.[94] One southern white sociologist noted this period as being so violent that regions of the country could be labeled "that part of the United States lying below the Smith and Wesson Line."[95]

Recollections by an eighty-year-old ex-slave, Ryer Mom Emmanuel who was freed at the age of six but lived throughout the bloody contentious years of Reconstruction is indicative of an emotionally ponderous, sometime self-deprecating lifestyle that many Freedmen accommodated themselves to.

> My mammy, she was de housewoman to de big house, en she say dat she would always try to mind her business, en she never didn' get no whippin much. Yes, man, dey was might good to my mother, but dem other what never do right, dey would carry dem to de cow den en make dem strip of dey frock, bodies clean to de waist. Den dey would tie dem down to a log en paddle dem wid a board. When dey would whip de men, de boards would often times have nails in dem.
>
> Hear talk dey would wash dem wid dey blood. Dat first hide dey had, white folks would whip it off dem en den turn round en grease dem wid tallow en make dem work right on. Always would inflict de punishment at sunrise in de morning fore dey would go to work.
>
> Den de women, dey would force dem to drop dey body frock cross de shoulders so dey could get to de naked skin en would have a strap to whip dem wid. Wouldn' never use no

board on de women. Oh, dey would have de lot scatter bout full of dem what was sot get whip on a morning....

I don' know as de white folks would be meaning to kill any of dey niggers, but I hear talk dey would whip dem till dey would die some of de time en would bury dem in de night. Couldn' bury dem in de day cause dey wouldn' have time. When dey would be gwine to bury dem, I used to see de lights many a time en hear de people gwine along singin out yonder in dem woods just like dey was burying buzzards. Us would set down en watch dem gwine along many a night wid dese great big torches of fire. Oh, dey ould have a fat lightwood tourches. Dese her big hand splinters. Had to carry dem along to see how to walk en drive de wagon to haul de body, Yes, child, I been here long enough to see all dat in slavery time.[96]

The killing of a black person during Reconstruction as during slavery was not a traumatic event for most white Americans, particularly southerners, and only incurred the wrath of the law when it infringed on property rights laws held sacred by plantation owners. In countless documented instances, murdering a black person or persons was such a low priority that often a legal response was not required or desired. Their violent demise at the hand of others was considered to be a game in which neither the victim's humanity or a responsibility for committing their murder was an act worthy of prosecution. Only when blacks sought and successfully revenged a murder by attacking whites was there a legal issue to be resolved.

In this regard, Brawley Gilmore recalled that

When I was a boy on de "Gilmore Place," de Ku Klux would come along at night riding de niggers like dey was goats. Ye sir, dey had 'em down on all-fours a crawling, and dey would fbe on dere backs. Dey would carry de niggers to Turk Creek bridge and make dem set up on de banisters of de bridge; Den they would shoot 'em offen de banisters into de water. I 'clare dem was de awfulest days I ever is seed.

A darky name Sam Scaife drifted a hundred yards in de water down stream. His folks took and got him outen dat bloody water and buried him on de bank of de creek. De Ku Klux would not let many of de niggers take de dead bodies of de folks no whars. Dey just throwdd dem in a big hole right dar and pulled some dirt over dem. Fer weeks atter day, you could not go near dat place, kaise it stink so fer and bad. Sam's folk's dey throwed a lot of "Indian-head" rocks all over his grave, kaise is ws so shallah, and dem tocks kept de wild animals from a bothering Sam.

Another darkey, Eli McCollum, floated about three and a half miles down de creek. His folks went dare and took out and buried him on de banks of de stream right by de side of a Indian mound. You can see dat Indian mound to dis very day.

De Ku Klux and de niggers fit at New Hope Church. A big rock marks de spot today. De church, it done burnt down. De big rock sets about seven miles east of Lockheart on de road to Chester. De darkies killed some of de Ku Klux and dey teak dere dead and put dem in Pilgrims Church. Den day sot fire to dat church and it burnt everything up to da very bones of the whites folks. And ever since den, dat spot has been known as "burnt Pilgrim"—da darkies left most of de folks right dar fer de bussards and other wild things to eat up. Kaise den niggers had to git away from dar; and dey didn't have no time fer to fetch no word or nothing to no folks at home. Dey had a hiding place not far from "Brunt Pilgrim." A darkey name Austin Sanders, he was carring some victuals to his son. De Ku Klux cotch him and dey axed him what he was a gwine. He lowed dat he was setting some bait for coons. De Ku Klux took and shot him and left him lying right in de middle of de road wid a biscuit in his dead mouth.[97]

While criminal justice for blacks via the courts was rare, it was unheard of when it concerned the interest of whites. In his classical work, *Reconstruction,* DuBois remarked that in most states, blacks were allowed to testify in courts, however these were cases involving blacks. In some states, this privilege included testifying against accused whites as long as both parties agreed to this arrangement.[98] This however was not the case in Mississippi, where criminal or civil justice for blacks simply meant the conversion of Mississippi's slave codes into black codes:

> All penal and criminal laws now in force in this State, defining offenses, and prescribing the mode of punishment for crimes and misdemeanors committed by slave, free Negroes or mulattoes, be and the same are hereby reenacted, and declared to be in full force and effect, against Freedmen, free Negroes or mulattoes, except so far as t he mode and manner of trial and punishment have been charged or altered by law.[99]

Criminalizing Blackness

In Opelousas, Louisiana, 1865 ordinances made it extremely harsh for blacks to exercise basic human or civil rights. With the cotton economy reeling from the effects of four years of intense civil war and periodic drought, whites argued that if imposing a sense of terror was necessary to keep the Freedmen laborers in their place, then so be it. And if the key component in this process was to prohibit black laborers from migrating elsewhere, thereby forcing them to fulfill their appointed task, then everything including terror was justified. In this spirit, Opelousas's ordinances proclaimed:

(1) No Negro or freedman shall be allowed to come within the limits of Opelousas without special permission from his employer, specifying the object of his visit and the time necessary for the accomplishment of the same.

(2) No Negro or Freedmen [who] shall be found on the street of Opelousas after ten o'clock at night without a written pass or permit from his employer, shall be imprisoned and compelled to work five days on the public streets, or pay a fine of five dollars.

(3) No Negro or freedman shall be permitted to rent or keep a house within the limits of the town under any circumstances, and anyone thus offending shall be ejected, and compelled to find an employer or leave the town within twenty-five hours.

(4) No Negro or freedman shall reside within the limits of the town of Opelousas who is not in the regular service of some white person or former owner, who shall be held responsible for the conduct of said freedman.

(5) No Negro or freedman shall be permitted to preach, exhort, or otherwise declaim to congregations of colored people without a special permission from the mayor or President of the Board of Police, under the penalty of a fine of ten dollars or twenty days' work on the public streets.

(6) No freedman who is not in the military service shall be allowed to carry firearms, or any kind of weapons within the limits of the town of Opelousas without the special permission of his employer, in writing, and approved by the Mayor or President of the Board.

(7) Any freedman not residing in Opelousas, who shall be found within its Corporate limits after the hour of 3 o'clock, on Sunday, without a special permission from his

employer or the Mayor, shall be arrested and imprisoned and made to work two days on the public streets, or pay two dollars in lieu of said work.[100]

Eighty-five-year-old Lucinda Davis of Tulsa, Oklahoma, recalled that in her youth in Spartanburg, the Ku Klux would raid her little homestead and try to enforce similar codes by attempting to scare blacks into believing the existence of dead Confederate spirits. Recalling one spirit terrorist who proclaimed that he hadn't any water since he was killed at Manassas Junction during the early years of the Civil War, Davis remembered that

he asked for water and he just kept pourin' it in. Us think he sure must be a spirit to drink dat much water. *Course* he not drinkin' it, he pourin' it in a bag under he sheet. Mamma never did take up no trunk with spirits so she knowed it just a man. Dey tell us what dey gwine do iffen we don't all go back to us massas and us all agrees an den dey all disappear.

Den us move to New Prospect on de Pacolet River, on de Perry Clemmons place. Dat in de upper edge of de county and dat where de second swarm of de Ku Klux come out. Dey claim dey gwine kill everybody what am Republican, my daddy charge with bein' a leader amongst de niggers. He make speech and instruct de niggers how to vote for Grant's first election. De Ku Klux want to whip him and he have to sleep in a hollow log every night.

Dey's a old man name Uncle Bart what live about half mile from us. De Ku Klux come to us one night, but my daddy done hid. Den I hear say de gwine go kill old man Bart. I jump out de window and shortcut through dem woods and warn him. He get out de house in time and I save he life. De funny thing, I knowed all dem Ku Klux spite dey sheets and things. I knowed dey voices and dey saddle hosses.

Dey one white man name Irving Ramsey. Us play fiddle together lots of time. When de white boys dance dey always wants me to go to play for dey party. One day I say to dat boy, "I done knowed you last night." He say, "What you mean?" I say, "You one dem Ku Klux." He want to know how I know. I say, "Member when you do under the chestnut tree and say, "Whoa, Sont. Whoa, Sont, to your hoss?" He say, "Yes." And I laugh and say, "Well, I'se right up in dat tree." Dey all knowed I knowed de den, but I never told on dem. When dey seed I ain't gwine tell, dey never try to whip my daddy or kill Uncle Bart no more.[101]

Extrapolating lessons of survival from a harsh political environment, Lucinda Davis like many other blacks continually demonstrated levels of inner strength and resistance to what many whites hoped would be a wasted and ignoble life:

I ain't never been to school but I just picked up readin' With some my first money I ever earn buy me a old blue-back Webster. I carry dat book wherever I goes. When I plows down a row I stop at de end to rest and den I overlook de lesson. I 'member one de very first lessons was, "Evil communications corrupts good morals." I knowed de words "evil" and "good" and a white man explain the others. I been done use dat lesson all my life.[102]

The social and political distance between Davis and the political apparatus of the state that attempted to determine her lifestyle were vast and compelling. Daily intrusions of racial conflict and murder that invaded her psyche were distant, unimportant and impersonal for those who thought they could define empowerment and self esteem for the Freedmen. The Lucinda Davises of the south were not expected to be socially or politically responsible on any level, nor were they expected to extract any inner strength or political resistance from what many concluded was a marginal existence. However a closer exami-nation of racial violence throughout this era indeed indicates that Davis (like others) sus-pected that a war of attack and retaliation was on the horizon.

Violence between the newly enfranchised black and ex–Confederate soldiers and their sympathizers was so intense that within an eighteen-month period from January 1866 to June 1867, 197 murders and 548 cases of aggravated assaults were reported throughout South Carolina.[103] Within York County, South Carolina, from November 1870 to Septem-ber 1871 the Klan followed a weekly schedule when raiding the cabins of black homestead-ers. Though the exact number of blacks and whites killed during these forays is unknown, an estimated eleven murders were committed and more than six hundred cases of whip-pings, beating and other kinds of assaults were reported during this period.[104] Historian Albion Tourgee noted that racial hostility reached such levels of intensity that blacks and their white allies became prime candidates to be "shot, stabbed, hanged, drowned, muti-lated ... tortured beyond conception" thereby adding to the more than three thousand out-rages that had occurred within an interval of six months in 1867.[105] By 1871, a southern states convention declared that while 1500 to 1600 murders were committed in Georgia, through-out the eleven states of the defunct Confederacy, approximately 20,000 murders occurred during this period.[106] Armed white violence against an essentially unharmed black popu-lace was so prolific and apparently of little concern for President Johnson that one pro–John-son paper, the *Memphis Daily Appeal,* even opined, "If one had the power ... it would be a solemn duty for him to annihilate the race."[107]

Lawlessness and attempts at racial genocide against southern blacks was endemic and decisively cruel. It traumatized those who resisted with inadequate weapons and it degraded others who attempted to seek a compromise in the face of its onslaught. It turned daytime friendships into nightly enemies. White farmers who were displaced by the Reconstruc-tion Act of 1867 joined organizations such as the Ku Klux and forced their white tenants to attack black tenants, or themselves be brutalized. Black churches were burned while white-owned farmlands, barns and cotton gin houses were torched nightly in retaliation. Black women were assaulted and raped while men of both races periodically slept out in the woods rather than be surprised by night-riding raiders.[108] In this regard black-owned newspapers tended to be circumspect when reporting violent attacks possibly initiated by Freedmen, while conservative white papers were explicit in their detailing of Negro out-rages. For example, in an article related to incendiarism the black-owned and pro–Repub-lican *South Carolina Leader* published the following:

> Mr. Editor — A most destructive fire occurred here [Darlington, S.C.] on Sunday morning. It was discovered at daybreak in the store of Mr. Early. The buildings being of wood, the fire spread with great rapidity, and did not cease until more than thirty houses were destroyed, among which were eighteen stores, the Court-house, hotel and a number of residences. There was not engine, and the insufficient water rendered it impossible to check the progress of the flames. The efforts of the soldiers, especially those of the 30th Mass., could not have been surpassed. The office of the Darlington Era was burned. The press was lost, but the types saved. Different rumors are afloat as to the origin of the fire. It has been attributed by some to the carelessness of an intoxicated clerk, — Some say a colored man set the fire; others that the soldiers did it. Against the last supposition it may be urged that the gentleman on whose premises the fire originated was a favorite with he soldiers, and not at all obnoxious to them.[109]

TABLE 5. WHITE AND BLACK VIOLENCE IN TEXAS, 1865–1868

	White–Black	Black–White	White–White	Black–Black
Killing	499	15	241	48
Assault/battery and aggravated assault and battery	487	9	38	90
Whipping	126	—	—	—
Shooting	81	5	17	3
Assault: intent to kill	61	2	47	17
Assault	50	3	13	5
Threatening to kill	45	—	11	4
Robbery	29	1	6	2
Shooting at	28	1	5	5
Threatening to shoot	15	—	1	1
Stabbing	14	—	1	—
Driving from crop	11	—	—	—
Other*	78	6	46	14
TOTALS	1,524	42	426	189

*There were forty-eight cases where unknowns, Indians or Mexican Americans were involved. Texas population 1870: 818,579. Blacks: 253,475. Whites: 564,700.[114]

Source: "Criminal Offenses Committed in the State of Texas." Assistant Commissioner, Austin, vols. 11–13, Records of the Bureau of Freedmen, Refugees, and Abandoned Lands, Texas, Records Group 105 (National Archives); *The Vital Statistics of the United States,* Ninth Census (1870) (3 vols; Washington, D.C., 1872), 11,560,608. Table from Barry Crouch, "A Spirit of Lawlessness," in Nieman, p. 54.

However, in an article related to the murder of a Savannah, Georgia, "white boy" the southern pro–Democratic conservative *Courier* was unambiguous about who the guilty parties were:

> The white boy who so mysteriously disappeared the other day has been found today, murdered by the negroes near the city. His gun and clothes were gone, and it is supposed that he was murdered and robbed. The perpetrators of this foul deed are unknown. There is great excitement in the city. Parties have been out three days hunting the body, and frequently met armed bodies of negroes, who halted them.
>
> Parties are now out scouring the country in search of the murderers. Robberies and assaults on whites coming into the city by negroes are of hourly occurrence. The negroes in and around the city are thoroughly armed and organized.[110]

In Georgia, Florida, Alabama, Mississippi and Texas, violence was rampant. In Texas, the Secretary of State reported to the Senate that in his state alone, some "905 homicides had taken place in the two years ending in 1870, and he believed that if all the facts were known, the total would be 1500. In 1870, after the new State government was organized, it was officially reported that 2,970 persons were arrested and charged with murder, and two to even murders were often attributed to the same individual."[111] In addition, the 1870 census indicates that 253,475 blacks lived in Texas, however the annual death rate for blacks from white violence from 1865 to 1868 averaged 65.4 per 100,000. If one examined data pertaining only to black males whose population was 126, 278, the violence-specific death rate would be 131.5 per 100,000. By narrowing this violence to the fifteen to forty-nine years of age range the rate indicated is 290.4 deaths per 100,000 or 1 percent of the entire black male population who were killed during the early years of Reconstruction in Texas alone![112]

Many whites claimed that most of this violence occurred within the black communities, that is to say, it was black-on-black crime, and underscored this assumption with a parable claiming, "If a nigger kills a white man, that's murder. If a white man kills a nigger, that's justifiable homicide. If a nigger kills another nigger, that's one less nigger."[113] To the extent that assaults of any kind were accurately reported, the following figures are suggestive of criminal activity in post–Civil War Texas that was primarily aimed at the suppression of the black populace.

While the 1865 to 1868 statistics from Texas (top of page 145) suggest a limited number of black-on-white attacks in the area of killings, assaults and battery, it is interesting to note that the statistics do not reveal any instances of black-on-white whippings, threats to kill or shoot, stabbing or driving from tending their crops! Yet we read that resistance and retribution by blacks to white violence occurred throughout the south, though in the face of overwhelming odds.

In Guilford County, North Carolina, just two years after the war, on hearing the news that a black man was killed by his white employer, black citizens "organized themselves into a regular armed company" and marched to the employer's home. When the employer refused to come out, they fired volley after volley of gunfire into the house. Their actions so excited the white community that the *Greensboro Herald* warned that the Negroes seemed willing to "bring on a war of the races in earnest. Let the war commence, and in three months time, not a vestige of the African race will be found in the South."[115] Attempts by black federal soldiers from 1865 to 1868 to impose a semblance of law and order throughout the towns and countryside were met by violent resistance from white police, and a more violent guerrilla campaign began to emerge. Enraged whites who viewed black economic and political assertiveness as a threat to their own well-being quickly and correctly noted that their perceptions of the compliant, befuddled Freedmen was becoming day by day less a reality. Thus the following report in the *Wilmington Herald* complaining about the social attitudes of colored troops are not surprising:

> Two companies of the 40th Regiment United States Colored Troops [Regulars] Colonel Miles, commanding, arrived in this city on the Wilmington and Weldon Rail Road, Wednesday evening, *en route* for Charleston, where we learn they will be stationed. A portion of the regiment to which these troops belong, are stationed at the forts below this place, being the same which were landed from the steamer that went ashore on New Inlet Bar recently. The remaining portion we are informed, are at Morehead City. During the night before last and the forenoon of yesterday, straggling parties of the detachment passing through were strolling about the streets and committing depredations of a character calculated to annoy, disturb and injure the citizens. We are informed that several stores were entered by bands of these stragglers and bold robberies committed, in the very face of the owners. Abusive language accompanied these actions, and the owners of the goods thus stolen, on remonstrating with the soldiers on their action, where threatened with their lives. This, we suppose is but a foretaste of what we are to expect when military law assumes full sway.[116]

In November 1867, the *Greensboro Herald* reported that after a fight which resulted in the killing of a black man at a circus and menagerie in Greensboro,

> a large crowd of negroes rushed up and seized Curry [accused white murder], and were using him very roughly, and it is unknown what they would have done had it not been for

the timely interposition of our brave and fearless Marshall ... while the prisoner was being conveyed to jail, the negroes followed in large gangs clamoring for his life. Some two hundred formed in front of the court house armed with pistols, clubs, etc., and threatened to wrest the prisoner from the hands of the officers and put into execution their own version of the *Lynch law*,

but were persuaded to cease their demonstrations.[117]

Minimizing the murder of a black citizen as a grievous event, the *Herald* endeavored to bolster the white community's sense of control by asserting that "we think it high time that some precautionary measures should be adopted by the citizens," no doubt in keeping the blacks in their place.[118]

As noted earlier, while the term "lynch law" was generally an euphemism for mob rule that ended in the hanging death of one or more persons, it was rarely utilized by southern blacks as a means of retribution. Its most telling use was by southern whites as a means to not only terrorize entire segments of the black population, but placate many conservative whites sense of political and personal gloom. Social scientist William A. Sinclair described the relationship between mob rule and lynching as

mobs torture human being and roasted them alive without trial and in defiance of law and order; mobs shoot down women and children who have never been charged with a crime, and against whom there is no suspicion, — it is enough that they are Negroes. Mobs take possession of the streets of great cities and assault and shoot down innocent colored people, driving them from their homes and burning their property ... Mobs intercept and hold up the regularly constituted officers of the law, take prisoners for their possession and shoot them to death. Mobs break into jails and take out prisoners and hang them, sometimes in the jail yard, and riddle their bodies with bullets. Mobs even invade the sacred precincts of the courtroom, and during the actual process of the trial, take prisoners from the custody of the lawful authorities and shoot them in the very temple of justice, or hang them in the court-yard in the presence of judge, jury, and court officers, amid the shouts and cheers of hundreds, and, at times, thousands of people.[119]

Newspaper descriptions of a lynching in local and northern newspapers were not only indicative of low-intensity warfare between blacks and whites, but generally denoted a violent unrestrained intimidating context that southern black communities and hamlets lived under. However, periodically other indicators appear that suggested not all African Americans were threatened, beaten or killed into submission. For example, a July 4, 1871, article in the *New York Times* titled, "Outrage by Armed Negroes, One man killed and another two ladies wounded," describes the actions taken by armed blacks who undoubtedly prevented a lynching:

On Saturday last twenty-five armed negroes went to the plantation of Angus Red, in Barnwell County, South Carolina, about twelve miles below Augusta, on the Savannah river, and fired a volley into his residence, killing Thomas A. Lowe, and seriously wounded Red and his wife and mother. After disarming Red, the negroes returned to Paul T. Hammond's plantation, where the Deputy Sheriff tried to arrests them, but without success, as they refused to disarm. The negroes however, promised to go to Aiken and stand an investigation. One of the parties implicated was arrested here this evening. His version is that Red and Lowe attempted to chastise a negro for stealing from the premises of the former, but the negro escaped from them and returned with an armed band, who did the shooting by way of retaliation. The affair causes uneasiness and alarm. The negro arrested in this city says he is a school-teacher, and was on his way to Aiken to deliver himself up to the authorities.[120]

Note the writer's stylistic cues as to who is at fault in this incident. In doing so he placed blame upon the "Negroes" (in lowercase N) right to bear arms. In another incident, on July 1, 1871, the *Pontotoc Equal Rights* in Pontotoc, Mississippi, reported on a virtual shootout between Klansmen and the townfolk:

> On last Friday night, or rather Saturday morning, between twelve and one o'clock, the writer was awoke by his name being called and a knocking at his front door. It proved to be two of his friends, who informed him that there were between twenty five and thirty Ku Klux in town, that a few gentlemen had collected and intended to demand their surrender, and requested them to get up and go with them, which was immediately complied with. As we approached where the other gentlemen were standing, we heard about one hundred and fifty yards off on a back street the born and singular and indescribable sound made by the Klan, who were then coming in our direction.
>
> It was proposed, and agreed to, that Chancellor Pollard should demand their surrender. He handed his gun to one of the party, and advancing towards them, commanding that they should surrender. A pistol was discharged by one of the Klan, which fire was immediately returned by our party, when the Ku Klux turned and commenced a rapid retreat. They were headed off at a cross street when they again fired and were fired upon, this time one of them was unhorsed. He was found lying upon his back in a street which is the courthouse square, apparently dead. After removing his black mask it was discovered he was not dead, and gave his name as Richard Dillard. He was a white man living about eight miles from this place.
>
> A physician was sent for, who recommended his removal to some place where his wounds could be examined, and he was taken to a room on the lower floor of the jail.
>
> His disguise was taken off. It consisted of a blouse and pantaloons having a stripe of white about one inch broad running down all the way on each side, under these was his ordinary clothing. His hat was made of some white substance, high and round. After removing the rest of his clothing it was found that his shirt along the back was completely saturated with blood caused by six buckshot wounds. One in the back of the neck, near the shoulders; one in the hip, and four in the side. He positively declined giving the names of any of the Klan, said there were thirty in town, and that he fell where he was shot. He lived two or three hours, when death took place.
>
> We cannot commend too highly the chivalrous conduct to Judge Pollard and the rest of the gentlemen engaged, eight of whom in open fight and without shelter defeated thirty Ku Klux. Five horses and mules were captured-three of them wounded. A pistol was found, spurs, a saddle, and two pair of saddle-bags containing four everyday hats, besides some fifteen suits of disguises, hats, masks, etc., thrown away along their line of retreat for miles. From the number of horses without riders which a portion of the Klan was seen leading two or three miles from town, it is reasonably supposed that several others were killed and wounded.[121]

Sexual Terror: The Rape of Mrs. Roda Ann Childs

Black women were particularly vulnerable to murderous assaults and sexual abuse by night-riding Klansmen. Though accurate statistics on the number of rapes committed by night riders against black women is difficult to obtain, the following sparse table of reported violence against black women in Texas from 1865 to 1868 is indicative of an entrenched perverse attitudes aimed at blacks.

Table 6. Violence against Texas Black Women Committed by Whites, 1865–1868

	Incidents
Assault and battery	76
Aggravated assault and battery	48
Murder	15
Whipping	12
Assaulting and rape	9
Shooting and assaulting	9
Threatening to kill	6
Shooting at	3
Holding in slavery	2
Robbery	1
Cutting off ears	1
Abduction	1

Source: "Criminal Offenses Committed in State of Texas," Assistant Commissioner, Austin, vols. 11–13, Records of the Bureau of Freedmen, Refugees, and Abandoned Lands, Texas, Record Group 105 (National Archives). All tabulations by Barry A. Crouch, "A Spirit of Lawlessness," Nieman.

Despite a number of economic and political rationales that could be offered up to explain these kinds of attacks, deeper psychological impulses appear when examining testimony submitted to investigating agents of the Bureau of Freedmen, Refugees, and Abandoned Lands.

In early January 1866, Mrs. Roda Ann Childs, a field contract laborer in Spaulding County, Georgia, gave a sworn deposition to the Freedmen's Bureau detailing her brutal assault by Klansmen. She and her husband had retired for the evening when they were visited by night riders who they assumed were Klansmen. Fully aware of the impending danger to her husband rather than herself, Roda distracted the riders while her husband escaped from the rear of the cabin.

> They then seized me, and tied me, and took me some distance from the house, where they bucked me down across a log, stripped my clothes over my head, one of the men standing astride my neck, and beat me across my posterior, two men ho'ding my legs. In this manner I was beaten until they were tired. Then they turned me parallel with the lag, and one man placing his foot upon my neck, beat me again on my hip and thigh. Then I was thrown upon the ground and my breast, while two others took hold of my feet and stretched my limbs as far apart as they could while the man standing upon my breast applied the strap to my private parts until they were satisfied, and I was more dead than alive.
>
> Then a man supposed to be an ex-confederate soldier, as he was on crutches, fell upon me and ravished me. During the whipping, one of the men run his pistol into me, and said he had a great mind to pull the trigger, and swore they ought to shoot me, as my husband had been in the "god damned Yankee army," and swore they meant to kill every black son of a bitch they could find that had fought against them. They then went back to

the house, seized my two daughters, one 14 and the other 17 years old, and beat them, demanding their father's pistol, and upon failure to get that, they entered the house and took articles of clothing as suited their fancy and decamped. There were in this affair eight men, none of which could be recognized for certain.[122]

Not all visits on isolated rural homesteads ended in this manner, as many Klansmen quickly realized, particularly in Union and Newberry counties of South Carolina where they would learn that not all blacks were easy targets. Those Freedmen who chose to fight did so with an assurance that their numerical advantage was generally an asset, and failure to not resist meant being brutalized, forced into refuge in another state or death.

The Case of Miles Johnson

When interviewed by the congressional committee on Ku Klux Klan activity in South Carolina, Miles Johnson, a black laborer who lived in a rural community known as Leonidas, about fifteen miles from the village of Newberry, had vivid recollections about the events of June 18, 1871. On retiring for the evening, he heard a group of nightriders approach his neighbor's house. The riders demanded that his neighbor put his head out of the window, which he refused to do. Almost instinctively Johnson knew that there was trouble in the air.

Within a few minutes these riders, who Johnson now assumed were raiding Klansmen, reached his house. Still in his pajamas Johnson stationed himself on a table that stood in the room between the front and back door. A simultaneous assault was made upon both doors by the intruders, but being heavily barred it was impossible to push either of these doors in. Finally, they got an ax and after a few blows broke the front door to the cabin. Johnson now prepared to greet the intruders and was armed with a heavy Navy Colt revolver, but when the front door came down he immediately hid under a nearby table. One of the party then threw a lighted match into the room, and immediately two of the men entered, whereupon Johnson stood up, placed his pistol close to the head of one of them and fired. The man fell and in great confusion his companions dragged him out and he heard them say, "Hold up his head." Johnson then fired his second shot into the crowd of whites, which by now had come around to the back door. He wasn't sure what damage this shot caused, however the raiders returned fire, sending ricocheting lead throughout the house. Six balls fired into the front door splintered it and became lodged in the heavy wood. At this point, Johnson made a quick exit out of the rear door when the party left for the front one where the "Ku Kluxer was shot."[123] Staying overnight in the woods, Johnson returned to his home the next day and remained there until Monday night when he walked about thirty miles and took the cars for the state capital in Columbia.[124]

In another tragic attack, Abraham Chicks, a black preacher living in Goshen Hill township, located in the lower part of Union County, South Carolina, was kidnapped from his home by a gang of raiders who tortured Chicks by hanging him by his thumbs until he told them where Lewis Thompson, a black preacher, lived. After this brutal treatment the raiders proceeded to Thompson's home where they took him out "since which time nothing has been seen or heard of him."[125]

Throughout this period, newspapers' accounts contemplating an inevitable "war of the races" was debated by pundits on both sides of the political spectrum. One particular delegate at a Texas state convention in 1868 was so positive about an impending race war, he declared, when it did occur, "there would not be a black man left to tell the tale."[126] Bravado sentiments aside, in other regions of the south actions by groups of armed Freedmen were challenging enough to make traveling from one town or city to another problematic. By 1868 rising levels of highway robberies and more politically motivated assaults were occurring daily and although not necessarily suggestive of open warfare between the races, the possibility of a form of limited warfare between groups of white and blacks was no longer simply conjecture. In a Savannah (Georgia) *News and Herald* article the reporter discusses an incident, in an instructive manner for traveling whites, about a nearly violent confrontation between armed blacks and whites.

> Early yesterday morning a number of farmers, while on the Augusta road coming to town and about ten miles distant was hailed by one party of negroes some two hundred in number. The gentlemen did not rein up immediately, whereupon the Negro who had been walking up and down the road with a double-barreled gun on his shoulder assumed the position of a challenging sentinel and ordered them to halt. The part halted and demanded to know the cause. They were informed that the Negroes had orders to stop all persons passing along the road and make them contribute bread and whiskey , and if they didn't have the articles must give money, in order that they could be purchased. The party of gentlemen were well armed and refused to comply with the demands of the Negroes, and they seeing that the gentlemen were ready to defend themselves, let them pass on. They had not gone far before they came to a creek, the bridge over which had been taken up doubtless to cause wagons to stop, and then the owners could be assaulted and robbed at leisure. Our party repaired the bridge and came into town. But for their determination they would have been robbed and most probably, roughly handled.[127]

After describing the incident, the reporter then contemptuously suggested a racial remedy by postulating:

> It is supposed that these negroes were sent to repair it and not white men being there to control them, concluded to levy a contribution upon all passers-by. A sufficient force should be sent down to arrest all who can be recognized as being among them, and all caught should be severely dealt with. Nothing but speedy and severe punishment will teach the negroes that they must behave themselves.[128]

Carl Schurz, President Andrew Johnson's envoy to investigate conditions within the southern states, made yet another assessment of the coming race war by advising that a "Negro insurrection" was not probable

> as long as the Freedmen were assured of the direct protection of the national government. Whenever they are in trouble, they raise their eyes up to that power, and although they may suffer, yet as long that power is visibly present, they continue to hope. But when State authority in the south is fully restored, the Federal forces withdrawn, and the Freedmen's Bureau abolished, the colored man will find himself turned over to the mercies of those whom he does not trust. If then an attempt is made to strip him again of those rights which he justly thought he possessed, he will be apt to feel that he can hope for no redress unless he procure it himself. If ever the Negro is capable of rising, he will rise then. Men who never struck a blow for the purpose of gaining their liberty, when they were slaves, are apt to strike when their liberty once gained, they see it again in danger.
> However great the patience and submissiveness of the colored race may be, it cannot be

presumed that its active participation in a war against the very men with whom it again stands face to face, has remained entirely without influence upon its spirit.[129]

Not wanting to speculate on the outcome and or political implications of an insurrection by blacks and the responding efforts by the government to suppress it, Schurz admittedly agreed that "it would inflict terrible calamities upon both whites and blacks, and present to the world the spectacle of atrocities which ought to be foreign to civilized nations." Yet, he added, any conclusion that questioned whites' eventual dominance was unthinkable! In his view, "the Negro, in his ordinary state, is docile and good-natured" and only when disturbed will he become "engaged in a bloody business ... it is difficult to say how far his hot impulses would carry him."[130] As for southern whites, Schurz opined that one simply had to review their already contentious nature to understand the extent they would resist any insurrection by blacks. Out of necessity it would be a "war of extermination, revolting in its incidents, and with ruin and desolation in its train" for both races.[131]

A somewhat opposing view was pursued by jaded editors in newspapers such as the *Free Man's Press*, a Republican-oriented tabloid started three years after the Civil War in Austin, Texas. Wearily, the editors commented that continual talk about race wars, and claims of "Negro insurrection" had been overblown "harmless bugaboo's" of the old south for half a century. The real question, they maintained, was not an immediate or even possible insurrection by Freedmen, but "what is to become of the mixed bloods; to which side will they gravitate" in any bloody struggle for power?"[132] Whether the issue of "mixed bloods' was truly a significant political factor is debatable, however the continued existence of Republican institutions such as the Union Leagues and Freedmen Bureau in recalcitrant Democratic states such as Texas was an important issue for most southern whites.[133] Instinctively they realized that because these institutions were instructing blacks on the importance of being organized, disciplined and secretive, the interest of whites was being undermined. Conversely, these same traits when exemplified by the Ku Klux or similarly constituted organizations were understood to be necessary characteristics for political survival and development.

Rumblings of Resistance

In August 1868 the editors of the *Free Man's Press* concluded that in a free country, secretive organizations were not needed, and in fact were undesirable if individual liberty was sacrosanct. However, the editorial went on to surmise that if a society became so unlawful that basic human rights are systematically disrespected, ignored and circumvented by secret societies while civil laws were also abridged, it was then the right of "Union men to organize and join together."[134] This editorial also exclaimed that in a society saturated with all kinds of secret societies, one would be foolish not to look after their own interest! "We believe every patriotic man who is wrong[ed] to see the terrible and dangerous condition of our country, well acknowledge that the patriotic society known as the Union League is not only a necessity, but a blessing to the recently enfranchised colored men."[135]

Established in the north during early years of the Civil War and eventually southward after the war, the Union Leagues of America were an outgrowth of northern Republican intent to establish a series of political clubs throughout the black belt communities of the south. In South Carolina, some eighty-eight chapters were spread throughout the black communities.[136] As in other southern States, they rapidly became a network of radical Republican political clubs that were organized to challenge entrenched white terrorism and the Democratic Party's reluctance to accept the ex-slaves' inclusion and enfranchisement as citizens.

In a time when group affiliations among blacks were becoming increasingly important to their sense of self-esteem, local rural churches in alliance with Union League chapters generally acted as the connective tissue for community development. It bound local folk to organizations who in turn attempted to express and resolve those immediate crisis that individuals by themselves felt helpless to resolve. It gave those who were ex-slaves a sense of empowerment to overcome their present crisis. And though the leagues increasingly provided blacks with a psychological umbrella, their emergence began to rival the southern black church as a center for social activity.

Membership in the Union League of America was generally high by the black community, though it maintained the trapping of a secretive organization. However while advertisements in black-owned newspapers requesting Freedmen to join a variety of organizations suggested the emergence of strong community-based organizations that were separate and apart from the league. As early as 1866 it was common to see, as shown below, "special notices" columns in black newspapers advertising organizations who while not outwardly militant, were organized and most important had overlapping memberships with those groups who were armed.[137]

G. U. O. O. F.

FRATERNAL LODGE NO. 1064

Attend a regular Meeting of your Lodge on Tuesday,
April 3rd at 7 o'clock p.m.
By order of N.G. Eow-tf   A.J. Ransier, Secretary

ATTENTION COMPANY B

HOME GUARDS — Attend a regular meeting of your
company on Tuesday next at Bonum Hall.
By order JOHN BONUM, John C. Desverveys, O. S.

MUTUAL AID ASSOCIATION

A regular monthly meeting of your association will be held
on Monday evening, inst. 7 o'clock at Bonum Hall.
By order of President,
March 30, 1866   M. SIMONDS, Sec.

HAYDEN LODGE

NO. 8, A. F. M. — A regular communication of your lodge
will be held on Wednesday evening next, at half-past 7 o'clock.
Punctual attendance is particularly requested.
By order W.M.   M.J. SIMONDS

While elaborate organizational rituals and passwords were developed to keep their meetings free from spies, a major effort was made to help its most timid members feel secure within the league. Appealing to a sense of group (albeit racial) loyalty, allegiances were consummated through elaborate rituals and a multiplicity of officers with badges and sashes[138]:

These clubs also provided political banquets and barbecues, and arranged political processions that were most attractive to the Freedmen and annoying to the white Democrats. These activities involved wearing of sashes and badges, the building of floats, and the loud beating of drums. At a night parade in Holly Springs [Mississippi], the Negroes wore red oilcloth caps with red feathers, red sashes, and enormous red and blue badges. Torches and transparencies completed the equipment. At a barbecue in Lawrence county, the members of the League formed into a large procession and marched in double file around the court house and under a cross of blue cloth, bowing as they passed beneath it.[139]

Needless to say, efforts by Democrats and otherwise conservative whites to destroy the leagues were persistent and once the leadership of a local club was identified, there were attempts to either kill or drive them from the state. Furthermore demonstrations of this sort caused many whites to feel that time-honored social mores of blacks' deference toward them were being violated and as such, would eventually lead to a more violent interaction between the races. In fact, some historians have concluded that the Union Leagues were disliked more than the Freedmen's Bureau due to their clandestine meetings and mysterious initiation rites.[140] For sure, in the hostile social environment which was Reconstruction, any word that a growing number of organized blacks were able and willing to not only defend themselves but pursue political and economic goals by aggressive armed action, simply inflamed the imagination of an already frightened white populace. An example: A published description of a 1877 Union League meeting did little to relieve white Mississippians fear about blacks political designs:

It was in these secret meetings that the fabulous tales of forty acres and a mule originated, and confiscation ideas made some of the leading subjects for discussion. Lands were apportioned by imagination, and fine rebel mansions seized by hope. Gentlemen of African descent saw themselves rear back with all the pomp and dignity of princes in their old masters' carriages ... civil rights bills were to be passed by Congress, that would allow them to occupy front seats in white churches, sit at the same table with their former masters, and be respected with all the modern civilities in their parlor and drawing rooms.[141]

Whether the issue was their right to walk on sidewalks rather than being forced to the middle of the road, or one's use of the franchise, efforts to intimidate blacks into submission exploded in the streets, the fields and the legislative houses all throughout the south:

In black communities, both in the cities and in the countryside, men and women who had been slaves only two, three, and four years earlier reenacted some of the scenes of the American Revolution. Long lines of them, preceded by fife and drum and an American flag, marched to the polls to vote for delegates to new state governments and in Congress. Black men organized under the Republican party banner and the Union League.[142]

On election day in 1868 in Apling County, Georgia, out of a necessity to protect themselves from attack, approximately one hundred black men armed with rifles, pistols and clubs arrived at the county seat after a twelve mile walk to cast their votes for a Republican candidate. Without this show of arms, they never would have been allowed to approach the voting office to implement their newly acquired franchise.[143] Similarly, in Yazoo, Mississippi, racial oppression was so rampant that "it was hazardous for blacks to wear [Ulysses S.] Grant and Colifax buttons. And even when some where beaten and stripped of the buttons, they still insisted on wearing them at all costs, for failure to do so meant almost voluntary return to slavery."[144] Some women walked twenty or thirty miles into town to get a button and wear it openly, in defiance of their husbands' advice. In spite of this defiance, blacks in Yazoo were not allowed to walk on sidewalks, but only "in the middle of the street where other niggers go." For whites, this was a formality to be recognized and honored on every level when it came to blacks.[145]

Notwithstanding southern mores, The *Richmond Planet* reported many Mississippian blacks were no longer intimidated by or respectful of southern white etiquette, and on an increasing number of occasions, as in Utica, Mississippi, violently resisted what they considered to be odious restrictions:

> A terrible, tragedy occurred at Utica, Mississippi, Sunday 12th inst. It seems that a white man, named Beverly Robinson was escorting a white lady, and Bob Broom, colored was escorting some colored ladies. It was said that Robinson was forced from the side-walk.
>
> Later the white man accompanied by their friends attacked Broom, who was also accompanied by his friends. This colored party were prepared for them and fired, killing Dr. Holliday and wounding Frank Wallace and Armand white, all white. Of course it is claimed that the attack was sudden and no resistance was made by the whites. They ran as they would generally do if they received their just deserts oftener.
>
> Broom of course was found guilty and a band of 200 men took him out and hanged him in a cemetery yard. The other colored men escaped. It is this kind of dealing with southern Bourbons that will bring about a change.
>
> We must have martyrs and we place the name of the fearless Broom on that list.[146]

Racial violence on the streets of Utica, Mississippi, was symptomatic of the Freedmen's rejection of a world in which their personal esteem and self-fulfillment was continually threatened and when possible curtailed. Similarly demonstrations by Freedmen for parity either in the work place or in the public arena was immediately attacked and ridiculed while both privately and publicly condemnation of them as Americans was automatic and expected. For many Freedmen, Republicans and indigenous people few alternatives for an honorable lifestyle without armed resistance were available. This fact was highlighted in Robeson County, North Carolina, with the exploits of a racially diverse band of guerrilla fighters led by a Lumbee Indian, Henry Berry Lowrie.[147]

Well known for successful exploits in fighting Klansmen and federal troops alike from 1867 to 1874, Lowrie was often referred to as the Robin Hood of Robeson County.[148] Exhibiting a total disregard for reputed Klansmen, Democrats and white or black conservatives, Lowrie and his raiders dramatically challenged existing notions of white racial superiority by utilizing armed guerrilla attacks from bases deeply secured in North Carolina's dismal swamp region. His exploits are described in the next chapter.

5

Organized Resistance

They are distributing arms, Winchester rifles, all through the south now, and it is their intention to put a rifle into the hands of every white man who is a Democrat, and to carry the election in South Carolina in 1872 by the bullet and the dagger of the assassin.
— *The New National Era*, February 9, 1871

The Henry Berry Lowrie Raiders

Concerns by conservative whites about a coming race war in South Carolina were continually heightened by fears that the black population not only in South Carolina but throughout the south would eventually seek a more organized and forceful response to violent abuses being waging against them by organizations such as the Red Shirts, the Brotherhood, the Knights of the White Camellia, and the Innocents. This is exactly what occurred by the early 1870s when an armed anti–Klan force of Lumbee Indians, whites and blacks under the leadership of Henry Berry Lowrie banded together to wage a guerrilla war in Robeson County, North Carolina, against the Ku Klux Klan and its supporters.[1]

Portrayed in both the black and white newspapers as the son of a "full blooded Indian and a mulatto [black] woman," Lowrie and his companions were identified in newspapers from North Carolina to New York as a prime example of a spreading "reign of terror" that was sweeping throughout the south. A few newspaper accounts, however, depicted Lowrie and his fellow raiders as Robin Hood prototypes who after being harassed by hostile governing forces, sought refuge in an inaccessible area of the country, the Dismal Swamp area near Lumberton. Though the similarity between the English folk hero of Sherwood forest and an American bandit suggest more than a bit of reality, Lowrie and his band of guerrilla fighters were viewed by many blacks and Lumbees as upholders of justice during a period when extreme judicial and political violence appeared to rule the day.

During the early years of Reconstruction, rioting and murder of blacks by whites in cities such as Memphis and New Orleans in 1866, New Orleans and St. Landry, Louisiana, in 1868 and Camilla, Georgia, in 1868 undoubtedly convinced many southern blacks and certainly some indigenous groups that only by establishing an effective violent response to terrorist gangs such as the Klan could any semblance of order by established.[2] Ironically, the social context from which armed anti–Klan groups such as the Lowrie raiders emerged was not only the end result of compelling political analysis by disparate political entities who concluded that armed resistance to terrorism was possible but that any such resistance simply underscored the federal government's inability or lack of desire to do so. With this said, the emergence of Lowrie's raiders as an effective guerrilla force was a natural and direct response to centuries-long white racial privileges.

Birth of a Legend

Descriptions of Lowrie's personality are varied and mythical. One biographer described the muscular Lumbee and his fellow raiders as being courteous bandits, who were "restrained" while conducting highway robberies, even to the extent that if it was apparent that their victims could not afford a total loss of possessions, they then sought a negotiated settlement. Legend asserts that often receipts were given, thereby exempting their prey from any further robbery for a specified period of time.[3] Though his benevolent demeanor is suggestive of a cavalier nature, it in no manner diminished the violent context from which Lowrie and his fellow raiders emerged.

In 1909, another chronicler of nineteenth-century North Carolina history described Lowrie as a twenty-six-year-old who having a easy smile "generally playing over his countenance when quiet but when aroused [it] was a smile of a demon."[4] He was said to "wear a dark goatee, with his hair straight back and black *like* a Indian's. Being five feet ten inches high, and weighing about one hundred and fifty pounds, physically he was well knit, straight backed, with arms and shoulders fitting on a deep, broad chest not reflecting any flaw in his frame." In brief, the writer claimed "he was like an India rubber ball ... he was elastic all over." There is also the hint that "when he converses, he talks like an illiterate man, conversant with no books except of nature, and human nature," and that in his dress "he was rather careless and negligent. He generally wore calf-skin boots, a woolen frock coat or blouse, breeches or trousers of the same material, i.e., mostly Salem or Kentucky jeans, with a wide brimmed felt hat."[5]

A somewhat less Quixotic but still interesting description of Lowrie was that of "a coon hunter."[6] The *Lumberton Robesonian* gave its readers a glance of his "cool" countenance when it reported that

> We learn that on Monday morning last Mr. Oakley McNeill, residing near Scuffletown, in this county, was out before day coon hunting. About daylight his dog "treed," and Mr. McNeill was proceeding to the spot for the purpose of securing the game, when he heard some one walking through the darkness in the same direction. Supposing this person to be one of the outlaws Mr. McNeill, became alarmed and retired.
>
> Having occasion, soon after breakfast, to go to Moss Neck depot, Mr. McNeill was sitting on the platform at the depot conversing with one or two gentlemen who were present, when suddenly the notorious outlaw, Henry Berry Lowry, made his appearance, bearing in his hand a dead coon, which he presented to McNeill, saying that, as it was "treed" by his dog, the game rightfully belonged to him.
>
> The outlaw then asked Mr. McNeill to lend the dog to him for a short time, as he

wished to engage in the sport of coon hunting. Mr. McNeill declined to lend the dog, as he expected to use him himself for the same purpose, but informed the outlaw that he had another dog at home equally good for coons, which he thought would follow him, and which he would be willing to lend. After a little further conversation the outlaw bade Mr. McNeill and friend a good morning, and sauntered leisurely away.[7]

However, another contemporary of Lowrie described him in a manner more characteristic of one skilled in the art of guerrilla warfare:

In regard to his arms: a belt around his waist kept in place five six barreled revolvers-long shooters; from this belt a shoulder strap passes up and supports behind, slinging style, a Henry rifle, which carries the extraordinary number of sixteen cartridges. In addition to theses fifty-two charges, he carried a long blade knife and a double-barrelled shot gun, his whole equipment weighing not less than eighty pounds. His main object in thus equipping himself was doubtless to stand a long campaign, or to be ready with almost an arsenal at his command. With all his armor on he could run, swim, stand weeks of exposure in the swamps, walk day and night and take sleep by little snatches, which in a few days would tire out white or Negro. Being fond of blood he has waged for the past ten years a savage predatory warfare against the county, State, Confederate and United States authority.
    Without advantages other than nature gave him, without fear, without hope, defying society, he carried out his tactics in a peculiar way, impressing the whole population with his superiority, power and influence as a brigand leader and executive spirit.[8]

Born near Pembroke, North Carolina, Lowrie was of mixed Lumbee, African and Scottish ancestry. His great-grandfather was a major landholder and Methodist supporter of the Whigs during the American Revolution. This political stance placed him in immediate opposition to his Tory or loyalist neighbors, and led to some level of conflict throughout the war. Similarly, during Andrew Jackson's presidency, the Lowrie family had problems with the federal government as Jackson pursued a forced removal policy of native peoples from south-eastern states to western territories beyond the Mississippi River. Those who stayed or refused to move, such as the Lowrie family, found themselves with diminished social and civil rights that placed them barely above the status of the enslaved Africans.[9] As one historian put it, "Piecemeal they had lost their lands, their civil rights, and their social status. Now at last the line that separated the brown-skinned labor conscript from the black skinned negro slave must have seemed a subtle legal distinction indeed![10]

With the beginning of the Civil War, Confederate forces began to impress indigenous labor for the construction of forts around the mouth of the Cape Fear River complex in North Carolina. This decree was implemented due to a yellow fever epidemic that sent most poor white laborers and plantation owners fleeing inland or northward for higher and healthier ground. When it was suggested that the enslaved population as well as local indigenous population might be used for this work, planters complained that

(a) use of slaves in this manner would strip and already limited labor force from the production of needed food supplies from plantations if the south was going to fight an effective war with any chance of winning.

(b) exposing their property to this deadly diseases would be financial irresponsible.[11]

Eluding the Confederate governments' dragnet for conscripted labor, Lowrie joined a group of Lumbee runaways led by his older brother, William. Hiding in the vast Dismal

Swamp, these runaways were eventually viewed more seriously by Confederate forces as an unmanageable and seditious Lowrie band.[12]

Throughout the latter months of the Civil War, Lowrie's band of runaways began to demonstrate their effectiveness as an anti–Confederate guerrillas force that actively assisted escaping federal soldiers and officers from a nearby Rebel prison camp in Florence, South Carolina. In a short time, the guerrilla force had expanded enough to make armed attack against the local Confederate home guard. They became so effective that the region became a pro–Union enclave in North Carolina.[13] As one of the youngest members of the guerrilla band, Henry attracted attention to himself by first assassinating a Confederate postmaster who was also serving as a scout for the Home Guard, and then killing a conscription officer who had recently killed three of his first cousins.[14]

In the spring of 1865 with the war's end just a few months away, Lowrie's father, Allen Lowrie, and his two brothers, William and Sinclair, were captured, charged and tried by a Confederate military tribunal in Robeson County for stealing produce from a local farmer, Bob McKenzie. The items in question were hog meat that was previously placed in shocks of corn by a slave at McKenzie's home, and a bolt of cloth that McKenzie claimed was purchased in Wilmington. Convicted without the opportunity to testify in their own behalf, both Allen and his sons were sentenced to be shot.[15] Though apparently charges of thievery in a time of war was employed as the rational for conducting a "military tribunal," a more probable reason for this trial was the group's violation of conscription laws and suspected support for harboring Union soldiers.[16]

In any case, Sinclair was released and Allen and William Lowrie were led outside the courtroom in military fashion by the local Home Guard. They were forced to dig their own graves, stand in front of them and then were summarily shot. However, the graves were not dug wide or deep enough, so a local militiaman was told to "jump on top of the bodies to make them fit in the graves." Hiding about fifty yards away in nearby bushes, Henry observed this entire episode while the rest of the family was locked in McKenzie's smoke house. Returning later that night to his father and uncle's grave and with the vivid recollection of their murder and desecration just hours earlier by Confederate Home Guards, Henry swore that every person involved in this murder would come to the same fate. Though the bodies were later reburied in family plot, vengeance was utmost in Henry's mind.[17] The following morning, March 6, 1865, the bodies of William and Allen were dug up, washed and prepared for a traditional burial. The divide between tolerance and war had now disappeared.[18] From this moment on, the Lowrie band was no longer simply resisting conscription, they were now at war with the Confederacy.[19] In a series of daring attacks on the Robeson County courthouse in Lumberton, they were able to secure guns and ammunition that were used on raids against prosperous pro secessionist planters throughout the county.[20]

Six years later in October 1871, a *New York Times* article alerted the public with a brief description of a "North Carolinian outlaw" who had survived the Civil War and was successfully defying both state and federal attempts to curtail his attacks against the Ku Klux Klan supporters and conservative Republicans. The name Henry Berry Lowrie was fast becoming synonymous with armed resistance among the Lumbee people, African Americans, as well as some poor whites. Fascinated by the bravado and daringness of Lowrie's armed attacks against conservative Democrats, Klansmen, North Carolina's militia and federal troops, both northern and southern newspapers supplied the public with continuous updates and details of what was quickly becoming a war of resistance by Lumbees, African Americans and any sympathetic whites throughout North Carolina.

In a republished article from the *Washington Chronicle* in the *New York Times* titled "Lowrey and His Gang — The Authorities Defied — Pursuit by the Soldiers," resistance against the Klan and its supporters largely in Robeson County is described in simplistic terms that essentially criminalizes their actions as acts by a gang of outlaws.[21] Underscoring an ability of the "Lowrey gang" to defy capture by both state and federal troops for several years, the article ignored a central issues for the resistance: Lowrie's abhorrence for corrupt Republican officials and North Carolina's black codes! Readers are instead given a biographical description of Lowrie as a kind of colorful criminal, who was primarily motivated by a blood vendetta.

> During the war, in 1862, Allen Lowrey, said to be a full blooded Indian, residing in the little village of Scuffletown, and a son of his were murdered by confederate troops, the charge being that of harboring rebel deserters and Federal soldiers.
>
> Lowrey's wife was a bright mulatto woman, by whom he had eight sons. One of these, *Henry Berry Lowrey*, though but fifteen years of age when his father was shot, swore he would avenge the death of parent and brother. Henry was charged soon after with killing a man named Barnes, for which he was tried and sentenced to be hanged. He broke out of jail, but was subsequently arrested and lodged in irons in the prison at Whitesville, Columbus County. From this he effected his escape also and fled to the woods, where he has remained till the present day.
>
> A year after the surrender a party of disguised men killed Sheriff King of Lumberton, and robbed him of a large sum of money. Lowrey and several former associates were suspected of the crime. Some of those suspected were caught and hung by a mob; others fled to the woods and joined Lowrey to avoid punishment. The band now consists of Henry Berry Lowry the leader; Stephen L Lowrey, Thomas Lowrey, Boss Strong, Andrew Strong, and George Applewhite and two or three others.
>
> Several efforts have been made to capture them, but have proved ineffectual. A number of persons engaged in hunting the outlaws have been shot, and a terrible state of affairs exist in the county because of their depredations. In the spring of last year a company of militia surrounded the gang near Scuffletown, and found all of them drunk but Lowrey and Applewhite. The company fired upon them, and Applewhite was wounded and fell. Lowrey roused his men, returned the fire with his right arm, and bore Applewhite, the wounded man, off on his left, and they all escaped.
>
> Lowrey, it is said, wears a belt with several knives and pistols, carries a double-barrel gun on each side, and a carbine that shoots sixteen balls, in his hand. His men are all armed well, and provided with a supply of ammunition.
>
> Scuffletown is an old settlement of Indians and free Negroes. The population of ten square miles exceeds 4,000 people. It is thought that many of the residents are in sympathy with the outlaws, and lend them assistance and provide food and ammunition. The majority of these people, however, it is stated are as anxious to effect the capture of these desperadoes as the community generally can be.
>
> Last summer the authorities of Robeson County, suspecting that the relatives of the gang were harboring them, and knew of their whereabouts, proceeded to Lumberton. On the way the outlaws fired upon the Sheriff's posse, killing three and wounding another severely. Failing to effect the release of his family, Lowrey sent a message to Lumberton, stating that he would give the Sheriff till ten o'clock the following day to release them, and if this was not done he would drench the county in blood. The order was obeyed by the authorities, and the women and children returned to Scuffletown.

The next outrage committed by Lowrey was the murder of Mr. Lucas, a few days ago. The band has perpetrated several depredations of late, and damn and defy the authorities. These desperadoes are determined never to be taken alive by the authorities. Lowrey, it is said, swears he will spill his blood near or upon the spot his father shed his own. They prowl about the country, often in open day, and prey upon the people. Many citizens of Robeson have seen and conversed with Lowrey and other members of his gang, and demanded a breakfast, dinner or supper, and the demand is generally granted. Lowrey says all he asks is to be let alone — he knows he will be shot or hung if caught — and he will harm no one that does not harm him or his associates.

Members of both political parties are active in lending the authorities assistance to capture the band. Adjt. Gen. Gorman, of this State, is now in Robeson, County, and has a detachment of United States soldiers, with a company of militia, engaged in hunting the gang. It is hardly probably that they can be captured until winter, and then not until they are frozen, starved, or driven out of that section of the country.[22]

Attempts by the local sheriff or county militia could neither abate attacks by Lowrie's raiders nor effectively keep him or his compatriots in jail once captured. A noted example of this occurred years earlier during Lowrie's marriage ceremony to Rhoda Strong on December 17, 1865. In the presence of several hundred wedding guests, Lowrie was arrested by former members of the Confederate Home Guard who eight months after the Civil War were reconstituted as the county militia! Accused with killing James Barnes who once served as a scout for the Confederate militia, Lowrie was taken to and jailed in Whiteville, North Carolina, where in a short period of time friends were able to smuggle in a file that allowed him to escape. Conservative Republican governor Jonathan Worth was so enraged when he learned of Lowrie's escape that he offered a $300 reward for his capture, dead or alive.[23]

Faced with an ever growing anger by local whites, particularly those associated with the militia, Lowrie and his compatriots concluded that they either had to surrender to the local authorities and negotiate a reconciliation or resume resistance activities that were perfected during the war. They choose the latter.

Northern newspaper accounts reporting on the phenomena of armed Negro, Quadroon and Indian resistance in North Carolina generally highlighted the outlaw aspects of anti–Klan attacks. North Carolinian newspapers on the other hand tended to discuss the Lowrie gang success from a trickery perspective, rather than emphasizing the guerrilla's apparent military skill. In addition, many northerners were troubled by Lowrie's successful resistance occurring at a time when congressional investigations into Ku Klux Klan outrages throughout South Carolina, Georgia and North Carolina were also convening! In fact, newspaper accounts describing violent attacks against blacks and Republicans by groups similar in philosophy with the Ku Klux also vied for newspaper space with articles depicting the war against native tribes in western plains.[24] And while both conservative Republican and Democratic pragmatist concluded these accounts of resistance to either Klan terrorism or the Indian wars needed to be closely monitored, an important issue to resolve was which form of resistance to white hegemony and authority was least tolerable?

For most southern white Americans the issue was unquestionably clear. By characterizing southern blacks and Native Americans as outlaws and bandits the issue of political control was simplified to a workable axiom: open resistance to white American hegemony was indisputable evidence of lawlessness, sedition, and criminal intent or behavior. As a consequence, any propagation of defensive violence against the state or its designated officials justified in the minds of southern conservative elements the need to regulate these unstable social elements by any means necessary.[25] Similarly, punitive measures by extralegal organizations such as the Ku Klux, the Knights of the White Camellia, and the Brotherhood, no matter how disagreeable or criminal, were viewed just as necessary in the south as the U.S. Cavalry's pacification efforts were in the western plains. In this regard, Missouri's Democratic party leader Frank Blair and candidate for vice president on the Horatio Seymour ticket in 1868 expressed the sentiments of many when on a campaign tour he stated that whites should be allowed to reorganize the government, eliminate the Reconstruction Act of 1867, and rid themselves of "a semi barbarous race of blacks who are worshippers of fetishes, and polygamists," who if given the opportunity would "subject the white women to their unbridled lust."[26] Though his statement was later condemned by Republicans as treason, Blair undoubtedly felt neither threatened nor uncomfortable in expressing these sentiments among his colleagues.

However, for federal troops and North Carolina's state militia, Lowrie's raiders could not be rationalized away with vehement proclamations or rousing politically inspired campaigns as one lengthy article in the November 1, 1871, *New York Times* explained:

Matters at last reached such a pass that Gov. Caldwell ordered out the militia of the county, supplied them with arms and ammunition, and put them on a war footing, under command of Adjutant-General Gorman, of the State forces. A large number of United States troops then in North Carolina for the suppression of the Ku Klux Klan outrages, the Governor applied for two companies to aid in the capture of Lowrey and his band. These were furnished, and on or about the 1st of August last [1871] the united commands were moved into Robeson County, fully determined either to make prisoners of the famous outlaws or to exterminate them.

During the past three months, the exploits of the Lowreys are declared to have been more imprudent and numerous than ever. One day Lowrey appeared alone in a bateau [flat-bottom row boat used in low-swamp water areas] in Lumber River, and rowed directly into the presence of a detachment of United States troops, who were encamped on the bank. The soldiers began to fire upon him, but Lowrey promptly laid down in the boat in such a manner as to careen her over, and present her bottom to his foes; and thus protected deliberately paddled himself out of danger.

On another occasion, this audacious ruffian who seems to have a quite a humorous turn, actually made his solitary way into a militia camp by night, cut his name on the stock of a musket, and left a complimentary note for Gen. Gorman, to the effect that his, i.e., Lowrey's inspection of the camp had been most satisfactory, and that the discipline was excellent.

Still another time he met a squad of troops directly in the high-road. They happened, by some mischance, to be unarmed, and the bandit was bristling with revolvers. He looked them coolly in the face, and walked off, unmolested, into the woods ...

Robeson County, North Carolina has for some time been the scene of a remarkable drama. A gang of brigands, whose lair is in the midst of almost impassable swamps, have for years carried on their depredations, and laughed at all attempts to arrest them. It is said that they have committed no fewer than twenty-five murders, besides other crimes, apart from their ordinary profession of robbery. Many expeditions have been formed for their capture, but they have ended, in each case, with humiliating failure. Of course there are reasons for this singular state of things.

In the first place the men are halfbreeds, or rather from descriptions, we should say quadroons, and are connected by blood and sympathy with most of the population that immediately surrounds them.

Again, the nature of the country favors their lawless proceedings in an extraordinary manner. Their retreat lies among swamps and islands, and to penetrate either even for a friendly purpose would be extremely difficult. It is said, too, that all preparations for their capture by officers of the law or soldiers have been speedily telegraphed to the bandits by signals known only to the initiated. To this is attributed the invariable defeat of every attempt to surprise them.

Even these exploits, dazzling as they may seem, have since been outdone. We are now informed, on the authority of the North Carolina Press, and subsequently on that of Gen. Gorman, that Lowrey sent a letter to Gorman proposing a flag of truce and a personal interview. For reasons that were satisfactory to himself. The General assented; and the strange spectacle was presented of an officer in command of United States troops holding parley with a murderer and a thief, and taking into consideration, if he did not agree to terms of amicable composition...[27] [see Appendix F for the continuation of this article].

The *Times* article observed that "Accounts of what has happened since are rather conflicting. One authority declared that the military have been withdrawn, and another that the Lowrey party are supposed to have eluded their vigilance and fled from the State."

While the *Times* account of Lowrie's raiders placed an emphasis on the outlaw's shrewdness, later that October 1871, North Carolina's largest daily newspaper, *The Morning Star,* published a letter General Gorman sent to his superior that explained in an even less magnanimous manner why his military campaign against Lowrie's guerrillas was a total failure.

Our operations against the outlaws were rather after the manner of hunting deer. the soldiers and citizens were mixed in small detachments and sent in the swamps and pine fields in those areas more frequented by the banditti, and especially in the vicinity of the house of the wives of the outlaws, four of whom are married, and two of whom have children.

In the meantime when Col. Wishart and myself used every means in our power to obtain definite information concerning the haunts and whereabouts, and acted promptly on the meager information we were able to obtain. We succeeded in gaining the promise from several parties to give us information, and the only times we came anywhere near running upon the outlaws was by this means. But we quickly saw out force as inadequate in numbers. It was impossible for all to leave camp at once, and the various places which should have been watched were to numerous for the small force we had at our command. Only about twenty volunteers responded to the call, and of that number only two or three were sufficiently acquainted with the outlaws to know them when they saw them, and I was in constant dread that some innocent individual would be shot in the swamps who supposedly belong to the gang ...

After one trial in the swamps with this detailed militia, I became convinced that they were utterly useless for the purpose. They were given three days rations, and sent out under proper guides to certain points but on arriving at the designated points either made [look-out] for the outlaws, or [made] so much noise that their whereabouts, if the hunted were in the vicinity, were made aware of the fact, and hence could easily evade them. Many of them also, after staying not only one night, quite their comrades and either returned to camp or proceeded immediately home. Some of the militia were also placed with portions of the troops whose duty it was to drive certain swamps and bays where at was probable the outlaws were hiding, but after getting out of sight of the troops in the evergreens, quietly sat down, and let the balance of the command move on, and then returned to camp and reported that they "got lost" from the rest. After this attempt, I despaired of the utility of the militia, [and] readily assented to their wish to return home to their wives in the perils of child birth, sick children and untended crops. There were a few exceptions to this general incompetence, but all promptly deserted us when permission was granted....

After this I determined to attempt the capture of the outlaws with the available force I had of volunteers and troops, and trust to fortune and some good opportunity to lead the gang into our clutches, although I knew that it would be almost an accident if such an event happened, unless they were betrayed by some of their class, an event Col. Wishart and myself endeavored to produce.

The U.S. troops were as efficient as it was possible for them to be and Col. Mendenhall, Lieut's Humphires and Harris seemed as anxious to effect his [Lowrey's] capture as any of the volunteer force, and used every means suggested by us to that end. Many of the volunteers however became disheartened at the want of cooperation on the part of the citizens, and gradually abandoned the enterprise. Until during the fifth week, only seven men, including Col. Wishart and McLean, remained with us. When this occurred the troops and their commander became disheartened and was convinced that with only that number of volunteers, hardly sufficient to act as guides, their efforts were fruitless, and wouldn't continue [on]. Having been sent there only when cooperation was [received] by the citizens, I reported the state of affairs to the commanding office of the department, who ordered their recall, and thus ended the campaign[28] [see Appendix G for the preceding paragraphs of Gorman's letter].

In February 1872, Lowrie's raiders robbed a store in Lumberton, and instead of sequestering only food, as was their habit, they took a safe containing $22,000.[29] Although this was the last time the Lowrie band was seen in public, during the following year, members of his band were either gunned down or simply disappeared, thereby carrying to the grave secrets about Lowrie's whereabouts. As time passed rumors began to circulate as to Lowrie's fate. Judged by both his enemies and admirers as a remarkable individual, imaginary tales abounded as to his fate. Detractors prayed that he was killed and devised accounts on how this occurred, while others gave credence to rumors that he escaped from Robeson County with the money obtained in the robbery, only to then drown in the swamps! Another persistent rumor claimed that he was shot accidentally by one of his own men.[30] Sixty-five years later on April 2, 1937, the great-nephew of Henry Lowrie, Dr. Earl C. Lowrie gave a presentation at the auditorium of the Cherokee Indian Normal school in Pembroke, were he claimed that his uncle Henry was still alive. The *Wilmington Morning Star* reported that Dr. Lowrie claimed:

That Henry Berry Lowry, leader of a band of outlaws for whom rewards aggregating $18,000 at one time were offered, escaped from Robeson county in the disguise of a federal soldier, drew pay from the government for 4 years as a soldier before his discharge in Norfolk, Va. Four years from then, he went from Norfolk to the state of Florida and is still living today at the age of 92.[31]

Queried by reporters as to Henry's escape from Robeson County, the nephew explained that while he would not reveal his uncle's exact location he had few qualms about providing his interpretation of his uncle's ingenuity and skill as a guerrilla fighter. Dr. Lowrie explained that by Christmas 1871, every man in the county to whom Henry had planned to administer retribution for the murder of his relatives had been killed, with the exception of two who fled the county and another who became unbalanced.[32] At this point Henry supposedly told his fellow raiders that their work had been completed and suggested that they leave the county. Deciding to remain in the Scuffletown area, Henry predicted that within two years all of them would be dead, a prediction that proved to be true. Sometime during this period, Henry allegedly conceived of a plan to fake his own death and escape from North Carolina. After Henry explained to his wife how "unreasonable it would be for him to remain longer" in Robeson County, he left her some money and then departed sometime in early 1872. Dr. Lowrie then states that:

> Short of funds, Henry Berry planned a trip to Lumberton where the safes of the sheriff's office and of Pope and McLeod [businesses] were robbed of $25,000. [A witness to the robbery, Mrs. Norment reported that the sheriff's safe was left in the streets of Lumberton.] En route home, Tom Lowry [one of the raiders] shot a rabbit, removed its drains [insides], and dashed then out at Steve's [another raider] home. A gun fired off. Henry Berry removed most of his arms and fled. A dummy of straw was placed in a pond back of the home of Steve, and it was related that Henry Berry had been killed by his own gun. Many of the curious came there and saw that dummy but none but his mother was allowed to see the head. Lumber was obtained from a saw mill for the stated purpose of building a coffin in which to bury Henry Berry. Jesse Oxendine [another raider] was employed to build the box. With the box, the remaining members of the gang went from a point near Union Chapel to the home of Peter Dial, near Harpers Ferry, where the boards were removed and made into a cart. No trace of the burial was ever found and the dummy was unstuffed, its straw thrown into a pond.[33]

Regardless of the veracity of this account, or the fact that Henry's brother, Reverend Patrick Lowrie, who was a delegate to the Republican state convention in 1872, announced that his brother and Boss Strong, Henry's bodyguard and closest friend were both dead, unverifiable accounts placed Henry in Atlanta, New York, California and elsewhere. Even Lowrie's wife Rhoda insisted until her death in 1909 that Henry was still very much alive.[34]

Wherever truth lay in the saga of Henry Berry Lowrie and his fellow raiders, one biographer was able to succinctly write:

> He struggled against injustice, and he helped preserve the ethnic identity of his people. Before Lowry, the Lumbee had been poor and powerless. Regarding the Lumbee and blacks as racially inferior, whites denied them equal protection of the law. Lowry gave the Lumbee justice, and the courageous exploits of the Lowry band instilled in the Indians a sense of pride and a confidence in their ability to control their lives.... In the late nineteenth century, whites began to appreciate the Indian ancestry of Lumbee, although their racist attitude towards nonwhites remained fixed.[35]

As late as 1874, highly descriptive accounts of suspected raids by the Lowrie gang were published in northern and southern newspapers such as the *New York Times* and North Carolina's *Lumberton Robesonian*.[36] These raids no doubt led to timeless accounts of Lowrie's raiders as heroic if not mythic guerrilla fighters waging armed struggle against the forces of evil and racism. And though the *Times* and *Robesonian* called attention to "the murderous doing of the Lowrey gang," and the seemingly inefficient tactics by General Gorman and his command to capture their nemesis, the *Fayetteville Eagle* was careful not to suggest that these highly successful attacks by armed nonwhite gangs were weakening white Democratic hegemony in North Carolina. These journals however warned the white populace about "censorious" remarks often heard on the street by "dandified clerks in the city counting-room who would say, 'Why don't those people rise up and extirpate the Lowrie gang? If I was there, I could very easily stop this thing.'"[37] However, the *New York Times* decision to publish General Gorman's critical assessment of why Lowrie's raiders were so successful, and the apparent ineffectiveness of his militia and military forces, either knowingly or not gave a clarion call to white terrorist groups like the Ku Klux, the White League, the Knights of the White Camellia and their sympathizers that an effective new threat to white hegemony was in the making. As one astute newspaper correspondent put it,

> Perhaps no people have been so scourged as the people of Robeson [County], nevertheless they have been abused and vilified. The dandified clerk in the city counting-room would say, "Why don't those people rise up and extirpate the Lowrie gang? If I was there, I could very easily stop this thing." The stroller along the side-walks made similar remarks. Even dignified and cautious people sometimes made censorious remarks of Robeson county. A multitude of talkers afar off from the terrible scenes enacted by this Lowrie band had this and that to say about the good people of Robeson County. Curt, petulant and sarcastic saying passed from the mouths of *bomb-proof assailants*, but through it all the killings went on. Not one of the captious critics of Robeson suffered one iota in purse or person. They were afar off, although sometimes trembling. We take this opportunity, the killing of the last outlaw, to say to the country at large, what we know to be strictly true, that there is no more courageous, industrious, whole-souled people in the world than the citizens of Robeson, and all through the Lowrie war, whether under the command of a United States officer, or the Sheriff, they conducted themselves with the courage and a high sense of public duty. The obstacles these people had to encounter in suppressing the Lowrie gang is not a property of the bomb-proof critic or the side-walk loafer, but it is province of truth and history to delineate these facts.[38]

Though armed political struggle by the Lumbee, African Americans and whites in Robeson County was in many ways atypical to what the rest of Reconstruction America experienced, a socially explosive message was delivered to the nation's political pundits. It was however symptomatic of a repressive social environment that defined any act of resistance by nonwhites as criminal insanity. In such a state of affairs organized resistance by southern blacks to white terrorism was traditionally underreported, minimized, or buried under a jargon of criminality. When instances of violent resistance or retaliation by blacks did occur, they had to overcome a number of encumbrances if they expected to be successful. For example, primary among the prerequisites for a successful retaliation was that their attack had to be conducted with extreme violence, unmerciful in its implementation and swift. Furthermore, because there generally was little backup or reinforcements and reserves to rely on, two factors were critical in any armed clash with whites:

(a) The Freedmen's general inability to secure an adequate number of quality weapons or sufficient ammunition for a sustained level of combat. This of course was not the case for hostile white state militias and their allied terror gangs who were directly involved in an armed conspiracy against the Freedmen and consequently had access to ammunition and weapons otherwise denied the black population.[39] In fact, under the infamous black codes it was unlawful for blacks, who were not in the military and therefore not under white control, to buy or carry guns and ammunition.[40]

(b) Dissimilar to the indigenous Lumbee people of North Carolina, the psychological importance of defending one's traditional lands and culture was *not* a part of the Freedmen's rational for resistance; personal and group survival for eventual social integration was. Consequently the subtle but significant disconnect between survival and traditional lands is critical as are the differences between the political-cultural goals of assimilation and separatism.

Immediate as this problem was for southern blacks, a still more pressing problem laid at the feet of a moribund black leadership who earnestly believed that armed resistance was either hopeless or suicidal. Accommodating themselves to what they viewed as the reality of white dominance, any notion of armed resistance, regardless of those who were brutalized or killed as a result of terrorism, was out of the question. Remarking on this phenomena, historian John Hope Franklin explained,

> One of the really remarkable features of the Negro leadership was the small amount of vindictiveness in their words and their actions. There was no bully, no swagger, as they took their places in the state and federal governments traditionally occupied by the white planters of the south. The spirit of conciliation pervaded most of the public utterances the Negroes made. In his first speech in the South Carolina convention Beverly Nash asserted that the Southern white man was the "true friend of the black man." Pointing to the banner containing the words, "United we stand, divided we fall," Nash said, "If you could see the scroll of the society that banner represents, you would see the white man and the black man standing with their arms locked together, as the type of friendship and union which we desire.[41]

They made it known that while a strategy of political parity with conservative whites was essential for survival, it did not include organized self-defense units! One local leader even exclaimed to a white colonel: "I beg of you, do not leave us. You are our chief, if not our sole, dependence ... stay with us; lead us and guide us."[42]

For black spokesmen who deliberated in this manner, creating a social consciousness that publicly and privately advocated armed defense of one's home and community was secondary to finding an accommodating peace with both southern Democrats and deceptive Republican conservatives. And though this political position was fraught with weakness and naïveté, many black spokesmen immediately following the Civil War maintained a view similar to that of the 1865 Virginia Convention of Colored People, which held political rights were the *only* critical issue in any defense of the race. Nonetheless, within five years, the Colored National Labor Convention had to realistically concluded that it was necessary to publicly state that the Republican party wasn't totally interested in their political or economic domination of the south.[43]

If this wasn't problematic enough, in the face of continuous brutal attacks by white terrorist groups, northern army officers commanding black and white troops commonly deferred to the concerns of the allegedly disposed southern white gentry. This obligated many southern blacks to conclude that whites, be they military officers or conservative Republicans, were at best unreliable allies, and that the only recourse was to rely on their own abilities, resources, numbers and a will to resist if any semblance of freedom was to be realize.[44]

The Darien Insurrection

A good example of some black leaders' confusion if not antipathy on the issue of self-defense and armed retaliation to white terrorism occurred in Darien, Georgia, just a few months before the end of the nineteenth century. In an event that was eventually known as the Darien Insurrection, black farmers in McIntosh County, demonstrated that contrary to what many whites and some blacks wanted to believe, successful armed resistance against Klan-like groups was not only possible but probable in specific circumstances.[45] However, as with Henry Berry Lowrie and his raiders some twenty years earlier, acknowledgment of blacks' retaliation against white gangs was inconsistent and for many incomprehensible. Southerners as well as the rest of the nation were clearly more familiar with detailed newspapers accounts about obnoxious blacks being brutalized or lynched, rather than reports indicating armed resistance or retaliation by Freedmen. Yet over the thirty years since the end of the Civil War, an interesting trend was occurring. Besides the obvious warning that reports of armed resistance by blacks or indigenous people historically portended for white Americans in generals, increasingly these accounts were highly suggestive that retaliation by southern blacks to racist provocation was more likely to occur when they had managed to obtain a strong level of economic autonomy and political mobilization.[46]

This was progressively more evident in the last two decades of the nineteenth century, when relentless racial strife was punctuated throughout the south with over 100 lynchings in Georgia alone between 1881 and 1898, while terror gangs known as whitecappers in 1899 roamed the state killing and whipping blacks for a variety of alleged crimes, but not without growing or organized resistance.[47] As a result, an examination of Georgia's *coastal* regions (Table 7 and Table 8) indicated that increased land ownership by blacks was indicative of a deeply entrenched economic infrastructure, social identity and a willingness to resist Klan-like attacks with retaliatory violence.[48]

In attempting to explain the infrequency of gang violence against coastal blacks, one historian suggested that while southern apologist argued it was from "lingering paternalism," it was more likely a reaction to the nonpassive response by coastal blacks to whites' attempts at intimidation. As one observer noted, coastal blacks "retained modest political rights, a modicum of economic independence, durable community bonds and therefore were less vulnerable to many non-violent forms of coercion. [But] whites could not lightly turn to violence because they recognized they were not dealing with a cowed and impotent black population."[49]

For example, in the spring of 1896, an editorial in the *Springfield* (Massachusetts) *Weekly Republican* newspaper described an event in Manatee County, Florida, that provided evidence of blacks success in defending themselves against white terror:

> Some days ago the son of the county sheriff and the son of a poor Negro quarreled and the black was the victor in a boy's fight. Thereupon the sheriff and a number of *brave* whites, fully armed, went to the negro's cabin at night and demanded that the boy be handed over to them.
>
> Knowing what would be his probable fate, the Negro refused to surrender his son. On the contrary he seized a gun and when the white mob fired upon the house he returned the fire and killed the sheriff. Then the whites in a rage picked up a log and rushed upon the cabin door to batter it in, and another shot from the negro's gun killed another white man and fatally wounded a third.

TABLE 7. BLACK FARMLAND OWNERSHIP IN COASTAL GEORGIA, 1900

	Number of Black Farm Owners	Total Number Black Farmers	Percent of Total Black Farmers
Bryan	144	267	53.9
Camden	403	571	70.6
Chatham	171	426	40.1
Glynn	97	119	81.5
Liberty	793	1138	69.7
McIntosh	243	313	77.6
TOTAL	1851	2834	65.3

Source: Federal Census, *Agriculture, 1900*: 68–71.

TABLE 8. LYNCHINGS OF BLACKS BY REGION AND DECADE, GEORGIA, 1881–1930

	Mountain	Piedmont	Black Belt	Southern	Coastal
1881–1890	5	5	20	26	1
1891–1900	7	12	45	35	5
1901–1910	0	9	41	40	3
1911–1920	4	8	69	52	0
1921–1931	0	2	20	13	4*
TOTAL	16	38	195	166	13

Source: Tables were adapted from *Black Freedom/White Violence 1865–1900* by Donald Nieman, p. 31, and from "The Darien Insurrection of 1899," W. Fitzhugh Brundage, pp. 16–35.

The mob retreated for reinforcements, and the Negro took his boy and gun and made off for the swamps. At last accounts he had not been captured and tortured to death, but in lieu of this, the noble and manly whites were going about the country firing into the cabins of innocent and defenseless blacks, burning up the homes of some, killing others, and ordering a general exodus of Negroes, threatening a boycott on employers of labor who would not discharge their Negro help.[50]

In July 1899, racial violence exploded in Darien when Matilda Ann Hope, a young white woman, swore to an affidavit that charged her black neighbor, Henry Delegale, of raping her during the previous winter, thus causing her to give birth to a black child. Hearing of the charge Delegale turned himself in to the authorities and pleaded innocent to the charges. Though many residents in the area tended to discount Hope's charges, the reality was that under such a situation, Delegale's life was under imminent danger. The county sheriff, Thomas Blount, decided that by moving Delegale to Savannah, he would ensure that his prisoner received a trial, and not the vengeance of a mob. However, an armed group of Darien blacks prohibited this from happening, arguing that any attempt to move Delegale would simply ensure that he would be killed en route by racist gangs.[51]

African American fears in this regard were not misguided. From 1880 to 1930, 118 of 453 lynching victims in Georgia occurred while the prisoner was in transit to jail![52] The

Savannah Morning News went so far as to admit that "safekeeping" by the authorities of black prisoners "meant death to the accused on a swing limb somewhere between Darien and Savannah."[53]

To ensure that this would not happen, a group of blacks from Darien organized themselves into a protective militia to protect Delegale against any incursions by white mobs. Taking up defensive positions outside the jail, they let it be known that neither a white mob nor the sheriff would move the prisoner without an armed fight. Representing a cross-section of the black populace in McIntosh County, landowning families, day laborers, saw mill workers and domestic servants saw in Delegale themselves, and acting in a "collective spirit" to protect him demonstrated a determination to safeguard their fellow kinsmen and by implication their own political and economic independence.[54] As the *Savannah Morning News* commented, "Some of the best farms are owned by the Negroes themselves. It is known among the Negroes that should a prolonged difficulty with the whites occur, the black men would have sufficient food to sustain them supplied from the farms either by black owners or tenants."[55] The paper also noted that, coastal blacks had become "perfectly independent of the white man."[56]

Darien had a population of approximately 1700 people, of which approximately 1000 were blacks. Having a high level of economic wherewithal, Darien blacks were able to support a nascent but vocal political machine in McIntosh County that began under the tutelage of Tunis G. Campbell. Described derogatively by whites as a "black carpetbagger," Campbell laid the foundation for political activism and racial cooperation organization that eventually provided the model for active resistance to white extremists and terrorists.[57] His efforts bore fruit on August 22, 1899, when as a result of a previous agreed on signal, the ringing of the Baptist church bell summoned over 100 armed blacks to Darien's jail to protect Delegale. Intimated by their presence, the Darien Dragons, a local conservative white militia, remained out of sight, but did wire Georgia governor Allen D. Chandler to send state militia troops as quickly as possible. Chandler immediately ordered up 200 men and 6 officers of the state militia, First Infantry Regiment.[58]

Told that an imminent "race war" was in the making, the train traveled "at a furious pace, exceeding a mile a minute for much of the trip, [and] delivered the troops to Darien shortly after dusk" on the same day.[59] When the state troopers arrived they immediately assessed the presence of an armed black militia surrounding the jail, however neither side fired. Once the black farmers were assured that Delegale would not be lynched by a white mob, they consented to the state guards transporting the prisoner to Savannah.[60]

This highly sensitive confrontation would have terminated peacefully had it not been for the bruised feelings of the local white inhabitants and authorities who felt that those who led the armed "black mob" should "feel the weight of the strong arm they have defied, and that punishment shall be meted out to them."[61] On August 25, two deputies, Robert Townsend and O. Hopkins, took it on themselves to travel out of town to the Delegale homestead, where they were confronted by Delegale's two sons, John and Edward. Newspaper accounts claim that after a few sharp words and threats, the Delegale sons were ordered to surrender. Deputy Hopkins was said to have made a move toward his gun and at that precise moment someone from inside the house, "open[ed] fire with a shotgun, killing Townsend and severely wound[ing] Hopkins."[62] The very next day the *Savannah Press* headlines warned,

RACE WAR IMMINENT;
TROUBLE NOT ENDED,
Entire First Regiment Lift Savannah Again
For Darien;

Col. Lawton Depart for the Seat of Trouble
at Head of Command.

BRUNSWICK TROOPS UNDER ARMS,

Voting Delegale Captured Today — Effort to Wreck
Train to Savannah Wednesday.

COMING OF NIGHT IS NOW DREADED.[63]

One would suspect that such an act by blacks would have immediately propelled Darien whites into a frenzy; however, no lynchings or further bloodshed occurred, though feelings in both the black and white communities were tense. The reasons for this are instructive because those conditions were necessary for blacks' successful use of violence and their ability to curtail a response from white mobs.

When Alexander R. Lawton, the commanding officer of the State Guard, heard about the confrontation he first attempted to nullify any further violence by racing to the Delegale homestead before the white militia arrived. Cunningly, the matriarch of the Delegale family petitioned the State Guard to protect the family from any white mobs that were surely preparing to raid the homestead. Second, a plan was quickly formulated between the Delegale family members and the State Guard whereby family members would be placed temporarily under protective custody and moved into Darien's jailhouse, thereby forestalling any direct attack on the homestead. Needless to say, while most of Darien's blacks were agitated about the necessity of such a plan and saw it as an affront to their civil rights and dignity, other black leaders, having a more constrained response, valued this nonviolent approach.

At this point, religious community leaders from varying black denominations including a local federal collector of customs for Darien found reasons to join forces.[64] Though all of them enjoyed tolerable if not excellent reputations in the white community, not surprisingly they were curiously and conspicuously silent during the previous week's violent confrontations. They now collaborated with Col. Lawton, the federal collector of customs in Darien, on a circular that when widely distributed throughout McIntosh County strongly petitioned that blacks refrain from any acts that might incite white violence, and that they recognize that the troops were not present solely to protect white interest.[65] However, of more immediate concern for these prominent black community leaders was their second circular that advised, "black women to abstain from all words that may incite rashness or may be abusive. And by all means let every man see to it that no colored woman shall show her face at the courthouse or on the streets thereto."[66] Similar ensuing statements by a prominent but accommodating black leadership surmised that their public stance as articulated by the second circular would "bring back to our city and county that peace and harmony between the races with which in the past we have been so signally blessed."[67] Alas, neither liberal or conservative whites were comforted by these appeasing tactics.

When Delegale's case was reviewed in Savannah, the court chose to first address the charges against those who were arrested for the killing and wounding of the deputies, and only then proceed with the rape charge. In the first trial, twenty-three alleged rioters were convicted, while charges on forty others were dropped. Fines ranged from $250 to $1000, and a prison term of twelve months and hard labor were meted out. John and Edward Delegale received life sentences, and their brother and sister were acquitted. The jury also concluded that Henry Delegale was innocent of the rape charge that had precipitated the conflict and was subsequently released.[68] However once sent to Brooks County convict camp in south Georgia, the convicted Delegales and other rioters (including two women) suffered harsh treatment and barely survived their imprisonment.[69] The women, Louisa Underwood and Maria Curry, were hired out and served their prison sentence at the James sawmill at Adrian, Georgia, in violation of Georgia's laws pertaining to woman prisoners.[70]

Assessing Armed Resistance

Assessing what benefits were derived from resisting threats and actual attacks by white mobs is always relative to what might have been lost if no resistance was attempted. In the case of Darien, though an all-white State Guard in conjunction with local white militias did ensure a dominant military presence, McIntosh County whites also realized that some blacks were confident enough to reject whites' paternalist strategies, largely because they enjoyed a level of economic security derived from strong community bonds. Seemingly these factors were enough to give skilled black workers in the lumber and naval stores industry as well as independent farmers a significant role in McIntosh county's economic development, notwithstanding their sense of emotional investment and autonomy beyond the philosophy of physical survival.[71] For these African Americans, a duplicity in their economic situation was such that while survival was premised on respect from others and the upholding of black community's self-interest, there was still among some a strong need to placate white fears, as DuBois observed.

> He would not bleach his Negro soul in a flood of white Americanism, for he knows that Negro blood has a message for the world. He simply wishes to make it possible for a man to be both a Negro and an American, without being cursed and spit upon by his fellows, without having the doors of opportunity closed roughly in his face.[72]

Organized militancy to the point of armed resistance by African Americans was not lost on those whites who were cognizant enough to know that any display of militancy by blacks was indicative of their ability to fashion for themselves a response to provocations. In addition, white Americans were being increasingly forced to recognize that once blacks obtained a resourceful economic base, they could not easily be cowed or rendered impotent by the propagandizing efforts of terrorists. As a result, it was now apparent that throughout the Low Country region of Georgia and South Carolina, reliance on the mob to subdue blacks was increasingly nonfunctional *unless* supported by sympathizing federal troops or state militia.

With this said, many southern black leaders were again uncomfortable with this state of affairs. Undecided about the necessity for self-defense, when pushed to take a stand on the issue, they waffled. An example of this occurred in April 1870, when reputed black nationalist Martin Delany allegedly informed South Carolina's Democratic conservatives, "keep your Ku Kluxers away from me," and he would be "willing to strike hands with you in maintaining a free, honest and pure government in South Carolina!"[73] This conspicuous yet naive attempt to place trust in an agreement with southern conservatives was roundly denounced by many prominent nonconformist black leaders such as Frederick Douglass, who knew only too well the dangers this invited. Douglass, who was not an advocate for slave rebellions before the Civil War, on this occasion criticized Delany's comments by stating, "I cannot agree with you in denouncing colored men for going armed to political meetings in South Carolina, assault compels defense." Moreover, Douglass proclaimed that he wasn't going to advocate "that blacks act as lambs while whites acted as wolves!"[74] Stressing African Americans' right to retaliate against their enemy, Douglass recalled his own fight with a slavebreaker some thirty years earlier:

> I was a changed being after that fight. I was *nothing* before; I was a man now. It recalled to life my crushed self-respect and my self-confidence, and inspired me with a renewed determination to be a Freeman. A man, without force, is without the essential dignity of humanity. Human nature is so constituted, that it cannot *honor* a helpless man, although it can *pity* him; and even this it cannot do long, if the signs of power do not rise.
>   He can only understand the effect of this combat on my spirit, who has himself incurred something, hazarded something, in repelling the unjust and cruel aggressions of a tyrant.[75]

Notwithstanding Douglass's comments, there were those who continued to favor Delany's perspective of hopeful eradication of a confederate way of life through debate and legislation! For them, morality, tolerance and trust eventually united responsible men into an economic and political alliance that ensured the creation of a democratic and reconstructed south. This, they argued, was the best option. However, the reality of continuing murderous attacks by terrorist gangs and mob violence forced the question: racial survival at what cost?

Expelled black Georgia representative Henry B. Turner said it plainly, "I am here to demand my rights, and to hurl thunderbolts at the men who would dare to cross the threshold of my manhood." Turner also advocated that blacks should emigrate to West Africa and went on to assert that blacks did not ask for those conditions that force them to retaliate violently against attackers, and would gladly rejoice in being accepted as full citizens. However, if continually forced to do, they will retaliate against those desiring to restore white rule in Georgia by violence.[76]

History is instructive on this question of armed defense and retaliation, especially when rural black farmers demonstrated a willingness to resist nightly terror raids by white marauders and retaliated in kind despite a limited number of weapons. Moreover, when organized resistance did occur as with Lowrie's raiders and the Darien insurrection, a tacit message was conveyed to local whites that was instantly understood as a threat to their own safety. Accordingly, many impending racial crises were abated or minimized once blacks indicated that they would not be demoralized or intimidated. Conversely, when conservative whites became heartened by blacks' seeming submissiveness, a different message was being conveyed, a message that all too often resulted in an unrestrained, unremitting and relentless desire by terrorists to vent a sundry of abuses on their black victims. Within this context, southern whites' deep-seated psychological cravings for relief from melancholic sensations of social, political and personal distress vibrated through an array of violent acts and rituals against generally a defenseless black populace.

Calhoun's Dilemma

Finding a rationale to explain white America's time-honored social psychological maladjustment toward nonwhites requires an understanding of the very premise on which the nation was conceived. Succinctly put, the enfranchisement of European males into the newly constructed American republic of the eighteenth century affirmed not only their political independence from foreign rule but dramatically proclaimed in law the enslavement of Africans and the displacement and near total genocide of an indigenous population.[77] Not a paradigm for peaceful coexistence, this eighteenth-century political construct established a basis for unequal development while favoring racial preferential status for any European desiring to make the most of what law and martial power could provide when ordinary natural abilities and talents were otherwise lacking.

Contrived in this manner, one's racial background has been an ever present prescription for power and control in America. As a consequence, the remarks of many early eighteenth-century American patriots have become the mandates for late nineteenth-century terrorists. For example, Senator John C. Calhoun, an outspoken South Carolinian and southern ideologue, continually harangued his countrymen in his own inimical manner on the American Declaration of Independence:

> In my speeches and writings, I mounted an ideological counterattack against the subversive doctrines of the Declaration of Independence, which sanctions revolution and chaos. It was this most dangerous of all political error, I pointed out, that had given birth to abolitionism, to the deep and dangerous agitation which now threatened to engulf our political institutions. Therefore the sentiments in the Declaration had to be discredited and destroyed. They are nothing, I contended, but glittering generalities and self-evident lies. A good example is its assertion that all men are born free and created equal. This is an illogical absurdity. *Men* are not born; *infants* are born and they are not born free. They are incapable of freedom, being destitute alike of the capacity to think and act, without which there is no freedom. They are also subject to the dictates of parents, society, and State. Nor is it less false to hold that men are born "equal." They are not in any sense. The whole idea of equality is sentimental rubbish. *Inequality* and *slavery* are the achievements of human progress. There never has yet existed a wealthy and civilized society, from that of ancient Greece to our own, in which one portion of the community did not, in point of fact, live on the labor of the other.
>
> Let me make my position clear: I care nothing about slavery, it is entirely a secondary question with me. In three hundred years' time there will not be a nigger on the face of the globe. As the Indian is new retreating before our civilization, so the nigger will gradually be eliminated and his place taken by a higher and more intelligent race, it is only a question of time. I advocate slavery in the South because it is a guarantee of stability and the supremacy of the white race.[78]

In 1890, some 120 years later and a civil war in between, the congealed hatred of thousands of Calhoun acolytes forced many Americans to scrutinize the anguish that these obdurate-styled words had wrought. Commenting on this development, one New Orleans newspaper columnist stated, "Last week in Fayette County, Georgia, in an affray between colored and whites, provoked by the latter, eight Negroes were killed and six wounded. Eight whites were shot, but only one fatally. However deplorable these affrays, it is refreshing to see the Negro defending himself, but, he must learn to shoot straight."[79]

The same incident, published in the *Richmond Planet* one week earlier, detailed a level of black resistance that most other papers, black or white, disregarded or ignored as if it were the plague.

A fatal riot occurred at Starr's mill-pond in Fayette County, at 3 o'clock this afternoon. Four Negroes were killed and six wounded, two of whom are reported dying. Eight whites were shot but it is thought only of them fatally, making eighteen in all killed and wounded. Pete Griffin (white) is reported dangerously shot. A darkey selling wine on the occasion became engaged in a war of words with a white man about the purchase of some wine, which resulted in the Negro getting cut.

From this quarrel was taken up by others until Griffin became involved with a Negro who had a gun but who did not care to use it. Anderson Williams, another Negro told him that (if he will not use it) to shoot this damn scoundrel, give him the gun, and he would shoot him himself.

He took the gun and emptied its contents into Griffin's chest and bowels. He was immediately shot in the neck and died in a few minutes. The shooting became general. After emptying their weapons a demand was made of a merchant for more ammunition. He refused to sell, but the infuriated rioters ran roughshod and helped themselves to all he had. There were over 500 people on the ground, and it is a mystery that the shooting was not more fatal in the results.[80]

Recognition of the federal government's reluctance and in many cases inability to enforce punitive actions against terrorist-like actions, the presence of a generally unarmed southern black population was tantamount to blacks' subjugation or at worst political and physical genocide. To be disarmed in the presence of an armed unsympathetic adversary was in itself a provocative act. Furthermore, in South Carolina, as with most southern states, spontaneous, irrational violence against blacks was so common that guaranteed protections by the fourteenth and fifteenth amendments to the Constitution were ignored as a natural course of action. What is seldom discussed is that open complicity by southern state officials with terrorist gangs tended to foster the creation of a class of black citizens who, once terrorized and periodically whipped, accommodated themselves to their immediate attackers and then eventually whites in general! Those who resisted as in Darien or in numerous hamlets throughout the south, acquired their assertiveness by either finding a way to jettison a life time of perverse social conditioning or living as did Lowrie, outside the pale of white trust and control.

Low Country Resistance

Black Carolinians were relatively successful in forestalling widespread massacre by armed whites due to specific social environmental factors that were not generalized throughout other southern black communities. For example, a careful examination of violent racial confrontations during the post–Civil War years indicate that there were thirty-three major racial revolts in which a single life or more was lost.[81] A closer analysis of these clashes indicate that a number of important prerequisites were present as necessary conditions for successful armed defense during these confrontations.

(A) In 70 percent of the riots, blacks made up a majority of the population in the area of conflict.

(B) In a region that was overwhelmingly rural, 42 percent of the riots occurred in cities with a population over 5000.

(C) Over a third of the racial riots occurred within two weeks of an election and five erupted on election days (Savannah, Georgia, in 1868; Baton Rouge, Louisiana, in 1870; Macon, Georgia, in 1872; Eufaula, Alabama, in 1874; and Mobile, Alabama, in 1874.) Consequently a high sense political focus was present among the black electorate.

(D) Fifty-five percent of the riots began with an attempt by whites to break up a black political meeting or keep blacks from voting. In such instances, there was a critical mass of blacks to either defend or act aggressively in retaliation to provocative acts by whites.

(E) In 73 percent of the riots, blacks fought back at least initially, and usually until they were overwhelmed due to superior white numbers, firepower, military experience, communications, weaponry, connivance of those in authority, abandonment by the federal government, blacks ignorance, poverty and inexperience.[82]

On a number of occasions Charleston became the site of pitched hand-to-hand battles between blacks and whites. As the historic site where armed rebellion against the federal government began on April 12, 1861, Charleston was considered to be the heart and soul of southern white gentility, breeding and power. However, four years later this mecca of southern aristocratic power suffered what many considered to be the unforgiving indignity of having the first black regiment of Union soldiers officially recruited during the Civil War, the Massachusetts 54th Regiment, march victoriously through the streets of Charleston right up to the symbol of Confederate military might, the Citadel, with the freed black populace cheering them on.

On this day, Martin R. Delany, a major in the 52nd U.S. Colored Troops, recalled his first impressions on entering Charleston:

> In entered the city, which, from earliest childhood and through life, I had learned to contemplate with feelings of the utmost abhorrence, a place of the most insufferable assumptions and cruelty to the blacks; where the sound of the lash at the whipping post, and the hammer of the auctioneer, were coordinate sounds in thrilling harmony, that place which had ever been closed against liberty by an arrogantly assumptuous despotism....
>
> For a moment, I found myself dashing in unmeasured strides through the city, as if under a forced march to attack the already crushed and fallen enemy. Again I halted to look upon the shattered walls of the once stately but now deserted edifices of the proud and supercilious occupants. The haughty Carolinians, who believed their state an empire, this city incomparable, and themselves invincible, had fled in dismay and consternation at the approach of their conquerors, leaving the metropolis to its fate. And but for the vigilance and fidelity of the colored firemen, and other colored inhabitants, there would have been nothing left but a smoldering plain of ruins in the place where Charleston once stood, from the firebrands in the hands of the flying whites.... Whatever impressions may have previously been entertained concerning the free colored people of Charleston, their manifestation from my advent till my departure, gave evidence of their pride in identity and appreciation of race that equal in extent the proudest Caucasian.[83]

Needless to say, this was a bitter political reality for most if not all of Charleston's white residents. Expectedly, furious impassioned battles between Freedmen and a recalcitrant white populace occurred on almost a daily basis. One major confrontation occurred in

THE "IRREPRESSIBLE CONFLICT"—CHARLESTON, SOUTH CAROLINA, July 28, 1866.—[SKETCHED BY A. R. WAUD.]

The "irrepressible conflict": Blacks and whites fight over who shall dominate Charleston's Battery Park on weekends. LIBRARY OF CONGRESS PRINTS AND PHOTOGRAPHS DIVISION, WASHINGTON, D.C.

Charleston's central market just a few months after the Confederate surrender. On Saturday, July 8, 1865, James Bing, a well-known and respected black vendor in the city's central market, and a white customer became involved in a disagreement that exploded into violence and eventually culminated in Bing's death and the wounding of several whites in the market area. When nearby soldiers from the Massachusetts 5th Regiment and the 21st U.S. Colored Troops were summoned to investigate the violence, they soon clashed with a white regiment of New York Zouaves who were also sent to the scene. Fighting between these three military units quickly spread and soon involved civilians. Within an hour, the entire downtown area of Charleston was entrapped in violence as enraged blacks attacked incensed white soldiers and civilians wherever they could find them. Pandemonium continued on throughout the weekend and only abated early Monday morning.[84] This would not be the last full blown interracial violence in Charleston, South Carolina.

One year later during the summer of 1866, racial clashes were again occurring and in heightened intensity. In Charleston's historic Battery Park, overlooking Fort Sumter, black and white youth clashed on a daily basis to determine which racial group would dominate use of the park.[85] In what many white southerners considered sacred ground, Battery Park with its cannons still facing Fort Sumter, was a symbol of Confederate resistance to the dictates of the federal government. However, with the emergence of a partially enfranchised black populace at war's end, embolden black youth cared little about Confederate symbols and less about the sensitivity of Charleston's white populace. Though these tensions were felt throughout every facet of Charleston's populace, battles by rock-throwing youth on

Sunday afternoons over the use of this park became symbolic of a much larger struggle. A visiting aristocrat to Battery Park in the spring of 1866 noted that the park with its music and strollers had given way on Saturday's to non-noble lineage young ladies and their gentlemen companions. However on Sundays the "ethiops spread themselves on the Battery."[86]

At the heart of this antagonism was Charleston's majority black population, particularly those black merchants who after the war had established significant commercial interest and trade unions apart from the white populace. They were by their presence a cause for white's anxiety. Perceived fears of being dominated and the possibility of violent retribution for past wrongs haunted Charleston's white communities.[87] With day-to-day interactions between the races being difficult at best, there was the additional presence of the offshore black Sea Islander Gullah population who immediately after the war's end attempted to repossess vacated land by ex-slaveowners, and as one planter noted, drove "the hatred of some white people for the colored race almost to a frenzy."[88]

Faced with this history, Charleston's white youth, carrying out the edicts of their time, exhibiting the anxiety and fears of their elders, saw in themselves the need to protect the only way of life they knew, in the only spiritual home they could possibly conceive of, Charleston. Having ex-slave children challenging this space was not only unthinkable to them, but instructive as a training ground for a life long struggle, to keep the nigger down!

For black youths, thrown rocks and fists during these early clashes eventually gave way to more serious considerations on armed resistance. For them, the struggle for racial esteem was a fight for physical and psychological survival. In this regard, their strength was sharply challenged by the brazenness but weakness of an enemy who sniped about them in fearful wonder whenever blacks decided to demonstrate purposefulness and a steady aim.

6

Literary Provocateur:
A Case Study of John A. Leland

That hatred springs more from self-contempt than from a legitimate grievance is seen in the intimate connection between hatred and a guilty conscience.[1]

A Voice from South Carolina

After four years of civil war, with some 600,000 dead and countless thousands wounded, the north and the south found themselves entwined in bloody attempts at Reconstruction. Though securing effective racial hegemony over its nonwhite populace was the goal for both northern and southern white political infrastructures, to accomplish this "an alliance of northern and southern capital" as well as "political alliances across sectional lines" had to be established by any means necessary.[2] To facilitate this process, appeals to a distraught ex–Confederate leadership, sympathizers and Ku Klux–like terrorist gangs were made through newspapers, pamphlets, theatrical performances and books. Novels such as Thomas Jefferson Jerome's *Ku-Klux Klan No. 40*, Thomas Nelson Page's *Red Rock*, and N.J. Floyd's *Thorns in the Flesh: A Voice of Vindication from the South*, sought to placate the most aggrieved white southerners by asserting

It should not be denied that outrages, or rather acts of violence that were fully justified by the crimes committed, were perpetrated here and there, by mobs of persons styled "Ku Klux Klans," acting under sudden impulses of outraged feeling; nor can it de denied by the *well informed*, that these, when they greatly exceeded the bounds of a proper punishment for the crime committed were called to account by the "Knights of the Golden Circle," the "Knights of the White Camelia," the "Angles of Avenging Justice," the "Spirits of the Lost Clan," or the "Centaurs of Caucasian Civilization." The reader can have his choice of names. Nor can it be successfully denied that "The Order" did more to prevent horrible crimes and to tide civilization of the negroes over the fearful period of anarchy referred to, than could have been done by the Freedman's Bureau and all the troops, — or twice the number, — stationed in the South, even had all the officials been wise men and true Christians and patriots, which was very, very far from being the case, as all fools who did errands have testified and can testify....

The writer has nothing more to say concerning the so-called "Ku Klux Klan," but he claims that the mere fact that the country, particularly the cotton and sugar belts—from the Chesapeake to the Rio Grande, was not drenched in the blood of riots and assassinations, during the period of reconstruction and rehabilitation, proves the Southern white people to be possessed of a civilization having certain qualities of excellence which, no matter what may be the brilliant destiny of the leading human race in the future, can never be surpassed while men shall continue to be frail and fallible. And he here records the prediction that the time will come when the candid and unprejudiced historian, who has thoroughly informed himself respecting the period extending from 1859 to 1884, as he glances back at the wrongs and outrages of the past, ... will greatly whisper to the invisible guardian spirit at his side: "Ah, noble people! As political brethren, they were generous, magnanimous and forgiving; as military foes, they were chivalrous and brilliant; but under the numberless wrongs and persecutions which succeeded their downfall they were sublime!"[3]

By 1870, southern propagandists were quickly fashioning a number of rationalizations for the continued existence of a political ethos that envisioned the south as a separate political and cultural entity within the United States, a nation within a nation. Though the secessionist-minded Confederacy was defeated after four years of warfare, its economic infrastructure was vital to a postwar development of the nation. With this in mind, southern white patricians initiated a social dialogue that indicted both the Freedmen and white Republicans as culpable in exhausting the nation with four years of civil war. These astute political pundits quickly realized that by shrewdly associating black political involvement and economic development with social disorder, southern whites' guilt about their military defeat could be minimized.[4]

Interesting enough, a parallel analysis by black and white Carolinians also recognized that it wasn't northern *brotherly* love for the ex-slave or *hatred* of slavery that propelled federal interest to pursue the war to its bloody conclusion, but rather an inability by Lincoln's wartime administration to develop a workable political and economic solution between divided regional interest, some of whom advocated slavery and others who sought what they considered were the best interest of white wage laborers.[5] With the termination of hostilities, the freed African posed an even greater problem as an economic spoiler who supposedly could no longer be sold, bought, bartered or traded. They were now a numerical entity that threaten to dramatically obliterate assumed white patterns of social order and dominance throughout the south and beyond.

With this as a threat, southern conservative and Democratic newspapers along with a sympathetic northern conservative wing of the Republican Party mounted a national campaign that unleashed a steady barrage of racially inspired invectives characterizing blacks as incompetent, bungling political dupes for radical Republicans. Central to this analysis was the following supposition: Lacking a history outside slavery, blacks were racially incompetent in seeking or exercising power and authority on a local or national level, especially over whites.[6] Accordingly, it was understood that the responsibility for governing occurred at birth and as a result was an innate, God-given mandate for whites! For those who needed visible or material confirmation of this fact, a racist credo declaring no matter how poor whites may be, they could never become a nigger, was enough!

Refusals to accept this thinking constituted not only a physical threat to social order, but a psychic dismissal of those mythologies that for centuries decreed white racial privilege as a divine axiom. In the midst of this national post–Civil War struggle, a leading proponent of thinking was John Adams Leland, a conservative member of South Carolina's democratic academic elite, an enthusiastic apologist for the Ku Klux Klan and a major propagandist and ideologue who fashioned southern racist sentiments into a literary format on terror.

The Terrorist Word

In 1879 John Leland authored a treatise titled *A Voice from South Carolina: Journal of a Reputed Ku-Klux,* in which he expounded on the evils of Republican Reconstruction, particularly within the spiritual heart of the Confederacy, South Carolina. Written as a diary, Leland presented the reader with a glimpse of his views and thought processes as a southern educator. Utilizing metaphors, parables, allegoric representations and selective imagery, he constructed a historical rational of the postbellum period that rescued fellow white Carolinians from "African rule both State and Municipal." This he explained was necessary at a time when social conditions in his beloved state were so horrendous that "Sampson, shorn of his locks, was not more completely in the hands of *his* Philistines."[7] With this as his approach to history, Leland attempted to succinctly describe who the enemies of southern whites were, while establishing the boundary lines for any future political intercourse.

As a graduate from both Williams College in Massachusetts and South Carolina College in Charleston, holder of a doctorate degree, professor and chair of the Mathematics and Astronomy Department at South Carolina's Military Academy, the Citadel, and as president of the Laurensville Female College in Laurens, South Carolina, Leland, the self-proclaimed southern gentleman dedicated his seminal work to "the Women of South Carolina."[8] In doing so, he attempted to merge his own sense of chivalry and contempt of Republican "moral mania" with a level of cynicism and personal despair that ultimately concluded even "the lowest Ku-Klux would have blushed to have acknowledged the most obnoxious Negro."[9] With this as his mantra, *A Voice from South Carolina* ridicules Republican reconstruction efforts, but not without first asserting his own credentials as author of "Journal of a reputed Ku Klux!"[10]

Fashioning a writing style replete with the patrician appeals of a politically deposed antebellum plantation class, while reviewing a litany of events that he asserts are examples of northern abuses of southern sensibilities, Leland attempts to address the critical questions of the day particularly for southern white Democrats; how will national conciliation be acquired and who shall rule? This style of political liturgy, forged with expressions of chivalry, cynicism and terror proved to be a powerful and lethal weapon when introduced by an astute writer and orator such as Leland, for it also implies notions of southern whites' innate superiority over blacks in all things political, economic and cultural.

For example, Leland's linguistic style describes an apocalyptic South Carolina, replete with abuses that forced him to sacrifice his standing as an educator by publicly admitting a reputed association with the Ku Klux Klan. In this regard, it is important to note that

Leland's use of the word reputed is singularly important for it affords him a political rational of *intent by association* while not identifying him as an active member of, as he put it, "those lawless and reckless spirits, to be found in almost every community — particularly after a protracted and disastrous war."[11] Nevertheless when official charges of lawlessness, violence and murder were cast his way as a result of his participation in the Laurens riot of 1870, he was incarcerated on the charges of conspiracy and murder.[12]

Describing the circumstance and events that led to the Laurens County riot in the third person, Leland proclaimed that his reputation was still unblemished by the riot, and that even when the citizenry of Laurens were queried by investigators as to character of those arrested, he was one of three identified as being "above all suspicion of complicity with rowdyism."[13] Insisting that his claims of innocence were above reproach, and that his arrest was simply a judicial farce, Leland stressed how even the prosecuting attorney agreed that he and three others were actually trustworthy enough to "be bailed out till the November term of court." Criticizing local Republicans for conspiring against him and his cohorts, he implies that the prosecutor was influenced, "on a whisper from Joe [Crews]," an aggressive local Republican political figure, to believe that Leland was trying to incur favor due to his position as a college president when in fact, Leland avows, it was Crews's actions that were irresponsible, dangerous and a threat to public safety! To forestall any more rioting, the court commissioner decided to remand all of the prisoners, including Leland, and move the trial to the U.S. Circuit Court in Charleston.[14] From this relatively small but bloody incident, Leland's reputation s a protector of southern Democratic ideals began to rise.

Admittedly having a reputed association with the Ku Klux Klan precluded any objective historical writing on Leland's part. If anything, it nominated him as a vigilant supporter of a militant arm of the southern Democratic political party. By 1872, he was accused by South Carolina's radical Republican leaders of being not only a secretive member of the Ku Klux, but a murderer and a staunch southern conservative ideologue who planned to win in defeat what the south lost in military conflict — control over black labor. In this regard, Leland's work aspires by implication and metaphor to revitalize in southern whites a sense of defiance toward those who would demean and trample on what he considered were "the time honored rights of the great Anglo Saxon race."[15] In line with this thinking, he praised South Carolina's political leaders as a pantheon of men whose supreme virtue and sacrifice had nobly tolerated existing in a world filled with the weak and irreverent. Seemingly understanding their pain, he professed:

> South Carolina can proudly point to a galaxy of historic names, who have illustrated her fame in every period of her past history. Through these her voice has already been heard in tones which will reach the latest posterity.
>
> In the dark days of the revolution, this voice could be heard in such clarion notes as her Moultries, her Sumters, and her Marions could utter, to electrify new life in her people, though overrun and all but conquered.
>
> In the formation of the government, it has been heard, in no faltering accents, from her Pinckneys, her Laurenses, her Rutledges and her Heywards — equals among equals — statesmen, who were jealous of her liberty so dearly purchased. These only consented to her association with her sister colonies, when they thought this liberty was hedged in by every safeguard which human wisdom could devise.
>
> It has been heard in the halls of State and Federal legislation, from the tongues of Calhoun, Hayne, McDuffie, Preston, and a long list of worthies, whose names will ever adorn

the annals of the past. Giants in intellect, who could embellish profound and ennobling statesmanship and patriotism, with unsullied integrity, and the purity of the high-toned gentleman.[16]

Enraptured by South Carolina's past, Leland warned his readers to be cognizant of current dangerous social transgressions, which were nurtured by historical neglect. Contending that when the "barbarian hordes press hard against the barriers of civilization," they do so by disregarding any semblance of respect for the past as they hurriedly construct the future. Viewing himself as the voice of reason and sagacious discernment, he laments white South Carolinians' fate:

But this potent voice has long been hushed, and her approaching "centennial year" will find her in habiliments of mourning — silent and sad. Most of her sisters who began the race with her, and very many of those younger ones, who are but of yesterday, and who owe so much to her sacrifice of blood and treasure, will then be rejoicing in their prosperity, and have already invited the whole world to witness their progress and their greatness. She, almost alone of the "Old Thirteen," will turn her face to the wall, and will feel no responsive throb to the rejoicing over this national jubilee.

In one short century, she seems to have run her whole career of rises, progress, decline and fall. She has the same bright sky above her, as in her palmist days; the same broad rivers flowing from her mountains to the seaboard; the same fertile soil and genial climate ...

Her most bitter enemies must admit that her, so-called, leaders have maintained a dignified silence since her fall. Even those who watch so assiduously to catch up and pervert every chance expression of Ex-President Davis, have found nothing to report from them. These gentlemen show that it is the part of true manhood to *endure* what is unavoidable, as well as to *dare*; and that fortitude is, in many respects a higher virtue than bravery.[17]

He ends this supplication by throwing *his own* sacrificed soul on the consciousness of good South Carolinians whom he anticipates would quickly recognize that

This "Voice from South Carolina," comes from one of her humble sons, whose earnest desire is to cling but the closer to her side in the day of her humiliation. He feels irresistibly impelled to publish to the world that the grand old State, declared to be free, sovereign and independent, a hundred years ago, is now deposed, gagged, and trampled in the dust. Her seat and name has been usurped by a brazen-faced strumpet, foisted upon her "high places" by the hands of strangers; her proud monuments of the past, all begrimed and vandalized; her sacred treasury thrown wide open to the insatiable rapacity of thieves and robbers; and her bright escutcheon blackened by every crime known to the decalogue.

All these, too, have been the legitimate fruits of deliberate legislation on the part of her sister States, in congress assembled; people, like herself, by the descendants of that glorious old Anglo-Saxon race, whose achievements on this continent have filled the world with amazement and admiration. Could our common ancestors ever have foreseen this? Can posterity ever account for the "madness of the hour," in States, having the same lineage, combining to drive one of their number from the fold of civilization into the dark despotism of African rule? And yet, South Carolina to-day presents the terrible picture of a great American State abandoned to the tender mercies of her former slaves, exasperated and maddened by the teachings and guidance of foreign mercenaries and native desperadoes.[18]

The October 20, 1870, riot that Leland and others were charged with inciting stemmed primarily from charges that they had conspired to prohibit potential black voters from participating in the Laurens County elections for state officers, and that Leland personally "had murdered several colored citizens" during the civil unrest.[19] Leland's recollections as well as local newspapers accounts of the ensuing racial clash at the polling boxes is instructive in that it illuminates southern whites' general attitude on the question of voting rights for Negroes and blacks' entitlement to armed self-defense. However in Leland's recounting of events that led to his arrest, he claimed that "the majority of the adult male population of the town, then present were arrested; and, at first, shut up in the court house." He further asserted that "as soon as this congregation, without reference to sects, was assembled in this unusual place, by forcible means, we were marched in procession, through Main Street to the residence of the Honorable Joseph Crews."[20]

Though the veracity of Leland's testimony is left up to the reader's discretion, his introduction of Joseph Crews as a "vile character" and recognized leader of the radical wing of the Republican Party in Laurens County is intriguing. Leland demeaning characterization of Crews is emphasized by declaring that he is "a base and vile trader" who before the Civil War had a questionable and stained reputation for "making his bread by trafficking in negroes, and with negroes."[21] From this affiliation, Crews had supposedly developed an appreciation of "*their* peculiar characteristics" and in due time after the war, made additional money by acting as liaison between the two racial communities. By befriending blacks, Crews quickly became recognized in the state capital (Columbia) as an individual of worth and eventually became a legislator, a commissioner of elections, a military aid to the governor and a trial justice. Leland finally concludes that Crews in effect became a useful individual for Republican interest while living within the Democratic pearl of the ex–Confederacy, South Carolina.[22]

More important for Leland was that as a county leader in the Republican Party, Joe Crews was entrusted with full powers to organize and equip the county militia, Republican Union Leagues and conduct limited military exercises with black soldiers when deemed necessary for the public's safety. In this regard, Leland cynically noted that:

> A complete program of military barbecues was arranged for the summer, always to be attended, armed and equipped, as the [party] law directed. It was his haranguing at these barbecues that first fired the colored heart.
>
>   Some of his speeches were listened to by respectable citizens, who testified in the public prints of the day, and over their own signatures, to his highly incendiary diatribes. Among very many other things, he advised the laborers, now that they had arms in their hands, to seize whatever of the crops they thought they ought to have, and if any fuss was made, they could easily burn them out, as matches were cheap. That *they* now had the power, and the white man must be taught to know his place.
>
>   Under such teachings as these, it was not to be wondered at, that companies of colored militia, in going to, and returning from these gatherings, with arms in their hands, should be insolent, and sometimes even violent towards their former owners. There were many instances of insults offered to ladies, while riding in their carriages over the public roads; and of indignities the most gross, perpetrated by them, on the premises of some obnoxious farmers.[23]

It is therefore not surprising to learn that Leland's account of what occurred on election day in Laurens County is laced with racial invectives. Describing the mangers of the elections as radical Republicans, he admits that with the exception of a few minor incidents, "everything went on quietly and peacefully until eleven o'clock." However, he claims at this time, a citizen (white) and a constabulary (black) had a few nasty words to say to each other that resulted in a fistfight. Other reports claim that it was when the Constable called a local white "a tallow-faced son-of-a-bitch" that the trouble began in earnest.[24] From this moment on events occurred quickly:

> A friend of the citizen, pistol in hand, went up to the scene of the fight, to see fair play, as he said. Seeing that his friend had got the best of the fight, he was about to return his pistol to its case — under his coat, and attached to a belt behind — when it was accidentally discharged. A cry was immediately heard among the Negroes, "they are firing upon us!" and together, they all disappeared in the armory. Soon guns were seen protruding from the windows up stairs, in the direction of the public square, immediately in front; and a volley of some twenty guns was fired.
>
> There was quite a sprinkling of men on the square, and yet "nobody was hurt." This is easily account for. These bold militia men thought their only agency was in "cocking the gun and pulling the trigger," and that the blood-thirsty bullet would itself seek its victim independently of all aim.[25]

The effect of this volley, Leland maintains, was to send white citizens running in all directions, some looking for safety, while still others reached for their weapons in responses to what they perceived of an attack by blacks.[26] Warming to his literary task, he mockingly asserts:

> The effect of the volley on the scattered crowd was startling enough. A hornet's nest suddenly turned over, could not have produced more flying to and fro, or more rage and venom among the assailed. Some ran for their arms-secreted near by, the day before, in case of an emergency-shot-guns from the show cases, were seized and loaded on the double quick; others with no arms at all but walking canes and brick bats all rushed madly for the front door and windows of the armory. These yielded readily to the furious onset of the whites, and similar openings in the rear opened as readily to the mad outset of the blacks. It was no fight at all; for as soon as these sable warriors saw the determined rush for their stronghold, they instantly dropped their sixteen shooters on the floor, made a break for the back windows and doors, and this eye-witness avers that they made the quickest time on record down the declivity in the rear.
>
> It seems that some of our boys who had served from Bull Run to Appomattox could not resist the temptation for some sharp shooting at a foe; but they declared that a black target, changing its level every second so amazingly, afforded them a poor chance to show their skill. There was only one struck fatally on the retreat, and he lingered for several days. Two others, shot in the building, made up all the casualties of its famous affair.[27]

Though Leland admits being a witness to the riot, his version differs substantially from that of the state prosecutor, the indictment and reports from local newspapers. While Leland's inability to attribute good aim to blacks defending themselves may be indicative of a deeper reluctance on his part to accept any form of resistance or martial ability by blacks as justified, the *Daily Phoenix* newspaper reported the following:

> A black man showed his head on a balcony, and a bullet from the square dropped him dead to the ground below. The whites then rushed the armory, broke the door ... the

blacks fired through the weather board as they retreated. Two white men and a little boy were wounded. Two black men were wounded as they retreated.[28]

Testifying that on the day of the riot he was walking with his students from the nearby female college in Laurens, Leland maintained that because the wind was blowing in the opposite direction he was not able to see or hear any confusion or shooting in the town square two streets away! Several witnesses placed him not only at the site of the riot, "shooting and cussin and swearin," but testified that he was seen shooting several times near the spot where a black man was killed.[29]

Denying these claims, Leland reiterated that while he wasn't responsible for the shootings and killings, he totally supported the actions of "enraged citizens" of Laurens against the "irresponsibility" of the blacks, whom he referred to as "Sambo," "Cuffy" and "Boy."[30] Using racially laden metaphors to define the real culprits was meant to indicate to those who supported the curtailment of blacks' aggressive behavior, that he too was of similar mind, though careful enough to minimize any actual involvement in any killings. With this said, the Laurens College president wasn't adverse to claiming that "there is no doubt, that what [afterward] became the 'Ku Klux,' were in their origin, simply organizations for self defense, similar to those in Laurens, just before the outbreak on October 20th 1870."[31] Yet in a remorseful letter to a friend, a deeply concerned Leland lamented about his future and the necessity for white South Carolinians to maintain what he called an interminable fight against "hell," and one's glorious remembrances of a honorable past: "You may break, you may ruin the vase, if you will, But the scent of the roses will hang round it still."[32]

Racial Celebration as Propaganda

As a consummate political pundit and propagandist, Leland also understood that many of his closest contemporaries longed for a return when southern economic growth, founded on the strength and resiliency of slavery, would once more indulge itself in an intemperate form of political elitism and racial dominance. However, Leland of all persons also understood that though the re-enslavement of blacks would never happen, the need to codify southern traditions into laws that would fashion white privileges into a philosophy of white racial hegemony was paramount. This he surmised was essential if any creation of a postwar southern economic and political ethos was to be salvaged. In this respect the success or failure of his brand of literary terrorism hinged on an ability to link the ideas, needs and purposes of terrorist gangs such as the Ku Klux with numerous social, material and philosophical expectations of southern and possibly northern white Americans. In this respect Leland understood that by propagandizing and celebrating race, two important issues would be addressed.

First, for those white south Carolinians needing clarity on what should be the proper way to respond blacks assertiveness and possible insurgency, advice would be provided with ample demonstrations if necessary. Second, racial propagandizing fostered an emotional and highly subjective context that underlined the "righteousness" of attempt secession premised on white racial prerogatives. From this perspective the demise of the Confederacy was safely cushioned within protective hyperbole particularly when Leland confidently proclaimed:

The "bills of mortality" tell a sad tale of many of these who had passed the meridian of their powers; reminding us, mournfully, of what is so often sung thoughtlessly:

> for freedom now so seldom wakes,
> the only throb she gives,
> Is when some heart indignant breaks,
> to tell that still she lives.[33]

Additional reflections by Leland are laced with both nostalgia and foreboding as he attempts to articulate his southern brethren's anguish, an anguish that even as he wrote threaten to turn the entire south once again into an open battlefield. Not inclined to disguise his own certainty that slavery was morally just, he reminded his readers and no doubt his female students at Laurens College that slavery was a fundamental law of the land in 1787, and all efforts aimed at its eradication are indicative of one's disloyalty to the government. He also argued, as if the Civil War had not settled this issue, that a closer examination of northern morality reveals contradictory ideals:

> as long as slavery and the slave-trade continued to be sources of profit, the conscience of the majority slept quietly enough over their great enormities. After a more full development of their appropriate industries, it was found that the slave was an incubus, and he was quietly shipped and sold where his services were regarded as still indispensable. Being thus happily relieved of his presence, and reimbursed for his pecuniary value, they abolished the institution in their own States; and these same consciences *then* became most painfully sensitive to the sins of their neighbors, on whom they had palmed their whole load of *fancied guilt*.[34]

Though the term "fancied guilt" placed the blame for slavery's conception and perpetuation in the Americas, Leland's major thesis focused on an unending struggle between southern claims for sovereign and delegated state constitutional rights, and the federal government's assumptions about its own enumerated rights and prerogatives.[35] Though publicly Leland advocated the former, he bridled at the possible stigma of being an insurrectionist who once advocated rebellion, but in the postwar era could possibly be thought of as a demagogue seeking civil strife! In response to such implications, he continually reminded his critics that the original thirteen states never relinquished their right to remedy faults with federalism by seeking disunion! Employing the testimony of a Rev. Thornwell who attended South Carolina's 1860 convention on secession, Leland sought to buttress his claim that the eventual eleven states that seceded from the Union did so by evoking their constitutional prerogatives:

> That there was a cause, and an adequate cause, might be presumed from the character of the convention which passed the Ordinance of Secession, and the perfect unanimity with which it was done. The convention was not a collection of politicians and demagogues. It was not a conclave of defeated place-hunters, who sought to avenge their disappointment by the ruin of their country. It was a body of grave, sober and venerable men, selected from Every pursuit in life, and distinguished, most of them, in their respective spheres, by every quality which can command confidence and respect. It embraced the wisdom, moderation and integrity of the bench; the learning and prudence of the bar; and the eloquence and learning of the pulpit.
>
> It contained retired planters, scholars and gentlemen, who stood aloof from the turmoil and ambition of public life, and were devoting an elegant leisure to the culture of their

minds, and to quiet any unobtrusive schemes of Christian philanthropy. There were men in that convention utterly incapable of low and selfish schemes, who, in the calm serenity of their judgments, were as unmoved by the waves of popular passion and excitement, as the everlasting granite by the billows that roll against it. There were men there who would listen to no voice but the voice of reason; and who would bow to no authority but what they believe to the be authority of God.

There were men there who would not be controlled by "uncertain opinion," nor be betrayed into "sudden counsels"; men who would act from nothing, in the noble language of Milton, "but from mature wisdom, deliberate virtue, and the dear affection of the public good." That convention, in the character of its members, deserves every syllable of the glowing panegyric which Milton pronounced upon the immortal Parliament of Great Britain which taught the nations of the earth that resistance to tyrants was obedience to God. Were it not invidious, we might single out names, which, wherever they are known, are regarded as synonymous with purity, probity, magnanimity and honor. It was a noble body, and all their proceedings were in harmony with their high character. In the midst of intense agitation and excitement, they were calm, cool, collected and self-possessed.

They deliberated without passion, and concluded without rashness. They sat with closed doors, that the tumult of the population might not invade the sobriety of their minds. If a stranger could have passed from the stirring scenes with which the streets of Charleston were alive, into the calm and quiet sanctuary of this venerable council, he would have been impressed with the awe and veneration which subdued the rude Gaul, when he first beheld, in senatorial dignity, the conscript-fathers of Rome. That in such a body there was not a single vote against the Ordinance of Secession; that there was not only no dissent, but the assent was cordial and thorough-going, is a strong presumption that the measure was justified by the clearest and sternest necessities of justice and of right. That such an assembly should have inaugurated a radical revolution in all the external relations of the State, in the face of acknowledged dangers, and at the risk of enormous sacrifices, and should have done it without cause, transcends all the measures of probability. Whatever else may be said of it, it certainly must be admitted that this solemn act of South Carolina was well considered.[36]

Within this historical prism, various segments of southern white society assumed that their way of life was not only historically correct but indispensable in forging a societal equation that ensured their political and economic survival. Leland noted that the way the Union was constituted,

Not the Union which South Carolina had made sacrifices, neither was this the government for the maintenance for which she had plighted her faith and her sacred honor. She had unanimously entered into a solemn league, and covenant with homogeneous States and allies, in solemn convention assembled; again, in solemn convention assembled, she as unanimously withdrew from this union, when it was revolutionized into a consolidated government, controlled by a hostile party. And yet this solemn and formal expression of the sovereign will of the whole people of a State, has been branded as a "Rebellion"; and the secession of ten States from a revolutionized Union, has been stigmatized as an "insurrection!"[37]

Such an analysis assumed that any deviation by whites *or* blacks from this social contract would be disloyal to the ethics of God and race. Similarly, to be labeled a Republican or an obnoxious black was conterminous with being a Judas.

In addition to these national issues, paternalistic concerns by whites about blacks presupposed that the latter lacked dominion over their own well-being, and as a consequence were incapable of any viable input in the affairs of state. The argument once postulated then asked, how were blacks able to obtain the skills needed for governing or fulfilling positions of responsibility if they have no history or experience of empowerment? Judge Edward Frost at the South Carolinian constitution convention even proclaimed that any incompetence among Freedmen was not of their own making, but the fault of white southerners! Frost queried, "did he [the Freedmen] make himself ignorant? ... Did he ever have a chance to choose his station in life?" Wasn't learning how to read or write an "act of insubordination?"[38] Yet others asked, weren't blacks already functioning in some aspects of government but as Republicans dupes? And if so, how could they be trusted to standup to any white man, Republican or Democratic?[39]

As expected, inquiries of this sort allowed Leland to cite "intolerable annoyances" as examples of his frankness. He opined that the federal government's creation of the "Freedom's Bureau, emerging from its embryo on the Sea Islands, and spreading its filthy meshes all over the State," is reason enough to warrant further suspicion about Republican law makers.[40] Admonishing any conceivable support for the Freedmen's Bureau, Leland suspects and then charges malfeasance:

> These were, at first, mere swindling machines in the hands of sharpers afterwards part contrivances were superadded for the political bondage of the Blackman, far more galling than world-abused "chains of slavery." These man-traps furnished appropriate schooling for that rapacious crew who afterwards reveled in the treasury of the State. Here Scott [General Scott of the Freedmen's Bureau] and his congenial colleagues received that impervious coating over everything like conscience, which fitted him and them for the open robbing of public funds.[41]

Leland and the African American Soldier

Varying his attack, Leland also demeans the abilities and performance of black soldiers in the Civil War. Ignoring the battlefield records of Colored Regiments from states such as Massachusetts, as well as the First South Carolina Colored Volunteer Regiment that was formed by Union forces as early as 1862 on Hilton Head Island,[42] repudiating history he alleges:

> it may be remarked that these colored garrisons, so profusely scattered over the State, rejoiced in the high-sounding title of "57th," "59th," & "Massachusetts Regiments," and some explanation seems necessary for the fact that Massachusetts Regiments were so exclusively selected to march over South Carolina soil, *after the surrender*.[43]

Sensing his readers' distress with blacks ascendancy from enslavement to killers of Confederate soldiers, he warms to his task and reassuringly explains:

> In the malarial regions near Port Royal [Beaufort, South Carolina], including most of the Sea Islands, the slaves employed in the culture of ride and cotton constituted the very lowest type of the African race in the State. They were for the most part the immediate descendants of the latest importations of native Africans brought to our shores, in the constitution to the "slave trade." These were generally worked in large gangs, having but little intercourse with the whites. For example, Governor Aiken owned more than one thousand of them, on his Island of Jehossee, and with the exception of his overseer, his

physician, and the Methodists preacher, they seldom saw a white man from one Christmas to another.

Now, these were the fields from which Massachusetts swelled the numbers of her regiments, with the rank and file, who could not even speak her vernacular. The officers of these regiments may have belonged, and probably did belong, to the "cod fish aristocracy," but all the privates were the genuine Cudjoes and Cuffees of this class—familiarly known as "Gullah negroes."

Their language was an unintelligible jargon to these officers, and nothing short of the "bounty-cash" could have induced them to undertake the drilling of these thick-skulled, semi-savage soldiers.

These garrison commands afforded appropriate training for the richer spoils of the Freedmen's Bureau, into which these self-sacrificing patriots so quickly retired, on the cessation of hostilities; and to which they so tenaciously clung, as long as there was a dollar of congressional appropriation in their treasuries.[44]

Leland's flawed perception of blacks involvement in their fight against chattel enslavement is only surpassed by his feigned ignorance of "Gullah Negroes'" raison d'être. For Leland, the existence of what he styled as a "codfish aristocracy" and their "unintelligible" black soldiers not only inflamed his strong racial bias but shaped his sense of class conflict with northern liberal whites. And while a portion of Leland's formative education occurred in Massachusetts, the heart of New England's codfish aristocracy, it was the Massachusetts 54th Regiment's heroic record in the war that hit a nerve and now unraveled his sensibilities. For example, when word of Leland's death reached the elite military academy of the south, the Citadel, where he taught for nearly eight years, a tribute to his life was prepared and published by the institute's Colonel J. P. Thomas. In his tribute an interesting reference was made to Leland's somewhat mundane military duties during the Civil War, where as a major he was assigned to what in essence was rear guard duties:

> Following the bent of his aroused sensibilities, Major Leland, now formally laid aside the dress of the civilian, for the harness of the soldier. Bringing together a number of choice spirits, he promptly organized a company known as the "Trenholm Rifles." As part of Manigault's Battalion, the company did good service near the mouth of the classic Santee, until the disorganized Conscription Act led to the disbandment of the corps. After this Major Leland, whose figure unfitted him for regular military campaigning. Engaged in desultory State service, and the last years of the war found him in the vicinity of Walhalla, in command of several detachments of State Troops, and charged with the duty of guarding against threatened raids from Tennessee and with other military work.[45]

The likelihood that a southerner with Leland's sentiments and seemingly "unfit figure for regular military service" would ever understand the opinions of Union Private Thomas Long of the 1st South Carolina Volunteers is slight, particularly when the combat-experienced private made his reasons for fighting in the Civil War abundantly clear: "Suppose you had kept your freedom without enlisting in dis army; your chillen might have grown up free and been well cultivated so as to be equal to any business, but it would have been always flung in dere faces—'Your fader never fought for he own freedom.'"[46]

Witnessing the fall of Charleston on February 17, 1865, to "Cudjoe" and "Cuffee" was both a psychologically debilitating and ghastly spectacle for the likes of Leland. It was truth turned to ashes as the "rights of the conquerors" and the "sickening tales of private property seized for government use, or no known use at all, and of private rights insulted and outraged by the elevation of the slave to the position of master" disparaged his secessionist soul.[47] This rage was obviously not shared by the black population, as one witness described:

> While the proud metropolis—the Confederates Holy of Holies—still smoldererd, the Union forces took possession of the harbor defenses—Forts Sumter, Ripley, and Moultrie, and Castle Pinckney—which has so valiantly withstood all previous efforts. A few hours later, at ten in the morning, Lieutenant Colonel A.G. Bennett, of the *Twenty-First U.S. Colored Troops*, reached the city by rowboats from Morris Island and demanded that the mayor formally surrender. The latter quickly sent word of his acquiescence. Bennett acknowledged the reply and added: "My command will render every possible assistance to your well-dispose citizens in extinguishing the flames."
>
> Then into the stricken city marched the Union soldiers, the *Twenty-First U.S. Colored Troops*, followed by a detachment of two companies of the *Fifty-Fourth Massachusetts*. The Bay State Negroes had distinguished themselves at Battery Wagner [Fort Wagner], where they had led the charge, and at Olustee, where they had held back the victorious enemy until a new battle line could be formed. And then for more than a year they had been lying in sight of Charleston. The other Negro soldiers who marched into the city were members of the old *Third* and *Fourth South Carolina Regiments,* many of whom had been numbered in 1860 among Charleston's nearly 18,000 slaves. Now theirs was the high privilege of being the first Federal troops to enter the proud capital city of South Carolina, their own birthplace.[48]

Charles Coffin, a reporter from the *Boston Journal,* became totally enraptured by the historic implications of this moment when he wrote:

> and on this even memorable day they made manifest to the world their superiority in honor and humanity. Here were ex-slaves, with the old flag above them, keeping step to freedom's drum beat, up the grass-grown streets, past the slave shambles, laying aside their arms, working the fire-engines to extinguish the flames, and, in the spirit of the Redeemer of men, saving that which was lost.[49]

On March 21, 1865, another correspondent from the *New York Times* described Charleston's liberation in more detail:

> The occasion was a grand celebration by the freed people of Charleston in honor of their release from bondage. The affair was gotten up under the auspices of Brevet Maj. Gen. Saxton; Brig. Gen. Hatch, commandant of the district; Col. Stewart L Woodford, Commandant of the district; Lieut. Col. A.G. Bennett, Twenty-first United States Colored Troops, Rev. Mr. French; Mr. James Redpath, Superintendent of Schools, and numerous other officers and civilians interested in the good work, of caring for, and aiding the colored population, not only in this city, by wherever they may be located.
>
> On the Sunday preceding the day of the celebration, assembled at Zion Church, that arrangements were in progress to give them an opportunity of manifesting their delight at the new freedom they were enjoying. This announcement, made by Col. Woodford, was received with prolonged shouts and deafening cheers, and all present showed by the eager manner in which they entered into the spirit of the proposition that the affair so far as they were concerned, should not be a failure. And every one who witnessed the proceeding of Tuesday will join in saying that they were not a failure.
>
> The designated place for assembling was at the Citadel-square, and at 12 o'clock, not only the space within the enclosure, but the streets on either side were crowded with men,

women and children, all preparing to form themselves into a procession. At 2 o'clock, the number of people thus assembled reached four thousand, and shortly after that hour, the colored Marshals, who had previously performed the duty assigned them of arranging the school children into companies, and the trade and other organizations into divisions, took their position in the line, and everything was ready for the start.

First in the procession came two colored Marshals on horseback, each wearing badges, and rosettes of red, white and blue. They were followed by an organization of about fifty butchers, who carried their knives at their sides, and in front of them displayed a good size porker.

Next in order came the Twenty-first Regiment United States Colored Troops, Lieut. Col. Bennett, Commanding, preceded by a band. The regiment turned out in nearly full force, and presented a very fine appearance. The music discoursed by the band was very credible, and added much to the general effect of the whole proceedings.

A company of school boys, the leading boy carrying a banner with the device, "we know no masters but ourselves," followed the military, and after them came a car of liberty drawn by black horses and decorated in the most gorgeous manner with flags, steamers and banners. Within the car were seated thirteen young girls, costumed in white, with colored trimmings, and each wearing a white head-dress. As the car passed along, it was saluted by the spectators on each side of the street with cheers, which were acknowledged by the occupants with cheers, which were acknowledged by the occupants with smiles and the waving of handkerchiefs.

The preachers, elders, Sunday-school teachers and bible societies of the various colored denominations in the city formed the next feature in the procession. Then appeared eighteen hundred school children, boys and girls, with their white teachers walking beside them, and displaying mottoes, of which, "We know no cast or color," "The Heroes of the War: Grant, Sherman, Sheridan, Gillmore, Terry, Thomas, Farragut, Dahlgren, Porter," are only a sample.

Throughout the march they observed good order, and showed by their joyful countenances that they thoroughly appreciated the improved change which has been worked out for them. The tailors, carrying shears as the emblem of their trade, and the coopers, with hoops in their hands, turned out in large force. After them came the firemen, there being no less than ten organizations represented in the line. They were dressed in red shirts, with belts around their waists, and made an attractive feature in the procession.

The various Trade Association, including painters, blacksmiths, carpenters, wheelwrights, barbers and others, all came in regular order. These were followed by a cart drawn by a mule, and containing an auctioneer, who was standing over two women seated on a block, with their children standing about them. A boy was also in the cart, whose office was to ring a bell with all the energy possessed. the cart bore the announcement: "A number of Negroes for sale"; and as it moved along the auctioneer would appeal to the crowd for a bid, making use of the phrases which are usually heard in a Negro auction-room. For instance, the bystanders were repeatedly informed that such a one was an excellent cook, or an expert seamstress, or a valuable field-hand, and that some one of the number had run the price up to an extravagant amount-in Confederate money, of course. Attached to the cart was a long rope tied to which was a number of men and women.

Next was a hearse, bearing a coffin, and having the inscriptions: "Slavery is dead"; "Who owns him?" "No one." "Sumter dug his grave on the 13th of April 1861." The hearse was followed by mourners dressed in deep black. Fifty sailors with their officers, a company of wood sawyers, a band of newspaper carriers, and several clubs and associations brought up the rear of the procession. At intervals throughout the line were displayed the American colors, kindly furnished for the occasion by rear-Admiral Dahlgreen.

The route taken was through the principal street of the city below the citadel, and the length of the procession is estimated to have been about three miles. The carriages of Gen. Hatch, Gen. Saxton, and Col. Woodford, were frequently halted and their occupants cheered. Whenever the American flag was passed it was honored with shouts and the waving of handkerchiefs and caps. Stands had been erected at the Citadel square for the accommodation of speakers, but in consequence of rain the addresses were postponed. At a little after dark the proceedings terminated and the participants returned to their homes.

Charleston never before witnessed such a spectacle as that presented on Tuesday of last week. Of course, the innovation was by no means pleasant to the old residents, but they had sense enough to keep their thoughts to themselves. The only expressions of dislike I heard uttered proceeded from a knot of young ladies standing on a balcony, who declared the whole affair "shameful," "disgraceful." The colored people themselves were wild with enthusiasm, and as an evidence of their patriotism it is stated that no less than hundred were enrolled as recruits in the United States service on that one day.[50]

Notwithstanding the pomp and circumstances created by northern celebrations within a generally hostile southern environment, or the role of some 180,000 noncitizen African soldiers and sailors in defeating Confederate forces, the steely experiences of the Civil War fused a number of social pathologies and cultural political predispositions into a tenuous peace. Augmented by the demands of an expanding northern industrialized war economy, institutionalized racism persisted as a stratagem for economic hegemony between victor and loser. That is to say, after four years of war in which over 600,000 soldiers were killed, unresolved racial power relationships were now transferred into what would be an interminable conflict over racial empowerment. Though the Civil War officially ended on April 9, 1865, and millions of Africans were no longer enslaved, the nearly 200,000 colored troops who fought and survived the conflict soon realized that the line between victor and vanquished was far from being settled in 1865.[51] In fact, it was an unremitting hatred for blacks and nonconservative Republicans that motivated southern secessionists, propagandists and educators such as Leland to proclaim that any return to normalcy first required an immediate reinstatement of Anglo-Saxon law and tradition. Accordingly, Leland's book, written in a style reminiscent of many southern white writers of that era, yearned for an idealized "old virtuous South," where survival of the fittest ruled, and most important, all *others* knew their place in the order of things! While neither of these craving would ever be attainable, they bore the old south's mythological stamp of racial privilege and its unmistaken social prerequisites for southern white privilege, social etiquette, political independence and racial separation.[52] As one historian put it, Southern whites bitterness ran deep and many felt "slavery was dead, but slavery was what the Africans were meant for, and something as near as possible to slavery was what they were going to get. The South might have been defeated in war, but her resources for racial oppression were by no means exhausted."[53]

Leland's Literary Terrorism

Embedded in *A Voice from South Carolina* is Leland's glorification of "the old thirteen" colonies as the foundation of all that was pure, in which South Carolina he affirms was the cornerstone: "In one short century, she seems to have run her whole career of rise, progress, decline and fall. She has the same bright sky above her, as in her palmist days;

the same broad rivers flowing from her mountains to he seaboard; the same fertile soil and genial climates."[54]

From this analysis, nostalgia functioning in the defense of an idea was clearly meant to promote emotional thoughts and discussions about a past *American* century filled with exalted struggles against an evil and formidable British foe. Now, almost a hundred years and two rebellions later, historical events had found a new scribe in Leland! Envisioning himself as the quintessential patriot, Leland expressed his own particular "shame" and "fancied guilt" as contributing factors that led to the disintegration of the Union into one Confederate the other federal, when lamenting, "Tis Greece: But living Greece no more."[55]

Constructing a philosophical affiliation with ancient Greece was indeed a very bold strategy for a revisionist such as Leland. By depicting parallels between ancient Greece and America's southern states, he postulated a number of relationships; namely, that Greece's class and caste system and its mythological constructs were comparable to nineteenth-century western slave societies and the notion of a pax Americana.[56] However, those who accepted his moralizing discourses on "that glorious old Anglo-Saxon race" undoubtedly forgot, didn't know or chose to ignore Greece's cultural indebtedness to ancient Egypt! In this regard, author Ronald Segal reminded us that

> Most southern whites, however, had no such prosperity to protect. Yet they were encour-
> aged to believe that whatever their particular circumstances, they were the beneficiaries
> and guardians of a singular civilization, one of stability and harmony and graciousness,
> whose very existence depended upon the system of slavery. A favorable comparison with
> the slave-owning culture of ancient Greece affected especially those few who were rela-
> tively well educated. On small farms and in workshops, more influential was the favorable
> contrast between southern society and the predatory capitalism of the industrial North.
> More influential still was the connection between slavery and color, which gave to the
> meanest white, without hope of a single slave to call his own, a sense of superiority to the
> multitude of blacks.[57]

Very much in line with this analysis, Leland envisioned South Carolina's white population as the last vestige of a superior culture, that while overwhelmed by the forces of evil, struggles on to survive as the beleaguered sentry for humanity and southern white Christian values. Emphasizing this point, he allegorically alludes to the emotions of a repenting son, who in seeking to protect his grieving mother, proclaims "this voice from South Carolina comes from one of her humble sons, whose earnest desire is to cling but the closer to her side on the day of her humiliation."[58]

Of course, not every observer of the ex–Confederacy was as enamored as Leland in describing the south's "humbled sons." For instance, one traveler in northern Alabama reported on the bitterness between struggling yeomen farmers and poor whites who predominated numerically in region dominated by the planter class,

> They are ignorant and vindictive, live in poor huts, drink much, and all use tobacco and
> snuff; they want to organize and receive recognition by the United States government in
> order to get revenge — really want to be bushwhackers supported by the Federal govern-
> ment; they wish to have the power to hang, shoot, and destroy in retaliation for the
> wrongs they have endured; they hate the "big nigger holders," whom they accuse of
> bringing on the war and who, they are afraid, would get into power again; they are the
> "refuge," poor white element of low character, shiftless, with no ambition.[59]

However, existing alongside millions of southern whites who mourned their inert Confederacy was Leland's moralizing polemics that explicitly pitted the rights of "abused" whites against the immediate threat posed by African rule in South Carolina! Warning whites to be psychologically ready for the coming racial Armageddon and a triumphant Denmark Vesey–type rebel, *A Voice from South Carolina* assails the development of "despotic African rule" in the Carolinas and elsewhere.[60] Formulating a message instituted to instill a sense of moral urgency, Leland warned:

> When the passions of men shall have had time to cool down, and the deadly hate so long cherished shall have died out with the generation who have fomented it, the course of South Carolina, in what is called her secession mania, will not appear so reckless and mad as our present [northern] school histories represent it. The *moral mania* on the other side will then come more prominently forward, and even their posterity will wonder at the madness that ruled the hour. Slavery was the occasion of all this mania on both sides, and posterity will know the facts of the case, without being distempered by *morbid sentiment*.[61]

By implication his reasoning decreed that the Civil War was a mistake, a misguided venture into "moral mania" by men of the same cloth, who in their passion did not realize that it was the slave and conspiring abolitionist who divided the Union! It is they, Leland argued, who bore full responsibility for the present calamity, mischief and destructive terror. In a sense, his belittling of liberal whites' "morbid sentiment" and "moral mania" over their *own* slave property attested to his own fundamental pro-slavery stance:

> It will not then be forgotten, that, at the time of the adoption of the constitution , *all* of the States were slave-holding, with a single exception: that slavery was fully recognized and guaranteed in the fundamental law of the land, and that all efforts at its abolition were really acts of disloyalty to the government.[62]

As a member of an articulate and educated southern class, Leland's views on race and class were generally shared by most southern whites. He was astute enough to realize that speech as well as the written word with its array of metaphors and semantic strategies could be used to shape and manipulate human reactions once given the proper social framework. In this respect his personal experiences were the ultimate framework on which he immersed himself in real and figurative battles between the forces of good and evil. These battles as he saw it were largely waged by a succinct use of political propaganda that reshaped humans' perception of reality and hence their actions. This he assumed was true for both the ex-master and the ex-slave.

From this skewed perspective, *A Voice from South Carolina* addressed a number of exigencies faced by returning Confederate soldiers: destroyed plantations, devastated houses, wasted cattle and the freeing of the slave. Discerning that nothing could inflame the passions of these battle-hardened war veterans than newspaper or journal articles depicting "indignant" suffering white women who lost their husbands, sons and fathers to the Confederate cause, he envisions an emotional scene in which returning southern soldiers find devastated homesteads and a "motley gang, miscegenation and open concubinage [now] the prevailing habits of the *new settlers*."[63] With this as his social framework for Reconstruction, he cleverly presupposes that the Confederate warrior knew that "his impulse was to put his family and all he held dear, as far as possible from this moral pestilence. It could be his home no longer," as aliens threatened southern life and traditions, and rule the day.[64]

In allegoric fashion Leland continues on to describe South Carolina's famed city of Charleston not as a port city but as a virtuous female, who once opened her "loving" proud arms to all, but who now laid raped, beaten, and infested by the "peculiar rights of the conquerors."[65] Symbolic descriptions of this sort, devised to elicit a spirited rush of southern nationalism, also alerted devotees that the sacredness of a once-proud land that was personified by Robert E. Lee, John C. Calhoun, slavery and chivalry was now imperiled and all should petition as he did, "Father, forgive them; they know not what they do."[66]

Although poetic at times, Leland's verbiage in describing southern virtue was often in direct conflict with historical data. For example, his use of Biblical phrases and characters such as Sampson as analogies for South Carolina's post–Civil War period is ludicrous, yet symptomatic of a deeper malaise that for centuries southern whites labored under: a psychological love-hate impasse with the enslaved that ultimately raised questions as to southern whites' psychological inadequacy as enslavers. For example, historian T.J. Stiles noted in his study on terrorism and interracial relationships during American slavery that "the relationship between master and slave was complicated, contradictory, and sometimes unsettling."[67] He further notes that "Slave-owners entertained a convoluted, paradoxical outlook. On the one hand they believed that blacks were intrinsically inferior; on the other, they implicitly acknowledged their humanity."[68] If this observation is correct, it was the Africans' sense of their own humanity that whites felt a need to control by force. Addressing this concern, Frederick Douglass wrote, "If a slave has a bad master, his ambition is to get a better; when he gets a better, he aspires to have the best; and when he gets the best, he aspires to be his own master."[69]

In addition, Leland's figurative use of the terms "motley gang," "miscegenation," and "concubine" to describe the African female materialized as an attempt to dismiss the victim role of enslaved females in the institutionalized miscegenation's slave-owners world of rape. This of course is intriguing coming from the president of a women's college, albeit for white females. Though Leland dedicated his book to the "Woman of South Carolina" it was a futile attempt to replace the villainous reality of sexual assault and violence visited on enslaved women with a self-indulgent reference to southern white women by a pampered, vindictive aristocracy.[70] This kind of pandering and excessive manipulation of reality is instructive as to what can occur in a world of illusory virtuosity where the once proud are defeated yet see demons at every turn. Social psychologist Robert Bales noticed that in such volatile situations:

> The culture of the interacting group stimulates in each of its members a feeling that he has entered a new realm of reality — a world of heroes, villains, saints, and enemies — a drama, a work of art. The culture of a group is a fantasy established from the past, which is acted upon in the present. In such moments, which occur not only in groups, but also in individuals responses to works of art, one is "transported" to a world which seems somehow even more real than the everyday world.[71]

In the case of South Carolina, persecution as perceived by the Lelands of the south, was ultimately the result of an onslaught of "demons" such as "scalawags," "carpetbaggers," "radical Republicans," and "niggers" who had to be resisted by spirited men called Ku Klux. Similarly, he claims that once the war had terminated, no animosity or revenge was felt by southerners toward the Negro; for they "behaved admirably during the four long years — when almost all domestic interests had been left to their care and management — and the whites felt grateful to them" for that![72] This changed, Leland claims, once the actions of "scoundrels and carpetbaggers" won the day and destroyed an otherwise balanced relationship between the races.[73] Finally and incredulously he declares:

> The Negro was, in no way, responsible for his emancipation, nor was generation of whites [1860–65] responsible for his past servitude. Both parties had been born under the institution of slavery, and there were no heart-burnings nor feelings of revenge, until these were sown in their hearts by designing scoundrels. If these carpetbaggers had been starved out, as they easily might have been, and the two races left to themselves, there would have been a continuance of that harmony which had resulted from mutual dependence and mutual good will.[74]

As pointed out earlier, the psychological dilemma for southern whites hinged on the argument that Africans were inanimate objects, something devoid of true human responses, a being that could only be led by patronizing whites or deluded by conniving northern white radicals. However convenient this argument might have seemed to Leland and his associates, its reasoning was seriously flawed when economic development within black communities gained strength and momentum. For example, the impact and growth of black newspapers with their prolific black writers and politically involved editors was profoundly significant, particularly in organizing the underground railroad and emigration movements to Canada and Haiti throughout the antebellum years of 1827 to 1861. In a few instances they even openly advocated support for armed slave revolts.[75] In fact, the development of social institutions by free blacks during slavery not only ensured their survival after the Civil War but constituted a social development that defied cultural and certainly business expectations of the day, while implicitly suggesting that given the opportunity, black Americans might become an economic or political threat to white dominance in the future.[76] These efforts and others, no matter how small in numbers, contradicted Leland's thesis of an apathetic, inanimate black populace.[77]

Nevertheless southern whites' disregard of these prima facie facts revealed a vital intellectual weakness in southern racist mythology: its general failure to curtail the intellectual abilities and dispositions of Freedmen in the face of white racism and mythology. In fact one historian noted that after emancipation, "The average ex slave tried to get away from whites as [well] quickly as he could. Radical Reconstruction did little to slow this rush toward separatism ... Over the course of Reconstruction the percentage of blacks who owned land increased from nearly nothing to 20 percent, while white landownership dropped by 13 percent."[78] Not surprisingly, many mid–nineteenth-century whites asked how it was possible that a supposedly inferior race, living for centuries in substandard social conditions as slaves, could suddenly articulate opinions so clearly as did Frederick Douglass and a multitude of other fugitive blacks.[79] In his autobiography, *My Bondage, My Freedom*, Douglass addressed this very question by revealing a letter he sent to his publisher in 1855, in which he laid the issue to rest for those who doubted his abilities:

> I see, too, that there are special reasons why I should write my own biography, in preference to employing another to do it. Not only is slavery on trial, but unfortunately, the enslaved people are also on trial. It is alleged, that they are, naturally inferior; that they are so *low* in the scale of humanity, and so utterly stupid, that they are unconscious of their wrongs, and do not apprehend their rights. Looking then, at your request, from this stand-point, and wishing everything of which you think me capable to go to the benefit of

my afflicted people, I part with my doubts and hesitation, and proceed to furnish you the desired manuscript; hoping that you may be able to make such arrangements for its publication as shall be best adapted to accomplish that good which you so enthusiastically anticipate.[80]

White South Carolinian Fears

White Americans marginalizing of African Americans' civil and human rights throughout the south and in much of the north was generally rationalized away to be a result of their low intellectual capabilities and inferior cultural attributes. This belief was reinforced by a dogma of intolerance that restricted most white Americans' understanding of racial conflict to be either what they have read in newspapers or information they received through conversation. Consequently, what was considered common and time-tested knowledge on race, slavery and Reconstruction was more often than not information premised on orchestrated political agendas.

This was the case in South Carolina were a persistent post–Civil War secessionist-minded white population of varying class backgrounds now confronted the political and economic vigor of an ex-enslaved population determined to shed over 250 years of imposed racial subjugation. Within this political cauldron, propagandists similar to Leland reminded their white constituents that irrespective of what ones social status was vis-à-vis the slave before Appomattox, in those minuscule or grand things of daily life, race would forever be the primary denominator, definer and arbitrator of social position. In this fashion new recruits to the Ku Klux Klan in 1867 were charged with the following order:

> Our main and fundamental objective is the *maintenance of the supremacy of the white race* in this Republic. History and Physiology teach us that we belong to a race which nature had endowed with an evident superiority over all other races, and that the Maker, in thus elevating us above the common standard of human creation, has intended to give us over inferior races a dominion from which no human laws can permanently derogate.[81]

With the enemy clearly targeted and an enraged white populace's symbols of dominance now seemingly defined by official Ku Klux mandates, challenges by audacious blacks on a daily basis forced the Lelands of South Carolina to lecture, harangue and otherwise incite southern whites to use violence as a means of halting blacks' enfranchisement. Bemoaning the times, Leland explains,

> South Carolina was particularly odious as the leader in Secession. Whatever justification or appeal came from her borders, fell on ears most unsympathizing, and the stereotyped reply, "served her right!" was the only satisfaction vouchsafed. Her slaves were in a vast majority, more than three to two in the aggregate, and in some sections of her low country, as many as ten to one. The congressional policy of reconstruction, therefore, has not only revolutionized her government and closed her record as one of the "old thirteen," but has changed her caste among the peoples of the earth, as far as legislation can do so. A native from the wilds of Africa could, at that time, have reached higher stations, and enjoyed greater privileges and immunities, than any of her native-born sons of the great Anglo-Saxon family.[82]

Concerns about social if not physical displacement was very much grounded in the physical fear of southern whites of the native "from the wilds of Africa." With the abolition of slavery by the Thirteenth Amendment, the ratification of the Fourteenth Amendment and its due process and property rights provisions, and then the enactment of the Fifteenth Amendment's voting rights constructs in 1870, the sinews of political control appeared to ever so slowly favor "the native" majority in South Carolina. For whites living in Florida, Mississippi, Louisiana and South Carolina, where blacks constituted a strong numerical majority, the implications were immense.[83]

This alarming situation was but a prelude to "the slaves'" elevation and political equality with (if not dominance over) their former owners. Advocating that whites must resist any such attempts for black empowerment, Leland blamed "thick-skinned, heartless, zealous carpetbaggers" and black Republicans for creating a cruel situation that was "sowing suspicion, enmity and even deadly hate between the races," a situation that he emphatically believed had transformed the "inoffensive Sambo" into a political instrument for Republican use.[84] The problem as he saw it was getting white Carolinians to revise their fear of being a beleaguered helpless minority into that of an organized physical force that could resist a vengeful and impassioned black majority. He implores his readers to accept the notion that quickness of mind, stealth and assertiveness were not exclusive characteristics of a particular strata of whites, but innate attributes of all whites regardless of their class background.

As if a Confederate military defeat never occurred, Leland condemned any recognition of black enfranchisement, choosing instead to infer that the "old thirteen" of 1776 was betrayed by Republicans when they placed the "native from the wilds" above the "native-born sons" of America.[85] With this as his vision of Reconstruction, the native African was an annoyance, an alien, a bothersome thing, a social irritant, an interloper, but most significantly an economic competitor and a visual reminder of social, political and cultural differences within the nation.

Commenting on this kind of anxiety, social psychologist J.A.C. Brown observed that extreme expressions and demonstrations of ethnocentric behavior, similar to Leland's, often occur when the legitimacy of a social philosophy is at stake. When this happens, forceful violent deeds are rationalized as necessary defensive acts that in time forge a stronger sense of group solidarity. As a result:

> Frustrated people need to hate because hatred when shared with others is the most potent of all unifying emotions: as Heine wrote; "What Christian love cannot do is effected by a common hatred." Psychologically speaking, what happens is that, when an individual is frustrated in his attempt to reach a goal, aggression naturally arises, probably with the original function of massing all his energies to overcome the obstacle. But when this cannot be done, the aggression must be turned in one or both of two directions: inwardly against the self, or outwardly against a substitute object.[86]

Similarly, Leland utilized a style of language that endeavored to reduce his readers' political options to a common denominator, anti–Republicanism. Any deviation from this way of thinking had to be crushed. Accordingly, ex-overseers, traders, planters, white merchants, ex–Confederate soldiers, indigent whites, household mothers and their children had to be persuaded and if need be terrorized to accept the notion that it was an unholy union of black Republicans and white abolitionists that conspired and forged the nation's disintegration into civil war, the demise of the Confederacy and the folly of postbellum Reconstruction![87] Tragically, the veracity of these assertions were of no immediate concern for advocates of southern white empowerment. Their only concern was that enough blacks and whites would be so enraptured by Ku Klux ideology and its notions of invincibility that they would overlook the Klan's essential weakness and inept racist mythology. This however would not be the case as armed resistance by individuals and organized groups of Freedmen throughout the latter half of the nineteenth-century rose to the challenge and in doing so established a heroic legacy of armed resistance to racist oppression.

Epilogue

Throughout the nineteenth century, armed attacks by antislavery activists and later antiracist forces against terrorist elements have seldom received open praise from an otherwise sympathetic African American population. This was the case on October 16, 1859, when John Brown led eighteen men in an attack against slavery by assaulting the United States Federal Arsenal and Armory at Harpers Ferry, Virginia. This was also the case when twenty-eight years earlier Nathaniel Turner led a band of raiders in a deadly attack on slave-owning families in Southampton, Virginia. Similarly, only muted praise was offered or discussed in black newspapers when blacks, whites and indigenous rebels under the Lumbee leadership of Henry Berry Lowrie and his guerrilla fighters fought against racist paramilitary groups such as the Ku Klux Klan throughout the 1870s to 1890s. In addition, little has been written explaining why Lowrie's armed struggle against the Ku Klux Klan throughout in North Carolina was generally successful or how black farmers in Darien, Georgia, were able to secure a level of respect between themselves and local whites. By not fully understanding how the philosophy of armed resistance and retaliation emerged as an effective tool for Freedmen during reconstruction, the unwary traveler through the past might easily fall victim to the mythological ravings and analysis of distorted history.

It is apparent that when detailed examination of historical data from Reconstruction is weaned from nineteenth-century newspapers, archives and personal diaries, examples of armed resistance by African Americans to racist provocations is available. However, compiling this data requires of the researcher an ability to understand that most acts of resistance by blacks to either racist provocations or defense of their homes or family was masked by official labels and statistics indicating criminality! As a result the armed bandit outside of town may not be that much different in motivation from the mugger who robbed a gentleman walking down King Street in Charleston. They both were responding to a system that neither created, yet were condemned to survive in. Similarly, the sharecropping Freedmen who was awakened at night to find Klansmen or others at their cabin door were considered criminals if they proceeded to fire their pistol or rifle in self-defense. New Orleans Innocents who paraded with flags depicting a black man held to the ground by a white man with a knife to his neck were not viewed as inciting racial conflict but simply practicing their constitutional right to demonstrate. It is also apparent that while increased forms of institutionalized racism and provocative actions by local citizens precipitated racial clashes in the late 1860s, fundamental social or political causes beyond that of violated social mores and tradition were not addressed by either conservative or liberal newspapers editors. Though the notion of white criminality was unknown when it came to the issues of racial prerogatives, blackness as a social and political concept became criminalized through the actions of extralegal organizations and supporting state laws. By 1868 ensuing discussions by Freedmen on available legitimate forms of day-to-day resistance to personal infringements increasing (from the perspective of conservative whites) became relegated to acts of criminality. For many Americans regardless of racial background, legitimate armed resistance by nonwhites in any context as a response to racism was absent and consequently unthinkable, yet it occurred.

Thus both Louisiana and South Carolina Freedmen who rejected the notion of having to stand up or outside a streetcar due to their color were labeled by conservatives as troublemakers or criminals. Conversely, whites injured after an altercation with discriminated blacks were quickly converted into victims of an outrage! Even more revealing are a paucity of articles in the Freedmen press that would even consider legitimizing reports of armed blacks defending themselves against white gangs. This observation is even more significant in that it suggests that while some editors were concerned about the limits of their First Amendment rights, others were worried about violent repercussions. Tragically one of the unspoken realities of being black in America during the latter half of the nineteenth century was the forced ambivalence that some narrators felt impelled to portray when it came to the issue armed self-defense. Consequently, succeeding generations attempting to fully comprehend the exigencies of Reconstruction and Ku Klux terrorism were confronted with the challenge to get past the mythologies of a past era.

Part of the social historians dilemma is that not until recent years has the perception of a freedom fighter been associated with black Americans or their struggle against racist elements within America itself! The image of armed blacks killing members of the Ku Klux is not part of American folklore. The concept for many whites and undoubtedly black Americans was an anathema. Better understood or tolerated is the image of a lynched Freedmen. Thus, one of the unspoken realities of being black in America is having an awareness of white America's historical reluctance about the portrayal of race and armed social conflict. Unfortunately, resulting assumptions made about American democracy preclude serious discussions on terrorism by Americans against Americans. As a result, armed resistance by black Americans to attacks by pro–American but antiblack groups during Reconstruction and afterward were consistently depicted as criminal! As expected, when armed resistance appeared effective, inquiries pertaining to the political efficacy of armed resistance by blacks were then excessively debated, analyzed and evaluated within the constructs of the dominant institutional structures as a social problem.

An even more contentious observation is observed when evaluating how this salient issue is portrayed in educational institutions. For example, one can speculate on the frequency that text such as William Styron's novel *The Confessions of Nat Turner,* John Lofton's *Insurrection in South Carolina: The Turbulent World of Denmark Vesey* or a lesser known but important work, *Black Freedom/White Violence, 1865–1900,* edited by Donald Nieman, are cited for their important analysis on the conditions and personalities that are shaped by terror-framed social environments. In this respect American history books have generally forgotten, overlooked or minimized the efforts of its native black sons and daughters in their fight against American home-grown terrorism. Even more grievously, when vigorous response by blacks, people of color or antiracist whites *are* addressed, they are portrayed as mad men, criminals or misguided adventurers. This was the situation when Lowrie and his band of raiders were depicted as Robin Hood types, devoid of political clarity but saturated with personal vendettas and uncontrollable blood thirsts! Similarly, with the exception of recently published studies, radical white antislavery activists such as John Brown were and are depicted as mad men, psychotic, extreme religious zealots who easily led groups of duped blacks and traitorous whites into misadventures, such as the 1858 attack on Harpers Ferry.[1]

Even more egregious are the forgotten names, biographies and testimonies of black men and woman who participated directly and indirectly in armed resistance efforts against extreme racial oppression throughout the centuries of American slavery. Few Americans able are able to identify the raiders at Harpers Ferry or why the attack occurred. Fewer even realize that those blacks who participated in the attack; Dangerfield Newby, Shields Green, John Anthony Copeland, Jr., Lewis Sheridan Leary, and Osborne Perry Anderson where the predecessors to almost 200,000 black soldiers who eventually fought against slavery just sixteen months later. Furthermore, years later when history books underscored the brilliance of American poet laureate Langston Hughes, they seldom mentioned that it was his grandmother Mary Sampson Patterson Leary's recollections about her first husband, Lewis Sheridan Leary, who fought against slavery at Harpers Ferry that aided Hughes in his own political development and understanding of the workings of racism.[2] Though one can only speculate about the influence this knowledge had on Hughes's thoughts and creative expression as a writer and poet, one biographer did write:

> He was too young as a schoolboy to place in historical perspective some of the events his grandmother related, but the remembrance of them remained with him. On one occasion she took him to Osawatomie, where John Brown lived; there, three years before she died, he saw her seated on the speaker's platform with Teddy Roosevelt, honored as the last surviving widow of John Brown's raid on Harpers Ferry.[3]

Years later in a letter to Arthur Spingarn, a friend and avid collector of books and archives about African Americans, Langston underscored the importance of knowing this history, "I didn't know any of the things you told me about Sheridan Leary in your letter. I am mighty glad to have those facts, and it was surely good of you to look them up for me. I wish I had been old enough to learn more from my grandmother before she died."[4]

On the other hand, many Americans black and white are familiar with an almost folkloric ardor, secessionist notables of the Confederate States of America, such as Robert E. Lee, Jeb Stuart, and Jefferson Davis![5] The implications of these historical priorities are very apparent: the continued absence in literature of African Americans as armed freedom fighters against slavery and racial terrorism is not by accident, but symptomatic of an attempt by many scholars and institutions to view this kind of historical representation within the educational curriculum with disgust. Needless to say, institutional fear of what such testimonies might depict about America's bloody battle with racial phobias is not as troubling as the nations continued receptiveness of terrorist symbols as an acceptable facet of Americana.

However unfortunate it may be, social political history interpreted by educators and with the mindset of a John Leland will always be saturated in mythological triumphs and ascribed racial authority. This was certainly the case after the Civil War when philosophy's of social truth, power retention and ascribed racial hegemony were synonymous primarily because they rested on rationalized pillars of human aggression. In this respect, psychologist John Crayton reminds us that

> Human aggression is most dangerous when it is attached to the great absolutarian psychological constellations, the grandiose self and the archaic omnipotent object. The most gruesome human destructiveness is encountered, not in the form of wild, regressive and primitive behavior, but in the form of orderly and organized activities in which the perpetrators' destructiveness is alloyed to absolute conviction about their greatness and with their devotion to archaic omnipotent figures.[6]

Ironically, notwithstanding their attack on the federal government and losses during the Civil War, southern secessionist easily discerned that America's vision of greatness and manifested destiny was still *their* birthright! With this as an assumed social truth, Leland's *A Voice from South Carolina,* as well as Ella Gertrude Thomas's diary, *The Secret Eye,* were unquestionably convenient vehicles created to establish a world that perpetuated an American vision premised on racial and indeed class privilege. In fact, their individual testimonies are significant not because of any supposed notion of historical accuracy, but because they provided later generations with a detailed *subjective* recitation on what *they* believed to be the *truth* in their time!

Lacking the ability to walk in Ella Thomas's shoes, one must value her succinctly written diary as a valuable insight into the daily household dilemma of a postbellum, former slave-owning plantation family on the path to financial ruin. Surrounded by social confusion and political disruption, Ella's diary exudes both personal fear and uncertainty about the future, yet portends a deeply felt commitment to southern class values and her beloved Confederacy, particularly when she wrote:

> I am writing history for you my children and your mother tells you now of her interview with the man whom she *"most delights to honor"* — tells you of our President Jefferson Davis, dearer far dearer now in the hour of defeat than he was when Chief magistrate of the Southern Confederacy. How I sympathized with our fallen chieftain in his degradation when he was taken through our streets closely guarded, no woman in that hour of peril to wave her handkerchief to him to make sign of sympathy and men so crushed by defeat that the closed carriage passed by crowds who dared not to cheer him for fear of sharing his fate. We could do nothing else for you my President and we did all we could. We named our boy for you, our boy who during the firsts year of the war I never dreamed of calling for our successful chief, but we felt honored in identifying ourselves with him in his change of fortune.[7]

Though Ella's testimony on a deadly southern fantasy facilitates our understanding of life for a certain class of southern *whites* in the aftermath of civil war, surely those *black* soldiers who captured Jefferson Davis or those watching him pass through the streets as a captive held quite a different view. What thoughts roamed through *their* minds' eyes about the Confederacy? They too were southerners. And while Ella was certainly not writing for them, unfortunately little testimony exist of the world from their perspective. Yet one can speculate as to the derision if not outright contempt held for their prisoner or Confederates in general.[8]

Ultimately millions of southern whites and secessionists in particular were soon confronted with the reality that the deadly fantasy which they were weaned on since childhood had now gone terribly wrong. And though the Ella Thomases of the south penned wretched and despairing thoughts in diaries for posterity, neither their testimony nor nostalgia could eliminate or neutralized the terror-filled experiences of Ku Klux victims. However, thoughtful analysis on Ku Klux terror and its supporters do raise additional questions about the processing of information in stressful situations such as what was occurring in the latter part of nineteenth-century America.

For example, we know that an individuals understanding of an event is critically affected by the way information is received and transmitted. Moreover, varying historical periods were replete with different methodological constructs by which events and information were converted into meaningful data. Knowing the time and speed in which events are processed, reviewed and understood within identifiable historical contexts such as nineteenth-century southern America is critical when assessing or giving meaning to events or people within that period.[9]

Correspondingly, *time* as a measurable entity in nineteenth-century America, especially in southern states, was different from many other parts of the country. Words, sentences and conversations occurred in response to different stimuli, and as a result how information was received and analyzed during the nineteenth century was considerably slower than today.[10] Understanding this phenomenon is critical when discerning how decisions were rendered 150 years ago. In the south as in many agricultural regions, information and opinion-making processes occurred more often from mediation, contemplation and reflection that eventually was restructured and streamlined into data and eventually knowledge.[11] This process was essential for the maintenance of a sense of community. That is to say, communication and information processing helped define community networks. In fact, the concept of community was established by the effective development of face-to-face verbal networks that in turn fostered a community's sense of order and well-defined expectations. A more critical analysis of these southern rural and town networks reveal a meaningful hierarchy of moral, social and power relationships among community members that in itself became important to information transmission.[12]

For propagandists like John A. Leland, communication linkages within a southern parochial and colloquial social structure such as Laurens, South Carolina, were vital for his efforts to get community folk to make the correct associations for what *he* deemed should be the proper development of postbellum South Carolina. In this regard his decision to evaluate South Carolina through *A Voice from South Carolina*'s journal format was similar to Ella Thomas's diary in that both methods were highly subjective, and in specific instances, almost gospel-like in their appeals. While their candor and reasoning rarely complemented each other, they acquiesced to the emotional needs of a vanquished order, the Confederacy. In spite of this, every repudiation of the Freedmen's presence by southerners such as Leland and Thomas inadvertently admitted to the ex-slaves' saliency as a political, economic, intellectual, physical and psychological threat! Thus, a quixotic notion of racial preeminence combined with an infectious form of social paranoia filled the pages of their respective works, compelling the reader to envision a *frightening* fulfillment of an apocalyptic prophecy — tyrannical African rule![13]

With this said, an even more serious predicament existed for the Lelands and Thomases of the south in that total Freedmen enfranchisement by 1870 was no longer a theory but a

distinct possibility. This being the case, any resulting recognition of the ex-slaves' humanity immediately challenged southern whites' childhood illusions and adult obsessions about
the character of a supposed Sambo, Cudjoe and Cuffee![14] The paradox of course was that
for white Americans, whether they were southern Democrats, northern conservative Republicans or die-hard secessionist or liberals, it was agreed that it was far better to have a compliant nonaggressive, deferential dependent stereotype "sambo"-type Freedmen in
government or business than one who was self-reliant, assertive and vengeful, one who conservatives feared would assuredly establish a troublesome nonwhite hegemonic political
challenge! Assuredly apologists for the Confederacy would have suggested it was better to
have a compliant Harriet Beecher Stowe novel, *Uncle Tom's Cabin, or Life Among the Lowly*
(1852), as a literary model for the future, than Martin Delany's description of a successful
rebel leader in his novel, *Blake: or, The Huts of America* (1859). Better a black South Carolinian conservative like William Beverly Nash in the state legislature than an anticonser-
vative and undefeated Lumbee guerrilla leader like Lowrie who roamed the countryside!
In this respect southern conservatives anticipated that by temporarily supporting deferential black leadership, whites and blacks could be induced to generally accepting these stereotypes as the only acceptable models for social tranquility. While much of this reasoning
was premised on centuries of class and racial dominance, it was primarily an analysis float-
ing on a sea of mythology, or as Ralph Ellison noted, "And as always when the belief which
nurtures a great social myth declines, large sections of society become prey to superstition.
For man without myth is Othello with Desdemona gone: chaos descends, faith vanishes
and superstitions prowl in the mind."[15]

Though Leland's interpretation of Christian values, Grecian history and seething
Anglo-Saxon ethnocentricity reinforced the likelihood of racial conflict, without racial
social stratification throughout the south open violent class warfare among white Americans would have occurred. Through the promoting of racial and caste differences, southern
propagandists similar to Leland were able to provided a necessary social disguise for an
emerging capitalist structure that concluded; any fostering of racial alliances among both
rural and urban workers was a problematic and political, albeit socialist threat that needed
to be averted. A speaker at the 1869 Philadelphia Labor Convention either purposely or
inadvertently clarified the danger for astute industrialist and planters when he posited the
following observation:

> To any one who has watched the deliberations of this congress of artisans and working-
> men, one peculiar fact stands out in a bold relief, viz., that the barriers of class and caste
> have been broken down, so far as the laboring classes of the country are concerned, if we
> are to take the solemnly-avowed sentiments of this body as indicative of the feelings that
> exist among the constituencies therein represented. For the first time in the history of this
> nation a convention has been held in which working-men and working-woman, white and
> black, loyalist and ex-rebels, have met together upon terms of perfect equality, for the pur-
> pose of taking deliberative action on vital questions affecting equally the interest of all.[16]

Unquestionably neutralizing this type of nascent interracial cooperation between urban
workers and rural farmers was paramount among conservative southern propagandists, if
white intraracial struggle over class and ethnic domination was to be avoided. Race therefore as a social and political construct became a critical factor in eliminating nonwhite
Americans from equal participation in the affairs of the nation, as federal laws protecting

the Freedmen were minimized, circumvented, ignored or otherwise reneged on. In similar fashion, Ku Klux mythology and propaganda descended on the languishing spirit of a frustrated, angered and terribly deceived southern white population who contrary to their mythological notions of honor and integrity, tragically designed an unparalleled type of moronic violence during Reconstruction and called it valor! Out of this milieu, nineteenth-century American terrorism as a deadly fantasy embodied by the Ku Klux was nourished and institutionalized to become a major violator of American civil and human rights.

Appendix A:
A Planter's Letter to
The New York Times

Alternative forms of labor, such as the use of Chinese laborers, were also discussed in this *New York Times* letter, August 16, 1869, p. 2, col. 6.

The experiment of introducing coolie labor, now so much the rage, I fear, will not for many years prove successful. The Negro is no fool. He understands that coolie labor is intended to supersede him, or as a means to coerce him into the planter's terms. He will not willingly submit to be driven from old home, or to accept a bare subsistence by the introduction of the stranger.

Now to a comparison of the best of negro and coolie labor. This year the wages of a "full hand" on the coast and islands of South Carolina are from $50 to $70 per annum, with the usual reaction, viz, three pounds of bacon, one peck of meal or grist, one quart of molasses and a pint of salt per week, and such quarters as the plantations afford, a garden spot, and from one-half to one acre of land for his corn and potatoes. Where the hands are employed by the year, they perform task-work. These task are the same they performed for their old masters, and is the only relic of the old 'regime' that they will recognize. The task are not heavy, and a good hand can, by going to the fields at daylight, get through with his task by noon, and do it well. The balance of the day they devote to their own corn and potato patches....

Call the average wages paid during the year on a cotton plantation $60; the rations will cost the planter $40; making the cost of a full hand $100.

The coolie costs, to begin with, for passage, profit to importer, etc., $100 and his wages from $12 to $15 a month — say, for the year, $160; cost of his rations, consisting of rice, fish, pork. Etc., will not be less than $40; add yearly proportion of advance — say one-fifth, $20, amounts to $200. In case the coolie dies or runs away, the whole advance is lost, making $300, or three times the cost of negro labor. The only advantage the planter has is that he can keep his coolies in the field all day, or from sun to sun, but can the weak and inexperienced coolie do as much work during day, and do it as well as the Negro, who was born with the hoe in his hand, can do in half the time? I think not, for the first year at least. The negro, physically, morally and mentally is by far superior to the coolie, and if conciliated and fairly treated by the planter, is the cheapest and most intelligent laborer for the South. What is demoralizing the laborers of the South is the "share system" and the "two days" system and this arises from no fault of the planter, but is the consequence of his poverty. Stripped of everything save land, by the war and the emancipation of his slaves, he has not the ability to pay wages, and since the war, nearly every planter on the coast and islands has had hard work to feed his family on the plainest food, and only cornbread and bacon could be found for months on the board, where, before the war, all the luxuries of the world were common.

On the "share system," by which the Freedmen are to receive a portion of the corn and cotton — usually one-third the cotton and one-half the corn crop — usually one-third the cotton and one-half the corn crop — he is fed by the planter, and the cost of his rations is deducted from his share of the cotton crop at the end of the year. In many instances during the last three years, when the crop has been sold, he has learned that he has eaten, up his share of the cotton, and in some instances is in debt; this result being caused by the ravages of the caterpillar, and bad seasons, and not by any bad faith on the part of the planter, who has made one bag of cotton when he should have made ten. Nevertheless, the negro is very suspicious, and imagined himself wronged by his employer, and determines that he will not work again on the "share system," so he falls into the "two days system," which is to say, he agrees to pay the planter for the rent of generally three acres of poor land, two days labor per week. These two days' labor in many, I may say in most instances are given with reluctance, and performed in the most careless and slovenly manner, and in many cases are not performed at all.

I have seen this year, in June, the cotton choked by grass and doomed to destruction, on this system, and the planter helpless and fated to another year of poverty and suffering. As the poverty of the planter compels him to adopt such expedients as the "share system" and the "two days system," so the poor Freedmen, on the "two days' system," are compelled to neglect not only their own patch of corn and cotton, which frequently is overrun with grass but in order to get corn and bacon with which to keep their families alive, they engage with the more fortunate planters in the vicinity, who can pay wages, in money or food, and this the poor planter loses his two days' labor, or has it performed in such a manner as to be productive of nothing.

The white man is decidedly the superior of the negro, and in any conflict between the two races, the negro must go to the wall. The American African is superior to the Mongolian, and in a conflict between those races the Mongolian goes down. The introduction of the coolies into the South must necessarily, owning to the poverty of the planters, be very slow. The hostility of the negroes against the coolies will be from the start, and without the armed assistance of the whites, the latter will be driven from the country. To introduce the coolies in numbers sufficient to cultivate the cotton and r ice crops of the South to their full extent — say five millions — would require fifty years, and an utter extermination of the Negro, leaving the country in the meantime a howling wilderness. Are the planters aware of the fact that by our immigration laws, no immigrant laborer can be held to serve for a longer period than twelve months, no matter what the contract, or how much has been advanced him. Without a change in these laws eh is a free man at the end of twelve months' service.

How can our Sea Island cotton planters pay $12 to $15 per month, besides rations, to coolies at the present price of the staple —from 40c to $1 per pound — against Egyptian competition, where a few cents per day is paid to laborers? Are we not deluding ourselves by believing that we possess the only soil and climate suitable to raise the long stable cotton? Already we have been surprised at the progress made in Egypt in the quality and quantity of her cotton, every year showing an improvement in the length of the staple. Samples of "Egyptians" were exhibited lately in Charleston that the best judges there could not tell from some of our best medium sorts, and superior to Floridas. Every year this improvement and increase of production is going on in Egypt and other countries, and competing more and more successfully with our own Sea Island cotton; and not-withstanding "we have the only belt of country in the world suitable for the production of fine cotton," we see year by year the prices for our finer sorts running done in Liverpool. Soon we shall be compelled to abandon growing of the finer sorts of long staple and confine our efforts to medium qualities: and how long we can do that against the competition of the cheap labor of Egypt and other countries who can tell? All this the planter will say is an argument in favor of cheap labor. So it is, but do we get it by paying coolies $12 to $15 per month, and feeding them besides?

The only way to have cheaper labor than we have in the negro is in the apprentice system of Cuba, where the coolie is held for eight years and paid $4 per month. Will our legislators give us this system? I judge not from the opinions lately expressed against the coolie trade. What the South most needs to make her prosperous is capital. With capital the planter can manage and control the present laborer. Where her pays him in cash and promptly, and keeps good faith with him, his work is satisfactory, and the negro civil, obedient and respectful. Who raised the past year's crop 2,500,000 bales, and who is raising the prospective 3,000,000 bales of the present year? Not the coolie — not the white man — but the negro produced this vast amount of wealth for the country. What a commentary upon the too-prevalent fashion of abusing the negro for his idleness, etc. Does the country want 5,000,000 bales of cotton? Let capitalist furnish the money to worthy and intelligent planters, and the country will get them. Do we wish to avoid the vices and evils of paganism and all the political and civil trouble that must follow the introduction of the coolie? Furnish the capital that is so abundant at the North, and you will not only get the cotton, but you will do more for the benefit of the negro, by making him happy, contented and prosperous than all the efforts of the fanatical zealots have done for him in the last twenty years.

Wappoo

Appendix B: Excerpt from *The Prostrate State* by James Pike

It is the uniform testimony of experience and observation that the pure black is the best man. The admixture of white blood does no good, but the contrary. The half-breed is more treacherous, more passionate, more vicious, more delicate in constitution. But the black is a child of vice and ignorance and superstition in South Carolina as well as in Africa. What he might have been capable of, under different conditions than those in which he has ever existed, it is useless to inquire. Races of men exhibit the same general characteristics from age to age.

The question which concerns us is, not what might be, or what is some remote future may be, but what now is. The negro is suddenly thrust into conspicuous prominence in our political system, and it is his present condition, qualities, habits, propensities, that we have to deal with, and we are now all alike deeply interested with his former masters in considering the problem of his character. He is certainly not the kind of man, and his race is not the race, for whom our political institutions were originally made; and it is already a serious question whether he is the man, or his the race, for which they are adapted. We have buy barely entered upon the experience which is to furnish a solution of this question, It is one we need to study and try to master.

The overshadowing mass of black barbarism in the South hangs like a portentous cloud upon the horizon. The country boldly confronted the question of slavery and as boldly destroyed it. It is gone, and gone forever. No man wishes to restore it. Not even in South Carolina is that man to be found. The best thinkers of the South to-day tell us they bless God for the war. It was necessary to get rid of slavery. But for slavery, they believe, the original slave States of the South would be among the greatest and most flourishing of all our commonwealths. It is the negro who has been the innocent cause of their despoliation. It is the negro that rest like an incubus upon them. Their viral forces pulsate under ribs of iron which will not give them play. It is the man from Africa who today bestrides them like a colossus. He came in helplessness, he has risen in strength. He was the servant of South Carolina; he has become her master.

These are the appalling facts that make it important and necessary that the Negro should be studied and understood by the whole country. It is not a question for South Carolina merely, it is a question for the nation. For it is a question of the predominance and antagonism of races. If it be true that this is not a white man's government, is it true of any State that it shall be a black man's government? It is a question for statesmanship to answer whether it can be expected that the white man will long stand passively by and see all the power of legislation wielded by the inferior race. And more: whether he can be expected to witness patiently the still more exasperating spectacle of the ignorance and venality of the blacks, bearing sway over the intelligence, probity, and honest manhood of the State. There is a more element in every State. There is its conscience, its sense of right, its hatred of wrong. These are it genuine and unconquerable revolutionary forces. Once roused, we have a State on fire, and a fire which politics and politicians are always powerless to quench. It is the fanaticism of justice, which the stars in their courses sustain, and against which no attribute of the almighty takes part.

We only disposed of one phase of the negro question in abolishing slavery. The great perplexity of establishing just relations between the races in the negro States is yet to be encountered. And it comes upon the country under a cloud of embarrassments. It has to be settled under the growing urgency an doubtful solution of the question whether the great mass of the black population at the South is not now mentally and morally unfit for self-government, and whether the progress of events will not force a modification of the original reconstruction acts— not based upon race or color or previous condition, but upon other considerations yet to be evolved and elucidated.

Fancy the moral condition of a State in which a large majority of all its voting citizens are habitually guilty of thieving and of concubinage. Yet such is the condition of South Carolina. Are we to be told that the civilization of the nineteenth century has nothing better to propose than this for the government of one of the oldest and proudest States or the American Union?

As it is morally, so it is intellectually. These same rulers of a great State, speaking of them as a whole, neither read nor write. They are as ignorant and as irresponsible in the exercise of their political functions as would be the Bedouin Arab of the desert, or the roving Comanches of the Plains, if called upon to choose the rulers of New York or Massachusetts. Is this the self-government for which a war of seven years was waged, in which the best blood of a nation was shed, and to secure the results of which a written Constitution was painfully elaborated by its wisest and most conscientious men, in order that justice and liberty might forever be maintained in the States of the model American Republic? Tell us what government of any civilized state of the Old World, if imported into South Carolina, would be as oppressive upon, and as unfitted for, the 300,000 white people of that State, as that which now curses it under the name of republican!

Appendix C: Testimony of Elias Thomson Regarding Klan Activity

Spartanburg, SC, July 7, 1871. In *Report of the Joint Select Committee Conditions on Affairs in the Late Insurrectionary Southern States,* 13 vols. (Washington, 1872), *House Report,* U.S. 42nd Congress, 2nd Sess., 1871–1872, vols. 3–5 (Subcommittee on South Carolina), pp. 411–416.

The next question was, "Who did you vote for?" I told them I voted for Mr. Turner — Claudius Turner, a gentleman in the neighborhood. They said, "What did you vote for him for?" I said, "I thought a good deal of him, he was a neighbor." I told them I disremembered who was on the ticket besides, but they had several, and I voted the ticket. "What did you do that for?" they said. Says I, "because I thought it was right." They said, "You thought it was right? It was right wrong." I said, "I never do anything hardly if I think it is wrong; if it was wrong I did not know it. That was my opinion at the time, and I thought every man ought to vote according to his notions." He said, "If you had taken the advice of your friends you would have been better off." I told him I had. Says I, "You may be a friend to me, but I can't tell who you are." Says he, "Can't you recognize anybody here?" I told him I could not, "In the condition you are in now I can't tell who you are."

One of them had a very large set of teeth. I suppose they were three-quarters of an inch long. They came right straight down. He came up to me and sort of nodded. He had on speckled horns and calico stuff, and had a face on. He said, "Have you got a chisel here I could get?" I told him I hadn't, but I reckoned I could knock one out, and I sort of laughed. He said, "What in hell are you laughing at? It is no laughing time? "I told him it sort of tickled me, and I though I would laugh. I did not say anything to them for a good while. "Old man." Says one, "have you got a rope here, or plow-line, or something of the sort?" I told him, "Yes, I had one hanging on the crib." He said, "Let us have it." One of them says, "String him up to this pine tree, and we will get all out of him. Get up, one of you, and let us pull him up, and he will tell the truth." I says, "I can't tell you anything more than I have told. There is nothing I can tell you but what I have told you that you asked me."

One man questioned me all this time. One would come up and say, "Let's hang him a while, and he will tell us the truth." Another them came up and said, "old man, we are just from hell. Some of us have been dead ever since the revolutionary war." Another one said, "We have heard your conversation for the last six months. I came up from under your kitchen floor just this night, and I have heard your conversation a good while." I was not scared, and said, "You have been through a right smart of experience." "Yes," he says, "We have just come from hell." I said, "If I had been there I would not want to go back." One says, "Have you heard a wild goose holler lately?" I said, "I heard one the other night." Said he, "That is one of us coming over and looking down to see what you have been doing this time." I said, "You must fly, then." He says "When we start we can go a long ways." And then said, "How far is it to Asheville?" I said, "About sixty miles." He said, "How far to Spartanburgh?" I says, "Ten miles." He says, "We have got to go to Spartanburgh to-night, and from there to Ashville before daylight.' It was then about 2 o'clock. I says, "You have a long trip." He says, "This is no laughing time." I says, "If anything tickles me I always laugh, no matter how it is."

Then they made me get down on my knees and told me to pray. I told them I was not a praying man, and didn't feel like it, and could not pray. Another put a pistol to my head and says, "Get down." I got down on one knee. I said, "I can't pray." One of them said, "Let us shoot him." Some six or seven of them pointed pistols at me, and I thought they were going to shoot. They said, "Commence praying; your time is short." I said, "I can't pray."

They let me stand on my knee some time. One said something to the rest, and they went off to the others. One spoke to the others in some kind of Dutch talk — I could not understand it — and they all consulted together, and came back to me and said, "Old man, which would you rather have, six hundred lashes over your shirt, or five hundred lashes without your shirt, or be shot or hanged?" Say's I, "Gentlemen, I have no choice. If you are going to do either one, either one will do me, do it now and make an end of me. But what have I done?" "You have done a d — — d sight," one says. I said, "I don't know what it is. I do not trouble anybody around me, and they all know me, and they can bring nothing against. I was always said to me a good boy by Dr. Vernon that raised me." He says,

"Who says so but you?" I says, "Anybody will say so." One of them says, "He has got a d — — d good influence. Didn't you bribe anybody to go your way?" Says I, "No sir." "How did you vote?" I told him I voted for Mr. Turner. I did not say anybody else but Mr. Turner all the time. He said several times, "Who else?" I never said anybody else but Mr. Turner. He say to me, "Have you given advice to vote your say?" "No sir, I will tell you what I have done. I was with the parties the same day of the election, and I said to them, won't you vote for Mr. Turner, and ain't you going to vote for Mr. Turner, but I could not make them do it." He says, "You have had a good influence; we must correct you a little." I told him I did not think that was any harm at all. He say, "We considere that it is." I thought they were not going to trouble me all this time.

I still kept in good spirits and laughed occasionally. They all got together again and consulted, and one says, "Let's go." I was standing and one says, "Come, old man, come with us." I did not know what the were going to do with me. They went on with me thirty or forty steps from the house where we were standing, close to the house. Right in the road one says, "Jerk me a limb off that tree." One ran and jerked a limb off a pretty heavy one, with two prongs to it. He says, "Pull off your shirt," "What for?" says I. "Pull off your shirt." He says, "Don't you ask me anything." I didn't pull it off. "If you don't pull it off, says he, "I will shoot you in a minute. I will shoot a hole through you big enough for a rat to go through." I just turned it over my head. I had on only my drawers and my shirt. Then they hit me such cuts. Then they hit me with thirteen of the hardest cuts I ever got. I never had such cuts. They hit me right around the waist and by my hip, and cut a piece out about as wide as my two fingers in one place.

I did not say a word while they were whipping, only sort of grunted a little. As quick as they got through they said, "go to your bed," and they started away. One of them says, "Look here, what are you going to say when anybody asks you about this?" "What can I say, sir?" He says, "What are you going to say?" I says, "I will have to say something." "Are you going to tell them that we have been here?" I says, "What else can I say?" "Can't you tell a lie," says he, "and say nobody has been here?" Says I, "That would not be right." "Can't you do it?" I told him I could do it. He said. "Just let us hear of this thing, and when we come back we will not leave a piece of you." That was the end of it. They left then, and got on their horses and went away.

Appendix D: Remarks of Judge Hugh Bond Regarding Klan Activity

Spartanburg, SC, July 7, 1871. In *Report of the Joint Select Committee Conditions on Affairs in the Late Insurrectionary Southern States,* 13 vols. (Washington, 1872), *House Report,* U.S. 42nd Congress, 2nd Sess., 1871–1872, vols. 3–5 (Subcommittee on South Carolina), pp. 1983–1984.

There is abundant proof of the nature and character of the conspiracy. Evidence of nightly raids by bands of disguised men, who broke into the houses of Negroes and dragged them from their beds—parents and children — and, tying them to trees, unmercifully beating them, I exhibited in every case. Murder and rape are not infrequent accompaniments, the story of which is too indecent for public mention. The persons upon whom these atrocities are committed are almost always colored people. Whatever excuse is given for a raid, its conclusion was almost accompanied by a rebuke for the former exercise of the suffrage, and a warning as to the future exercise of the right to vote.

But what is quite as appalling to the court as the horrible nature of these offenses is the utter absence on your part, and on the part of others who have made confession here, of any sense or feeling that you have done anything very wrong in your confessed participation in outrages, which are unexampled outside of the Indian territory.

Some of your comrades recite the circumstances of a brutal, unprovoked murder, done by themselves, with as little apparent abhorrence as they would relate the incidents of picnic, and you yourselves speak of the number of blows with a hickory, which you inflicted at midnight upon the lacerated, bleeding back of a defenseless woman, without so much as a blush or a sigh of regret. None of you seem to have the slightest idea of, or respect for, the sacredness of the human person. Some of you have yourselves been beaten by the Klans without feeling a smart, but the physical pain. There appears to be no wounding of the spirit; not such sense of injury to yourself as a man as would be felt by the humblest of your fellow-citizens in any other part of the United States with which I am acquainted.

There the citizens upon whom such outrages were perpetrated, stung to madness by the insult to his manhood, would be swift to follow the wrong-doer to the end of the world to make him atone for it. You make excuse for this in your statement to the court that you are very ignorant; that the Klans would have beaten you, and even killed you, had you refused to join them in their crimes. Some of you now particularly before me have actually suffered for your refusal, before you really united in membership with them. The court, in an endeavor to recognize some features of humanity in you, have considered these facts which you plead to excuse. You have grown up in a country where slavery existed for a long time, and where the whipping-post was a standing institution.

To see blacks flagellated was no unusual occurrence. The scene often viewed, with its novelty, lost its revolting effect. And when it came to be understood that the human person was not so sacred in the colored man as to secure immunity from outrage, it did not take it long to lose its sacred character in yourselves, and in all other men who, like the colored man, was obliged to labor. It must be from this cause that your indifference to wrongs among freemen would stir a fever in the blood ... arises.

And then you tell us that you differ from many other portions of the country in this, that it has always been obligatory upon you, and the class to which you belong to look to persons of wealth and education for command, and that you, in your ignorance, had to follow such persons implicitly.

It will appear strange to your fellow-countrymen who read your story, and that of your confederates, however willing they may be to believe you, that so large a portion of the young white men of your country can be in such a state of abject slavery to the men of property above them, as to be willing to commit murder at their command.

In no case has there been any resistance to these midnight raiders except on the part of the colored people.

You say some of you "laid out" in the woods night after night, and have hidden yourself in thickets to escape thee marauders. None of you, however, have had the manliness to defend your firesides from the assaults of these lawless men. There has not been, on your part, so far as the evidence shows, an assault and battery committed in defense of family and home and all that freemen hold dear.

Admitting all you have said to the court to be true, while the story of your condition and of your participation in these outrages through fear is painful enough, the facts do not excuse you. They may palliate, in some degree, your offense, but they cannot justify you. The punishment the court awards you is partly inflicted that you may learn that no amount of threats or fear of punishment will justify a man in unprovoked violence to another, unless the danger threatened to the wrong-doer be imminent or actually present at the time of his wrong doing, and even then the danger must be of present great bodily harm, and of death itself, before some of the criminal conduct confessed would be justified.

It does not excuse you for participating in this conspiracy and raiding upon inoffensive colored people — dragging them from their beds, beating some, and hanging others— that you had notice if you did not join the Klan would visit you.

You are bound to run the risk or seek means of protection rather than do violence to your neighbor. The law and your fellow-citizens look to you to make this threat of violence difficult to execute by a manly resistance or an enforcement of the law. You had no right, when you could escape, to make the price of your security the violation of your neighbor's.

Appendix E: Excerpt from the Oral History of Mary Anderson

Federal Writer's Project: North Carolina Slave Narratives, Mary Anderson, no. 3220086, pp. 20–26.

We had good food, plenty of warm homemade clothes and comfortable houses. The slave houses were called the quarters and the house where master lived was called the great house. Our house had two rooms each and master's house had twelve rooms. Both the slave and white folks buildings were located in a large grove one mile square covered with oak and hickory nut trees. Master's house was exactly one mile from the main Louisburg Road and there was a wide avenue leading through the plantation and grove to master's house. The house fronted the avenue from the main road you traveled west.

The plantation was very large and there were about two hundred acres of cleared land that was farmed each year. A pond was located on the place and in the winter ice was gathered there for summer use and stored in an ice house which was built in the grove where the other buildings were. A large hole about ten feet deep was dug in the ground; the ice was put in that hole and covered. A large frame building was built over it. At the top of the earth there was an entrance door and steps leading down to the bottom of the hole. Other things besides were stored there. There was a still on the plantation and barrels of brandy were stored in the ice house, also pickles, preserves and cider.

Many of the things we used were made on the place. There was a grist mill, tannery, shoe shop, blacksmith shop, and looms for weaving cloth. There were about one hundred and sixty-two slaves on the plantation and every Sunday morning all the children had to be bathed, dressed, and their hair combed and carried down to master's for breakfast. It was a rule that all the little colored children eat at the great house every Sunday morning in order that master and missus could watch them eat so they could know which ones were sickly and have them doctored.

The slave children all carried a mussel shell in their hands to eat with. The food was put on large trays and the children all gathered around and ate, dipping up their food with their mussel shells which they used for spoons. Those who refused to eat or those who were ailing in any way had to come back to the great house for their meals and medicine until they were well. Master had a large apple orchard in the Tar River low grounds and up on higher ground and nearer the plantation house there was on one side of the road a large plum orchard and on the other side an orchard of peaches, cherries, quinces and grapes. We picked the quinces in August and used them for preserving. Master and missus believed in giving the slaves plenty of fruit, especially the children.

Master had three children, one boy names Dallas, and two girls, Bettie and Carrie. He would not allow slave children to call his children master and missus unless the slave said little master and little missus. He had four white overseers but they were not allowed to whip a slave. If there was any whipping to be done he always said he would do it. He didn't believe in whipping so when a slave got so bad he could not manage him, he sold him.

Master didn't quarrel with anybody, missus would not speak short to a slave, but both missus and master taught slaves to be obedient in a nice quiet way. The slaves were taught to take their hats and bonnets off before going into the house, and bow and say, "good morning Master Sam and Missus Evaline." Some of the little negroes would go down to the great house and ask them when it was going to rain, and when master or missus walked in the grove the little negroes would follow along after them like a gang of kiddies. Some of the slave children wanted to stay with them at the great house all the time. They knew no better of course and seemed to love master as much as their own mother and father. Master and missus always used gentle means to get the children out of their way when they bothered them and the way the children loved and trusted them was a beautiful sight to see.

Patterollers [slave patrols] were not allowed on the place unless they came peacefully and I never knew of them whipping any slaves on masters' place. Slaves were carried off on two horse wagons to be sold. I have seen several bring back slaves, once he brought back two boys and three girls from the slave market.

Sunday was a great day on the plantation. Everybody got biscuits on Sundays. The slave women went down to masters for their Sunday allowances of flour. All the children ate breakfast at the great house and master and missus gave out fruit to all. The slaves looked forward to Sunday as they labored through the week. It was a great day. Slaves received good treatment from master and all his family. We were allowed to have prayer meetings in our homes and we also went to the white folks church. They would not teach any of us to read and write. Books and papers were forbidden. Master's children and the slave children played together. I went around with the baby girl Carrie to other plantations visiting. She taught me how to talk low and how to act in company. My association with white folks and my training while I was a slave is why I talk like white folks.

Betti Brodie married a Dr. Webb from Boylan, Virginia. Carrie married a Mr. Green of Franklin County. He was a big southern planter.

Master and missus then went into the house got two large armchairs put them on the porch facing the avenue and sat down side by side and remained there watching. In about an hour there was one of the blackest clouds coming up the avenue from the main road. It was the Yankee soldiers, they finally filled the mile long avenue reaching from master's house to the main Louisburg road and spread out over the mile square grove. The mounted men dismounted. The footmen stacked their shining guns and began to build fires and cook. They called the slaves, saying, "You are free." Slaves were whooping and laughing and acting like they were crazy. Yankee soldiers were shaking hands with the negroes and calling them Sam, Dinah, Sarah and asking them questions. They busted the door to the smoke house and got all the hams. They went to the icehouse and got several barrels of brandy, and had such a time. The Negroes and Yankees were cooking and eating together. The Yankees told them to come on and join them, they were free. Master and missus sat on the porch and they were so humble no Yankee bothered anything in the great house. The slaves were awfully excited. The Yankees stayed there, cooked, eat, drank and played music until about night, then a bugle began to blow and you never saw such getting on horses and lining up in your life. In a few minutes they began to march, leaving the grove which was soon as silent as a grave yard. They took master's horses and cattle with them and joined the main army and camped just across Cypress Creek one and one half miles from my master's place on the Louisburg Road. When they left the country, lot of the slaves went with them and soon there were none of master's slaves left. They wandered around for a year from place to place, fed and working most of the time at some other slave owner's plantation and getting more homesick every day.

The second year after the surrender our master and missus got on their carriage and went and looked up all the negroes they heard of who ever belonged to them. Some who went off with the Yankees were never heard of again. When master and missus found any of theirs they would say, "Well, come on back home." My father and mother, two uncles and their families move back. Also Lorenzo Brodie, and John Brodie and their families moved back. Several of the young men and women who once belonged to him came back. Some were so glad to get back they cried, "cause fare had been might bad part to the time they were rambling around and they were hungry. When they got back master would say, "Well you have come back home have you," and the Negroes would say, "Yes master." Most all spoke of them as, missus and master as they did before the surrender, and getting back home was the greatest pleasure of all. We stayed with master and missus and went to their church, the Maple Springs Baptist church, until they died. Since the surrender I married James Anderson. I had four children, one boy and three girls.

Appendix F.
"The Lowrey Bandits"

"The Lowrey Bandits," *New York Times*, November 1, 1871.

In Gen. Gorman's own words:

"On their second message to the same effect being received, I concluded to risk an interview, and learn the object they had in view. In a few days I was told, after consenting to meet them, if I would go unattended, through a swamp some three or four miles from camp, it was possible that they would meet me, and on the next day, without informing any but col. W. of my intention, I proceeded thither, unarmed except with a repeater, and unattended.

"I met them on that occasion, and had conversation of over an hour with the entire gang, which consisted of Henry Berry Lowrey, Thomas Lowrey, Stephen Lowrey, Andrew Strong and Boss Strong. When I first saw them they were sitting on a log awaiting my promised presence. They were all heavily armed — Henry Berry Lowrey, the leader with a Spencer rifle and a double barreled gun, while within his belt were five repeaters. The balance of the gang had each two double guns and from three to five repeaters. All of them I believe also carried a bowie knife. I am told that this is the usual complement of arms which they generally carry.

"They were exceedingly respectful to me during the interview, and stated that their object in wishing a conference was to know if it was possible for me to grant them some terms. They expressed themselves as sick and tired of their manner of life, and longed to be free from their present peril and uncertainty, and stated that if they were allowed, t hey would depart the territory of the United States."

After hearing all the rest of the story we are almost surprise to be told that this proposal was not at once agreed to. Gen. Gorman, however informed his interlocutors that the matter was not to be thought of. He added that if they would surrender they should not be molested, except by due course of law; that he would guarantee them a fair trail by jury, and that the best of legal talent should be employed in their defense. Further than this he really could not go. The brigands listened with much courtesy, and warming into the geniality that comes of social intercourse, assured the General that they would refrain from ambushing or "bushwhacking" any of the troops under his command, unless indeed, they should be "cornered," in which event it was their intention to "die game.' This said, they withdrew-obligingly refraining from cutting the General's throat as a preliminary to their departure; which, as he was quite alone, they might readily have done, and which would certainly have been altogether in keeping with their ordinary taste and custom.

Appendix G: Letter from General John C. Gorman Regarding the Lowrie Bandits

The *Morning Star* (Wilmington, N.C.), October 28, 1871, p. 2, cols. 1 and 2.

They live, as a general thing, by tending boxes (by getting out crude turpentine), cutting the timber for rafts in winter, and doing odds jobs for the more thrifty farmers who live a few miles from them. There are exceptions to this general rule, when they have good farms of a hundred or more acres, well cultivated, and where the honesty, sobriety and good behavior of the owners are above reproach. Prominent among such are Patrick, Calvin and St. Clair Lowrey, brothers to three of the outlaws, and several others.

In the section [area] to which I allude [Scuffle Town] there are perhaps 200 families who compose the main part of a class of people to which the outlaws belong. Being mixed breeds between the white man, black and Indian, many retain in a remarkable degree the Indian characteristics in their color and form, and are said to possess all the natural shrewdness belong to the Indian.

They live generally from hand to mouth, in a state of much poverty, in log houses, with slab roofs, with little or none of the comforts of civilized life. The locality derived its name long before the war [Civil War], I suppose from the divers *scuffles* which occurred amongst them, they bearing the name of being quite belligerent in character-as well as the scuffle it evidently took for them to procure an honest living off their two acres cultivated potatoes.

Only some three or four white farmers continue to live on their farms among them, and these are constantly preyed upon by the outlaws for provisions which they give without much demand and barely a whisper. Having been fleeced of their property and living in a constant state of dread and uncertainty, not knowing what time of the day or night they may be visited by the outlaws, it is alleged by both the outlaws and those who have previously hunted them that they are an object of suspicion.

Some two or three white men have married mulatto women, and live on places in the neighborhood with their wives, and are assisting in the further mixture of the race. The whole race is more or less connected by blood, and some five or six family names constitute they majority of the inhabitants, the Lowreys, the Oxendines, and Chavises being the largest in number. It is asserted and my experience rather goes to prove the assertion that nearly this entire community are in active sympathy with the outlaws, many doubtless through fear, others from prejudice, and the balance from ties of fraternity and blood.

All without exception, lend no aid whatever in the capture of the gang, and never report their hiding places or whereabouts, and will not even mention the fact when they see them, until sufficient time has elapsed to place the outlaws beyond the reach of pursuit. However it is positively affirmed that any movement made by officers of the law and others to capture the banditti, is speedily telegraphed by signals known only to the initiated, and by divers other means, whereby they are enabled to elude pursuit. From this cause is attributed the invariable failure of the parties to surprise the gang, or any time to catch them unawares. Besides this, the entire people, living as they do upon the edges of the swamps and bays, which in winter are almost islands surrounded by water, have numerous paths and short cuts from house to house, which they almost invariably follow instead of the road, and they are by this means enabled to communicate with the outlaws much sooner than parties who go the ordinary roads to reach any place at which they may suppose them to be. These trails and paths ramify the swamps and pine fields bewildering to the unacquainted, and many of them are scarcely distinguishable to the uninitiated.

During my stay of five weeks in that section, I think I visited alone or with a detachment of men, nearly every house in the outlaws' domain, and took especial pains to inform myself as to the feelings and expressed opinions of the people. There was nothing sullen in their behavior to me or to the troops. They were free in speech, and without exception expressed a wish for the troubles of the locality to end, but almost invariably refused to lend any assistance toward the capture of the outlaws, even for pay or reward. Nearly all complained of the harsh treatment they had in times past received from parties who ostensibly hunting the banditti, and they repudiated any alliance or fraternity of feeling between themselves and the gang. Their protestations in the majority of cases, however, I believed to be deceitful and without a particle of sincerity, as their sympathies would naturally crop out occasionally in their conversation.

As I could not obtain volunteers, I was determined to call out a portion of the militia, and made an appeal to them to promptly come forward and cooperate with me, and for this purpose made a requisition upon the Colonels of the 58th and 59th regiments. But the call was but feebly responded to. The people had been called upon so often, so many fruitless attempts had been made, that they had no faith in any such measures, and all were averse to moving. The militia law is so defective that my authority to force them out, was doubted, and I did not attempt it seriously. I however received about ninety unwilling recruits from two regiments, the larger majority of whom reported to camp without arms, ammunition or blankets, and had to be fed from the meager stores which the Commissioners had furnished me for the volunteers.

Chapter Notes

Note to Preface

1. Olsen, Otto H., "The Ku Klux Klan: A Study in Reconstruction Politics and Propaganda." In Nieman, David G. (ed.) *African American Life in the Post-Emancipation South, 1861–1900*. New York: Garland Press, 1994, p. 242.

Notes to Introduction

1. LeLand, John A., *A Voice from South Carolina: Journal of a Reputed Ku-Klux*. Walker, Evans & Charleston, S.C.: Cogswell, 1879, p. 12.

2. Nieman, Donald G., *Black Freedom/White Violence, 1865–1900*, vol. 7. New York: Garland Publishing, 1994.

3. DuBois, W.E.B., *Black Reconstruction in America, 1860–1880*. New York: Atheneum, 1983, p. 541.

4. Ibid.

5. *The Constitution of the United States*. National Constitution Center, Philadelphia, PA, July 1995.

6. Hine, Darlene Clark, William C. Hine, and Stanley Harrold, *The African American Odyssey*. New Jersey: Prentice Hall, 2003, p. 287.

7. Bennett, Lerone, Jr., *Before the Mayflower: A History of Black America*, 6th ed. New York: Penguin Books, 1988, pp. 233–34. Bennett states that voter registration (males) for 1867 in South Carolina indicated that 80,000 were blacks and 46,000 were whites. Blacks were in the majority in 21 of the 31 counties. This meant that in the first Reconstruction legislature, 85 were black and 70 were white. Blacks were in the majority in every legislative session. They were able to establish two black Lieutenant Governors (A.J. Ransier and R.H. Gleaves), a Secretary of State (F.L. Cardozo) and were able to send numerous representatives to Congress throughout Reconstruction. In Mississippi, voter registration indicated 60,000 were blacks and 46,000 were whites. In Louisiana, voter registration roles indicated that 84,000 were blacks and 45,000 were whites. And in Florida some 16,000 blacks were registered to vote as compared to 11,000 whites. In terms of legislative power Mississippi, Louisiana and Florida were also able to replicate similar political suc-

cess as did South Carolina. To a lesser degree, North Carolina, Alabama, Georgia and Virginia were able to send representative to Congress during this period.

8. DuBois, W.E.B., *Black Reconstruction in America: An Essay toward a History of the Part Which Black Folk Played in the Attempts to Reconstruct Democracy in America, 1860–1880*. New York: Atheneum, 1983, p. 383.

9. Singletary, Otis A., *Negro Militia and Reconstruction*. Austin: University of Texas, 1957, p. 3.

10. Stiles, J.T., *Jesse James: Last Rebel of the Civil War*. New York: Knopf, 2002, p. 162. Lonnie Athens, *The Creation of Dangerous Violent Criminals*. London: Routledge, 1989. For an application of Athens' work to a military setting, see Richard Rhodes, *Why They Kill: The Discoveries of Maverick Criminologist*. New York: Knopf, 1999, pp. 286–312.

11. Ibid.

12. Ibid.

13. Ibid., p. 103.

14. Ibid., p. 163.

15. Ibid., p. 163; Michael A. Bellesiles, "The Origins of Gun Culture in the United States, 1700–1865," *Journal of American History*, 83, no. 2 (Sept. 1996); J.T. Stiles, ed., *Robber Barons and Radicals: Reconstruction and the Origins of Civil Rights* (New York: Berkley, 1997), 26; Otis A. Singletary, *Negro Militia and Reconstruction* (New York: McGraw-Hill/University of Texas Press, 1971), p. 3.

16. Nieman, p. 244.

17. Leland, pp. 11–23.

Notes to Chapter 1

1. Randall, William Pierce, *The Ku Klux Klan: A Century of Infamy*. New York: Chilton Books, 1965, p. 6–7. Note: Randall states that John B. Kennedy, one of the six original members of the Ku Klux Klan (Calvin E. Jones, Frank O. McCord, Richard R. Reed, John C. Lester, and James R. Crowe) "had briefly attended Centre College in Kentucky, where he must have observed some of the details of fraternity structure. He recalled from his study of Greek the word, *Kuklos*, meaning a band or circle." Crowe "suggested splitting Kuklos into two and chang-

ing the final letter to x, yielding, *Ku Klux."* Then Lester remarked that "all six members were of Scottish descent, proposed that *Clan* be added, spelt with a *K* for consistency; and he tentatively tried out the combination, *Ku Klux Klan.*

2. Trelease, Allen W., *White Terror: The Ku Klux Klan Conspiracy and Southern Reconstruction.* New York: Harper & Row, 1971, p. 62. Trelease writes, "There is abundant evidence that the primary role in spreading the Ku Klux Klan was played, not by General Forrest and his cohorts, but by the Southern Democratic newspaper press. It carried favorable news items concerning Klan activities in Tennessee and faithfully chronicled its appearance in other states, near and distant. Sometimes these events were reported straight, without comment or approbation, but often the Klan was treated as a fascinating and potentially useful agency to combat the evils of Radicalism and Negro ascendancy. Only a few Democratic papers opposed the idea from the beginning, whereas many openly or implicitly encouraged its growth and its organization locally."

3. Stiles, p. 240–41.

4. Carter, Dan T., *When the War Was Over: The Failure of Self-Reconstruction, 1865–1867.* Baton Rouge: Louisiana State University Press, 1985, p. 22. Carter writes, "White southerners of influence and position might regret — even deplore — the mistreatment of former slaves, but they were quick to insist that the greater threat was posed by the 'insolence' and 'insubordination' of the millions of blacks in their midst. And however much it might horrify the more refine sensibilities of New England newspapermen, the continued tendency of white southerners to resort to pistol, bowie knife, or gutta percha cane to settle their personal disputes aroused little alarm. If the victor was a southern gentleman and the victim an impudent northern newspaperman, such incidents might even seem pleasantly exciting."

5. Leland, John A., *A Voice from South Carolina: Journal of a Reputed Ku Klux.* Charleston, S.C.: Walker, Evans & Cogwell, 1879, p. 13.

6. *New National Era.* February 2, 1871.

7. Carpenter, R.B., *42nd Congressional Committee on Affairs in the Southern States,* 1878, p. 238.

8. Lester, John C. and David L. Wilson, *Ku Klux Klan: Its Origins, Growth, Disbandment.* Nashville, 1878, p. 78.

9. Buckley, Gail, *American Patriots: The Story of Blacks in the Military from the Revolution to Desert Storm.* New York: Random House, 2001, p. 116.

10. Borman, Ernest G., "Fantasy and Rhetorical Vision," *Quarterly Journal of Speech,* December 1971, p. 406.

11. Williams, Alfred, *Hampton and His Red Shirts.* Columbia: Ayer, p. 21.

12. Graff, Harvey, *The Legacies of Literacy: Continuities and Contradictions in Western Culture and Society.* Indiana University Press, 1987, p. 356.

13. *120 Years of American Education: A Statistical Portrait* (ed. by Tom Synder), U.S. Dept. of Education, Office of Educational Research and Improvement, National Center for Education Statistics, 1993. However, literacy can be defined by at least two standards. Quantitative literacy is defined as the ability to read at a certain school grade level, i.e., sixth grade, and measured by a specific standardized test. However, qualitative literacy standards suggest that literacy is determined by one's ability to function within a predetermined context. From this perspective, racial, gender, class and social political factors may determine whether an individual is defined as literate.

14. Ibid., p. 361.

15. Reddin, Debra van Tuyll, "Nineteenth-Century Georgia Newspapers." *New Georgia Encyclopedia,* Sept. 19, 2000.

16. Trelease, p. 63. The author states, "Southern Republican editors obviously wrote as outsiders. Quite naturally, they seldom retailed anecdotes about thirsty ghosts and superstitious blacks, regarding them as impolitic and often false, if not unfunny and in bad taste. From the start their curiosity concerning the order (Ku Klux) was mixed with apprehension and condemnation, for the Klan was patently directed against them. And once the Klan began to commit outrages, Republican papers reported them as fully as possible, together with appeals for law and order and for government action to suppress them. If they occasionally exaggerated the degree of terror, for effect or through misinformation, the fault was insignificant compared with the massive conspiracy to stifle the truth which the Democratic press engaged in."

17. Malcomson, Scott L., *One Drop of Blood: The American Misadventure of Race.* New York: Farrar Straus Giroux, 2000, p. 366.

18. Kinshasa, Kwando M., *Emigration vs. Assimilation: The Debate in the African American Press, 1827–1861.* Jefferson, North Carolina: McFarland, 1988, p. 115; Lewis A. Dexter, ed., *People, Society and Mass Communication* (New York: Free Press, 1964) pp. 418–21; Graff, p. 69. The author states that, "While illiteracy for free blacks was approximately 43 percent in 1850 and virtually 100 percent among slaves, recent studies on word-of-mouth communication suggest that information is received by peasant groups through such a network. It is also suggested that 100 percent illiteracy rate for slaves is highly suspect. 'In general, the word-of-mouth network is the newspaper of the peasant.' It is not that the upper classes do not receive word-of-mouth information; but it is relatively less important. Consequently, the lower-class-free black, being in less contact with communications media, put more emphasis on oral communication as a source of information. In this regard, one can assess the importance of "cultural modernization" in urbanized areas, and its relationship to a populace's identification with 'characteristics indicative of modernity, skill or sophistication."

19. Kinshasa, p. 118; Silvia Scribner and Michael Cole, "The Psychology of Literacy," *New York Times Book Review,* December 13, 1981, p. 1. "Historical research into nineteenth-century America has indicated that very little evidence exists that suggests people first became literate so as to rise socially, but rather, people who had risen socially tended to become literate."

20. Saville, Julie, *The Work of Reconstruction: From Slave to Wage Laborer in South Carolina, 1860–1870.* New York: Cambridge University Press, p. 174.

21. Ibid., p. 171; London Simons to CMDG. Genl., Nov. 10, 1867, Provost Marshall, letters received, Ser. 4280, Dept of the South, RG 393 pt. 1.

22. Saville, p. 171.

23. Ibid., pp. 150–51.

24. Doughty, col. Robert A. (ed.), *The West Point Museum: A Guide to the Collections.* Association of Graduates, Class of 1932, USMA, United States Military Academy, West Point, New York, 1987. The editor notes: "Zouaves were Union and Confederate soldiers who adopted their uniforms and name from French North African troops formed during the 1830s."

25. *Charleston Daily Courier,* October 18, 1866, p. 2, col. 2.

26. Saville, p. 144; Affidavit of J.D. Palmer, August 25, 1866, enclosed in vol. 254, Register of complaints, ser. 3309, Orangeburg, subordinate Field Office Records, RG 105 [A-7272].

27. Neiman, p. xi; William McKee Evans, *To Die Game: The Story of the Lowry Band, Indian Guerrillas of Reconstruction.* Syracuse: Syracuse University Press, 1995; *Report of the Joint Select Committee to Inquire into the Conditions of Affairs in the Late Insurrectionary States (Ku Klux Conspiracy)* (13 vols.) (Washington, DC: Government Printing Office, 1872).

28. Logan, Rayford, *The Betrayal of the Negro: From Rutherford B. Hayes to Woodrow Wilson.* New York: Da Capo Press, 1997, p. 7.

29. Trelease, Allen W., *White Terror: The Ku Klux Klan Conspiracy and Southern Reconstruction.* New York: Harper & Row, 1971, p. xlv.

30. Astor, Gerald, *The Right to Fight: A History of African Americans in the Military.* Cambridge, MA: Da Capo Press, 1998, pp. 43–55; William H. Leckie, *The Buffalo Soldiers: A Narrative of the Negro Cavalry in the West.* Norman: University of Oklahoma Press, 1997.

31. Carpenter, pp. 398–99.

32. Ibid.

33. Ibid.

34. Saville, p. 72. Saville notes that "Union general William T. Sherman's wartime Field Order 15, issued from Savannah in January 1865, stimulated this popular initiative. Setting aside territory on the mainland and sea islands lying southward from Charleston to the St. John's River in northern Florida for settlement and cultivation by former slaves, Field Order 15 has been aptly characterized as 'the most far reaching step taken toward the distribution of land from above' to emerge as wartime federal policy."

35. Ibid.

36. Magdol, Edward, *A Right to the Land: Essays on the Freedmen's Community.* Westport, CT: Greenwood, 1977, p. 126.

37. Ibid., pp. 126–27.

38. Ibid., p. 127.

39. Ibid., p. 128; Eugene D. Genovese, "Rebelliousness and Docility in the Negro Slave: A Critique of the Elkins Thesis," *Civil War History*, 13 (December 1967), 293–314; Stanley M. Elkins, *Slavery: A Problem in American Institutional and Intellectual Life.* Chicago: University of Chicago Press, 1959.

40. Magdol.

41. Ibid.

42. Ibid.

43. Ibid.

44. Hine, p. 184.

45. Carter, p. 147, from Sidney Andrews, *The South Since the War as Shown by Fourteen Weeks of Travel and Observation in Georgia and the Carolinas* (Boston, 1866), 22; J.P. Bardwell to Rev. M.F. Strieby, November 20, 1865, AMA, Mississippi, Reel 1.

46. Carter, p. 166.

47. *The Nation*, January 4, 1866, p. 15.

48. Ibid.

49. Saville, p. 147.

50. Jacques Ellul, *Propaganda.* New York: Knopf, 1965, pp. 58–59.

51. *New Orleans Tribune*, August 1, 1865, quoted in chapter "Shall We Have Land," in *A Right to the Land*, by Edward Magdol. Westport, Conn.: Greenwood, 1977, pp. 149–50.

52. Franklin, John Hope, and Alfred A. Moss, *From Slavery to Freedom: A History of African Americans.* New York: McGraw Hill, 1994, pp. 234–35. "Under the Southern Homestead Act of 1866, in Alabama, Mississippi, Louisiana, Arkansas, and Florida" land was distributed to all settlers, "regardless of race. Eighty acres were available for the head of each family. Within a year ex-slaves secured homesteads in Florida covering 160,960 acres, and in Arkansas they occupied 116 out of 243 homestead. By 1874 blacks in Georgia owned more than 350,000 acres of land."

53. Ibid., p. 150.

54. Ibid.

55. Ibid.

56. *The New York Times*, August 16, 1869, p. 2, col. 6. See Appendix A for full text.

57. Malcomson, Scott L., *One Drop of Blood: The American Misadventure of Race.* New York: Farrar Straus Giroux, 2000, p. 347–48. The author raises the critical issues, "The Civil War did nothing to undermine white faith in white destiny. The opposite seems to have been the case: as the nation coalesced between 1870 and 1900, regional differences gradually yielded tot a general whiteness. A belief in racial, often 'Anglo-Saxon,' destiny permeated the educated white classes and seems to have received passive assent among those with little or no education. In its strongest form, from Francis Lieber (who later recanted) through the Social Gospel prophet Josiah Strong and on to Theodore Roosevelt, militant Anglo-Saxonism tended to blend cause and effect: white dominated because it was their nature to dominate. What would belief in this require? First, there could be no debate, because one could not disprove a racial idea in its own terms. If whites fail to dominate, it was because they had failed to be sufficiently white. Thus the intense worry about racial mixture. The answers to racial questions (such as explaining white failure) had to be racial answers, otherwise racial thinking as a whole ceased to function. Second, there could be no free will. If an individual's racial destiny or responsibility was to embody his or her race-ness, then self-realization became the same as self-obliteration, and oneself a mere instance of the race, individually faceless and helpless. Finally, being in a naturally dominant race raises the question: What is the purpose of other races? Are they to be dominated forever? Or is the final goal of racial struggle the complete mastery of oneself as a white person — that is, ceasing to need the other races to define oneself; that is, in the case of a naturally dominate race, eliminating all others?"

58. Saville, p. 143.

59. Hine, p. 302.

60. Magdol, John, "Local Black Leadership," p. 136.

61. *The New National Era*, May 12, 1870, p. 2.

62. Ibid.

63. *The New York Times*, September 8, 1868, p. 1, col. 3.

64. *The Constitution of the United States of America*, Philadelphia, PA: National Constitution Center, 1995, pp. 25–27.

65. Magdol, "Rebirth of Community," pp. 98, 100–6; ""Shall We Have Land," p. 162.

66. Ibid., p. 110.

67. Ibid.

68. Records of the Assistant Commissioner for the State of Tennessee, Bureau of Refugees, Freedmen and Abandoned Lands, 1865–1869. National Archives Microfilm Publication M999 Roll 34, "Reports of Outrages, Riots and Murders." *Special Report on the late riot at Franklin, Tennessee.* By Brevet Major General and Commander W. Martin to Commissioner General O.O. Howard. July 15, 1867.

69. Ibid.

70. DuBois, pp. 559–60. DuBois claims that the initial success of the bank was "phenomenal and the deposits extraordinarily encouraging. They came from day laborers, house servants, farmers, mechanics and washer-

women, and the proverbial thriftlessness of the Negro seemed about to be disproven. North as well as South, the whites were agreeably surprised." This was about to change within a few years as "white planters regarded the Freedmen's Bank as part of the Freedmen's Bureau and did everything possible to embarrass it and curtail its growth."

71. Ibid., p. 208.

72. Franklin, John Hope, and Alfred A. Moss, Jr., *From Slavery to Freedom: A History of Black Americans*, 6th ed. New York: Alfred A. Knopf, 1988, p. 208.

73. Ibid.

74. Davis Tilson to Clinton B. Fisk, Memphis, August 18, 1865, "Freedmen Census of Memphis, 1865," in the *U.S. Selected Records of the Tennessee Field Office of the Bureau of Refugees, Freedmen and Abandoned Lands, 1865–1872*, in *Black Freedom/White Violence, 1865–1900*, ed. Donald Nieman, New York: Garland Publishers, 1994, p. 208.

75. Ibid., p. 210.

76. DuBois, p. 573.

77. Ibid.

78. Ibid., pp. 573–74.

79. *Nashville Dispatch*, July 12, 1866, a clipping in the State Historian's Papers, Record Group 29, TSLA, AD, Nashville; *Senate Journal of the Tennessee General Assembly, 1865–1866* (Nashville, 1866), p. 656; in *Black Freedom/White Violence, 1865–1900*, ed. Donald G. Nieman. New York: Garland Publishers, 1994, p. 210.

80. Ibid., p. 211; *Memphis Bulletin*, January 7, 1865; Jackie M Thomas, "Economic and Educational Activities of the Freedman's Bureau, 1865–1869" (M.A. thesis. Tennessee State University, 1960).

81. DuBois, p. 141.

82. Ibid., p. 139; *Congressional Globe, 39th Congress, 1st Session, Part 1*, p. 94.

83. *Memphis Argus*. August 24, 1865; Nieman, p. 212.

84. Ibid.; Tennessee Prison Records, Military, Criminal and Circuit Courts, 1831–1922.

85. *Charleston Daily Courier*, February 15, 1870, p. 4, col. 1–2.

86. Ibid.

87. Ibid.

88. Williamson, Joel. *After Slavery: The Negro in South Carolina during Reconstruction, 1867–1877*. New York: Norton, 1975, p. 246–47.

89. *Charleston Daily Courier*, September 2, 1868, p. 2, col. 3.

90. Ibid.

91. *Charleston Daily Courier*, November 12, 1868, p. 2, col. 3. In Joel Williamson's *After Slavery*, he writes, "The first president of the League in South Carolina was Gilbert Pillsbury, a long-time abolitionist who had first headed the military's school system in the Charleston area. Negroes must have found the Leagues entertaining. Visiting his low country plantation near Adams run in December, 1867, the Reverend Cornish found that "Sam—the then Negro boy that waited on me when I lived at the Hermitage on Edisto Island—...is now president of the Loyal League [sic] & a very influential character among the Negroes— is Sam Small" (p. 372); Diary, entry for December 3, 1867, from Dudley Taylor Cornish. *The Sable Arm: Negro Troops in the Union Army, 1861–1865*. New York: Longmans, Green, 1956.

92. *Charleston Daily Courier*, November 12, 1868, p.2, col. 2.

93. *Charleston Daily Courier*, October 21, 1868, p. 2, col. 3.

94. Ibid..

95. Burr, Virginia Ingraham (ed.). *The Secret Eye: The Journal of Ella Gertrude Clanton Thomas, 1848–1889."* Chapel Hill: Publisher, University of North Carolina Press, 1990, pp. 276–77.

96. Alexander, Adele Logan. *Homelands and Waterways: The American Journey of The Bond Family, 1846–1926.* New York: Pantheon Books, 1999, p. 172.

97. DuBois, p. 541.

98. Ibid., p. 600.

99. Foner, Philip S., *Frederick Douglass*. New York: Citadel Press, 1964, p. 311.

100. Ibid.

101. Mixon, Gregory, "Henry McNeal Turner versus the Tuskegee machine: Black Leadership in the Nineteenth Century." *Journal of Negro History*, vol. 89, no. 4, 1994, p. 363.

102. *The Journal of Negro History*, vol. LIV, no. 2, April 1969, "Address of Frederick Douglass at the Inauguration of Douglass Institute, Baltimore, October 1, 1865." (Documents) pp. 174–83. Edited by Philip S. Foner: Douglass discusses the importance of his recent conversion to understanding the importance of racially specific institutions in the black community: "The establishment of this institution may be thought by some a thing of doubtful expediency. There was a time when I should have thought it so myself. In my enthusiasm, perhaps it was my simplicity, it is not material which, I once flattered myself that the day had happily gone by when it could be necessary for colored people in this country to combine and act together as separate class, and in any representative character whatever. I would have had them infuse themselves and their works into the political, intellectual, artistical and mechanical activities and combinations of their white fellow-countrymen. It seemed to me that colored conventions, colored exhibitions, colored associations and institutions of all kinds and descriptions had answered the ends of their existence, and might properly be abandoned; that, in short, they were hindrances, rather than helps in achieving a higher and better estimation in the public mind for ourselves as a race.

I may say that I still hold this opinion in a modified degree. The latent contempt and prejudice towards our race, which recent political doctrines with reference to our future in t his country have developed, the persistent determination of the present Executive of the nation, and also the apparent determination of a portion of the people to hold and treat us in a degraded relation, not only justify for the present such associate effort on our part, but make it eminently necessary."

103. Carter, p. 7; Richmond *Whig*, February 11, 1865; Houston *Tri-Weekly Telegraph*, April 24, 1865; Columbia *Carolinian*, n.d., quoted in Yorkville (S.C.) *Enquirer*, February 1, April 26, 1865.

104. *The Random House Dictionary*, ed. Jess Stein. New York: Ballantine Books, 1980, p. 890.

105. DuBois, p. 620.

106. Ibid., p. 624.

107. James S. Pike, *The Prostrate State*, p. 66–7.

108. Saville, p. 145.

109. Ibid., p. 147.

110. Wharton, Vernon Lane, *The Negro in Mississippi, 1865–1890*. New York: Harper & Row, 1947, p. 139.

111. Ibid.

112. Ibid.

113. Ibid.

114. Ibid., p. 141.

115. Ibid., p. 142.

116. Leland, *A Voice from South Carolina*, p. 40.

117. Ibid.

118. Thomas, pp. 260–65.

119. Amon, Moshe, "The Phoenix Complex: Terror-

ism and the Death of Western Civilization," in *Perspective on Terrorism*, p. 15.

Notes to Chapter 2

1. Crouch, Barry A., "A Spirit of Lawlessness: White Violence; Texas Blacks, 1865–1868." In *African American Life in the Post-Emancipation south, 1861–1900*. Volume 7 entitled *Black Freedom/White violence, 1865–1900. Editor, Donald G. Nieman*. New York: Garland Publishers, Inc., p. 60. Crouch writes: "Texas white often killed blacks for no obvious reason other than racial hatred or the satisfaction of sadistic fantasies. Some reportedly shot Freedmen to "see a d — — d nigger kick" or because they just wanted to shoot a "damned nigger." Others shot them, apparently to test their skills as marksmen. The very presence of free blacks led to murders. In Grayson county, for instance, where blacks comprised only eighteen percent of the population and therefore were not a political threat, three whites murdered three Freedmen because, they said, they felt a need to "thin the niggers out and drive them to their holes. Texas anti-black violence, in the years 1865–1868 was significant because of its high yearly death toll and the percentage of the population affected. The Texas death rate for blacks during this era was more than twenty times higher than for Dallas, Houston and New York City in recent times. Probably due to the size of the state and the isolation of many sections, more than any other factors, white attacks on blacks were largely individual and only partially by groups. Certain patterns emerge however, in relation to the motivation behind the various categories of white violence."

2. Franklin & Moss, pp. 248–49.

3. Foner, Eric. *Reconstruction: Americas Unfinished Revolution, 1863–1877*. New York: Harper & Row, 1988, p. 283.

4. Ibid., pp. 283–85.

5. *Free Man's Press*. August 15, 1868 (Austin, Texas).

6. Fry, Gladys-Marie. *Nightriders in Black Folk History*. Athens, Ga.: The University of Georgia Press, 1991, p. 3. Fry explains that, "During and following the period of Black slavery in America, one of the means utilized by whites in controlling the Black population was a system of psychological pressure based on fear of the supernatural. The primary aim of such pressure was to discourage the unauthorized movement of Blacks, especially at night, by making them afraid of encountering supernatural beings. During slavery, this psychological control guarded against insurrection by discouraging nocturnal assembly; from the post–Civil War period to World War 1, the method helped to stem the tide of Black movement from rural farming communities in the South to the urban industrial centers of the North. Originally practiced during slavery by masters and overseers dressed as ghost, psychological control was later extended to the system of mounted patrols (or "patterollers") designed to monitor slave movement in antebellum days, the Ku Klux Klan of the Reconstruction era, and finally the night doctors. To their Black victims these groups were known as the night riders. Though they differed in disguises and stated aims, and even in point of time, all three adhered to a single cardinal purpose: the control of the Black through intimidation."

7. Ibid.

8. "Joint Investigating Committee of Public Frauds and Election of Hon. J.J. Paterson to the U.S. Senate — General Assembly of South Carolina at the Regular Session of 1877–1878." In DuBois, p. 676.

9. Trelease, p. 3.

10. Randel, William Peirce. *The Ku Klux Klan: A Century of Infamy*. Philadelphia: Chilton Books, 1965, p. 5.

11. Trelease, p. 430.

12. Op. Cit.

13. Op. Cit.

14. Brown, William Garrott, "The Ku Klux Movement." In *The Atlantic Monthly*, LXXX VII, 1901, pp. 636–37.

15. Fleming, Walter Lynwood (ed.), *Documentary History of Reconstruction*, 2 vols. Cleveland: Reprint Services Corp, 1906–7, p. 1, 229; Trelease, p. 4.

16. Blackburn, George M., "Radical Republican Motivation: A Case History." In *The Journal of Negro History*. Volume LIV, No.2 April, 1969, pp. 109–26.

17. *Nashville Press and Times*. July 12, 1866.

18. *Pulaski Citizen*, (Tenn.) August 10, 1866.

19. Trelease, p. 9.

20. Ibid.

21. Memphis *Bulletin*, August 12, 1868, p. 4.

22. Phillips, David. *Civil War Chronicles: Daring Raiders*. Metro Books, 1998. New York, p. 58.

23. Stiles, T.J. *Jesse James: Last Rebel of the Civil War*. New York: Alfred Knopf, p. 49. Stiles notes that, during the Civil War, Union efforts to fight against Confederate "weak and disorganized insurrectionist" military units was spotty at best. As the war progressed these irregular forces grew "smarter, tougher, angrier" and developed "more skills in the ways of partisan warfare." For example, from the Mississippi River to the Kansas border, "small bands continued a deadlier, if less pervasive, guerrilla struggle. They were not a new phenomenon. They, too, emerged from the slaveholding counties' secessionist fervor, which had grown out of the border ruffian mobilization. Under the pressure of the Union counteroffensive, these secessionist guerrillas broke into small cells that fought without central direction or official Confederate sanction, passing under the nickname of "bushwhackers."

24. Ibid.

25. Some confusion and mislabeling has occurred on this point of "southerners" being automatically assumed to be white, pro slavery and most important, pro secessionist. Historian T.J. Styles addressed this point in *Jesse James: Last Rebel of the Civil War*. New York. Alfred A. Knopf, 2002, p. 71. He noted; "Historians have often clouded the fraternal nature of Missouri's internal strife by calling Confederate sympathizers "Southerners." But their opponents were just as southern, having been born in Missouri, Kentucky, and other slave states. Indeed , some of the men who fought hardest for the Union, in Clay County and elsewhere, owned slaves. Better is the term "secessionist," or, to use the nickname of the times, "secesh." The rift between the two sides was ideological rather than cultural or geographic. The "secesh" believed slavery was under threat, and that it was more important than the nation itself. The loyalist did not see any danger to the peculiar institution , and in any case they cherished the sanctity of the Union above all else."

26. Trelease, p. 15.

27. Ibid

28. Hine, p. 125. The author notes that, "Almost half of the south's slaveholders owned fewer than 5 slaves, only 12 percent owned more than 20 slaves, and just 1 percent owned more than 50 slaves, Yet more than half the slaves belonged to masters who had 20 or more slaves. So, while the typical slaveholder owned few slaves, the typical slave lived on a sizable plantation."

29. Athens, Lonnie H. *The Creation of Dangerous Violent Criminals*. Chicago: University of Illinois Press, 1992, pp. 18–19.

30. *Charleston Daily Courier*, February 28th 1867, p.2, col. 3.

31. *Charleston Daily Courier*, February 16, 1867, p. 1, col. 3.

32. Ibid.

33. Ibid., p. 11.

34. *Washington Post*. August 13, 1905.

35. Lester, J.C. and D.L. Wilson. *Ku Klux Klan: Its Origins, Growth, Disbandment*. Cleveland: Scholarly Library Binding (Reprint Services Corp.) 1992, pp. 91–99.

36. Jones, col. Winfield. *Story of Ku Klux Klan*. Washington, DC.: American Newspaper Syndicate, 1921, p. 99.

37. Ibid.

38. Franklin & Moss, p. 112.

39. Borman, p. 404.

40. Lester, p. 198.

41. Leland, p. 121.

42. *Charleston Daily Courier*, September 1, 1868, p. 1, col. 1.

43. *Charleston Daily Courier*, August 26, 1868, p. 4, Cols. 2–3.

44. *Charleston Daily Courier*, November 14, 1868, p.2. col. 3.

45. Ibid.

46. Ibid.

47. *Charleston Daily Courier*, September 3rd 1868, p. 4, col. 3.

48. Williamson, Joel, pp. 263–4.

49. Trelease, pp. 49–51; 68–69; 81–88; 138–40.

50. Ibid., p. 640; However Nieman, writes: "the only group more feared than the *Innocents* was the *Knights of the White Camellia*, and although they apparently did not participate in the New Orleans riot, in any organized way, their presence surfaced nevertheless. Similar in every way to the Ku Klux Klan, the *Knights* was founded in 1867 in Louisiana, probably by Judge Alcibiades DeBlanc, its first leader. Members of Democratic clubs vehemently insisted that they were separated from the *Knights* primarily because they required a secret oath and because the *Knights* were not political, but had as their purpose white supremacy. The division line was often fine and being a member of a political club did not preclude membership in the *Knights*, and in fact frequently went hand in had." Nieman, p. 174–75 (notes).

51. Op. cit.

52. Trelease, pp. 93–94.

53. Ibid., p. 82.

54. Ibid., p. 131.

55. John Bonner to his mother, New Orleans, Oct 13, 1868. Bonner Family Papers. Department of Archives and Manuscript. Baton Rouge: Louisiana State University; Trelease, p. 133.

56. Ibid; Trelease, p. 132.

57. Trelease, p. 96–97.

58. Ibid.

59. Ibid.

60. *New York Times*. September 6th, 1868.

61. Hennessey, Melinda Meek, "Race and violence in Reconstruction in New Orleans: The 1868 Riot" in *Black Freedom/White Violence, 1865–1900*. by Donald G. Nieman. New York: Garland Publishers, Inc., 1994, p. 175.

62. Ibid., p. 176.

63. Ibid., p. 179.

64. Ibid., pp. 177–78.

65. Ibid., p. 181.

66. Ibid.; *New York Times*. November 7, 1868; *New Orleans Times*. October 28, 1868.

67. Ibid., pp. 133–34.

68. Neiman, p. 174.

69. *New Orleans Bee*. October 27–28 1868; *New York Times*. November 2, 1868; Nieman, p. 180.

70. Ibid.

71. Ibid., p. 135.

72. In *Black Reconstruction in America, 1860–1880* by W.E.B. DuBois, p. 461, he described Warmoth in the following manner, "It was this year that the new element of carpetbaggers began to be felt in Louisiana. Hitherto, there had been the planter class, the military authorities, and the free colored people, all striving for leadership of the Freedmen. Now cam the disbanded Union officers, the new small capitalist of the North, or those who represented them, although themselves without capital. Foremost among these was Henry Clay Warmoth. Warmoth took up his residence in Louisiana in 1865. He was a young Union officer, then only 23 years of age, and had an astonishing career. He was an unmoral buccaneer, shrewd, likeable, and efficient, who for ten years was practical master of the state of Louisiana. Hew represented those white men, Northern and Southern, currently called carpetbaggers and scalawags, who business it was to manipulate the labor vote, white and black." In *White Terror: The Ku Klux Klan Conspiracy and Southern Reconstruction*, Allen W. Trelease explains that "Ten days after his election as governor, Henry Clay Warmoth received a notice *Death* now awaites [*sic*] you." To fight against this direct threat to public order Warmoth was "authorized to organized a Militia, but he declined to do so. I would amount to arming one political party against the other, he explained, and he might have added more pertinently, arming the blacks against a white population which was already in a state of panic and near rebellion over the specter of a Negro rising." pp. 96–98.

73. Ibid., p. 135–36.

74. Nieman, p. vii–xi.

75. Lovett, Bobby L., "Memphis Riots: White Reactions to Blacks in Memphis, May 1865–July 1866." *Tennessee Historical Quarterly 38* (1979): 9–33. Reprinted in, *Black Freedom/White Violence, 1865–1900*. edited by Donald G. Nieman. New York: Garland Publishing, Inc., 1994, pp. 212–14.

76. *The New National Era*. January 5, 1871, p. 1, col. 2.

77. *The New Era*. August 4, 1870, p. 2, col. 5.

78. Ibid.

79. Ibid.

80. Hine, pp. 294–95.

81. Trelease, pp. 361–62.

82. Hine, p. 297. The author explains that "Many Republicans in the North lost interest in issues and principles and became more concerned with elections and economic issues. By the mid–1870s, there was more discussion in Congress of patronage, veterans' pensions, railroads, taxes, tariffs, the economy, and monetary policy than civil rights or the future of the South. Others, swayed by white Southerners' views of black people, began to doubt the wisdom of universal manhood suffrage. Many white people who had nominally supported black suffrage began to believe the exaggerated complaints about corruption among black leaders and the unrelenting claims that Freedmen were incapable of self-government. Some white Northerners began to conclude that Reconstruction had been a mistake."

83. Williamson, p. 264.

84. Ibid.; Edward Lipscomb to Smith Lipscomb, April 11, 1871. Edward Lipscomb Papers, Southern Historical Collection. Chapel Hill: University of North Carolina.

85. Foner, Philip S. and Ronald L. Lewis (eds.). *The Black Worker: A Documentary History from Colonial Times to the Present*, volume 1, The Black Worker to 1869, #17, p. 401. From the *Boston Daily Evening Voice*, August 17, 1866, "The Strike Against Colored Men in Congress Street," #17, p. 401. The author of the article asserted: "We should judge by the appearance of the blacks now

on the work that some of them were recently arrived from the South, and rather green at Northern work. The boss builder told us he paid them the same as he had paid the white men, and to our question whether they proved as capable hands he said he could not tell without further trial; but he should given them a pretty thorough trial before he hired Irishmen again. Irishmen should make a dispassionate note of this, and learn that when they strike against colored men, they do not hurt the colored men, but themselves only."

86. Stiles, p. 161.

87. Shapiro, Herbert, "Afro-American Responses to Race Violence during Reconstruction," *Science and Society* 36 (1972): 158–70. Reprinted in *Black Freedom/White Violence, 1865–1900*, edited by Donald G. Nieman. Garland Publishing, 1994, p. 165. The author states, "Negroes utilized every forum which offered a possible avenue towards protection of their rights. Hundreds of black witnesses played a remarkable role, coming forward to testify during the hearing on the Ku Klux Klan in 1871 and offering abundant evidence of the impact of Klan violence upon the south. They had no guarantee of protection after testifying. Spartanburg County, South Carolina, where hearing were held, had already been the scene of numerous Klan outrages. Yet 36 black witnesses appeared in Spartanburg to tell congressmen of the mayhem inflicted by the Ku Kluxers. These witnesses and many other blacks in North Carolina, Florida, Mississippi, Alabama and Georgia furnished the great bulk of the evidence which led the majority of the committee to condemn Klan violence."

88. Saville, pp. 125–26.

89. Carl I. Hovland, Irving L. Janis, and Harold H. Kelly, *Communication and Persuasion: Psychological Studies of Opinion Change*. New Haven: Yale University Press, 1953, p. 138.

90. *Joint Select Committee to Inquire into the Condition of Affairs in the Late Insurrected States: South Carolina-Court Proceedings*, 42nd Congress, 2nd Session, 1872, p. 1988.

91. DuBois, W.E.B., "The Shape of Fear," *North American Review* 223 [1926], 294–295.

92. Hine, pp. 296–97.

93. Ibid.

94. Ibid.

95. Singletary, Otis A. *Negro Militia and Reconstruction*. Austin: University of Texas Press, 1957, p. 37; J. Crews to Constable — . — Hubbard, July 8, 1870, quoted in *Report of Joint Investigating Committee on Public Frauds in South Carolina, 1877–1878*, p. 675; B.F. Eddin to — . — Thompson, July 31, 1875, quoted in A.T. Morgan, *Yazoo: On the Picket Line of Freedom in the South*, p. 452.

96. Saville, p. 144; Affidavit of J.D. Palmer, Aug. 25, 1866, enclosed in vol. 254, Register of Complaints, Ser. 3309, Orangeburg, Subordinate field Office Records, RG 105 [A-7272].

97. Saville, p. 9.

98. Singletary, pp. 30–31.

99. Ibid., p. 17; Henry Thompson. *Ousting the Carpetbagger from South Carolina*. Columbia, South Carolina: Bryan, 1927, p. 48.

100. Singletary, p. 17; James W. Patton, *Unionism and Reconstruction in Tennessee, 1860–1869*. Chapel Hill: University of North Carolina Press, 1934, p. 86; *Nashville Daily Times*. Jan. 16, 1865.

101. Williamson, p. 262.

102. Ibid.

103. Ibid.

104. Ibid.; Reports and Resolutions of the General Assembly of the State of South Carolina, 1870–1871, pp. 521–611.

105. Frazier, Franklin E. *The Negro in the United States*. New York. Macmillan, 1949, p. 145; Singletary, p. 152.

106. Singletary, p. 152; A. Alruthesus, *The Negro in South Carolina During Reconstruction*. Washington: Association for the Study of Negro Life and History, 1924, p. 190.

107. Singletary, p. 172.

108. *Charleston Daily Courier*, July 31, 1868, p. 4, col. 2; August 26, 1868, p. 4, col. 3; *Testimony of James B. Steadman*, KKK Testimony, vol. 2, pp. 1011, 1025; Saville, p. 173.

109. *Lalla Pelot Papers*. Duke University; Saville, p. 173; Singletary p. 101.

110. *Charleston Daily Courier*, July 27, 1867, p. 1. col. 2–5; Saville, p. 156.

111. Saville, p. 187.

112. General Orders no. 41, June 12, 1867, pp. 101–4, ser. 4126, 2nd Military District, RG 393 Pt 1, South Carolina. Saville notes that "In subsequent investigations, military authorities sentenced Ebby Johnson to two months confinement and W.Z. Wingate to thirty days' hard labor at a federal garrison, and ordered him to pay Dimery's daughter twenty-five dollars for his unnamed assault." p. 187.

113. Saville, pp. 187–88; Affidavit of Wade Hampton (not to be confused with future conservative Democratic South Carolina Governor Wade Hampton, 1876–1879) in *Patrick Fields v. Cordes.*

114. U.S. Secretary of War, Annual Reports, 1868, p. 403; Saville, p. 188. [Jan–Feb? 1867] and the enclosed Affidavit of James M. Cantwell, H.M. Henry to General H.B. Clitz, Jan. 8, 1868, Affidavit of Thomas H. Goodwin, Affidavit of Thomas Gadsden, George Lee to C.C. Bowen, Dec. 29, 1867, Affidavit of P.M.C. Earnest, Dec. 31, 1867, all in 2nd Military District, Letters Received, ser. 4111, RG 393 Pt 1 [SS-84].

115. D.T. Corbin. to Attorney Gen. Amos T. Akerman, Yorkville, S.C., Nov. 13, 1871. Justice Department source — Chronological file, South Carolina, RG 60, NA; *House Executive Documents*, 42nd Congress, 2nd Session, no. 268, pp. 5–17.

116. *Joint Select Committee to Inquire into the condition of Affairs in the Late Insurrected States: South Carolina-Court Proceedings*. 42nd Congress, 2nd Session, 1872, p. 1988.

117. Hall, Kermit L., "Political Power and Constitutional Legitimacy: The South Carolina KKK Trials, 1871–1872," *Emory Law Journal* (Fall 1984), 921; Letter from Hugh Lennox Bond to Anna Bond (June 14, 1871) (available in Hugh Lennox Bond Papers collection, Maryland Historical society; see George S. Bryan Biographical file, available at the South Carolina Department of History and Archives, S.C.). While Judge Hugh Lennox Bond of Baltimore, Maryland from the 4th circuit courts was a Republican, he was also noted for his political independence when interpreting the constitution, particularly amendments 2, 4 and 15 as they applied to the Ku Klux Klan trials in 1871. Shocked at the reported "outrages" by the Ku Klux and testimony rendered during the trials, he wrote his wife, Anna Bond, from South Carolina he hoped to punish the perpetrators "even if it means my own life to do so, ... I never believed such a state of things existed in the [U]nited [S]tates, ... I do not believe that any province in China has less to do with Christian civilization than many parts of this state." However, Judge George Seabrook Bryan was cut from another judicial cloth. Appointed by President Andrew Johnson in 1866, "this South Carolinian Whig-turned-Democrat was the

state's first Federal Judge following the civil war, [and] was previously a secessionist and slaveholder with ties of kinship and friendship to many of South Carolina's most influential families."

118. Rome *Weekly Courier*. Sept. 29, 1871; Columbia *Daily Phoenix*. Jan. 6, 10, 1872; Trelease, p. 414.

119. Ibid.

120. Reynolds, John Schreiner. *Reconstruction in South Carolina, 1865–1877*. Columbia: State, 1905.

121. Williamson, pp. 254–55.

122. Williamson, pp. 260–63; Hall, p. 921; Reynolds, pp. 179–217.

123. *U.S. Constitution, 2nd Amendment*: "A well-regulated Militia, being necessary to the security of a free State, the right of the people to keep and bear Arms, shall not be infringed." The Fourth Amendment proclaims: "the right of the people to be secure in their persons, houses, papers, and effects, against unreasonable searches and seizures, shall not be violated, and no Warrants shall issue, but upon probable cause, supported by Oath or affirmation, and particularly describing the place to be searched, and the persons or things to be seized." Hall, p. 921.

124. Ibid., pp. 1615–90.

125. Ibid.

126. Ibid.

127. Ibid. *Confession of Andrew Cudd*, p. 1987.

128. Ibid. *Confession of William Self*, pp. 1986–87.

129. John Schreiner Reynolds, *Reconstruction in South Carolina, 1865–1877* discusses one defendant, Dr. Edward T. Avery, whose attorney allowed him to escape certain conviction by running away. He was rearrested at his home many months later; however, sentence was never carried out and he simply forfeited his $3,000 dollar bond. He was pardoned in March 1874. Trelease, p. 516.

130. *Confession of William Self*, pp. 1986–87.

131. Hine, p. 220. The author notes that in the famous *Dred Scott* decision of 1857 this issue was debated in the Supreme Court and under the opinion of Chief Justice Roger Taney concluded that blacks had no rights: "They had for more than a century before been regarded as beings of an inferior order; and altogether unfit to associate with the white race, either in social or political relations; and so far inferior that they had no rights which the white man was bound to respect; and that the negro might justly and lawfully be reduced to slavery for his benefit." However, he was mistaken. Hine noted that "Though not treated as equals, free black people in many states had enjoyed rights associated with citizenship since the ratification of the constitution in 1788. Black men had entered in to contract, held title to property, sued in the courts, and voted at one time in five of the original states."

Notes to Chapter 3

1. Erikson, Erik. *Gandhi's Truth: On the Origins of Militant Nonviolence*. New York: Norton, 1969, p. 413.

2. *New York Times*. March 21, 1871, p. 2, col. 3.

3. *Truth and Reconciliation Commission*, p. 109.

4. Stiles, p. 240.

5. Stagg, J.A.C., "Klan Violence in South Carolina." In *Black Freedom/White Violence, 1876–1900*, edited by Donald Nieman. New York: Garland Publishing, 1994, p. 317.

6. Testimony of Mr. Elias Thomson. Spartanburg, South Carolina, July 7, 1871, in *Report of the Joint Select Conditions on Affairs in the Late Insurrectionary Southern States*, 13 vols. (Washington, 1872), *House Report*, United States 42nd Congress, 2nd Session, 1871–1872, vol. 3, 4 & 5 (Subcommittee on South Carolina) pp. 411–16 (cited hereafter as the *KKK Report*).

7. Ibid.

8. Ibid.

9. Ibid., p. 411.

10. Athens, p. 96.

11. Ibid.

12. Works Projects Administration (WPA) Files, "Slave Narratives" (Mary Wright, Christian, Ky). Gladys-Marie Fry, *Night Riders in Black Folk History*. Athens: Brown Thrasher Books, University of Georgia Press, p. 159.

13. Hine, p. 133.

14. "Life and Times of Frederick Douglass," p. 52, in Eugene D. Genovese, *Roll Jordon, Roll: The World the Slaves Made*. New York: Pantheon Books, Random House, 1974, p. 619.

15. Dodd, Pinkney. *KKK Report*, pp. 416–18.

16. Trelease, p. 404.

17. Ibid.

18. Ibid.

19. Ibid.

20. Ibid., p. 363.

21. Ibid., p. 406.

22. Morehead, Thomas. *KKK Report*. pp. 692–702.

23. Ibid.

24. Ibid.

25. Ibid.

26. Ibid.

27. Trelease, p. 367.

28. Ibid.; *KKK Report*, pp. 212, 1364–65, 1472, 1712–41.

29. Yorkville *Enquirer*. Feb. 16, 1871; *KKK Report*, pp. 208–9, 219; Trelease, p. 368.

30. Ibid.

31. Rainey, Amzi. *KKK Report*, pp. 278–81.

32. Ibid.

33. Trelease, p. 414; Rome *Weekly Courier*, Sept. 29, 1871.

34. Bond, Judge Hugh. *KKK Report*, pp. 1983–84.

35. *Harpers's Weekly Journal*. October 31, 1874, p. 901.

36. Janis, Irving L., "Effects of Fear Arousal on Attitude Change: Recent Developments," *Theory and Experimental Research*. (1972) pp. 280–86.

37. Ibid., pp. 278–81.

38. Ibid.

39. Ibid.

40. Samuel A. Agnew diary. Agnew, 1851–1902, was a South Carolina teacher and a part-time preacher. Southern Historical Collection, University of North Carolina.

41. Ibid.

42. Burr, pp. 291–93; Zenobia, the queen of Palmyra in Syria, 272 AD, was the subject off at least two novels prior to 1850.

43. Ibid., pp. 366–68.

44. Shapiro, Herbert. *White Violence and Black Responses: From Reconstruction to Montgomery*. Amherst: University of Massachusetts Press, 1988, p. 5; Jerry H. Bryant, *Victims and Heroes: Racial Violence in the African American Novel*. Amherst: University of Massachusetts Press, 1997, p. 54.

45. Hovland, Carl I. , Irving L. Janis and Harold H. Kelly, "Fear-Arousing Appeals," in *Communication and Persuasion: Psychological Studies of Opinion Change*. New Haven: Yale University Press, 1953, pp. 86–89.

46. Ibid., pp. 82–83.

47. Ibid.

48. Ibid.

49. Dollard, J., and N.E. Miller, *Personality and Psychotherapy*. New York: McGraw-Hill, 1950, p. 78; Hovald, James, and Kelly, p. 62.

50. Burr, p. 368.

51. Dollard, pp. 184–85.

52. *New York Times.* April 2, 1867, p.1, col. 5.

53. Ibid., p. 1, col. 7.

54. *New York Times.* June 23, 1870, p. 1, col. 4.

55. Tourgee, Albion W. *A Fool's Errand, by One of the Fools: The Famous Romance of American History* 1980, in William Peirce Randel, *The Ku Klux Klan: A Century of Infamy.* New York: Chilton Books, 1965, p. 164.

56. *The Colored Citizen.* May 19, 1866, p. 2, col. 4.

57. *Harper's Weekly.* December 17, 1864, p. 814.

58. Ibid., August 8, 1868, p. 512.

59. Ibid., October 24, 1874, p. 878.

60. Shapiro (1988) p. 5; Bryant, p. 54.

61. Carter, pp. 147–48. The author noted that "Underlying the assumptions of white southerners was their all-pervasive belief in the fixed and immutable racial inferiority of blacks. Few whites in the region felt the necessity of elaborating upon these racial convictions; they were simply accepted like the weather or the existence of god. Faced with the necessity of educating occupiers whom they believed hopelessly naïve, however, southern journalists and political leaders returned again to the well-worn antebellum "evidence" that had buttressed their proslavery arguments."

62. Trelease, p. 2.

63. Nobles, Wade W. *African Psychology: Towards Its Reclamation, Reascension and Revitalization.* Black Family Institute, 1986, p. 36.

64. Ibid., p. 39.

65. Bales, Robert. *Personality and Interpersonal Behavior*, p. 163, cited by Ernest G. Borman, "Fantasy and Rhetorical Vision," *Quarterly Journal of Speech* (Dec. 1972). p. 398.

66. Tomkins, Silvan, "The Psychology of Commitment: The Constructive Roles of Violence and Suffering for the Individual and for His Society," in *Antislavery Vanguard.* Princeton: Princeton University Press, 1965, p. 280.

67. Ibid., p. 9.

68. Fromm, Eric. *The Sane Society.* New York: Holt, Rinehart and Winston, 1960, p. 8, cited in Gerald Sorin, *The New York Abolitionist: A Case Study of Political Radicalism.* Westport, Conn.: Greenwood, 1971, p. 11.

69. Heberle, Rudolf. *Social Movements.* New York: Appleton-Century Crofts, 1951, p. 109, cited in Sorin, p. 7.

70. *Meridan Mercury.* July 7, 1868, cited in Vernon Lane, *The Negro in Mississippi: 1865–1890.* New York: Wharton, Harper & Row, 1965, p. 153.

71. DuBois, p. 673.

72. *South Carolina Leader.* December 18, 1865.

73. Hine, p. 274.

74. Ibid., p. 291.

Notes to Chapter 4

1. Reich, Walter (ed.), *Origins of Terrorism: Psychologies, Ideologies, Theologies, States of Mind.* Cambridge: Cambridge University Press and Woodrow Wilson International Center for Scholars, 1996, p. 60.

2. Steinberg, *The Ethnic Myth*, p. 33–35.

3. Ibid., p. 36.

4. Ibid.

5. Ibid.

6. DuBois, pp. 383, 431, 451, 487, 495; Hine, p. 287.

7. DuBois, p. 591.

8. Ibid., p. 704.

9. Duster, Troy, "What's New in the IQ Debate," *The Black Scholar* 25, no. 1 (1995): 27.

10. Haller, John S., *Outcasts from Evolution: Scientific Attitudes of Racial Inferiority, 1859–1900* (Carbondale: Southern Illinois University Press), p. 124.

11. Forner, Phillip Sheldon, and Ronald L. Lewis (eds.), Letter in the *Workingman's Advocate*, December 12, 1868. Reprinted in *The Black Worker: A Documentary History from Colonial Times to 1869*, Philadelphia: Temple University Press, 1978, pp. 371–72.

12. *The Boston Daily Evening Voice.* November 15, 1865.

13. *The Black Worker.*

14. Ibid., no. 15, May 15, 1866.

15. Ibid., no. 17, August 17, 1866.

16. Ibid., April 25, 1868.

17. *National Standard.* November 11, 1871.

18. Ibid.

19. Reprinted in the *National Anti-Slavery Standard.* June 24, 1865.

20. *New Orleans Daily Tribune.* November 30, 1865.

21. *National Anti-Slavery Standard.* February 10, 1866.

22. Ibid.

23. *Federal Writer's Project: North Carolina Slave Narratives*, Mary Anderson, no. 3220086, pp. 20–26.

24. Trowbridge, J.T. *A Picture of the Desolated States; and the Work of Restoration, 1865–1868* (Hartford, 1888), pp. 230–31, in *The Black Worker* no. 32.

25. Bishop, David W., "The Affirmative Action Cases: *Bakke, Weber* and *Fullilove,*" *Journal of Negro History* 67, no. 3 (fall 1982): 242.

26. *Amendment to the Constitution of the United States: 14th Amendment.* Philadelphia: National Constitution Center, July 1995.

27. Painter, Nell Irvin. *Sojourner Truth: A Life, a Symbol.* New York: Norton, 1996, p. 226.

28. Ibid., p. 227.

29. Ibid., p. 228; *The Boston Herald.* February 23, 1871.

30. Ibid., p. 227.

31. *Jackson (Mississippi) Daily Clarion.* June 24, 1866.

32. Painter, p. 228.

33. Ibid.

34. Ibid.

35. Forner and Lewis. *The Revolution.* October 1, 1868.

36. Painter, p. 231.

37. Ibid.

38. Sylvis, James C., *The Life, Speeches, Labors and Essays of William H. Sylvis* (Philadelphia, 1872), p. 82, in Forner and Lewis, *The Black Worker*, no. 20.

39. *New York World.* March 16, 1867.

40. Ibid.

41. *Charleston Daily Courier.* October 14, 1869, p. 1, col. 2.

42. Ibid.

43. Ibid.

44. *Charleston Daily Courier.* January 13, 1870, p. 4, col. 2–3.

45. Ibid.

46. Stiles, p. 156. However, Hine on p. 261 mentions the importance of "Special Field Order #15" issued by Union General William T. Sherman on January 16, 1865 (two weeks after the Thirteenth Amendment of the Constitution that terminated slavery) that announced Freedmen would receive land. "This military directive set aside a 30 mile-wide tract of land along the Atlantic coast from Charleston, South Carolina, 245 miles south to Jacksonville, Florida. White owner had abandoned the land, and Sherman reserved it for black families. The head of each family would receive 'possessory title' to forty acres of land. Sherman also gave the Freedmen the use of army mules, thus giving rise to the slogan, 'forty acres and a mule.' Within six months, 40,000 freed people were working 400,000 acres in the South Carolina and

Georgia low country and on the Sea Islands. Former slaves generally avoided the slave crops of cotton and rice and instead planted sweet potatoes and corn. They also worked together as families and kinfolk." Hine, p. 276, noted that "(Thaddeus) Stevens determined to provide Freedmen with land, introduced a bill in Congress in late 1865 to confiscate 400 million acres from the wealthiest 10 percent of Southerners and distribute it free to Freedmen. The remaining land would be auctioned off in plots no larger than five hundred acres. Few legislators supported the proposal. Even those who wanted fundamental change considered confiscation a gross violation of property rights. Instead, radical Republicans supported voting rights for black men. They were convinced that black men — to protect themselves and to secure the south for the Republican party — had to have the right to vote. Moderate Republicans, however, found the prospect of black voting almost as objectionable as the confiscation of land. They preferred to build the Republican party in the South by cooperating with President Johnson and attracting loyal white southerners."

47. *Charleston Daily Courier*, January 11, 1870, p. 2, col. 1.

48. Ibid.

49. Ibid.

50. Steinberg. *The Ethnic Myth*.

51. Blackburn, George M., "Radical Republican Motivation: A Case History," *Journal of Negro History*, 54, no. 2 (April 1969): p.114.

52. Ibid.

53. Ibid.; Mississippi did not endorse the Thirteenth Amendment to the Constitution that officially abolished slavery in the United States until 130 years later, on February 17, 1995, "In a symbolic vote Thursday the state Senate finally endorsed the Thirteenth Amendment to the U.S. Constitution, which says, in part: "Neither slavery nor involuntary servitude ... shall exist within the United States. House approval is expected next," in *USA Today*, Feb. 17, 1995.

54. Carter, Dan T. *When the War Was Over: The Failure of Self Reconstruction in the South, 1865–1867*. Baton Rouge: Louisiana State University Press, 1985, p. 25.

55. Woodson and Baker, p. 114.

56. Carter, p. 30; Sir Frederick Bruce to Earl of Clarendon, February 9, May 6, 1866, in Eric Forner (ed.), "Notes and Documents, Andrew Johnson and Reconstruction: A British View," *JSH*, 41 (1975): 368–69; John Y. Simon and Felix James (eds.), "Andrew Johnson and the Freedmen," *LH*, (1977): 74–75; John Cimprich, "Military Governor Johnson and Tennessee Blacks, 1862–1865," *THQ*, 39 (1980): 459–70; Hans Trefousse, *Impeachment of a President: Andrew Johnson, the Blacks, and Reconstruction* (Knoxville, 1975), 43.

57. Ibid.

58. Ibid.

59. Lacy, Dan. *The Whites Use of Blacks in America*. New York: Atheneum, 1972, from Senate Executive Documents, No. 2, 39th Congress, 1st session, pp. 21, 32, as quoted in Vernon Lane Wharton, *The Negro in Mississippi, 1865–1890*, p. 82.

60. *Macon Daily Telegraph*. February 22, 1866; *Atlanta Daily Intelligence*. October 1865, in Carter, pp. 216–17.

61. Bennett, pp. 224–25.

62. *The Loyal Georgian (Augusta)*. January 27, 1866, p. 2, col. 4.

63. Ibid., p. 2, col. 2.

64. *Macon (Georgia) Daily Telegraph*. January 9–11, 1866.

65. Quill, Michael J. *Prelude to the Radicals: The North and Reconstruction During 1865* (Washington, 1980), pp.

130–31; *New York Tribune*. November 30, 1865; *Cleveland Leader*. December 3, 1865; *Report of the Joint Committee on Reconstruction*, 11, xvii, in Carter, p. 228.

66. Ibid.

67. DuBois, W.E.B. *Black Reconstruction in America, 1860–1880*. New York: Atheneum, 1983, pp. 260–261.

68. McPherson, Edward. *A Political History of the United States During Reconstruction*, pp. 29–44; DuBois, *Black Reconstruction*, pp. 167–68.

69. Ibid., p. 168.

70. Truman, Ben C. *New York Times*. February 4, 1865, in Theodore B. Wilson, *The Black Codes of the South*. Montgomery: University of Alabama Press, 1965.

71. DuBois, p. 168.

72. Ibid.

73. Ibid.

74. Ibid., pp. 169–72.

75. Ibid.

76. Ibid.

77. Ibid.

78. Smallwood, Arwin D. with Jeffrey M. Elliot. *The Atlas of African American History and Politics: From the Slave Trade to Modern Times*. New York: McGraw Hill, 1998, p. 69.

79. DuBois, p. 171.

80. Ibid.

81. Ibid.

82. Ibid.

83. Ibid., pp. 171–72.

84. Ibid., p. 172.

85. Ibid., p. 136.

86. Ibid., p. 137.

87. Ibid., p. 173.

88. Ibid., pp. 173–74.

89. Ibid., p. 176.

90. Ibid., p. 176.

91. *Federal Writers' Project, Slave Narratives: A Folk History of Slavery in the United States from Interviews with Former Slaves*. Library of Congress Project, 1936–1938. Works Project Administration for the District of Columbia. Project #1885–1, Folklore, Spartanburg, South Carolina, Dist 4, June 10 1937. No. 390167. Interviewee, Mr. Brawley Gillmore. Interviewer, Caldwell Sims.

92. "A South Carolina Society," *Atlantic Monthly* 39 (June 1877): 681–82.

93. Ibid., p. 682.

94. Bennett, p. 271. The author states, "What were blacks doing all this time? They were groping in the whiteness that blinded them for a place of safety and black light. Some — the most courageous, the most desperate — stood alone and defied the marauding crowds and died, having done all that free and outgunned men and woman can do. Others banded together and went forth in small groups to test the white line, as patrols in the night test the main force of the enemy."

95. Brearley, H.C., "The Pattern of Violence," in *Culture in the South*, ed. W.T. Couch. Chapel Hill: University of North Carolina Press, 1934, pp. 678–92, from introduction in *Black Freedom/White Violence, 1865–1900*.

96. *Federal Writers' Project Slave Narratives*, Project # 1885, #390407. Interviewee: Mrs. Ryer Moms Emmanuel. Interviewer: Annie Ruth Davis. December 16, 1937. Claussens, South Carolina.

97. Ibid.

98. DuBois, p. 176.

99. Ibid., p. 177.

100. Ibid., pp. 177–78.

101. Yetman, Norman R. (ed.), *Voice from Slavery* New York: Holt, Rinehart and Winston, 1970, p. 115.

102. Ibid.

103. DuBois, p. 676.

104. Ibid.

105. Tourgee, Albion, quoted in Otis Singletary, *Negro Militia and Reconstruction*. Austin, 1957, p. 4.

106. Shapiro, Herbert, "Afro-American Responses to Race Violence During Reconstruction," in *Black Freedom/White Violence, 1865–1900*, vol. 7, Donald G. Nieman (ed.). New York: Garland Publishers, 1994, pp. 300–12.

107. Stiles, p. 176; as quoted in Patrick W. Riddleberger, *1866: The Critical Year Revisited*. Carbondale: Southern Illinois University Press, 1979, p. 179; McPherson, *Political History*, pp. 29–44.

108. DuBois, p. 676.

109. *South Carolina Leader*. March 13, 1866, p. 2, col. 6.

110. *South Carolina Leader*. September 4, 1868, p. 1, col. 2.

111. DuBois, p. 677.

112. Nieman, p. 33. This data does not include black women who made up 3 percent of black murders.

113. Ibid.

114. *Greensboro Herald*. August 26, 1869.

115. *Charleston Daily Courier*, March 16, 1867, p.1, col. 3.

116. *Greensboro Herald*. November 16, 1867.

117. Ibid.

118. William A. Sinclair, *The Aftermath of Slavery: A Study in the Condition and Environment of the American Negro*. New York: Arno Press and *New York Times*, 1969, pp. 4–5.

119. *New York Times*. July 4, 1871.

120. *New National Era*. June 1, 1871, p. 1, col. 3.

121. *The Loyal Georgian* (Augusta, Ga.). October 13, 1866.

122. *The New National Era*. July 6, 1871, p. 1, col. 4.

123. Ibid.

124. Ibid.

125. Ibid.

126. *Charleston Daily Courier*, September 4, 1868, p. 2, col. 3.

127. Ibid.

128. Schurz, Carl, "Report on the Condition of the South," in *The American Negro: His History and Literature*. New York: Arno Press and the *New York Times*, 1969, p. 37.

129. Ibid.

130. Ibid.

131. *The Free Man's Press* (Austin, Texas). August 15, 1868.

132. Hine, p. 278. Formed in 1867 by the Republican Party, "Union Leagues were social, fraternal, and patriotic groups in which black people often, but not always, outnumbered white people. League meetings featured ceremonies, rituals, initiation rites, and oaths. They gave people an opportunity to sharpen leadership skills and gain an informal political education by discussing issues from taxes to schools."

133. Ibid.

134. Ibid.

135. Franklin, John Hope and Alfred A. Moss, Jr. *From Slavery to Freedom: A History of African Americans*, 7th edition. New York: McGraw-Hill, 1994, p. 249.

136. *South Carolina Leader*. March 31, 1866, p. 2, col. 6.

137. Wharton, Vernon Lane. *The Negro in Mississippi, 1865–1890*. New York: Harper & Row, 1965, p. 165–67.

138. Foner, Eric (ed.), *America's Blue Past: A Reader in Afro-American History*. New York: Harper & Row, 1970, pp. 218–22; Hattie McGee, "Reconstruction in Lawrence and Jeff Davis Counties," *Publication of the Mississippi Historical Society* 11 (1970): 186.

139. Singletary, Otis A. *Negro Militia and Reconstruction*. Westport, Conn.: Greenwood, 1957, p. 10.

140. Ibid.

141. Magdol, "The Habits of Mutuality," p. 42.

142. Ibid.

143. Ibid.

144. Ibid.

145. *The Richmond Planet* (Va.). August 25, 1888, p. 2.

146. Henry Berry Lowry's surname is spelled differently depending on the text. In a 1909 publication entitled, *The Lowrie History, as acted in part by Henry Berry Lowrie the Great North Carolina Bandit*, published by Lumbee Publishing in North Carolina, his surname is spelled with an "ie" ending. However, a biographical source from the *Dictionary of North Carolina*, University of North Carolina, 1991, vol. 4, p. 104, spells his name Lowry. For sake of continuity I use Lowrie as his surname unless taken from a reference.

147. Powell, William S. *Dictionary of North Carolina Biography*. "Henry Berry Lowry," by William McKee Evans. Chapel Hill: University of North Carolina, 1991, vol. 4, p. 104.

Notes to Chapter 5

1. Magdol, "Legacy of a Slave," p. 32.

2. Nieman, pp. 81–117, 171–85, 207–31. On pages 186–187 Melinda Meek Hennessey in "Racial Violence During Reconstruction: The 1876 Riots in Charleston and Cainhoy" explained, "In all, thirty-three major riots, those in which more than a single life was lost, occurred during Reconstruction and, as a body, they display some interesting patterns. In seventy percent of the riots, blacks made up a majority of the population in the area; and in a region that was overwhelmingly rural, 42 percent of the riots occurred in cities over 5,000 population.... Over a third of the riots occurred within two weeks of an election and five erupted on election days. Fifty-five percent of the riots began with an attempt by whites to break up a black political meeting or to keep blacks from voting.... In seventy-three percent of the riots, blacks fought back at least initially, and usually until they were overwhelmed by superior white numbers and firepower. In some outbreaks, blacks badly outnumbered whites and in the first stages of the riot, they dominated. But for a multitude of reasons — superior white military experience, communications, and weaponry, connivance of those in authority, abandonment of blacks by the federal government, black ignorance, poverty, and inexperience to name a few — whites generally emerged the victors in these interracial clashes. The one significant exception to this was in Charleston County. In one minor and two major riots in 1876 and in several earlier racial disturbances, the Charleston County black community had the most sustained militancy of any riot-torn area during the Reconstruction period."

3. Powell, p. 105.

4. Page, E.E. *The Lowrie History as Acted in Part by Henry Berry Lowrie, the Great North Carolina Bandit*. Lumberton, North Carolina: Lumbee Publishing, 1909, p. 10.

5. Ibid., pp. 10–11.

6. *Morning Star* (Wilmington, NC). October 20, 1871, p. 1.

7. Ibid.

8. Ibid.

9. Powell, p. 104.

10. Evans, William McKee. *To Die Game: The Story of the Lowry Band, Indian Guerrillas of Reconstruction.* New York: Evans, Syracuse University Press, 1995, p. 36.

11. Powell, p. 104.

12. Evans, pp. 19–53.

13. Perdue, Theda. *Native Carolinians the Indians of North Carolina.* North Carolina: Division of Archives and Historic Rural Resources, 1985, p. 46; Evans, pp. 19–53.

14. Powell, p. 104.

15. Evans, pp. 7–18.

16. Perdue, pp. 45–49.

17. *Wilmington Morning Star.* April 3, 1937.

18. Evans, pp. 7–18.

19. Perdue, p. 46.

20. Ibid.

21. *New York Times.* October 17, 1871.

22. Ibid.

23. Powell, p. 104. Three years later, Lowrie attempted to come to terms with state and county officials by surrendering, with the promise that a fair adjudication of him and fellow raiders would be negotiated. However, while in jail he learned that a conspiracy between Republican and conservative forces to lynch him and it forced him to once again escape. *Morning Star.* October 11, 1971.

24. *New York Times.* April 2, 13, 1871; February 18, 1872.

25. *New York Times.* July 18 and November 1, 1871; *Morning Star*, August 4, 1871.

26. Stiles, p. 202; William E. Parrish, *Frank Blair: Lincoln's Conservative* Columbia: University of Missouri Press, 1998, pp. 248–60, quote, p. 254; Foner, *Reconstruction,* p. 340.

27. "The Lowrey Bandits." *The New York Times.* November 1, 1871.

28. Ibid., October 28, 1871.

29. Perdue, p. 49.

30. Ibid.

31. *Wilmington Morning Star.* April 3, 1937, p. 1.

32. Ibid.

33. Ibid.

34. Powell, p. 105.

35. Perdue, p. 49.

36. *New York Times.* February 24, 1874, May 4, 1874.

37. *The Fayetteville Eagle.* February 24, 1874.

38. *The Fayetteville Eagle.* February 26, 1874, p. 157.

39. DuBois, pp. 534–36, 670–84.

40. Ibid., p. 177–78.

41. Scheiner, Seth (ed.), *Reconstruction, A Tragic Era?* Florida: Krieger, 1968, p. 53.

42. Lynch, John R. *The Facts of Reconstruction.* New York: Ayer, 1969, p. 121.

43. Current, Richard N. (ed.), "Appeal of Virginia Negroes, 1865," in *Reconstruction, 1865–1877.* Englewood Cliffs: Prentice Hall, 1965, p. 20.

44. Daniel H. Chamberlain, "Reconstruction in South Carolina," in *Reconstruction in Retrospect.* ed. Richard N. Current. Baton Rouge: Louisiana State University Press, 1969, p. 89; Nieman, p. 303.

45. Brundage, Fitzhugh W., "The Darien Insurrection of 1899: Black Protest during the Nadir of Race Relations," in *African American Family in the South, 1861–1900* (African American Life in Post Emancipation South, vol. 8); Nieman, p. 16.

46. Nieman, p. 17.

47. Ibid., p. 18.

48. Ibid., p. 21.

49. Ibid., p. 30.

50. Ginzburg, Ralph. *One Hundred Years of Lynchings.* New York: Black Classic Press, 1997, pp. 9–10.

51. Nieman, pp. 20–21.

52. Brundage, Fitzhugh W., "Lynchings in the New South: Georgia and Virginia, 1880–1930." Ph.D. dissertation, Harvard University, 1988, pp. 123–36. In Nieman, p. 20; *Savannah Morning News.* August 24, 1899.

53. Ibid.

54. Ibid.

55. *Savannah Morning News.* August 27, 1899.

56. Ibid.

57. Nieman, p. 23.

58. Ibid., pp. 23–24. The First Infantry Regiment was comprised of several militia companies from Savannah, the Republican Blues, Irish Jasper Greens, German Volunteers, Oglethorpe Light Infantry, Georgia Hussars and the Savannah Cadets.

59. *Savannah Morning News.* August 25, 1899; Nieman, p. 24.

60. Nieman in *Black Freedom/White Violence, 1865–1900,* p. 35, n40, an interesting study on this kind of response by the black community is, "Blacks organized guards to protect jails in Hampton, Virginia in January 1889 and Richmond in May 1901. Near Norfolk, in 1904, intimidating white authorities called in the state militia to restore order after the black population reacted with fury to the lynching of George Blount, a politician and outspoken opponent of white supremacy. In the aftermath of other lynchings, blacks organized campaigns to raise money for the victims families and to protest white lawlessness." See Robert F. Engs, *Freedom's First Generation: Black Hampton, Virginia, 1861–1890* (Philadelphia, 1979), p. 195; *Richmond Dispatch.* May 8, 1901; *Richmond Planet.* May 11, 1901; *Portsmouth Star.* October 25–30, 1904; *Norfolk Virginia-Pilot.* October 25–November 1, 1904; *Richmond Times-Dispatch,* October 25–29, 1904.

61. Ibid.

62. Ibid. August 25 and 26, 1899; *Atlanta Constitution.* August 26, 1899.

63. *Savannah Press.* August 26, 1899.

64. Nieman, p. 27. This leadership was inclusive of a number of individuals who whites found tolerable, Revs. E.M. Brawley, Paul R. Mifflin, J.P. Davis all ministers in local Baptist churches, the Rev. J.D. Taylor of the Presbyterian Church, the Rev. G.W. Butler of the African Methodist Episcopal Church, the Rev. F.M. Mann of the St. Cyprian P. Episcopal Church, Charles R. Jackson, postmaster of Darien, S.W. McIver, chairman of the local Republican Party, and James L. Grant, editor of the *Darien Spectator.*

65. *Atlanta Constitution,* August 28, 1899; *Georgia Senate Journal,* pp. 112–25.

66. Ibid.

67. Ibid.

68. *Savannah Press.* September 1, 1899.

69. Ibid. McIntosh County Superior Court Superior Minutes. Book E., 1896–1905, 27–28.

70. Nieman, p. 29; *Darien Gazette.* February 24, 1900; *Third Annual Report of the Prison Commission of Georgia, 1899–1900* (Atlanta, 1900), 42; *Acts and Resolutions of the General Assembly of the State of Georgia, 1897* (Atlanta, 1898), pp. 71–76.

71. Nieman, p. 19.

72. DuBois, W.E.B. *The Souls of Black Folk.* New York: Library of America, 1903, pp. 8–9.

73. *Charleston Daily News.* April 28, 1870.

74. Foner, Philip. *Life and Writing of Frederick Douglass.* New York: Citadel Press, 1955, p. 278; Nieman, p. 309.

75. Douglass, Frederick. *My Bondage and My Freedom.* Chicago: Ebony Classics, Johnson Publishing, 1970, p. 190.

76. "Condition of Affairs in Georgia," 40th Congress, 3rd Session, *House Misc. Doc. no. 52,* p. 12; Nieman, p. 309; *Black Exodus: Black Nationalist and Back-to-Africa*

Movements, 1890–1910 by Edwin S. Redkey. New Haven: Yale University Press, 1969, p. 34. "But Africa was to be much more than a refuge for persecuted Afro-Americans." Turner saw the "fatherland" as a great symbol for the entire race, and he saw it primarily as a political symbol, for he was essentially a political man. In a time when blacks were being divested of political power and office in the United States [1880s], and when some black leaders were settling for subordinated patronage offices and personal economic gain rather than true political power, Turner still linked the fate of the Afro-American with politics. "I do not believe any race will ever be respected, or ought to be respected," he wrote, "who do not show themselves capable of founding and manning a government of their own creation."

77. Wills, Gary. *Negro President: Jefferson and the Slave Power.* Boston: Houghton Mifflin, 2003, p. xiii. Narrow constructions of the meaning of enslavement often obfuscate both the terror of the institution as well as its deeper meaning for white Americans. A good example of this is Wills's apologist explanation: "Like other southerners, [Thomas] Jefferson had to take every political step he could to prevent challenges to the slave system. That is why southerners made sure that slavery was embedded in the very legislative process of the nation, as that was created by the Constitution — they made the three-fifths 'representation' of slaves in the national legislature a non-negotiable condition for their joining the Union. This had nothing to do, necessarily, with approval of slavery in itself-only with the political use of it to fend off challenges to the southern economic base. One could feel revulsion against slavery as an institution, yet expend great energy in buttressing it — George Washington freed his own slaves at his wife's death, but labored mightily to place the nations capital in territory where it would be populated with slaves."

78. Oates, Stephen B. *The Approaching Fury: Voices of the Storm, 1820–1861.* New York: Harper Perennial, 1997, p. 58. Additional references to Calhoun's remarks were taken from "England's abolitionist designs and *Texas annexation" JCCP* 17:354–56, 18:273–78; *Diplomatic Correspondence of the United States: Inter-American Affairs, 1831–60* (selected by William R. Manning), 12 vols. (Washington: Carnegie Endowment for International Peace, 1932–39), 7:252–53; *JCCW*, 5:330–47; *JCCC*, 573–77, 579–80, 592–94, 647–48; Peterson, *Great Triumvirate*, p. 348; Capers, *Calhoun*, p. 221; John Niven, *John C. Calhoun and the Price of Union* (Baton Rouge: Louisiana State University Press, 1988), pp. 265–82. JCC's concurrent majorities: *JCC U&L*, 3–284; Peterson, pp. 338–39, 411–13. JCC's attack on Jefferson and Declaration: *JCCW*, 1:57–59, 4:507–12; *JCC U&L*, 565–70; Capers, p. 244. JCC cares "nothing for slavery": Redelia Brisbane, *Albet Brisbane* (reprint of 1893 ed., New York: Burt Franklin, 1969), 221–22; Peterson, p. 411. Richard Hofstadter, *The American Political Tradition and the Men Who Made It* (New York: Alfred A. Knopf, 1959), 67–91.

79. *The Crusader* (New Orleans). July 19, 1890, p. 1.

80. *The Richmond Planet* (Virginia). July 12, 1890, p. 3.

81. Hennessey, Melinda M., "To Live and Die in Dixie: Reconstruction Race Riots in the South," Kent State University dissertation, 1978, in Nieman, pp. 186–98.

82. Ibid.

83. Victor, Ullman. *Martin R. Delany: The Beginnings of Black Nationalism.* New York: Beacon Press, 1971, pp. 313–14.

84. Ibid. *Charleston Daily Courier,* July 10, 11, 13, 14, 1865.

85. Ibid.

86. Williamson, Joel, "The Separation of the Races During Reconstruction," in *Reconstruction: A Tragic Era?*, edited by Seth M. Scheiner. Malabar, Florida: Robert E. Krieger, 1968, p. 111, from the book, *After Slavery: The Negro in South Carolina During Reconstruction, 1861–1877* (Chapel Hill: University of North Carolina Press, 1965), pp. 274–81, 290–92, 298–99.

87. Stono Rebellion in 1739, Denmark Vesy's near insurrection in 1822.

88. Rose, Willie Lee. *Rehearsal for Reconstruction: The Port Royal Experiment.* New York: Oxford University Press,1964, pp. 360–65.

Notes to Chapter 6

1. Putney, Snell. *The Adjusted American* (by Eric Hoffer). New York: Harper & Row, 1964, p. 37.

2. Mixon, George, "Henry McNeal Turner versus the Tuskegee Machine: Black Leadership in the Nineteenth Century." *Journal of Negro History,* 79 (4) (Fall 1994): 363.

3. Floyd, N.J. *Thorns in the Flesh: A Voice of Vindication from the South, In Answer to "A Fools Errand" and Other Slanders.* Philadelphia: Hubbard Bros., 1884 (in William Pierce Randel's *The Ku Klux Klan: A Century of Infamy.* Philadelphia: Chilton Books, 1965, p. 172).

4. Carter, pp. 58–59, "The dynamics of postwar politics seemed to point: the enfranchisement of the freedman. Parson Brownlow of Tennessee, for example, had been a bitter antebellum and wartime racist. And quite apart from his own feelings on the subject, he was conscious of the anti-black sentiments of his East Tennessee constituency. (If the federal troops are removed, said a Knoxville unionist, 'buzzards can't eat up the niggers as fast as we'll kill them.') As late as April of 1865 he supported the colonization of blacks outside the state and he repeatedly complained of black depredations and 'insolence.' As he saw his political strength falter, however, he moved expediently during the summer of 1865 toward a reluctant acceptance of black suffrage. A small number of outmaneuvered Louisiana and Virginia unionist made a similar about–face in 1865 ... The racial attitudes of southern unionist were probably better and certainly no worse than those of their political opponents, but this racial fear and hatred from the outset undermined any basis for a genuine political coalition."

5. Zinn, Howard, *A People's History of the United States: 1492–Present.* New York: Perennial Classics, 1999, p. 235–36. "The Irish working people of New York, recent immigrants, poor looked upon with contempt by native Americans, could hardly find sympathy for the black population of the city who competed with them for jobs as longshoremen, barbers, waiters, domestic servants. Blacks pushed out of these jobs, often were used to break strikes. Then came the war, the draft, the chance of death. And the Conscription Act of 1863 provided that the rich could avoid military serviced: they could pay $300 or buy a substitute. In the summer of 1863, a 'Song of the Conscripts' was circulated by the thousands in New York and other cities.... When recruiting for the army began in July 1863, a mob in New York wrecked the main recruiting station. Then for three days, crowds of white workers marched through the city, destroying buildings, factories, street cars, homes. The draft riots were complex — anti black, anti rich, anti–Republican... On the fourth day, Union troops returning from the battle of Gettysburg came into the city and stopped the rioting. Perhaps four hundred people were killed. No exact figures have ever been given, but the number of lives lost was greater than in any other incident of domestic violence in American history."

6. Atlanta *Daily Intelligencer*. December 21, 1865; Capt. Garrett Nagle to Col. H.W. Smith, September 31 [*sic*], 1865, in BRFAL (Bureau of Refugees Freedmen and Abandoned Lands), South Carolina, Box 23; Philadelphia *Inquirer*, August 9, 1865, in Carter, p. 2102.

7. Leland, John A. *A Voice from South Carolina: Journal of a Reputed Ku-Klux*. Charleston: Walker, Evans & Cogswell, 1879, p. 32.

8. Thomas, Colonel J.P., "Tribute to Major J.A. Leland," in *South Carolina Military Academy: Association of Graduates, In Memoriam to the Dead of 1891–92*. Charleston: Walker, Evans & Cogswell, 1892 (The Citadel Archives & Museum, Charleston, South Carolina).

9. Leland, p. 87.

10. Ibid., p. i.

11. Ibid., p. 87.

12. Ibid., pp. 92–93.

13. Ibid., pp. 76–77.

14. Ibid., pp. 113–14.

15. Ibid., p. 144.

16. Ibid., pp. 12–14.

17. Ibid.

18. Ibid.

19. *Indictment Presented to the Grand Jury in General Sessions, October 1870*, Laurens County, State of South Carolina (Laurens Historical Society, Laurens, South Carolina).

20. Leland, pp. 92–93.

21. Ibid., p. 52.

22. Ibid.

23. Ibid., pp. 52–53.

24. *Indictment*, Oct. 1870.

25. Leland, pp. 58–59.

26. Ibid.

27. Ibid.

28. *The Daily Phoenix*. October 25, 1870.

29. Wright, J.N. *Some Recollections of 1870, 1871, and 1872*. (Published in 1918.) Archival material in the Laurens County Library, Laurens, South Carolina. Catalog number 107149.

30. Leland, p. 49.

31. Ibid., p. 87.

32. Ibid.

33. Ibid., p. 16.

34. Ibid., p. 18.

35. *The Constitution of the United States*. Philadelphia: National Constitution Center, 1995, p. 23. On this point Amendment 9 states that "the enumeration in the Constitution of certain rights shall not be construed to deny or disparage others retained by the people," and Amendment 10 states, "The powers not delegated to the United States by the constitution, nor prohibited by it to the States, are reserved to the States respectively, or to the people."

36. Leland, pp. 21–22.

37. Ibid., pp. 19–20.

38. Carter, p. 152; Sidney Andrews, *The South Since the War*, pp. 73–74; "Report of the [North Carolina] Committee on the Subject of the Freedmen, January 22, 1866," in Raleigh *Standard*, January 31, 1866.

39. Leland, pp. 166–84.

40. Ibid., pp. 33–34.

41. Ibid., p. 34.

42. Quarles, Benjamin. *The Negro in the Civil War*. New York: Da Capo, 1989, pp. 110–13. Before the first official regiment of black soldiers were organized in Massachusetts in the spring of 1863 after the January 1, 1863, Emancipation Proclamation, on Hilton Head Island, a Union General, David Hunter, against the war office or President Lincoln's "authorization had proceeded to recruit the first regiment of Negroes in the Civil War" on April 7, 1862. In Kansas, "another General who tried to jump the gun on the using of Negro troops was Jim Lane.... On August 6, 1862, Lane sent word to the astonished [Secretary of War] Stanton, 'I am receiving Negroes under the late act of Congress.' Lane was referring to an act that was passed three weeks earlier that authorized the President to receive *persons of African descent* into any military or naval service for which they might be found competent."

43. Leland, p. 34.

44. Ibid., p. 34–35.

45. Thomas, p. 18.

46. Quarles, p. 183.

47. Leland, p. 31.

48. Ibid., p. 326.

49. Ibid.

50. *New York Times*. April 4, 1865, p. 9.

51. McPherson, James M. *What They Fought For*. Baton Rouge: Louisiana State University Press, 1994, pp. 17, 27.

52. Williamson, p. 112. The author states, "Ultimately, the physical separation of the races is the least important portion of the story. The real separation was not that duochromatic order that prevailed on streetcars and trains, or in restaurants, saloons, and cemeteries. The real color line lived in the minds of individuals of each race, and it had achieved full growth even before freedom for the Negro was born. Physical separation merely symbolized and reinforced mental separation. It is true that vigorous assaults by one side or the other forced the enemy to yield his forward trenches and to alter slightly the precise line of the color front. It is also true that material changes in post–Reconstruction Southern society pushed the trenches into areas which had not existed before. This often gave the illusion of basic change, of a breakthrough by the dominate whites in the war of races, whereas, actually, it merely represented the extension of the old attitudinal conflict onto new ground, only to bring with it the stalemate that marked the struggle elsewhere."

53. Brogan, p. 351.

54. Leland, p. 12.

55. Ibid.

56. Ibid., p. 13.

57. Segal, Ronald. *The Black Diaspora: Five Centuries of the Black Experience Outside Africa*. New York: Farrar, Straus and Giroux, 1995, p. 54.

58. Leland, p. 13.

59. Brogan, p. 364.

60. John Lofton discusses Denmark Vesey's conspiracy for armed insurrection in South Carolina and possibly Georgia in 1822. Some twenty years in the making the plot was 'discovered' a day before the planned revolt on June 16, 1822. *Insurrection in South Carolina: The Turbulent World of Denmark Vesey*. Yellow Springs, Ohio: Antioch Press, 1964.

61. Leland, p. 17.

62. Ibid..

63. Ibid., p. 29.

64. Ibid., p. 18.

65. Ibid., p. 29.

66. Ibid., p. 32.

67. Stiles, p. 42.

68. Ibid.

69. Ibid.; Douglass, *Narrative*, p. 103.

70. Leland, dedication page.

71. Bales, Robert. cited in "Fantasy and Rhetorical Vision," by Ernest G. Borman, *Quarterly Journal of Speech* (Dec. 1972): 398.

72. Leland, p. 41.

73. Ibid.

74. Leland, p. 41.

75. Kinshasa, pp. 68–89.

76. Kinshasa, Kwando M. *Emigration vs. Assimilation: the Debate in the African American Press, 1827–1861.* Jefferson, NC: McFarland, 1988, p. 7.

77. Ibid.

78. Malcomson. p. 341.

79. Douglass. *My Bondage, My Freedom.* Chicago: Johnson Publishing, 1970, p. 2.

80. Ibid.

81. Brogan, p. 346.

82. Leland, pp. 43–4.

83. The 1870 black/white census date for South Carolina indicates 415,814 to 289,667, a difference of 126,147 favoring blacks. By 1880, the population ratio was listed as 604,332/391,105, the difference had grown to 213,227. In terms of political influence this indicated that of the thirty-one counties in the state, blacks outnumbered whites in twenty, from DuBois, pp. 371–72; J.H. Franklin and A. Moss, *From Slavery to Freedom: A History of Negro Americans,* 6th edition. New York: McGraw-Hill, 1988, pp. 227–38.

84. Leland, p. 43.

85. Ibid., p. 44.

86. Brown, J.A.C. *Techniques of Persuasion.* Baltimore: Penguin Books, 1963.

87. Leland, pp. 2–23.

Notes to Epilogue

1. Reynolds, David. *John Brown, Abolitionist: The Man Who Killed Slavery, Sparked the Civil War, and Seeded Civil Rights.* New York: Knopf, 2005.

2. Mary Sampson Patterson Leary was of African, French, and Indian ancestry. She and Charles Langston were married by the Reverend F.L. Kenyon in January 1869 at Elyria, Ohio (*Lorain County News,* January 20, 1869). Source from Faith Berry, *Langston Hughes: Before and Beyond Harlem.* Westport, CT: Lawrence Hill, 1983, p. 332.

3. Berry, p. 8.

4. Ibid., p. 8; See Jacob R. Shipherd, *History of the Oberlin-Wellington Rescue* (Boston, 1959). See also Aptheker, *A Documentary History of the Negro People in the United States,* 2 vols. (New York, 1963), 1:62; Benjamin Quarles, *Black Abolitionists* (New York, 1969), pp. 213–14.

5. Anderson, Osborne Perry. *A Voice from Harper's Ferry* (Atlanta: World View Publishers, 1974); Stephen B. Oates, *To Purge This Land with Blood: A Biography of John Brown* (Amherst: University of Massachusetts Press, 1970), pp. 243–306; Stan Cohen, *John Brown: The Thundering Voice of Jehovah* (Missoula, Montana, 1999), pp. 40–41; Edward J. Reneham, Jr., *The Secret Six: The True Tale of the Men Who Conspired with John Brown* (Columbia: University of South Carolina Press, 1997), pp. 200–13.

6. Crayton, John W., "Terrorism and the Psychology of the Self." In *Perspectives on Terrorism.* ed. Lawrence Zelic Freedman and Yonah Alexander. (Wilmington, DE: Scholarly Resources, 1983), pp. 33–41.

7. Burr, p. 370.

8. Quarles, p. 265.

9. Kinshasa, pp. 115–16. "Communication theory on information diffusion suggest that if successful socialization is to occur, critical attention should be given to: the amount and speed of the diffusion of items of information, to such factors as geographic distance from the point of origin of the message, time elapsed since the original infusion of the message into a commodity, size of the community ... [and] the degree of clustering with which the message was originally released, and appeals used."

10. Kinshasa, pp. 113–14. The author reminds us stemming from the enslavement period, most nineteenth-century informational communication within the African American communities occurred through a "multi-step flow, information diffusion, rumor transmission [process] — as it socialized blacks to the values and beliefs of an upwardly mobile class within the black community. Moreover, a subordinated class of free blacks, with [their] limited educational level and reliance upon face to face communication, was insufficient in number to retard the gradualist, accommodationist philosophy which stressed the familiar nineteenth-century homilies of education, moral rectitude and economic sufficiency."

11. Giddens, Anthony. *New Rules of Sociological Method: A Positive Critiques of Interpretative Sociologies* (New York: Basic Books), p. 104. The author argues that "the production of interaction has three fundamental elements: its constitution as 'meaningful'; its constitution as a moral order; and its constitution as the operation of relations of power."

12. Ibid., pp. 104, 118.

13. Leland, pp. 44–50.

14. Leland, p. 35.

15. Callahan, John F. (ed.). *The Collected Essays of Ralph Ellison* (New York: Modern Library, 1995), p. 96.

16. *The American Workman* (Boston), August 28, 1869; *The Black Worker: A Documentary History from Colonial Times to the Present.* vol. 1, "The Black Worker to 1869." Edited by Philip S. Foner and Ronald Lewis. (Philadelphia: Temple University Press, 1978), p. 414.

Bibliography

BOOKS AND CHAPTERS

Alexander, Adele Logan. *Homelands and Waterways: The American Journey of the Bond Family, 1846–1926*. New York: Pantheon Books. 1999.

Alruthesus, A. *The Negro in South Carolina During Reconstruction*. Washington, DC: Association for the Study of Negro Life and History. 1924.

Anderson, Osborne Perry. *A Voice from Harper's Ferry*. Atlanta: World View Publishers. 1974.

Andrews, Sidney. *The South Since the War as Shown by Fourteen Weeks of Travel and Observation in Georgia and the Carolinas*. Boston. 1986.

Astor, Gerald. *The Right to Fight: A History of African Americans in the Military*. Cambridge, MA: Da Capo Press. 1988.

Athens, Lonnie H. *The Creation of Dangerous Violent Criminals*. Chicago: University of Illinois Press. 1992.

Bennett, Lerone, Jr. *Before the Mayflower: A History of Black America*. New York: Penguin Books, 6th edition, 1988.

Berry, Faith. *Langston Hughes: Before and Beyond Harlem*. Westport, CT: Lawrence & Hill. 1983.

Brearley, H.C. *Culture in the South*. Chapel Hill: University of North Carolina Press. 1934.

Brown, J.A.C. *Techniques of Persuasion*. Baltimore: Penguin Books. 1963.

Bryant, Jerry H. *Victims and Heroes: Racial Violence in the African American Novel*. Amherst: University of Massachusetts Press. 1997.

Buckley, Gail. *American Patriots: The Story of Blacks in the Military from the Revolution to Desert Storm*. New York: Random House. 2001.

Buckley, Norman. *Congo Jack*. New York: Pinto Press. 1997.

Burr, Virginia Ingraham (ed.). *The Secret Eye: The Journal of Ella Gertrude Clanton Thomas, 1848–1926*. Chapel Hill: University of North Carolina Press. 1990.

Callahan, John F. (ed.). *The Collected Essays of Ralph Ellison*. New York: Modern Library. 1995.

Carter, Dan T. *When the War Was Over: The Failure of Reconstruction, 1865–1867*. Baton Rouge: Louisiana State University Press. 1985.

Cohen, Stan. *John Brown: The Thundering Voice of Jehovah*. Missoula, MT: Pictorial Histories Publishing. 1999.

Cornish, Dudley Taylor. *The Sable Arm: Negro Troops in the Union Army, 1861–1865*. New York: Longhams, Green. 1956.

Crouch, Barry A. "A Spirit of Lawlessness: White Violence: Texas Blacks, 1865–1868." In Nieman, p. 60.

Current, Richard N. (ed.). *Reconstruction, 1865–1877*. Englewood Cliffs: Prentice Hall. 1965.

_____. *Reconstruction in Retrospect*. Baton Rouge: Louisiana State University Press. 1994.

Dollard, J., & N.E. Miller. *Personality and Psychotherapy*. New York: McGraw-Hill. 1950.

Doughty, Robert A. (ed.). *The West Point Museum: A Guide to the Collections*. New York: Association of Graduates, the Class of 1932, USMA, United States Military Academy. 1987.

Douglass, Frederick. *My Bondage and My Freedom*. Chicago: Ebony Classics, Johnson Publishing. 1970.

_____. *Narrative of the Life of Frederick Douglass, an American Slave, Written by Himself*. New York: Penguin. 1968.

DuBois, W.E.B. *Black Reconstruction in American, 1860–1880*. New York: Atheneum. 1983.

Elkins, Stanley M. *Slavery: A Problem in American*

Institutional and Intellectual Life. Chicago: University of Chicago Press. 1959.

Ellul, Jacques. *Propaganda*. New York: Knopf. 1965.

Erikson, Eric. *Gandhi's Truth: On the Origins of Militant Nonviolence*. New York: W.W. Norton. 1969.

_____ (ed.). *America's Blue Past: A Reader in Afro-American History*. New York: Harper & Row. 1970.

Evans, William McKee. *To Die Game: The Story of the Lowry Band, Indian Guerrillas of Reconstruction*. Syracuse, New York: Syracuse University Press. 1995.

Fleming, Walter Lynwood (ed.). *Documentary History of Reconstruction,* 2 vols. Cleveland: Reprint Services. 1935.

Floyd, N.J. *Thorns in the Flesh: A Voice of Vindication from the South, in Answer to "A Fool's Errand" and Other Slanders*. Philadelphia: Hubbard. 1884.

Foner, Philip S. *Life and Writing of Frederick Douglass*. New York: Citadel Press. 1955.

_____. *Frederick Douglass*. New York: Citadel Press. 1964.

_____ & Ronald Lewis (eds.). *The Black Worker: A Documentary History from Colonial Times to the Present*. Volume 1. Philadelphia: Temple University Press. 1978.

_____. *Reconstruction: America's Unfinished Revolution, 1863–1877*. New York: Harper & Row. 1988.

Franklin, John Hope, and Alfred A. Moss. *From Slavery to Freedom: A History to African Americans*. 7th edition. New York: McGraw-Hill. 1994.

Frazier, Franklin E. *The Negro in the United States*. New York: Macmillan. 1949.

Freedman, Lawrence Z., & Yonah Alexander (ed.). *Perspectives on Terrorism*. Wilmington, DE: Scholarly Resources. 1983.

Fromm, Eric. *The Sane Society*. New York: Holt, Rinehart and Winston. 1960.

Fry, Gladys-Marie. *Nightriders in Black Folk History*. Athens: University of Georgia Press. 1991.

Genovese, Eugene D. "Life and Times of Frederick Douglass." *Roll Jordon, Roll: The World the Slaves Made*. New York: Random House. 1974.

Giddens, Anthony. *New Rules of Sociological Method: A Positive Critique of Interpretative Sociologies*. New York: Basic Books. 1976.

Ginzburg, Ralph. *One Hundred Years of Lynchings*. New York: Black Classic Press. 1997.

Graff, Harvey. *The Legacies of Literacy: Continuities and Contradictions in Western Culture and Society*. Indiana University Press. 1987.

Haller, John S., Jr. *Outcasts from Evolution: Scientific Attitudes of Racial Inferiority, 1859–1900*. Carbondale: Southern Illinois University Press. 1995.

Heberle, Rudolf. *Social Movements*. New York: Appleton-Century Crofts. 1951.

Hennessey, Melinda M. "To Live and Die in Dixie: Reconstruction Race Riots in the South." Kent State University dissertation, 1978. In Nieman, pp. 186–98.

Hine, Darlene Clark, William C. Hine, and Stanley Harrold. *The African American Odyssey*. New Jersey: Prentice Hall. 2003.

Hofstadter, Richard. *The American Political Tradition and the Men Who Made It*. New York: Knopf. 1959.

Hovland, Carl I., Irving L. Janis, and Harrold H. Kelly. *Communication and Persuasion: Psychological Studies of Opinion Change*. New Haven: Yale University Press. 1953.

Kinshasa, Kwando M. *Emigration vs. Assimilation: The Debate in the African American Press, 1827–1861*. Jefferson, NC: McFarland. 1988.

Lacy, Dan. *The Whites Use of Blacks in America*. New York: Atheneum. 1972.

Lane, Vernon. *The Negro in Mississippi*. New York: Harper & Row. 1965.

Leckie, William H. *The Buffalo Soldiers: A Narrative of the Negro Cavalry in the West*. Norman: University of Oklahoma Press. 1997.

Leland, John A. *A Voice from South Carolina: Journal of a Reputed Ku Klux*. Charleston, SC: Walker, Evans & Cogswell. 1879.

Lester, John C., & David L. Wilson. *Ku Klux Klan: Its Origins, Growth and Disbandment*. Nashville. 1878. (Reprint: AMS Press. 1971)

Lofton, John. *Insurrection in South Carolina: The Turbulent World of Denmark Vesey*. Yellow Springs, OH: Antioch Press.

Logan, Rayford. *The Betrayal of the Negro: From Rutherford B. Hayes to Woodrow Wilson*. New York: Da Capo Press. 1997.

Lynch, John R. *The Facts of Reconstruction*. New York: Ayer. 1969.

Magdol, Edward. *A Right to the Land: Essays on the Freedmen's Community*. Westport, CT: Greenwood. 1997.

Malcomson, Scott L. *One Drop of Blood: The American Misadventure of Race*. New York: Farrar Straus Giroux. 2000.

McPherson, Edward. *A Political History of the United States During Reconstruction*. Virginia: Negro Universities Press, 1969.

McPherson, James M. *What They Fought For*. Baton Rouge: Louisiana State University Press. 1994.

Nieman, Donald G. (ed.). *Black Freedom/White Violence, 1865–1900*. Vol. 7. New York: Garland Publishing. 1994.

Niven, John. *John C. Calhoun and the Price of Union*. Baton Rouge: Louisiana State University Press. 1988.

Nobles, Wade W. *African Psychology: Towards Its Reclamation, Reascension & Revitalization*. New York: Black Family Institute. 1986.

Oates, Stephen B. *The Approaching Fury: Voices of the Storm, 1820–1861*. New York: Harper Perennial. 1997.

_____. *To Purge This Land with Blood: A Biography of John Brown.* Amherst: University of Massachusetts Press. 1970.

Olsen, Otto H. "The Ku Klux Klan: A Study in Reconstruction Politics and Propaganda." In *African American Life in the Post-Emancipation South, 1861–1900,* ed. David Nieman. New York: Garland Press. 1994. p. 242.

Page, E.E. *The Lowrie History as Acted in Part by Henry Berry Lowrie, the Great North Carolina Bandit.* Lumberton, NC: Lumbee Publishing. 1909.

Patton, James W. *Unionism and Reconstruction in Tennessee, 1860–1869.* Chapel Hill: University of North Carolina Press. 1934. p. 86.

Perdue, Theda. *Native Carolinians: The Indians of North Carolina.* North Carolina: Division of Archives and Historic Rural Resources. 1985.

Phillips, David. *Civil War Chronicles: Daring Raiders.* New York: Metro Books. 1998.

Pike, James S. *The Prostate State.* New York. 1874. (Reissued 1935.)

Powell, William S. (ed.). "Henry Berry Lowry," by William Mckee Evans, in *Dictionary of North Carolina Biography.* Vol. 4. Chapel Hill: University of North Carolina. 1991.

Putney, Snell. *The Adjusted American.* New York: Harper & Row. 1964.

Quarles, Benjamin. *The Negro in the Civil War.* New York: Da Capo Paperback. 1989.

Quill, Michael J. *Prelude to the Radicals: The North and Reconstruction During 1865.* Washington. 1980.

Randall, William Pierce. *The Ku Klux Klan: A Century of Infamy.* Philadelphia: Chilton Books. 1965.

Redkey, Edwin S. *Black Exodus: Black Nationalist and Back-to-Africa Movements, 1890–1910.* New Haven: Yale University Press. 1969.

Reich, Walter (ed.). *Origins of Terrorism: Psychologies, Ideologies, Theologies, States of Mind.* Cambridge: Cambridge University Press & Woodrow Wilson International Center for Scholars. 1996.

Reneham, Edward, Jr. *The Secret Six: The True Tale of the Men Who Conspired with John Brown.* Columbia: University of South Carolina. 1997.

Reynolds, John Schreiner. *Reconstruction in South Carolina, 1865–1877.* Columbia, SC: State. 1905.

Riddleberger, Patrick W. *The Critical Year Revisited.* Carbondale: Southern Illinois University Press. 1979.

Rose, Willie Lee. *Rehearsal for Reconstruction: The Port Royal Experiment.* New York: Oxford University Press. 1964.

Savile, Julie. *The Work of Reconstruction: From Slave to Wage Laborer in South Carolina, 1860–1870.* New York: Cambridge University Press. 1996.

Scheiner, Seth (ed.). *Reconstruction, a Tragic Era?* Florida: Robert E. Krieger. 1968.

Schurz, Carl. "Report on the Condition of the South," in *The American Negro: His History and Literature.* New York: Arno Press and the *New York Times.* 1969.

Segal, Ronald. *The Black Diaspora: Five Centuries of the Black Experience Outside Africa.* New York: Farrar, Straus and Giroux. 1995.

Shapiro, Herbert. *White Violence and Black Responses: From Reconstruction to Montgomery.* Amherst: University of Massachusetts Press. 1988.

Shipherd, Jacob R. *History of the Oberlin-Wellington Rescue.* Boston: John P. Jewett. 1859. (Reprint. New York: Da Capo, 1972.)

Singletary, Otis A. *Negro Militia and Reconstruction.* Austin: University of Texas Press. 1957.

Sorin, Gerald. *New York Abolitionist: A Case of Political Radicalism.* Westport, CT: Greenwood. 1971.

Stein, Jess (ed.). *The Random House Dictionary.* New York: Ballantine Books. 1980.

Steinberg, Stephen. *The Ethnic Myth: Race, Ethnicity and Class in America.* Boston: Beacon Press. 1981.

Stiles, T.J. *Jesse James: Last Rebel of the Civil War.* New York: Knopf. 2002.

_____. *Robber Barons and Radicals: Reconstruction and the Origins of Civil Rights.* New York: Berkley. 1997.

Sylvis, James C. *The Life, Speeches, Labors and Essays of William H. Sylvis.* Philadelphia. 1872. p. 82. In Foner & Lewis (eds.), *The Black Worker.* #20.

Thomas, Colonel J.P. *South Carolina Military Academy: Association of Graduates, in Memorium to the Dead of 1891–92.* Charleston, SC: Walker, Evans & Cogwell. 1892.

Thompson, Henry. *Ousting the Carpetbagger from South Carolina.* Columbia, SC: Bryan Books. 1927.

Tomkins, Silvan. "The Psychology of Commitment: The Constructive Roles of Violence and Suffering for the Individual and for His Society." In *Antislavery Vanguard.* Princeton: Princeton University Press. 1965.

Tourgee, Albion W. *A Fool's Errand, by One of the Fools: The Famous Romance of American History.* Waveland Press. Cambridge: Harvard University Press (reprint edition). 1991.

Trelease, Allen W. *White Terror: The Ku Klux Klan Conspiracy and Southern Reconstruction.* New York: Harper & Row. 1971.

Victor, Ullman. *Martin R. Delany: The Beginnings of Black Nationalism.* New York: Beacon Press. 1971.

Wharton, Vernon Lane. *The Negro in Mississippi, 1865–1890.* New York: Harper & Row. 1947.

Williamson, Joel. *After Slavery: The Negro in South Carolina During Reconstruction, 1867–1877.* New York: Norton. 1975.

Wills, Gary. *Negro President: Jefferson and the Slave Power.* Boston: Houghton Mifflin Company. 2003.

Wright, J.N. *Some Recollections of 1870, 1871 and 1872.* Laurens, SC: Archival material in the Laurens County Library. Catalogue number, 107149. 1918.

Yetman, Norman R. (ed.). *Voice from Slavery.* New York: Holt, Rinehart and Winston. 1970.

Zinn, Howard. *A People's History of the United States: 1492–Present.* New York: Perennial Classics. 1999.

ARTICLES AND DISSERTATIONS

Bales, Robert. Cited in "Fantasy and Rhetorical Vision." By Ernest G. Borman. *Quarterly Journal of Speech* (December 1972): 398.

Bellesiles, Michael A. "The Origins of Gun Culture in the United States, 1700–1865." *Journal of American History* 83, no. 2 (September 1996).

Bishop, David W. "The Affirmative Action Cases: Bakke, Weber and Fullilove." *Journal of Negro History* no. 3 (Fall 1982): 242.

Blackburn, George M. "Radical Republican Motivation: A Case History." *Journal of Negro History* 54, no. 2 (April 1969): 109–26.

Brown, William Garrott. "The Ku Klux Movement." *Atlantic Monthly* 87 (1901): 636–37.

Bruce, Sir Frederick (to Earl of Clarendon) in Eric Foner (Editor). "Notes and Documents, Andrew Johnson and Reconstruction: A British View." *Journal of Southern History* 41 (1975): 368–69.

Cimprich, John. "Military Governor Johnson and Tennessee Blacks, 1862–1865." *Tennessee Historical Quarterly* 39 (1980): 459–70.

Duster, Troy. "What's New in the IQ Debate." *Black Scholar* 25, no. 1 (1995): 27.

Foner, Philip S. "Address of Frederick Douglass at the Inauguration of Douglass Institute, Baltimore, October 1, 1865." *Journal of Negro History* 54, no. 2 (April 1969): 174–83.

Genovese, Eugene D. "Rebelliousness and Docility in the Negro Slave: A Critique of the Elkins Thesis." *Civil War History* 13 (December 1967): 293–314.

Hall, Kemit L. "Political Power and Constitutional Legitimacy: The South Carolina KKK Trials, 1871–1872." *Emory Law Journal* (Fall 1984): 921.

Lovett, Bobby L. "Memphis Riots: White Reactions to Blacks in Memphis, May 1865–July 1866." *Tennessee Historical Quarterly* 38 (1979); In Nieman, pp. 212–14.

McGee, Hattie. "Reconstruction in Lawrence and Jeff Davis Counties." *Publication of the Mississippi Historical Society* 11 (1970): 186.

Mixon, Gregory. "Henry McNeal Turner versus the Tuskegee Machine: Black Leadership in the Nineteenth Century." *Journal of Negro History* 79, no. 4 (1994): 363.

Scribner, Silvia, & Michael Cole. "The Psychology of Literacy." *New York Times Book Review* (December 13, 1981): 1.

Shapiro, Herbert. "Afro-American Response to Race Violence During Reconstruction." *Science and Society* 36 (1972): 158–70; In Nieman, p. 165.

[Signed Anonymously, a South Carolinian.] "A South Carolina Society." *Atlantic Monthly* 39 (June 1877): 681–82.

Simon, John Y., & Felix James (editors). "Andrew Johnson and the Freedmen." *Lincoln Herald* (1977): 74–75.

Thomas, Jackie M. "Economic and Educational Activities of the Freedmen's Bureau, 1865–1869." M.A. thesis. Tennessee State University, 1860.

NEWSPAPERS

Atlanta Constitution
Atlanta Daily Intelligencer
Boston Daily Evening Voice
Boston Herald
Charleston Daily Courier
Colored Citizen
Columbia Carolinian
Columbia Daily Phoenix
Crusader (New Orleans)
Daily Phoenix
Fayetteville Eagle
Free Man's Press (Austin, Texas)
Georgia Senate Journal
Greensboro Herald
Harper's Weekly Journal
Houston Tri-Weekly Telegraph
Jackson (Mississippi) *Daily Courier*
Loyal Georgian (Augusta)
Macon (Georgia) *Daily Telegraph*
Memphis Argus
Memphis Bulletin
Meridan Mercury
Nashville Dispatch
Nashville Press and Times
Nation
National Standard
National Anti Slavery Standard
New Era
New National Era
New Orleans Bee
New Orleans Times
New Orleans Tribune
New York Times
New York World
Philadelphia Inquirer
Pulaski Citizen (Tennessee)
Raleigh Standard
Richmond Planet (Virginia)

Richmond Whig
Rome Weekly Courier
Savannah Morning News
Savannah Press
South Carolina Leader
USA Today
Washington Post
Wilmington Morning Star (North Carolina)
Yorkville (South Carolina) *Enquirer*

FEDERAL AND STATE ARCHIVAL RECORDS AND REPORTS

Acts and Resolution of the General Assembly of the State of Georgia, 1897. Atlanta, 1898.

Annual Reports, U.S. Secretary of War Reports, 1868.

General Assembly of South Carolina at the Regular Session of 1877–1888.

General Orders: No. 41, Military District, Record Group 393, PT 1, South Carolina.

Indictment presented to the Grand Jury in General Session. Laurens County, South Carolina, Laurens Historical Society. 1870.

Justice Department Source — Chronological File, South Carolina, Record Group 60. South Carolina.

Military District, Letters Received, Serial 4111, Record Group 393 Pt 1, South Carolina.

Records of the Assistant Commissioner for the State of Tennessee, Bureau of Refugees, Freedmen and Abandoned Lands, 1865–1869. National Archives Microfilm Publication.

Report of the Joint Investigating Committee on Public Fraud in South Carolina, 1877–1878.

Report of the Joint Select Committee to Inquire into the Condition of Affairs in the Late Insurrectionary Southern States. 13 vols. (Washington, 1872), *House Report*. U.S. 42nd Congress, 2nd Session, 1871–1872, vols. 3, 4, & 5 (Sub Committee on South Carolina).

Reports and Resolutions of the General Assembly of the State of South Carolina, 1870–1871.

Senate Journal of the Tennessee General Assembly, 1865–1866.

State Historian's Papers. Record Group 29, TSLA, AD, Nashville (Tennessee).

Tennessee Prison Records, Military, Criminal and Circuit Courts, 1831–1922.

Third Annual Report of the Prison Commission of Georgia, 1899–1900. Atlanta 1900.

Truth and Reconciliation Commission of South Africa Report. New York: Grove Dictionaries, 1999.

U.S. Selected Records of the Tennessee Field Office of the Bureau of Refugees, Freedmen and Abandoned Lands, 1865–1872. Nashville, Tennessee, 1866.

MANUSCRIPT COLLECTIONS

Department of Archives and Manuscript, Louisiana State University, Bonner Family Papers.

Federal Writer's Project: A Folk History of Slavery in the United States, from Interviews with Former Slaves. North Carolina Slave Narrative: Mary Anderson Recollections. South Carolina Slave Narrative: Brawley Gillmore, Ryer Moms Emmanuel.

Southern Historical Collection, University of North Carolina, Chapel Hill. Edward Lipcomb Papers, Samuel A. Agnew Diary.

Index